Statistics and Computing

Series Editors:
J. Chambers
W. Eddy
W. Härdle
S. Sheather
L. Tierney

Springer
*New York
Berlin
Heidelberg
Barcelona
Hong Kong
London
Milan
Paris
Singapore
Tokyo*

Statistics and Computing

Gentle: Numerical Linear Algebra for Applications in Statistics.
Gentle: Random Number Generation and Monte Carlo Methods.
Härdle/Klinke/Turlach: XploRe: An Interactive Statistical Computing Environment.
Krause/Olson: The Basics of S and S-PLUS.
Lange: Numerical Analysis for Statisticians.
Loader: Local Regression and Likelihood.
Ó Ruanaidh/Fitzgerald: Numerical Bayesian Methods Applied to Signal Processing.
Pannatier: VARIOWIN: Software for Spatial Data Analysis in 2D.
Venables/Ripley: Modern Applied Statistics with S-PLUS, 3rd edition.
Wilkinson: The Grammar of Graphics

Leland Wilkinson

The Grammar of Graphics

With 248 Illustrations, 169 in Full Color

 Springer

Leland Wilkinson
SPSS Inc.
233 S. Wacker Drive
Chicago, IL 60606-6307
USA
leland@spss.com

Series Editors:

J. Chambers
Bell Labs, Lucent
  Technologies
600 Mountain Ave.
Murray Hill, NJ 07974
USA

W. Eddy
Department of Statistics
Carnegie Mellon University
Pittsburgh, PA 15213
USA

W. Härdle
Institut für Statistik und
  Ökonometrie
Humboldt-Universität zu Berlin
Spandauer Str. 1
D-10178 Berlin, Germany

S. Sheather
Australian Graduate School
  of Management
PO Box 1
Kensington
New South Wales 2033
Australia

L. Tierney
School of Statistics
University of Minnesota
Vincent Hall
Minneapolis, MN 55455
USA

Library of Congress Cataloging-in-Publication Data
Wilkinson, Leland.
    The grammar of graphics / Leland Wilkinson.
        p.   cm. — (Statistics and computing)
    Includes bibliographical references and index.
    ISBN 0-387-98774-6 (alk. paper)
        1. Statistics—Graphic methods—Data processing.   I. Title.
    II. Series.
    QA276.3.W55   1999
    001.4'226—dc21   99-14731

Printed on acid-free paper.

Production managed by Mary Ann Cottone; manufacturing supervised by Jacqui Ashri.
Camera-ready copy prepared from the author's PDF files.
Printed and bound by Friesens Corporation, Manitoba, Canada.
Printed in Canada.

9 8 7 6 5 4 3 2 1

ISBN 0-387-98774-6 Springer-Verlag New York Berlin Heidelberg   SPIN 10712625

To John Hartigan and Amie Wilkinson

Who can hide in secret places so that I cannot see them? Do I not fill heaven and earth?
Jeremiah 23.24

Cleave a piece of wood, I am there; lift up the stone and you will find me there.
Gospel of Thomas 77

God hides in the smallest pieces.
Caspar Barlaeus

God hides in the details.
Aby Warburg

God is in the details.
Ludwig Mies van der Rohe

The devil is in the details.
George Shultz

Bad programmers ignore details. Bad designers get lost in details.
Nate Kirby

Preface

Before writing the graphics for SYSTAT in the 1980's, I began by teaching a seminar in statistical graphics and collecting as many different quantitative graphics as I could find. I was determined to produce a package that could draw every statistical graphic I had ever seen. The structure of the program was a collection of procedures named after the basic graph types they produced. The graphics code was roughly one and a half megabytes in size.

In the early 1990's, I redesigned the SYSTAT graphics package using object-based technology. I intended to produce a more comprehensive and dynamic package. I accomplished this by embedding graphical elements in a tree structure. Rendering graphics was done by walking the tree and editing worked by adding and deleting nodes. The code size fell to under a megabyte.

In the late 1990's, I collaborated with Dan Rope at the Bureau of Labor Statistics and Dan Carr at George Mason University to produce a graphics production library called GPL, this time in Java. Our goal was to develop graphics components. This book was nourished by that project. So far, the GPL code size is under half a megabyte.

I have not yet achieved that elusive zero-byte graphics program, but I do believe that bulk, in programming or in writing, can sometimes be an inverse measure of clarity of thought. Users dislike "bloatware" not only because it is a pig that wastes their computers' resources but also because they know it usually reflects design-by-committee and sloppy thinking.

Notwithstanding my aversion to bulk, this book is longer than I had anticipated. My original intent was to outline a new paradigm for quantitative graphics using examples from publications and from SYSTAT. As the GPL project proceeded and we were able to test concepts in a working program, I began to realize that the details of the system were as important as the outlines. I also found that it was easier to write about the generalities of graphics than about the particulars. As every programmer knows, it is easier to wave one's hands than to put them to the keyboard. And as every programmer knows in the middle of the night, the computer "wonderfully focuses the mind."

The consequence is a book that is not, as some like to say, "an easy read." I do not apologize for this. Statistical graphics is not an easy field. With rare exceptions, theorists have not taken graphics seriously or examined the field deeply. And I am convinced that those who have, like Jacques Bertin, are not often read carefully. It has taken me ten years of programming graphics to understand and appreciate the details in Bertin.

I am not referring to the abstruseness of the mathematics in scientific and technical charts when I say this is not an easy field. It is easier to graph Newton's law of gravitation than to draw a pie chart. And I do not mean that no one has explored aspects of graphics in depth or covered the whole field with illumination. I mean simply that few have viewed quantitative graphics as an area that has peculiar rules and deep grammatical structure. As a result, we have come to expect we can understand graphics by looking at pictures and speaking in generalities. Against that expectation, I designed this book to be read more than once. On second reading, you will discover the significance of the details and that will help you understand the necessity of the framework.

The best environment for learning more about this framework is GPL, available at *www.spss.com*. If you have the occasion to create graphics on the Web or the desktop using GPL, you will learn the significance of the details. GPL is the existence proof for the theory in this book. It is capable of creating more types of quantitative graphics than any other computer program.

Who should read this book? The simple answer is, of course, anyone who is interested in business or scientific graphics. At the most elementary level are readers who are looking for a graphical catalog or thesaurus. There are not many types of graphics that do not appear somewhere in this book. At the next level are those who want to follow the arguments without the mathematics. One can skip all the mathematics and still learn what the fundamental components of quantitative graphics are and how they interact. At the next level are those who have completed enough college mathematics to follow the notation. I have tried to build the argument, except for the statistical methods in Chapter 8, from elementary definitions. I chose a level comparable to an introductory computer science or discrete math text, and a notation that documents the algorithms in set terminology computer science students will recognize.

I intend to reach several groups. First are college and graduate students in computer science and statistics. This is the only book in print that lays out in detail how to write computer programs for business or scientific graphics. For all the attention computer graphics courses devote to theory, modeling, animation, and realism, the vast majority of commercial applications involve quantitative graphics. As a software developer, I believe the largest business market for graphics will continue to be analysis and reporting, despite the enthusiastic predictions (driven by conventional wisdom) for data mining, visualization, animation, and virtual reality. The reason, I think, is simple. People in business and science have more trouble communicating than discovering.

The second target group for this book comprises mathematicians, statisticians, and computer scientists who are not experts in quantitative graphics. I hope to be able to convey to them the richness of this field and to encourage them to explore it beyond what I have been able to do. Among his many accomplishments in the fields of graphics and statistics, William Cleveland is largely responsible for stimulating psychologists (including me) to take a closer look at graphical perception and cognition. I hope this book will stimulate experts in other fields to examine the language of graphics.

The third target group consists of statistics and computer science specialists in graphics. These are the colleagues most likely to recognize that this book is more the assembly of a large puzzle than the weaving of a whole cloth. I cannot assume every expert will understand this book, however, for reasons similar to why expertise in procedural programming can hinder one from learning object-oriented design. Those who skim through or jump into the middle of this book are most likely to misunderstand. There are many terms in this book – *graph*, *graphic*, *variable*, *frame*, *point*, *line*, *shape*, *scale* – that have unfortunately come to be overloaded in ordinary and technical discourse. I have taken care to define these terms when they first appear and then to refine the definitions in context later in the book. Preconceptions about these terms, however technical, can prevent one from following my argument. And those who have heard me talk about graphics algebra in meetings or colloquia need to keep in mind that algebra is only one of fifteen chapters in this book. Before drawing any conclusions, one should read the book from start to finish and attend to the details.

The popular saying "God is in the details," whose lineage I have traced on the frontispiece, has an ancient heritage. It is usually attributed in English to the architect Ludwig Mies van der Rohe, who probably was quoting the art historian Aby Warburg. Elizabeth Sears, a Warburg scholar, told me that Warburg's saying is "much quoted, its sources variously sought." She cited Kany (1985), who devoted an entire article to the topic. William Heckscher (1958) found a possible source in the 17th century humanist Caspar Barlaeus (see correspondents' notes in Safire, 1997). The idea has much older roots in Western culture, however. It is a corollary of an immanent creator – the opposite of an absconding God. Church fathers and rabbis discussed God's omnipresence along these lines in the first millennium, and I have cited a verse from Jeremiah that gives evidence of biblical roots. In our time, we have altered its meaning by focusing on our attending to details rather than on God being in them. I do not know if George Shultz is the first to have given the saying an ironic twist. He used the expression "the devil is in the details" when referring to the intricacies of the SALT talks in a speech to the Council on Foreign Relations. In retrospect, however, Shultz informed me that he may have been quoting some earlier wit. My favorite recent redaction is by a programmer at SPSS. Nate Kirby's observation that bad programmers ignore details and bad designers get lost in them captures for me the difficulty in creating a complex system.

This book was composed in Times® Roman and Italic with Adobe FrameMaker®. The quantitative graphics were produced with SYSTAT®. Rick Wessler drew Figure 7.23 with Caligari TrueSpace®. Figure 15.1 (also on the cover) was created originally in GPL. The remaining non-statistical diagrams and tables were drawn with tools in FrameMaker and Adobe Photoshop®.

I have many to thank. Dan Rope is one of the few individuals I have met who is both master designer and master coder. He gave me the rare opportunity to test almost every idea in this book in detail and contributed many of his own. The few untested ideas will probably be discovered some years from now when others program them, but they will not be Dan's fault. Dan Carr, my other GPL collaborator, taught me with examples. One graphic from Dan (he has done many) can teach me more about good design than some books.

The group once at Bell Labs and now at its descendent institutions has continued to be a unique source of inspiration. Bill Cleveland has energized and advised me for almost two decades; he wins the citation derby in this book. John Chambers, John Tukey, Paul Tukey, Rick Becker, Deborah Swayne, Andreas Buja, Allan Wilks, Daryl Pregibon, James Landwehr, Lorraine Denby, and Mark Hansen have listened encouragingly and repeatedly to half-baked ideas.

At Northwestern, Bruce Spencer, Shelby Haberman, Martin Tanner, Keith Burns, and Amie Wilkinson have provided critical advice and support. At the University of Chicago, Stephen Stigler, William Kruskal, Ron Thisted, Benson Farb, and Peter McCullaugh have done the same. My Yale cohorts Jerry Dallal and Bill Eddy have helped me over more years than the work in this book spans.

At SYSTAT, Dan Michaels and Steve Willie introduced me to object-oriented design. Tom Leuthner worked extensively with me on maps. Mark Bjerknes, Greg Mullins, Mike Pechnyo, and Sasha Khalileev helped alert me to graphical issues raised by Mac, DOS, Windows, UNIX, and other environments. Laszlo Engelman shared numerical and graphical tricks that continue to amaze me. Pat Fleury and MaryAnn Hill made sure I continued to think about the graphical needs of real users.

At SPSS, Jack Noonan, Ed Hamburg, Mark Battaglia, and Nancy Dobrozdravic provided me the environment needed to complete this project. Josh Barr, Matt Levine, Andrew Walaszek, Jay Jayaprasad, Matt Rubin, Rajesh Selukar, John Burkey, Scott Adler, Janice Krinsky, Sheri Gilley, ViAnn Beadle, Rick Marcantonio, Joel York, Keith Kroeger, Jing Shyr, Ming-Long Lam, Jim Cortese, Scott Sipiora, Dave Hess, Tex Hull, Kim Peck, John Fry, Bonnie Shapiro, Richard Oliver, and Hiroaki Minato contributed numerous suggestions.

Elsewhere, I have received support and advice from several colleagues. The most significant have been Robert Abelson (my dissertation advisor at Yale), Susanna Epp, and Helmut Epp. Jack Cohen and Louis Guttman, no longer here to guide me, are always in my thoughts.

Some have graciously taken time to read all or part of this manuscript. I thank Amie Wilkinson, Paul Velleman, Howard Wainer, Wendell Garner, Michael Kubovy, Stephen Kosslyn, Wayne Oldford, David Scott, Cynthia Brewer, Alan MacEachren, Dianne Cook, Jürgen Symanzik, Jim Russell, and Stephen Stigler. And I especially thank a series editor at Springer-Verlag who made the effort to tell me what was sense and what was nonsense so I could revise intelligently.

At Springer-Verlag, I thank John Kimmel. John is a gentleman. A gentleman (or gentlewoman) is someone who never needs to sign a contract. I finally signed one for this book, but it was many years after I knew, and I know John knew, that I would not publish this book with anyone but John. I also thank Mary Ann Cottone for gentle persistence in coordinating the production of an extremely complex four-color manuscript.

My wife Ruth VanDemark has patiently lived with this book through many nights and weekends. And, while thanking family, I must confess a special pleasure in joining my son-in-law Benson Farb as a Springer author. Benson tutored me in the rudiments of geometry.

Lastly, the two to whom this book is dedicated – my mentor and my daughter. John Hartigan made me feel at home during my visits to the Yale statistics department in the early 1970's and encouraged my steps. Amie Wilkinson urged me to keep walking and taught me new steps. John and Amie share a remarkable intensity and an ability, rare among mathematicians, to explain to people like me what they do. This book is only a shadow of what they gave.

Chicago, Illinois   Leland Wilkinson

Contents

1

Introduction

Grammar gives language rules. The word stems from the Greek noun for letter or mark ($\gamma\rho\acute{\alpha}\mu\mu\alpha$). And that derives from the Greek verb for writing ($\gamma\rho\acute{\alpha}\phi\omega$), which is the source of our English word **graph**. Grammar means, more generally, rules for art and science, as in the title of a book in my artist father's library, *The Grammar of Ornament* (Jones, 1856).

Grammar also has a technical meaning in linguistics. In the transformational theory of Chomsky (1956), a grammar is a formal system of rules for generating lawful statements in a language. Chomsky helped explain many surface characteristics of specific natural languages through a deep, universal structure. Chomsky's context-free grammar is the progenitor of modern computer language parsers.

This book is about grammatical rules for creating perceivable graphs, or what I call **graphics**. These rules are sometimes mathematical and sometimes aesthetic. Mathematics provides symbolic tools for representing abstractions. Aesthetics, in the original Greek sense, offers principles for relating sensory attributes (color, shape, sound, etc.) to abstractions. In modern usage, aesthetics can also mean taste. This book is not about good taste, practice, or graphic design, however. There are many fine guides to creating good graphics (*e.g.*, Cleveland, 1985, 1995; Tufte, 1983, 1990, 1997; Kosslyn, 1994). This book focuses instead on rules for constructing graphs mathematically and then representing them as graphics aesthetically.

The title of this book also recalls Bertin's *Semiology of Graphics* (1967), the first and most influential structural theory of statistical graphics. Bertin's work has pervaded my thinking. Semiology deals with signs. Although Bertin put his signs on paper, his work applies as well to digital signs.

Some of the rules and graphics in this book may seem self-evident, especially to those who have never written a computer program. Programming a computer exposes contradictions in commonsense thinking, however. And programming a computer to draw graphs teaches most surely the ancient lesson that God is in the details.

1.1 Graphics versus Charts

We often call graphics **charts** (from χάρτησ or Latin *charta*, a leaf of paper or papyrus). There are pie charts, bar charts, line charts, and so on. This book shuns chart typologies. For one thing, charts are usually instances of much more general objects. Once we understand that a pie is a divided bar in polar coordinates, we can construct other polar graphics that are less well known. We will also come to realize why a histogram is not a bar chart and why many other graphics that look similar nevertheless have different grammars.

There is also a practical reason for shunning chart typology. If we endeavor to develop a charting instead of a graphing program, we will accomplish two things. First, we inevitably will offer fewer charts than people want. Second, our package will have no deep structure. Our computer program will be unnecessarily complex, because we will fail to reuse objects or routines that function similarly in different charts. And we will have no way to add new charts to our system without generating complex new code. Elegant design requires us to think about a theory of graphics, not charts.

A chart metaphor is especially popular in user interfaces. The typical interface for a charting program is a catalog of little icons of charts. This is easy to construct from information gathered in focus groups, surveys, competitive analysis, and user testing. Much more difficult is to understand what users intend to do with their data when making a graphic. Instead of taking this risk, most charting packages channel user requests into a rigid array of chart types. To atone for this lack of flexibility, they offer a kit of post-creation editing tools to return the image to what the user originally envisioned. They give the user an impression of having explored data rather than the experience.

If a chart view is restrictive, how do we impose structure on a graphic view? The concept of a graphic is so general that we need organizing principles to create instances of graphics. We may not want to put a pie chart in a catalog, but we need to give users some simple way to produce one. For that, we need methodologies based on object-oriented design.

1.2 Object-Oriented Design

Many of the insights in this book were stimulated by a recent development in applied computer science called **object-oriented analysis and design** (Meyer, 1988; Rumbaugh *et al.*, 1991; Booch, 1994). Object-oriented design (OOD) involves a plethora of techniques and principles that often baffle those trained in classical procedural programming languages and software design. Its methodology resembles a search for the objects that throw shadows on the wall of Plato's cave. Good objects are hard to find.

1.2.1 What is OOD?

OOD uses a variety of strategies for making software flexible and reusable:

- **Objects** are basic components of systems. They represent relatively autonomous agents that go about their business doing things useful for each other and for the general community of objects that comprise the system. The names of some of the most widely used objects in contemporary OOD systems express this utilitarian perspective: **Factory, Decorator, Facade, Proxy, Iterator, Observer, Visitor** (Gamma *et al.*, 1995). These objects do things that are aptly described by their names. A factory builds things. A decorator applies patterns to things. An observer looks for messages. A visitor roams and brings gifts.
- Objects communicate with each other through simple **messages**. These messages are distributed throughout the system. Because they may float freely throughout system, instead of being confined to the rigid protocols of classical programs, they resemble the communications within a living community.
- Objects are relatively stupid. They do a few things very well, as do lobsters.
- Intelligence resides in the system, not in objects, because activities in concert have a life of their own that cannot be explained by separate, uncoordinated activities. For an OOD, as for life itself, the whole is more than the sum of its parts.
- Because objects are relatively stupid, they are also relatively simple and useful for a variety of purposes, even in new systems. Objects are often **reusable**, although this aspect of OOD has been oversold by some proponents.
- Because objects respond only to a few messages, and talk to other objects via simple messages of their own, what they do is **encapsulated**. Other objects have no idea how they work. And they don't care. They only need to know what to do with messages.
- Components of object-oriented systems are relatively **modular**. If parts of the system are discarded or malfunction, the rest of the system usually can continue to function.
- Objects can **inherit** attributes and behavior from other objects. This saves time and space in a well organized system, because we can derive instances of things from more general classes of things.
- Objects are often **polymorphous**. That is, they can be induced to do very different things by sending them different messages or combinations of messages. Their responses may even be unanticipated by their designer, but in an elegant system their responses will not usually be harmful.

Polymorphism also implies that objects don't care what type of data they process. They are flexible enough to return reasonable responses to all sorts of data. This includes the simplest response, which is not to respond. This kind of robustness is quite different from classical procedural systems which crash or cause other routines to crash when fed illegal or unanticipated data. Well-designed polymorphous objects are not perverse.

- OOD induces designers to **abstract**. Nate Kirby, an object-oriented programmer and designer at SPSS, has noted that bad programmers *ignore* details and bad designers *get lost in* details. To a designer, whenever a category or class of object seems fitting, it elicits thoughts of a more general category of which it is an instance. Because of this generalizing tendency, object-oriented systems are intrinsically **hierarchical**.

1.2.2 What is not OOD?

1.2.2.1 OOD is not a Language

OOD is not a programming language. Some languages, like Simula, Smalltalk, and Java, make it easy to implement objects and difficult to implement procedures. Others, like *C++*, enable development of both objects and procedures. And others, like *C*, Pascal, Ada, BASIC, Algol, Lisp, APL, and FORTRAN, make it difficult (but not impossible) to develop objects. Using a language that facilitates object specifications is no guarantee that a system will be object-oriented, however. Indeed, some commercial *C++* graphics and numerical libraries are translations of older FORTRAN and *C* procedures. These older routines are disguised in **wrappers** whose names are designed to make them appear to be objects. By the definitions in this book, a Java library with classes that are called PieChartModel, PieChartViewer, and PieChartController, is no more object-oriented than a FORTRAN program with three subroutines of the same names.

1.2.2.2 OOD is not a GUI

OOD has been associated with the development of modern graphical user interfaces (GUI's) because it is easiest to instantiate the behavior of an icon or graphic control through well-defined objects. OOD's can be implemented in scripting or command-based systems, however, and GUI's with behavior indistinguishable from object-driven ones can be programmed through direct calls to an operating system tool kit. It is extremely difficult (though not impossible) to infer the design of a system through its behavior.

1.2.2.3 OOD is not an Interactive System

While modern desktop systems tend to allow a user to interact with its components in a flexible manner, this has nothing to do with OOD. For example, Data Desk, the most interactive commercial statistics package (Velleman, 1998), is not based on OOD. This is not necessarily a drawback. Indeed, it can be an advantage. Data Desk's design has served the package well because it was conceived with a close attention to the capabilities of the operating systems under which it resides. The extent to which an OOD system is interactive depends on how controller classes are implemented. Without user controls, OOD systems may be relatively autonomous.

1.2.3 Why OOD?

OOD has failed to realize some of the more extravagant claims of its proponents in the last decade. In my experience, OOD has not brought increased reliability to the development process. Reliability of a system depends more on clean design and intensive testing early in the development process than on a particular design method. Nor has OOD given us increased portability of programs. Operating systems have evolved more rapidly in the last few years than ever before. Manufacturers' promises that their object **frameworks** (the objects programmers use for routine tasks) would remain immutable, or at least upward compatible, have not been kept. Nor has OOD given us more rapid and responsive software. It is hard to beat assembly language or *C* programs at execution time. While there are exceptions, it is generally true that the most attractive elements of OOD – encapsulation and polymorphism – usually penalize performance. Nor has OOD given us more rapid development schedules. Indeed, OOD can retard development because objects are often more difficult to conceive properly, and modifying pre-existing objects is more difficult than changing procedures. Despite the marketing hype for OOD, it is hard to beat the development cycles realized in some of the best Lisp and APL systems of two decades ago.

This last sentence contains the key to the one reason that, in my mind, an OOD paradigm is the best way to think about graphics. APL is ideally suited to developing small matrix algebra functions because it is a matrix functional language. It is unbeatable for prototyping numerical methods. Lisp is ideal for manipulating lists of words and symbols because it is a list processing language. OOD, on the other hand, is a natural framework for thinking about graphics because graphics *are* objects (Hurley and Oldford, 1991). We can see and touch these objects. Having a language like Java that naturally implements these objects is an added benefit. If none of this work appeared on a computer, however, I would still find the effort worthwhile. Defining objects helps organize thoughts.

1.3 An Object-Oriented Graphics System

A **graph** is a set of points. A mathematical graph cannot be seen. It is an abstraction. A **graphic**, on the other hand, is a physical representation of a graph. This representation is accomplished by realizing graphs with **aesthetic** attributes such as *size* or *color*.

An object-oriented graphics system requires explicit definitions for these realizations and rules for relating them to data and for organizing their behavior in a computational environment. If we are lucky, this graphics system should have generality, yet will rest on a few simple objects and rules. This book is an attempt to reveal the richness of such a system.

From the OOD perspective, graphics are collections of objects. If the messages between these objects follow a simple grammar, then they will behave consistently and flexibly. To introduce this idea, I will focus on three stages of graphic creation:

1) Specification
2) Assembly
3) Display

After introducing these stages, I will show how they work in an example.

1.3.1 Specification

Specification involves the translation of user actions into a formal language. The user may not be aware of this language, but it is required for an automated system to understand the graphic request. Another way of defining specification is to say that it is the deep grammar of a graphic. A graphic, unlike a picture, has a highly organized and constrained set of rules. A picture, of course, has its own rules, especially real pictures such as photographs and videos (Biederman, 1981). Nevertheless, an artist is privileged to bend the rules to make a point (Bosch, Dali, or Picasso, obviously, but also Rembrandt, Cezanne, or Close). And a special-effects technician may use tricks to make us think that a video or virtual scene is more real than what we observe in our daily lives. Not so with graphics. We have only a few rules and tools. We cannot change the location of a point or the color of an object (assuming these are data-representing attributes) without lying about our data and violating the purpose of the statistical graphic – to represent data accurately and appropriately. Consequently, the core of a graphics system must rest on specification.

Statistical graphic specifications are expressed in seven components:

1) DATA: a set of data operations that create variables from datasets,
2) TRANS: variable transformations (*e.g., rank*),
3) FRAME: a set of variables, related by operators, that define a space,
4) SCALE: scale transformations (*e.g., log*),
5) COORD: a coordinate system (*e.g., polar*),
6) GRAPH: graphs (*e.g., points*) and their aesthetic attributes (*e.g., color*),
7) GUIDE: one or more guides (*axes, legends*, etc.).

In most of the figures in this book, I will add a syntactical specification of the graphic in order to make the definition explicit. In an earlier version of this specification language (Wilkinson, 1996) I incorporated all aspects in a single algebra. The notation was unwieldy and idiosyncratic, however, so I have separated them into components. These components link data to objects and specify a scene containing those objects.

1.3.2 Assembly

A scene and its description are different. In order to portray a scene, we must coordinate its geometry, layout, and aesthetics in order to render it accurately. A statistical graphics computer program must be able to assemble a graphical scene from a specification in the same manner as a drawing or modeling program puts together a realistic scene from specification components. This book is more about specification than scene assembly, but it is important to think about assembly while learning about specification so that we do not confuse surface features with deep structures. How we build a scene from a specification affects how the result behaves. A scene can be dynamic or static, linked to external data or isolated, modifiable or immutable, depending on how we assemble it.

1.3.3 Display

For us to perceive it, a graph must be rendered using aesthetic attributes and a display system (*e.g.*, paper, video, hologram). Contemporary operating systems provide access to rendering methods, preferably through well-defined, abstract interfaces. Production graphics require little in this area other than basic drawing capabilities. Dynamic graphics and scientific visualization, on the other hand, require sophisticated designs to enable **brushing**, **drill-down**, **zooming**, **linking**, and other operations relating data to graphics. Becker and Cleveland (1987), Cleveland and McGill (1988), Cook and Weisberg (1994), and Swayne *et al.* (1998) introduce these issues. More recently, virtual reality displays and immersive environments have expanded the available aesthetics to touch and sound.

1.4 An Example

Figure 1.1 shows a graphic of 1990 death rates against birth rates per 100,000 population for 27 selected countries in a UN databank. The plot contains two graphic elements: a *point* (collection of points) whose labels show country names, and a *contour* of a kernel density estimate (Silverman, 1986) that represents the concentration of the countries. I have also included three *guides* that help us understand the graphics. The first is a general geometric object called a *form* that is, in this instance, a line delineating zero population growth. Countries to the left of this line tend to lose population, and countries to the right tend to gain. The other two are guides that delineate axes for the represented space. Other examples of guides are legends and titles.

The graphic is striking because it reveals clearly the patterns of explosive population growth. The density contours show two concentrations of countries. One, to the left, has relatively lower death rates and small-to-moderate birth rates. The second, in the upper right, has high death rates and extraordinarily high birth rates. The latter countries tend to be developing. I have kept the sample of countries small so that we can read the country labels. Adding other countries from the database does not change the overall picture.

FRAME: **birth*death**
GRAPH: *point(size(0), label(**country**))*
GRAPH: *contour.density.kernel.epanechnikov.joint(color.hue())*
GUIDE: *form.line(position((0,0),(30,30)), label("Zero Population Growth"))*
GUIDE: *axis1(label("Birth Rate"))*
GUIDE: *axis2(label("Death Rate"))*

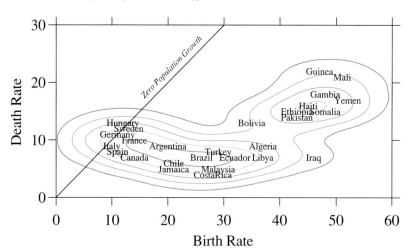

Figure 1.1 *Plot of death rates against birth rates for selected countries.*

1.4.1 Specification

The specification above the figure makes use of only FRAME, GRAPH, and GUIDE components. The data are assumed to have been organized in a cases-by-variables matrix, there are no transformations, and the coordinates are rectangular, so we can assume default settings. The first line of the specification defines the frame for the graph. We are crossing **birth** with **death** to produce a two-dimensional graph. The following lines show the two graphic elements in the plot: a *point*, and a *contour*. The *point* graphic actually does not show because its *size* attribute is set to zero. Normally, we would see symbols (perhaps dots) for each country. Instead, we have country labels for each point in the cloud set to the values of the variable **country** in the data. The *contour* graphic represents the density of countries in different regions of the frame. Where there are more countries near each other, the density contour is higher. These contours are computed by a kernel smoothing algorithm that I will discuss further in Chapter 8. The dot notation (*contour.density.kernel.epanechnikov.joint*) means that Epanechnikov kernel smoothing is one method of computing a contour. The different contours are given a *color.hue* aesthetic attribute based on the kernel density values at the level of each contour.

The guides consist of the line, the axes, and their corresponding scales and labels. The *form* guide is displayed with a line from (0,0) to (30,30) in the **birth*death** metric. This line is labeled with an associated text string ("Zero Population Growth"). In most of the figures, I will omit GUIDE specifications to keep the description simpler.

1.4.2 Assembly

Assembling a scene from a specification requires a variety of structures in order to index and link components with each other. One of the structures we can use is a network or a tree. Figure 1.2 shows a tree for the graphic in Figure 1.1. Each node in the tree, shown with a box, represents a type of object in Figure 1.1. Each branch in the tree, shown with an arrow, represents a type of relation between objects. The triangular-headed arrows represent "is a" relations. The diamond-headed arrows represent "has a" relations.

"Is a" relations provide a way to derive common functionality from one class. The result of such relations is **inheritance**. For example, an Axis is a Guide in the same sense that a piano is a keyboard instrument. Any aspect of a piano that has to do with being a keyboard instrument (having a sound produced by pressing one or more keys, for example) is inherited by other keyboard instruments. Any aspect of a piano that does not have to do with being a keyboard instrument (having hammers, for example) is not necessarily shared by other keyboard instruments (harpsichords pluck, pianos strike). If we derive common functionality from a general class, then a subclass can inherit skills from its parent without having to do any extra work. Tasks related to having keys, for example, can be defined and implemented in one Keyboard class. Tasks relating to guiding, such as relating numeric values to text strings, can be implemented in one Guide class. In a similar manner, the Contour and Point classes are both Graphs. They inherit capabilities that enable them to represent themselves in a frame.

"Has a" relations provide a way to group related attributes and functions under a class. The result of such relations is **aggregation**. For example, an Axis has a Scale, a Rule, and a Label in the same sense that a piano has a keyboard, strings, and pedals. The aggregation of these features and functions is what helps us distinguish a piano from other objects. In a similar manner, a Chart has a Frame, one or more Guides, and one or more Graphs. If we implement aggregation well, our objects will be small and efficient and our computer code will be comprehensible and modular.

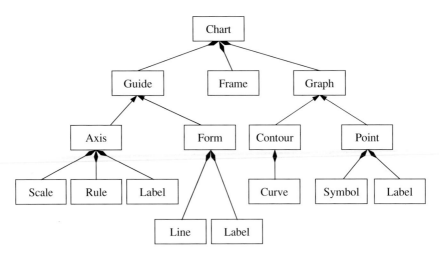

Figure 1.2 *Design tree for chart in Figure 1.1.*

1.4.3 Display

The tree in Figure 1.2, together with a set of rendering tools (symbols, polylines, polygons) and layout designer, provides a structured environment in which each object in a graphic can draw itself. There is no single agent needed to figure out all the rules for drawing each object.

A grammar of graphics facilitates coordinated activity in a set of relatively autonomous components. This grammar enables us to develop a system in which adding a graphic to a frame (say, a *surface*) requires no adjustments or changes in definitions other than the simple message "add this graphic." Similarly, we can remove graphics, transform scales, permute attributes, and make other alterations without redefining the basic structure.

1.4.4 *Revision*

Revision means, literally, to see again. For graphics, it implies that we want to change, query, and explore without having to go through all the work of specifying and creating a new graphic. By carefully separating the process of graph creation into hierarchical components, we enable a flexible environment that offers new views without recalculating every step in the system. And we can link controllers to any component or property in the system to provide direct manipulation of data, variables, frames, or rendering. If more than one graphic depends on the same sub-component, then they are linked as well.

Figure 1.3 shows an example. Even though the graphic looks different, the frame is the same as in Figure 1.1. I have omitted *point* and *form* and I have replaced *contour* with *tile* to represent a kernel density. The *hue* of each tile comes from the estimated density of the countries at that location. I have omitted the guides from this and subsequent specifications to save space. These will be discussed in more detail in Chapter 12.

DATA: **prop**=*proportion*()
FRAME: **birth*death**
GRAPH: *tile.density.kernel.epanechnikov.joint*(*color.hue*(**prop**))

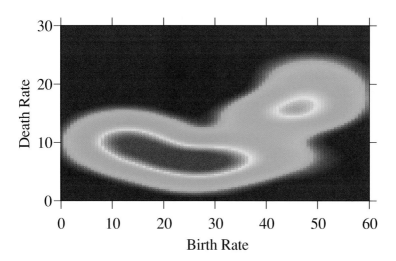

Figure 1.3 *Kernel density of death and birth rates*

Figure 1.4 adds a new variable to the specification of the point graphic in Figure 1.1. This variable, **military**, is the annual military expenditures per capita normalized as U.S. dollar equivalents. We are using this variable to determine the size of each symbol, so that size of plotting symbol represents military expenditure for each country.

FRAME: **birth*death**
GRAPH: *contour.density.kernel.epanechnikov.joint(color.hue())*
GRAPH: *point(size(**military**))*

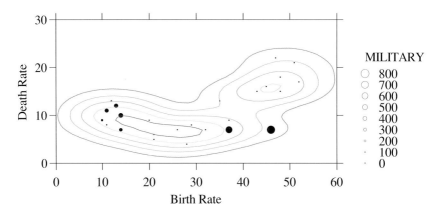

Figure 1.4 *Military expenditures vs. birth and death rates.*

Figure 1.4 conveys a rather troubling message. The highest relative military expenditures are often in the most rapidly growing, politically unstable countries. On the other hand, this statistic conceals the *absolute* level of military expenditures. The highest absolute levels of military spending are in advanced nations with larger populations.

Finally, Figure 1.5 shows a map of the difference between **death** and **birth** for the selected countries. The goal is to reveal the location of countries that are growing rapidly in population. I have used size of the plotting symbol to represent the magnitude of the difference (the few small negative differences have been set to zero). There are two sets of positioning variables that define the frame. The first, **lat** and **lon**, represent the location of the countries measured. These are used to plot the circles showing **death-birth** differences. The second, **latitude** and **longitude**, are used to denote the locations on the map that anchor the boundaries of the polygons defining the continental borders. The *point* and *tile* graphics use a *position* attribute to control which variables in the frame determine their position. And the *tile* graphic also uses a *shape* argument to set the shape of each polygon. It is assumed that a map polygon coordinate resource or file (*e.g.*, world.map) is available and indexed by a key stored in the variable **continent**. Finally, the dimensions are transformed with a *mercator* cartographic projection. The axes and grid lines respond to the projection, as well as the graphics in the frame. We will examine in Chapter 10 map projections that are better suited for representing the countries data.

TRANS: **bd**=*diff*(**birth,death**)
TRANS: **bd**=*max*(**bd,0**)
FRAME: **lon*lat+longitude*latitude**
COORD: *project.mercator*()
GRAPH: *point*(*position*(**lon*lat**), *size*(**bd**), *color*("red"))
GRAPH: *tile*(*shape.polygon*(**continent**), *color*("blue"),
　　　position(**longitude*latitude**))

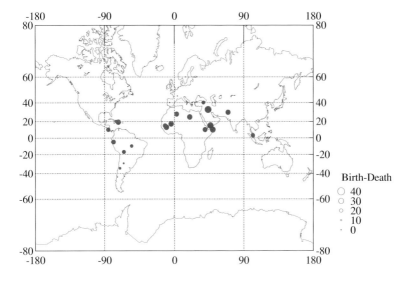

Figure 1.5 *Excess birth (vs. death) rates in selected countries.*

1.5 *What this book is not*

Because this book spans the fields of computer science, geography, statistics, and graphic design, it is likely to be misunderstood by specialists in different areas for different reasons. I cannot anticipate all of these reasons, but here are a likely few.

1.5.1 *Not a Command Language*

A cursory reading of this book might lead one to conclude that its purpose is to present a new graphics scripting language. Indeed, each figure is accompanied by a specification that resembles a command language. One impetus for this conclusion would be occasional similarities to existing quantitative graphics languages such as those in Mathematica[®], SYSTAT[®], S-Plus[®], and SAS-Graph[®]. These packages can produce a large variety of statistical graphics because they evolved to fulfill the needs of statisticians for sophisticated and flexible technical graphics. They were not developed with a comprehensive theory of graphics in mind, however. Often, their constructs have similar regularities because of the constraints of the graphics world. I owe a debt to all of these systems for being able to produce unusual graphics with them and to discover the common implicit structures. To appreciate the real difference between this and command-based systems, however, see Chapter 13.

Another conclusion one might draw after a brief glance is that this system is designed to be a static specification language instead of a dynamic, exploratory system. On the contrary, by regularizing the rules for graph behavior in graphics frames, it provides a richer environment for dynamic and exploratory graphics. This is especially true for paneled graphics, which are either avoided altogether in most dynamic graphics systems or hard-wired to specific data structures. In fact, the primary focus of my interest is in designing a system that is flexible enough to change state without re-specification. A naive approach to implementing such a system would be to create commands from user gestures, feed those commands to an interpreter, and then display the results. This method, employed in some existing packages, would indeed constrain it to be a static system. There is nothing in the theory presented in this book, however, to suggest that this is the best or even most appropriate implementation method.

1.5.2 Not a Taxonomy

Taxonomies are useful to scientists when they lead to new theory or stimulate insights into a problem that previous theorizing might conceal. Classification for its own sake, however, is as unproductive in design as it is in science. In design, objects are only as useful as the system they support. And the test of a design is its ability to handle scenarios that include surprises, exceptions, and strategic reversals. This book includes a few classifications, but they are in the service of developing objects that are flexible and powerful in a coherent system. Other classifications of the same problem domain are possible, but many of them would not lead to a parsimonious and general system. Some classifications have been attempted based on cluster analyses of ordinary users' visual judgments of similarities among real statistical graphics (*e.g.*, Lohse *et al.*, 1994). This approach may be useful for developing interfaces but contributes nothing to a deeper understanding of graphs. Customary usage and standards can blind us to the diversity of the graphics domain; a formal system can liberate us from conventional restrictions.

1.5.3 Not a Drafting Package

This system was not designed to produce any graphic imaginable. Indeed, the motivation is almost the opposite: to develop a closed system and *then* to examine whether it can produce both popular and esoteric graphics. I have tried to avoid adding functions, graphs, or operators that do not work independently across the system. There are doubtless many statistical graphics the system in this book cannot completely specify. We can add many different graphs, transformations, types of axes, annotations, etc., but there are two limitations we will always face with a formal system.

The first limitation applies to any free-hand drawing. Clearly, we cannot expect to use a formal data-driven system to produce sketches on cocktail napkins. It will always be possible to find creative designs that are not formally linked to data. The province of drafting systems is computer-assisted design (CAD) and desktop publishing (DTP). Those areas have their own rules driven more by the physical appearance of real objects than by the theoretical constructs of functional and data analysis.

The second limitation derives from the syntactical structure of the system itself. The operators in this system are capable, as we shall see, of producing a surprisingly wide variety of graphics, perhaps more than any other formal system or computer graphing program. On the other hand, one can imagine certain structures that may not be modeled by a language with the operators presented here. It is, after all, a closed system. This graphics system was designed with surveys of statistical graphics usage (*e.g.*, Fienberg, 1979) and existing commercial and scientific graphics software in mind. Nevertheless, one cannot over-estimate the inventiveness and ingenuity of real users when they display their ideas.

1.5.4 *Not a Book of Virtues*

This system is capable of producing some hideous graphics. There is nothing in its design to prevent its misuse. I will occasionally point out some of these instances (*e.g.*, Figure 10.24). That the system *can* produce such graphics is simply a consequence of its basis on the mathematical rules that determine the meaning of graphs, rather than on the *ad hoc* rules we sometimes use to produce graphics. These rules are not based on personal preferences but rather on the mathematics and perceptual dimensions underlying the graphics we draw in practice. These rules are just as capable of producing graphics for *USA Today* as for *Scientific American*.

This system cannot produce a meaningless graphic, however. This is a strong claim, vulnerable to a single counter-example. It is a claim based on the formal rules of the system, however, not on the evaluation of specific graphics it may produce. This is an essential difference between the approach in this book and in other texts on statistical graphics and visualization. I am much less interested in designing or evaluating specific graphics than in understanding the rules that produced them. Unless one specifies those rules explicitly, one cannot begin to claim that a particular graphic is meaningless or not.

I also cannot disagree strongly enough with statements about the dangers of putting powerful tools in the hands of novices. Computer algebra, statistics, and graphics systems provide plenty of rope for novices to hang themselves and may even help to inhibit the learning of essential skills needed by researchers. The obvious problems caused by this situation do not justify blunting our tools, however. They require better education in the imaginative and disciplined use of these tools. And they call for more attention to the way powerful and sophisticated tools are presented to novice users.

1.5.5 *Not a Heuristic System*

The title of this book is *The Grammar of Graphics*, not *A Grammar of Graphics*. While heuristic strategies are fun, pragmatic, and often remarkably adaptive, there is seldom reason to pursue them unless formal systems are shown to be deficient or elusive. It is sometimes fashionable to apply heuristics to well-defined problems in the name of artificial intelligence. If we take such an approach, it is our burden to prove that a heuristic system can accomplish everything a formal system can plus something more. Until we define the capabilities of a formal system, there is no way to make such a comparison.

Defining a formal system has practical implications in this field. Until recently, graphics were drawn by hand to represent mathematical, statistical, and geometric relations. Computer graphics programs, particularly scientific and mathematical plotting packages, have made this task much easier but they have not altered its *ad hoc* aspect. Nor have statistical and mathematical packages that generate more complex graphics contributed to our understanding of how they are created. Each new graphic in these programs was developed by an engineer who knew many of the rules in this book instinctively and applied them to a specific instance.

Now that **data mining** is popular, we need to be able to construct graphics systematically in order to handle more complex multivariate environments. Unfortunately, the sophistication of data mining algorithms far exceeds the graphical methods used in their displays. Most data mining systems still rely on pie, line, and bar charts of slices of **data cubes** (multi-way aggregations of a subset of a database). These charts fail to reveal the relationships among the entities they represent because they have no deep grammar for generating them. They are simply hard-wired to facets of the data cube. If we **drill through** the cube to view a different slice of the data, we still get a simple pie chart. A similar hard-wiring exists in displays from tree classifiers, neural networks, and other algorithms.

The remarkable consequence of building a closed formal system is that, while it solves more complex applied problems, it can appear more adaptive to the user. Paradoxically, closed systems often behave more "openly" than open systems. We should not confuse heuristics with flexibility. In the end, this book rests on what is perhaps an extreme position, but one I share with Jacques Bertin: designing and producing statistical graphics is not an art.

1.5.6 *Not a Geographic Information System*

This book includes several maps (*e.g.*, Figure 1.5). That might lead some readers to conclude that I regard it as the framework for a geographical information system (GIS). Indeed, I adopted from geographers some basic parts of this system, such as projections, layering, and aesthetic attributes (graphic variables). I believe that many statisticians interested in graphics have not given enough attention to the work of geographers. This situation has been changing recently, thanks to efforts of statisticians such as Daniel Carr and Linda Pickle, as well as geographers such as Mark Monmonier, Waldo Tobler, and Alan MacEachren.

The system in this book is not a model for a GIS, however, because geography and statistics differ in a crucial respect. Geography is anchored in real space-time and statistics in abstract dimensions. This is a distinction along a continuum rather than a sharp break; after all, there is a whole field called spatial statistics (Cressie, 1991). But this difference in focus clearly means that a system optimized to handle geography will not be graceful when dealing with statistical graphics such as Figure 11.16 and the system in this book would not do well if asked to provide a real-time tour through a geographical scene. There are many other consequences of this difference in focus. Geographers have developed topological algebras for scene analysis (*e.g.*, Egenhofer *et al.*, 1991), whereas I have employed a design algebra to model factorial structures. Geographers are concerned with iconography; I am concerned with relations.

Some geographers might disagree with my real-abstract distinction here. There is no question that the capabilities of a GIS can prove invaluable in visualizing abstract data. As Pinker (1996) has said, statistical graphics are often most effective when they exploit mental models that evolved as humans struggled to survive in a competitive world. But that brings me to my next point.

1.5.7 *Not a Visualization System*

This book includes some visualizations (*e.g.*, Figure 10.53). Scientific visualization uses realistic solid modeling and rendering techniques to represent real and abstract objects. I have taken advantage of some methods developed in the visualization literature. A visualization data-flow model is used for the backbone of this system, for example. And as with GIS, there is some cross-fertilization with statistics. Statisticians such as Dianne Cook, Jürgen Symanzik, and Edward Wegman (*e.g.*, Symanzik *et al.*, 1997) have employed immersive visualization technology developed by computer scientists such as Carolina Cruz-Neira and Thomas DeFanti (Cruz-Neira *et al.*, 1993) to display data.

We could define scientific visualization broadly to include GIS and statistical graphics. This would, I believe, vitiate its meaning. A better way to understand the differences between visualization and statistical graphics would be to compare visualization programs like PV~Wave[®] and Data Visualizer[®] to statistical graphics packages like SYSTAT[®] or S-Plus[®]. Going to extremes, we could even use a CAD-CAM engineering or an illustration package to do statistical graphics. Because we could does not mean we should.

1.6 Background

The scope of this book precludes an historical review of the field of statistical graphics. When designing a system, however, it is crucial to keep in mind the diverse and long-standing history of graphics and charts. Collins (1993) classifies historical trends in visualization, reminding us that the display methods used in modern computer visualization systems are centuries old. His illustrations, some dating to the 12th century, are especially informative. Collins shows that the principal contribution of the enormous recent literature on scientific visualization is its application to non-physical data rather than the displays themselves. Funkhouser (1937), Tilling (1975), Beniger and Robyn (1978), Fienberg (1979), Robinson (1982), Stigler (1983), Tufte (1983, 1990, 1997), and Wainer (1997) offer additional material on the history of statistical graphics that supports Collins' argument.

Others have investigated statistical graphics from a theoretical viewpoint, often providing ideas that are used in this book. Bertin (1967, 1977) is the pioneer in the area of modern graphic classification and design; his work underlies almost all of Chapter 7. Cleveland (1985) helped establish a framework for understanding the role of graphical elements in displays. Pinker (1990) proposed an information-processing model of graphical reading. Brodlie (1993) integrated concepts underlying both scientific visualization and statistical graphics. MacEachren (1995) extended Bertin's work by following systematic psychological and design principles. And Roth *et al.* (1995) developed a graphical system for querying and manipulating data. Their work, independent of mine and based on a different foundation, is nevertheless close in spirit to the content of this book.

1.7 Sequel

The remainder of this book will present each segment of this formal system. Chapter 2, particularly Figure 2.1, contains the outline for most of the book. I will begin by defining concepts through the task of constructing a pie graphic from data. The subsequent chapters proceed through the components of Figure 2.1, mostly from bottom to top. The title of each chapter is a major component. Chapter 3 covers data and datasets, including functions for organizing data. Chapter 4 covers variables and variable sets, the entities by which we define graphs. The next four chapters – Algebra, Geometry, Aesthetics, and Statistics – form the heart of the system. These are the four components that we assemble in practically any combination to construct a huge variety of graphics. Varset algebra comprises the operations that allow us to combine variables and specify dimensions of graphs. Geometry covers graphs and the creation of geometric objects from variables. Aesthetics are the sensory attributes used to represent graphics. And Statistics are the functions that allow graphs to change their appearance and representation schemes. Chapter 9 covers scales, which allow us to represent different measurement systems in graphics. Chapter 10 reviews coordinate systems, from polar coordinates to more complex map projections and general transformations. Chapter 11 covers facets, the coordinates that enable us to construct graphics of tables and tables of graphics. Chapter 12 deals with guides, such as axes and legends.

The remaining chapters investigate consequences of organizing our view of graphics through this system. Chapter 13 describes a graphboard – a user interface that allows us to construct and modify complex graphics interactively by taking advantage of the deep grammar of graphics presented in this book. Chapter 14 presents a graphics reader – a system that converts graphics to data. I will conclude with a case study of a famous chart in order to approach an answer to the question of the meaning of a graphic.

The titles of each chapter are (with the exception of the next) a single word. These words designate components that contain objects and behaviors more like each other than like those in other components. Not every one of these components is named in Figure 2.1 because some are subsystems or stages of the ones named. Nevertheless, it is reasonable to regard these chapters as cumulative, so it would not be easy to jump in at randomly selected locations. You may want to look ahead to see where applications fit into the system, but much of the terminology in later chapters depends on the definitions in the earlier.

2

How to Make a Pie

A pie chart is perhaps the most ubiquitous of modern graphics. It has been reviled by statisticians (unjustifiably) and adored by managers (unjustifiably). It may be the most concrete chart, in the sense that it *is* a pie. A five year old can look at a slice and be a fairly good judge of proportion. (To prevent bias, give the child the knife and someone else the first choice of slices.) The pie is so popular nowadays that graphical operating systems include a primitive function for drawing a pie slice. Nothing could be simpler.

Simple things usually deserve deeper examination. Despite the apparent simplicity of a pie, making one invokes almost every aspect of a graphics grammar. If we learn how to make a pie, we can create almost any statistical graphic. I will first present the general recipe for making a graphic and then I will go step-by-step through the process of making a pie, pausing occasionally for definitions.

Figure 2.1 summarizes the recipe for making a graphic. The vertical orientation of this figure resembles what used to be called a **data flow** model (Upson *et al.*, 1989), in which a set of data passes through a sequence of operations. This is not exactly a data flow, however, because the objects inside the rounded borders at each stage are not all transformations of data. The horizontal orientation represents agents of change. The "noun" objects in the rounded borders (Data, Dataset, Varset, Graph, Graphic) are transmuted by the "verb" function objects on the left (DataView, VarMap, Grapher, Aesthetic). Each noun object is also modified by the "adjective" transformation class attached to it on the right (Reference, Algebra, Coordinate).

I use grammatical parts of speech metaphorically to illustrate only the roles of these objects. In object-oriented design, we usually think of *any* object as a thing. Nevertheless, it is helpful to look in the definition of a noun object for "what it is." And it is helpful to look in the definition of a verb object for "what it does" to nouns. And it is helpful to look in an adjective definition for "how it modifies" nouns. All of the objects in Figure 2.1 are written in upper case because they are proper names. These proper names designate objects in a system that contain computer code or methods for doing various things. An aesthetic, for example, is a perceivable attribute such as size or color. The object Aesthetic, on the other hand, implements functions that assign aesthetics to objects in a computer program. It has to handle a number of related tasks, including indexing aesthetic attributes, packaging them so that a renderer can implement each appropriately, and so on.

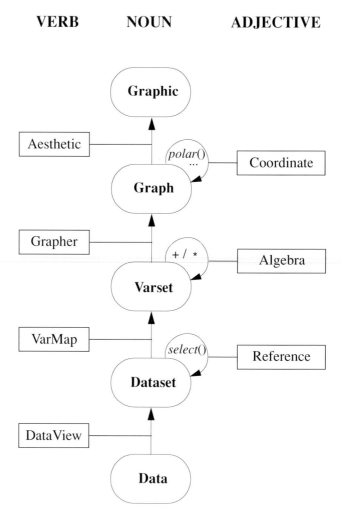

Figure 2.1 *From data to graphic*

It is important to keep in mind that Figure 2.1 is only one slice through the architecture of a system that produces graphics. As Booch (1994) indicates, an object-oriented system can be represented by a series of "orthogonal" object diagrams, each of which provides a different functional view of the system. Figure 2.1 gives us the ingredients and the dependencies among them, but it does not tell us how to assemble the ingredients. We could make some ahead of time, we could group them by type of task, or we could produce them in serial order. To keep things simple for now, I will use Figure 2.1 as a script for this chapter; we will assemble ingredients sequentially from bottom to top in the figure. At each stage, I will repeat the lower parts of Figure 2.1 so that you do not need to study the whole thing now, memorize it, or refer back later in the chapter. First, however, I will provide some elementary definitions of terms so that we can share a common notation.

2.1 Definitions

The following definitions are fairly standard. Because words like *relation* are used differently in various applications in mathematics, computer science, and statistics, I have tried to give them a common notation and structure wherever possible. This means that my notation may differ from that used in some specialized fields. Choosing a level of abstraction and a level of detail is not easy. I have tried to avoid abstraction when it does not suit our purposes and I have included terms only when they are needed for understanding the system.

2.1.1 Sets

A **set** is a collection of objects, which we denote by a capital letter (*e.g.*, X). An object in a set is called an **element** or a **member** of the set. We denote an element by a lower case letter (*e.g.*, x), and state that "x is an element of X" with the notation $x \in X$. The **null set** is an empty set, or a set with no elements. We denote the set of real numbers by R and natural numbers (integers greater than zero) by N. We use the notation $A = \{a: a \in R, a > 0\}$ to denote the statement "A is the set of a such that a is a member of the set of real numbers and a is greater than zero." If every element of a set A is also an element of set B, then A is a **subset** of B, denoted $A \subseteq B$. If A is a subset of B, but there is at least one element of B that is not in A, then A is a **proper subset** of B, denoted $A \subset B$.

Two real numbers a and b, with $a < b$, determine an **interval** in R. Two types of intervals are:

$(a, b) = \{x : a < x < b\}$ an open interval, and

$[a, b] = \{x : a \leq x \leq b\}$ a closed interval

We may also have intervals closed on the left and open on the right, or open on the left and closed on the right.

The **union** of two sets A and B, denoted by $A \cup B$, is the set

$$A \cup B = \{x : x \in A \text{ or } x \in B\}.$$

For example, if $A = \{1, 2\}$ and $B = \{2, 3, 4\}$ then $A \cup B = \{1, 2, 3, 4\}$.

The **disjoint union** of two sets A_1 and A_2, denoted by $A_1 \sqcup A_2$, produces a set whose members are tagged elements. A tagged element is one of the form $x{:}\$$, where $x \in X$ is the element and the symbol $\$$ is the **tag**. A tag is sometimes called an **identifier**; it may be a string, a numerical value, or another piece of information. For a disjoint union, we tag an element with the name of the set containing it. The elements of $A_1 \sqcup A_2$ are the tagged elements $x{:}A_i$, where x ranges over all elements of A_i and i ranges from 1 to 2. For example, if $A = \{1, 2\}$ and $B = \{2, 3, 4\}$ then $A \sqcup B = \{1{:}A, 2{:}A, 2{:}B, 3{:}B, 4{:}B\}$. Tags are only tags. They do not enter into numerical calculations.

The **intersection** of two sets A and B, denoted by $A \cap B$, is the set

$$A \cap B = \{x : x \in A \text{ and } x \in B\}.$$

If $A = \{1, 2\}$ and $B = \{2, 3, 4\}$ then $A \cap B = \{2\}$.

The (Cartesian) **product** of sets A and B, denoted by $A \times B$, is the set

$$A \times B = \{(a, b) : a \in A \text{ and } b \in B\}.$$

For our example, $A \times B = \{(1,2), (1,3), (1,4), (2,2), (2,3), (2,4)\}$.

We call (a, b) an **ordered pair** or a **tuple**. Although the notation is the same as that for an open interval, the meaning should be clear from context. We call $(a_1, a_2, \ldots, a_n)$ an **n-tuple**. We call the item a_i $(i = 1, \ldots, n)$ in an n-tuple an **entry**. The **degree** of an n-tuple is n. We denote the product set of n-tuples of the real numbers by $\boldsymbol{R}^n$.

A **finite set** is either the null set or a set for which there exists a one-to-one correspondence from it to the set $\{1, 2, \ldots, m\}$, where m is a positive integer. The **cardinality** of a finite set is m, the count of its elements. An **indexed set** is a set of the form $\{(1, a_1), (2, a_2), \ldots, (m, a_m)\}$.

2.1.2 Relations

Let A and B be sets. A **binary relation** R between A and B is a subset of $A \times B$. Given a tuple (a, b) in $A \times B$, we say that a is related to b by R if $(a, b) \in R$. An example is the relation between the set of real numbers $\boldsymbol{R}$ and itself given by $R = \{(x, y) : x \leq y, x \in \boldsymbol{R}, y \in \boldsymbol{R}\}$. Another example is the relation R between the sets

$A = \{$"boy", "girl"$\}$, and

$B = \{$"Mary", "John", "Jean", "Pittsburgh"$\}$, given by

$R = \{($"boy", "John"$), ($"boy", "Jean"$), ($"girl", "Mary"$), ($"girl", "Jean"$)\}$.

It is possible for some members of A not to be related through R to any member of B and possible for some members of B not to be related through R to any members of A.

An ***n*-ary relation** R on $A_1 \times A_2 \times \ ... \ A_n$ is a subset of $A_1 \times A_2 \times \ ... \ A_n$. Some authors notate such a relation by tagging, *e.g.*,

$$R = \{(a_{11}: A_1, a_{12}:A_2, \ ... \ , a_{1n}: A_n), \ ..., \ (a_{m1}: A_1, a_{m2}:A_2, \ ... \ , a_{mn}: A_n)\} \ ,$$

where $a_{ij} \in A_j$.

2.1.3 Functions

Suppose that to each element of a set A we assign a unique element of a set B. The collection of these assignments is a **function**, which is also called a **mapping** from A into B. To indicate that f assigns elements of B to elements of A, we write

$$f: A \rightarrow B$$

We call A the **domain** of f and B the **co-domain** of f. The element $f(a) \in B$ is the unique element in B that f assigns to $a \in A$. We call the set of these elements $\{f(a): a \in A \}$ the **image** of A under f or the **range** of f. Another way to describe a function (without naming it explicitly) is to use the symbol $\mapsto$. In this usage, "$a \mapsto b$" means "the function that assigns b to a."

An object that acts like a function is perhaps most easily understood as a black box that receives input and returns output. For every input, there is only one possible output. That output need not be a single number or string. The output is whatever form the elements of the co-domain B take. Many different inputs may produce the same output, but we may not have more than one tagged output for a given input. This black-box definition includes the function $f(x) = x^2$ as well as the function $f(a\ binary\ tree) = the\ list\ of\ its\ parent-child\ relations$.

2.1.4 Graphs

For each function $f: A \rightarrow B$ there is a subset of $A \times B$:

$$\{(a, f(a)): a \in A \}$$

that we call the **graph** of f. The graph of the function $f(x) = x^2$, where x belongs to the set of real numbers, is the set of all tuples (x, x^2), which is a subset of the crossing of the set of real numbers with itself. The graph of the function $f(a\ binary\ tree) = the\ list\ of\ its\ parent\text{-}child\ relations$ is the set of all tuples defined by $(a\ binary\ tree, the\ list\ of\ its\ parent\text{-}child\ relations)$, which is a subset of the crossing of the set of all binary trees with the set of all lists of parent-child relations. The graph of a function uniquely determines the function, and *vice versa*. For example, if (2,4) is the graph of f, then $f(2)=4$.

2.1.5 *Compositions*

A **composition** is a function formed from a chain of functions. Let $f: X \to Y$ and $g: Y' \to Z$ be functions for which the co-domain of f is a subset of the domain of g (*i.e.*, $Y \subseteq Y'$). The function $g \circ f: X \to Z$ defined by the rule

$$(g \circ f)(x) = g(f(x)) \quad \text{for all} \ x \in X$$

is the composition or **composite function** of f and g.

For example, if f and g are text string functions and the rule for f is *<capitalize leftmost letter>* and the rule for g is *<count number of capitals>*, then the following compositions are defined because all the inputs are members of the set of text strings and any output of f is a legal input for g.

$$g(f("Wow")) = 1$$
$$g(f("woW")) = 2$$
$$g(f("wow")) = 1$$
$$g(f("alec")) = 1$$
$$g(f("123")) = 0$$
$$g(f("")) = 0$$

The range of the composition is the range of g, namely the set of non-negative integers. Also, the null string is a member of the set of strings. If we implement these functions in a language like C, we must be sure to handle nulls properly.

2.1.6 *Transformations*

A **transformation** is a function $f: A \to A$ mapping a set A to itself. All transformations are functions, but not all functions are transformations. Because a transformation maps a set to itself, a composition of transformations is a transformation.

For example, if f and g are text string transformations and the rule for f is *<capitalize leftmost letter>* and the rule for g is *<append exclamation>*, then the following compositions are all transformations.

$$g(f(\text{"wow"})) = \text{"Wow!"}$$
$$g(f(\text{"Wow!"})) = \text{"Wow!!"}$$
$$f(f(\text{"wow"})) = \text{"Wow"}$$
$$g(g(\text{"wow"})) = \text{"wow!!"}$$
$$f(g(f(\text{"wow"}))) = \text{"Wow!"}$$
$$g(f(g(\text{"wow"}))) = \text{"Wow!!"}$$
$$f(g(\text{""})) = \text{"!"}$$

2.1.7 Algebras

An **algebra** is a collection of 1) **sets**, 2) **operators** on sets, and 3) **rules** for the combination of these operators. This definition includes algebras more general, limited, or abstract than the classical algebra underlying ordinary arithmetic on real numbers.

An operator generalizes the notion of transformation. An operator on a set X is a function defined on the set $X \times X \times \ ... \ X$ that returns a value in X. Operators are **unary** or **monadic** (having one argument, *i.e.* defined on X, and so a transformation), **binary** or **diladic** (having two arguments, *i.e.* defined on $X \times X$), or ***n*-ary** (having many arguments, *i.e.* defined on the n-fold crossing of X with itself). Algebraic rules specify how operators are to be composed. An example is the operator "+" on the set R defined by $(a, b) \mapsto a+b$.

2.2 Recipe

Now we will follow our recipe from beginning to end. Each subsection of this section will concern a noun object from Figure 2.1. And each subsection of those subsections will concern their associated verb and adjective objects. The definitions from now on will be for terms that are peculiar to this graphics system, although I will build on the standard definitions in the previous section.

2.2.1 Data

The ingredients of a graphic are **data**. Data are recorded observations of quantities, qualities, or relations. Data have no necessary organization or structure. They are simply a collection of information. Figure 2.2 shows this by enclosing in a dashed border the data from which we will make our pie.

Although we will create a pie for the females only, the data underlying a graphic must include relevant information about what the graphic represents. If anything, the data in Figure 2.3 are a subset of the data we need to construct our graphic. We need to read Morton and Price (1989) to understand fully what our graphic will mean. In a modern computer graphics system, it would not be unusual to include a **hypertext markup language** (HTML) copy of the book linked to the labels and slices of the pie in the on-screen graphic. I will focus only on the few variables needed to draw our pie in this chapter, but I will cover some of these issues further in Chapter 3.

We are accustomed to thinking of data as a row/column table of numbers or text, but such a table is a dataset, not data. A dataset and data can both reside in a computer – the former in a database and the latter in a free text file. A dataset and data can both rest on a desk – the former in an organized box of index cards or printed table, the latter in a pile of miscellaneous papers. In other words, a dataset requires an indexing system; data do not. Before we can proceed, we need to organize our data into a dataset.

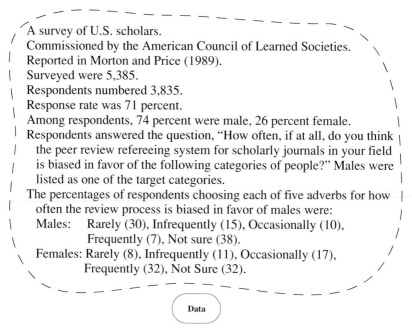

A survey of U.S. scholars.
Commissioned by the American Council of Learned Societies.
Reported in Morton and Price (1989).
Surveyed were 5,385.
Respondents numbered 3,835.
Response rate was 71 percent.
Among respondents, 74 percent were male, 26 percent female.
Respondents answered the question, "How often, if at all, do you think the peer review refereeing system for scholarly journals in your field is biased in favor of the following categories of people?" Males were listed as one of the target categories.
The percentages of respondents choosing each of five adverbs for how often the review process is biased in favor of males were:
Males: Rarely (30), Infrequently (15), Occasionally (10), Frequently (7), Not sure (38).
Females: Rarely (8), Infrequently (11), Occasionally (17), Frequently (32), Not Sure (32).

Data

Figure 2.2 Data

2.2.2 Dataset

A **dataset** is an indexed set of data. Each element in a dataset is called an **entry** or a **value**. Datasets are not always located in a single place or time. They are distinguished from raw data not by physical location but by indexing. Datasets are indexed by some scheme so that we can find data in them and associate data elements with each other. The object Dataset contains a dataset.

Figure 2.3 shows the dataset from which we will construct our pie. I have organized the data according to a tree because this is a popular form for documenting on-line or printed datasets and is a structure used in hierarchical da-

tabases. Other organizational models can be used, as long as we can locate the
information we need in order to create our graphic.

```
object: survey
      client: ACLS
      source: Morton and Price (1989)
      medium: mail questionnaire
      population: academics
      sample: convenience
            breakdown: stage
                  category: initial
                        count: 5385
                  category: final
                        count: 3835
                        breakdown: gender
                              category: male
                                    percent: 74
                              category: female
                                    percent: 26
      items: multiple choice
            ID: "Bias in reviewing"
                  text: "How often ... biased in favor of males?"
                  breakdown: response, gender
                        category: Rarely, male
                              count: 30
                        category:  Rarely, female
                              count: 8
                        category: Infrequently, male
                              count: 15
                        category: Infrequently, female
                              count: 11
                        ...
                        category: Not sure, male
                              count: 38
                        category: Not sure, female
                              count: 32
            ID: ...
```

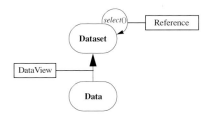

Figure 2.3 *Dataset*

2.2.2.1 DataView

A **data view** is a function that produces a dataset from a set of raw data. Different data views use different organizing schemes (*e.g.*, hierarchical, relational, topological). The DataView object implements data views by establishing an indexing scheme and associating data with the indices.

2.2.2.2 Reference

A **reference** is a mechanism for locating an object. In a computer, a reference points to an address in memory where an object is stored. In some computer languages (*e.g.*, C and C++), this address itself may be stored and manipulated; we call such a reference a **pointer**. In other languages (*e.g.*, FORTRAN and Java), the **name** of an object is its reference. In either case, a reference involves an operation on an index set of addresses.

The Reference object is a collection of functions that operate on index sets. These functions are all transformations; they operate on index sets and produce index sets. Some functions in Reference may permute indices, for example, so that a tree structure like that in Figure 2.3 could be converted to a sequential list of indices. Other functions in Reference may subset a dataset by converting some indices to null values (i.e. deleting them). We use functions in Reference to organize and filter out the data we need for creating variables.

We are ready for our next step in the recipe. To create a graphic, we need to work with variables rather than data. We need to be able to refer to *response* rather than a collection of strings such as "Rarely" or "Infrequently." For this, we need a varset.

2.2.3 Varset

Let $X_1, \dots, X_n$ be n sets. A **variable set**, or **varset**, is a set defined by:

$$varset[X_1, \dots, X_n] = \{[I, X_1, \dots, X_n, f]\} \text{ , where}$$

I is an index set $\{1, 2, \dots, m\}$,

m ranges over all the natural numbers N,

$f : I \rightarrow X_1 \times X_2 \times \dots X_n$, and

f ranges over all such possible functions.

A **variable** is a variable set of the form $V = varset[X]$. If X is a finite set, we say that V is a **categorical variable**. If X is a set of real numbers or tagged real numbers, then we say that V is a **continuous variable**.

An **instance** of a variable set is the tuple $[I_m, X_1, \ldots, X_n, f]$, where m is a natural number and the other terms are defined as above. An instance of a variable is the triple $[I_m, X, f]$. For example, an indexed list of 75 real numbers between -10 and 10 can be written as an instance of a variable $[I_m, X, f]$ in the following way:

$$varset[X] - \{[I_m, X, f] : I_m = \{1, \ldots, m\}, m \in N, f : I_m \to X \}$$

There are 75 rows in this table, so $m = 75$. The set X is the range of the interval $(-10, 10)$. If the list of data are labeled in order $x_1, x_2, \ldots, x_{75}$, then $f : I_{75} \to X$ is given by $f(i) = x_i$.

A variable set is a special case of a relation. Consider the relation

$$\{(a_{11}: D_1, a_{12}: D_2, \ldots, a_{1n}: D_n), \ldots, (a_{m1}: D_1, a_{m2}: D_2, \ldots, a_{mn}: D_n)\}$$

where a_{ij} are m tuples of attribute values measured on n domains D_j, with m representing the cardinality of the set (number of tuples), and n the degree of the relation (number of attributes in each tuple). A variable set requires that $a_{11} = 1, a_{21} = 2, \ldots, a_{m1} = m$. The set $D_1 = \{1, \ldots, m\}$ is called a **key** in a relational database system. Statistical packages sometimes call this key a **case number**.

Table 2.1 and Figure 2.4 show a variable set for making our pie. The rows and columns of this table are indexed, so that we can retrieve any entry (a_{ij}) by specifying its index. By this indexing, we can associate the response "Rarely" with the value 8, for example. We can also associate the identifier Response with the strings and the identifier Female with the numbers.

The object Varset contains variable sets. Although variable sets are special cases of a relation, this does not mean that Varset is a relational database system (Date, 1995). We may wish to implement parts of this system with a relational database, but there are performance and other considerations that may require other approaches. I will discuss some of these problems in Chapter 3 and Chapter 5.

Table 2.1

Key	Response	Female
1	Rarely	8
2	Infrequently	11
3	Occasionally	17
4	Frequently	32
5	Not Sure	32

Variable 1
name is **response**
label is "Adverb presented to respondents"
domain is {1, 2, 3, 4, 5}
range is {"Rarely", "Infrequently", "Occasionally", "Frequently", "Not Sure"}
instance (subset of domain-cross-range) is **response**
values of **response** are {(1, "Rarely"), (2, "Infrequently), (3, "Occasionally"),
                    (4, "Frequently"), (5, "Not Sure")}

Variable 2
name is *female*
label is "Percentage of responding females choosing adverb"
domain is {1, 2, 3, 4, 5}
range is [0, 100]
instance (subset of domain-cross-range) is **female**
values of **female** are {(1, 8), (2, 11), (3, 17), (4, 32), (5, 32)}

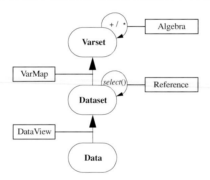

Figure 2.4 *Varset*

2.2.3.1 *VarMap*

A **variable map** is a function mapping a dataset to a variable set. This mapping is from a key index set to sets of values in a dataset. VarMap implements variable map functions. VarMap must accomplish the following tasks:

- Monitor the range of each variable in order to trap errors in the dataset. If a value in a dataset is out of range, for example, a VarMap must either know how to assign an appropriate value or inform clients that the value on the variable cannot be processed.

- Continue to return values correctly in the range for all possible values in the domain while the dataset itself is changing over time.

For our pie example, the ranges for our variables are one-to-one related to the corresponding data values in the dataset. This is not necessarily true, however. We might, for example, expect a reponse "Refuse to answer" that never occurred in our dataset. If we plan to hook up VarMap to different datasets or databases from different surveys to do pie charts in the future, we should include this value in the range of responses even if we have never seen it. Taking care to do this insures that we can trap illegal values and take appropriate action instead of producing a misleading graphic or undefined operation or exception.

2.2.3.2 Algebra

A general definition of an algebra is given in Section 2.1.7. The Algebra object implements an algebra on variable sets. It has three binary operators and a collection of associated rules. I will discuss them in Chapter 5. The output of Algebra is $varset[X_1, \ldots, X_n]$.

There is another object, not shown in Figure 2.1, that operates on Varset together with Algebra. This object, called Transform, is a set of monadic functions that transform variables. These are discussed in Chapter 4.

We do not need algebra to make our pie, however. We do not even need any variable transformations (such as changing percents to proportions), so I will proceed directly to the next stage. We have sets of variables. Now we need to create the geometry necessary to represent our pie.

2.2.4 Graph

A graph is defined in Section 2.1.4. The Graph object is a collection comprising a graph and the methods needed for representing it as a geometric object. This includes the information about the coordinate system in which it will be embedded and the function which is needed to create the graph itself.

Figure 2.5 shows the creation of a graph for our pie. The creation of a graph from a varset is handled by an object called Grapher. Grapher applies a desired graphing function to the variables in a varset and this results in a subset of a crossing of sets (the domain of the graphing function crossed with its range).

I will discuss the particular pie graph appearing in Figure 2.5 in more detail later in this section. At this point, it is enough to keep in mind that the indexed set called *graph* in the figure contains one interval in the range for every string value in the domain. This interval will define the geometric object that eventually is transformed into a pie slice. Every point inside a single pie slice can be traced back to one and only one of these intervals.

Graph:
{(1,"Rarely", [0, 8)), (2,"Infrequently", [0, 11)), (3,"Occasionally", [0, 17)),
(4,"Frequently", [0, 32)), (5,"Not Sure", [0, 32))}

Coordinates:

polar.theta() receives the *bar* graph and creates coordinates (ρ_i, θ_i) ,
where $\rho_i = 1$ and $\theta_i = 2\pi(x_i/100)$ for all points contained in *bar*().

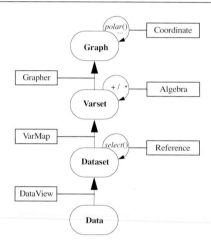

Figure 2.5 *Graph*

2.2.4.1 *Grapher*

A **graph** is a subset of a crossing of sets. The object called Grapher produces
a graph from a set of variables using a particular graphing function. Grapher
also sees to some other housekeeping tasks. One important task is to relate the
sets $X_1, \ldots, X_n$ in Varset to the dimensions of a geometric space in which the
graph will be embedded. We name these dimensions *dim1*, *dim2*, and so on. If
X_i is continuous, then $dim_i = \boldsymbol{R}$ and if X_i is categorical, then $dim_i = \boldsymbol{N}$.

We will use an interval graphing function called *bar*() for our pie. This
function receives a set of tuples for its input and outputs a set of tuples, each
of which contains one interval-valued entry. For our pie, Grapher feeds tuples
from Varset1 and Varset2 to the interval graphing function *bar*() in order to
create the graph shown in Figure 2.5. For example, the *bar*() function receives
the tuple (1, "Rarely") from Varset1 and the tuple (1, 8) from Varset2. For these
tuples, it outputs the tuple (1,"Rarely", [0, 8)). Notice the index is retained, and
the value 8 has been converted to the interval [0, 8). Because *bar*() is an interval-
valued function, it outputs intervals. Notice also that all the intervals overlap in

the graph in Figure 2.5. We are going to have to do something about this later; if we do not, all our pie slices will overlap. We *could* make a bar chart with these intervals organized this way, but we are in the pie business right now, so we will plan to take care of this problem later by stacking slices.

The first entry in each tuple *bar*() has made is the index we have been carrying along since we created the dataset, the second entry corresponds to **response**, and the third entry corresponds to **female**. Our graph has two dimensions. The first corresponds to the domain of the graph (**response**) and the second to the range (**female**). At this point, we need to relate this set to geometry.

2.2.4.2 Coordinate

When we use an *n*-tuple to denote a point in a space, we call its entries the **coordinates** of the point. A **coordinate system** is a scheme for locating a point in a space given its coordinates. This scheme includes 1) an **axis** for each dimension corresponding to a tuple entry, 2) a **scale** for each axis, and 3) a method for locating any point in the space given the values in its *n*-tuple. The best known coordinate system is called Cartesian coordinates. For ordinary two-dimensional Cartesian coordinates, the axes are two perpendicular straight lines. The scales are measured such that the **origin**, the location of the point $(0, 0)$, is at the intersection of the axes and such that equal differences between any two tuple entry values correspond to equal distances measured along the axes. The method for locating a point in the two-dimensional space is to find the location of each entry of the tuple on its corresponding axis and then find the intersection of the two straight lines that pass through these points and are parallel to the other axis.

We can construct other coordinate systems by modifying any of these three components. For example, instead of perpendicular straight lines for axes, we might pick oblique straight lines or even curves. We might choose a logarithmic scale instead of equal intervals on one or more of the axes. And we might use a method that employs intersecting curves instead of straight lines for locating a point. For our pie, we will use a polar coordinate system.

So far, the space linked to our coordinates has infinite extent. When we get around to drawing lines and other objects, we cannot draw forever. We could wait until later and clip lines inside a drawing window. This method works fine for rendering real geometric objects, but it is not a good idea for statistical graphics. As we shall see in Chapter 10, we should not include values outside our window when calculating statistical and other estimates. We need to clip sooner. For this type of model-based clipping, we will use something called a frame.

A **frame** is a coordinate system applied to tuples whose entries are limited to intervals. For example, a 2D Cartesian frame is a subset of the plane that is represented by the points with Cartesian coordinates (x, y), where x is in the interval $[a, b] = \{x : a \leq x \leq b\}$ and y is in $[u, v] = \{y : u \leq y \leq v\}$. If we choose to plot values on a scale from 0 to 100 in a region that is 10 centimeters wide, for example, we want to exclude from all computations any values less than 0 or greater than 100. The clipping produced by a frame is not based on physical (centimeter) coordinates. A frame is a bounded region. I will discuss this concept further in Chapter 6.

The frame for a particular graph determines how Grapher produces the graph. That is, Grapher limits its computations to those tuples that lie within the boundaries defined by the frame. If a frame changes by switching coordinate systems, for example, Grapher may need to recalculate the graph if it is using some statistical methods that are defined differently in different coordinate systems. I will discuss this further in Chapter 8 and Chapter 9.

The Frame object (not shown in Figure 2.1) contains information about the frame for producing a graph. This includes coordinates, scales, minima and maxima on each scale, and the indexes and references to dimensions of a space. All this is stored in a resource that is accessible to clients needing this information.

The Coordinate object in Figure 2.1 transforms graphs. It is used to represent graphs in rectangular, polar, and other coordinate systems. Coordinate transformations are limited to those that maintain the functional relationship between the domain and range of a particular graph.

The polar coordinate function used for our pie will convert rectangular objects to polar ones. When drawing is done, we will see a pie slice instead of a bar. The *polar.theta*() method sets the radius to a constant and maps a single variable (**female**) to the polar angle. Notice that the tuples in the graph are not transformed at this point. The polar transformation is bound to the graph to await transformation later when the graph is drawn. This allows more intelligent handling of text and other physical aspects of the rendering.

We now have a graph, but we cannot see it, hear it, smell it, or perceive it in any way other than parsing the set in Figure 2.5 and imagining it in our mind's eye. It is time to attach perceptible attributes (position on a plane, color, etc.) to the tuples in our graph.

2.2.5 Graphic

A **graphic** is a composite image of a graph under one or more aesthetic functions. The Graphic object is responsible for realizing the graphic in a display system. Figure 2.6 shows the graphic for our pie example. The *bar* graph has four associated aesthetic functions: *label*(), *color*(), *position*(), and *shape*(). The input to each of these functions is a graph plus the index of the entry in each tuple on which the function is to operate.

2.2.5.1 Aesthetic

An **aesthetic function** maps tuples or entries of tuples to strings or real numbers that serve as input to a physical display device such as a video screen, printer, or audio speaker. Aesthetic is an object that implements aesthetic functions. For example, if we wish to represent the value "Frequently" with the color red, we need to assign this string to a single value or tuple of values that is defined by the interface to a color generator. The interface to the generator determines the value we assign, whether it is 650 nanometers for a light source or the tuple $(1, 0, 0)$ for a (red, green, blue) color mixer.

In our example, the *label*() aesthetic function receives the set of tuples in the graph, separates out the entries corresponding to **response**, and outputs a set of tuples containing text strings for input to a printer/plotter. I define *label*() as an aesthetic function because it ouputs a value that produces a perceivable image (categorical text) when input to a display system.

The *color*() function works similarly, but it converts the same text strings to index values that point to a color table in the display system. I have used colored words to show this in the figure; those words should be interpreted as indices.

The *position*() function is an aesthetic that converts real-valued tuples to plotting coordinates on a display system. The *position.stack*() method of the *position*() function cumulates the intervals so that we will eventually end up with a stack of geometric bar objects that look like a set of stacked toy blocks. This is the stacking that I referred to earlier in Section 2.2.4.1. (To save space, I have omitted the variable name **female** from the GRAPH statement in the specification. If an argument is omitted from an aesthetic function, it is assumed to be taken from the FRAME statement.)

How do we get 2D blocks out of 1D intervals? That is the responsibility of the *shape.rect*() aesthetic function. This function takes the intervals and outputs display coordinates that delineate rectangles. I have used little rectangles to denote the result of this function. These rectangles are meant to represent coordinates for rectangles. Because display systems include geometric primitives such as bars and circles, our aesthetic functions ought to be written to take advantage of them as native objects whenever possible. Again, I have omitted **female** from *shape.rect*(). It is assumed from the frame.

The last thing we need is to apply our polar coordinate transformation before the rendering system actually draws our object. By postponing this operation as late in the pipeline as possible, we have made the system more flexible. The same code can produce a divided bar or pie. This is one example that follows one of my favorite maxims of good design, the title of an MIT AI Lab report, "Planning is just a way of avoiding figuring out what to do next" (Brooks, 1987).

Specification:

FRAME:**female**

COORD:*polar.theta*()

GRAPH:*bar*(*label*(**response**),*color*(**response**),*position.stack*(),*shape.rect*())

Graphic:

bar(*<aesthetic attributes>*) = ***perceivable graphic***

Aesthetics:

label(**response**): "Rarely" ↦ "Rarely", "Infrequently" ↦ "Infrequently",
        "Occasionally", ↦ "Occasionally", "Frequently" ↦ "Frequently",
        "Not sure" ↦ "Not sure"

color(**response**): "Rarely ↦ green, "Infrequently" ↦ blue,
        "Occasionally" ↦ yellow, "Frequently" ↦ red,
        "Not Sure" ↦ violet

position.stack(**female**): [0,8) ↦ [0,8), [0,11) ↦ [8,19), [0,17) ↦ [19,36),
        [0,32) ↦ [36,68), [0,32) ↦ 68,100)

shape.rect(**female**): [0,8) ↦ ▯ , [0,11) ↦ ▯ , [0,17) ↦ □ ,
        [0,32) ↦ ⬜ , [0,32) ↦ ⬜

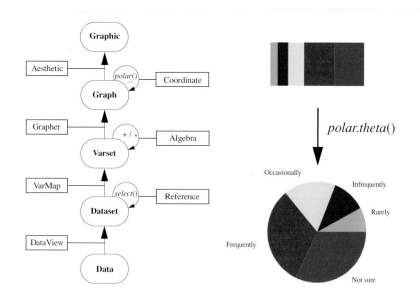

Figure 2.6 *Graphic*

2.3 Notation

Each graphic in this book is accompanied by a symbolic specification. As I have indicated, this specification is not a computer language or command system, although the syntax has been designed to fit naturally into a Java string-tokenizer and extended markup language (XML) environment. The main purpose of the specification syntax is to allow compact summarization of the components represented in Figure 2.1. When you examine a particular graphic, it is important to spend enough time on the specification to understand the meaning of the graphic. The meaning of a graphic is its specification and associated data.

2.3.1 Specifications

The specifications at the head of each graphic follow these conventions:

> **BOLD CAPITAL**: data objects
> ***bold italic***: variables
> **bold roman**: instances of variables (*e.g.*, finite samples)
> *light italic*: functions

Not every printed specification is sufficient for producing the entire graph shown in the figure. I have omitted details such as positioning of legends, annotation, and labeling of axes in order to focus on the fundamental structure of the graphics. In addition, I have occasionally used color to highlight graphical elements referenced by the text. This use of color does not always appear in the specification. Finally, I have used text sparingly in some places in order to emphasize the essential features of the graphics being discussed. Some of the graphics in this book lack the labels and other annotation that would be desirable for substantive publications.

For any graphic, the expression, attributes, and graphs will be represented in a multi-line notation that comprises the specification. The first line or lines contain the DATA functions that create variables from data. These are normally omitted if the data are assumed to be organized in a cases-by-variables matrix. The next lines give the TRANS specifications that define the transformation to be applied to the variables. These lines are optional if we assume an identity transformation. The next line is the algebraic expression that defines the frame, called the FRAME. This line is never optional. The next lines are the SCALE specifications that specify dimensions on which the graphs will orient themselves. The names of the dimensions used as arguments in this part of the specification are *dim1* and *dim2*. By convention, the indices for *dim* are taken from the order that the variables appear (left to right) in the FRAME specification. The SCALE specifications are optional if an ordinary interval scale is used on all dimensions. The next line or lines is the COORD that defines the coordinate system in which the graphs are to be embedded. This line is optional if we assume rectangular Cartesian coordinates. The next line or lines is the GUIDE specification for axes and legends and other guide notation. The remaining lines contain the graphing functions for the graphs appearing in the frame. These are denoted with the label GRAPH. For example, a two-dimensional scatterplot can be represented by:

DATA: **x** = **X**
DATA: **y** = **Y**
TRANS: **x** = **x**
TRANS: **y** = **y**
FRAME: **x*****y**
SCALE: *interval(dim1)*
SCALE: *interval(dim2)*
COORD: *rect(dim1,dim2)*
GUIDE: *axis1()*
GUIDE: *axis2()*
GRAPH: *point()*

or equivalently for this example,

FRAME: **x*****y**
GRAPH: *point()*

The DATA specification assigns a unique index to each element of the data objects **X** and **Y** using an index function. Sequential indexing is used in this example, so it can be omitted. The TRANS specification transforms the resulting variables. The identity transformation is used here, so it can be omitted. The FRAME specification determines the frame dimensions. The SCALE specification sets the scales for each dimension. Interval decimal scales (as opposed to, say, log scales) are used, so it can be omitted. The COORD specification sets the coordinate system. Rectangular coordinates are used, so it can be omitted. The GUIDE specifications determine two axes. These default to the dimensions in the frame, so they can be omitted. And the GRAPH specification includes any functional graphs.

2.3.2 Functions

Functions are notated in light italics, *e.g.*,

color()
position()
point.statistic.mean()
log()

Functions may be **overloaded**. This is a method for grouping under one name several functions that perform similar tasks but have different arguments. If we need to assign an index to a value of a variable, for example, we can make several versions of a function and name all of them *index*(). One version accepts real numbers, another accepts strings, and so on. By using the same name for each function and letting the system determine which version to use after examining the type of arguments, we can keep our design simple. For example, the following three functions return the same result (assuming the variable **group** contains a single value of either "red" or 0):

color("red")
color(0)
color(**group**)

Precise definitions of this behavior are required, but overloading is easy to implement in object-oriented languages like Java. It is more difficult (but not impossible) in languages like *C* and FORTRAN.

2.4 Sequel

The rest of this book examines Figure 2.1 in more detail. The next chapter starts at the beginning. It covers data and datasets, the classes of objects that are at the lowest stage of the graph creation hierarchy.

3

Data

The word **data** is the plural of the Latin *datum*, meaning a given, or that which we take for granted and use as the basis of our calculations. This meaning is carried in the French word for statistical data, *données*. We ordinarily think of data as derived from measurements from a machine, survey, census, test, rating, or questionnaire – most frequently numerical. In a more general sense, however, data are symbolic representations of observations or thoughts about the world. As we have seen, we do not need to begin with numerals to create a graphic. Text strings, symbols, shapes, pictures, graphs themselves, can all be graphed.

Older graphing systems required data to be stored in **flat files** containing row-by-column arrays of numerical observations on a set of variables. Spreadsheet graphics systems also arrange data this way. In these systems, the structure of the data determines the types of displays possible: line charts, bar charts, pie charts, or scatterplots. More recent object-oriented graphics systems assume their data are in a **data source**. And the most flexible systems provide an object-oriented interface to the data source which makes no assumptions about the underlying structure of the data. The graphing system itself has a **view** of the data that it uses for its initial mapping. This view may have no simple relation to the actual organization of the data source. In addition, the view may change from moment to moment because the system may be fed by a **streaming** data source. A well-designed graphics system must be able to handle this situation in order to avoid static views that can misrepresent the underlying data.

This chapter outlines three types of data: empirical, abstract, and meta. These types are distinguished by their sources and function. Empirical data are collected from observations of the real world. Abstract data arise from formal models. And metadata are data on data. Treinish (1993) provides further details on these types and elucidates them within the general context of graphics production. Fortner (1995) discusses empirical and abstract scientific data. I will first summarize data functions and then discuss these three types of data. I will conclude with a brief section on the emerging field of data mining and its relationship to the models needed to support a graphical system.

3.1 *Data Functions*

Table 3.1 lists some functions I will use in this chapter to create variables from datasets. I have assumed that the capital letters refer to column names (domain names) of a relation. The results of these functions are function variables.

As I mentioned in the last chapter, we could apply these functions to the contents of an object-oriented database as long as we devised a relational interface to insure that related sets are indexed properly. In any case, the actual referencing scheme we need is independent of the physical or formal organization of the data themselves.

Table 3.1 **Data Functions**

empirical	*abstract*	*meta*
sample(X, n, "<statistic>") *shape*(X$_1$,...,X$_n$,"<statistic>")	*iter*(first,last,step,rept) *series*("<func>", n) *count*(n) *proportion*(n) *percent*(n) *constant*(c, n) *string*("<string>", n) *rand*(n)	*link*(row,"<source>")

The empirical functions operate on columns of data. The *sample*() function implements sampling. Sampling methods include *sample.srs* (simple random), *sample.jackknife* (Tukey, 1958) and *sample.boot* (Efron & Tibshirani, 1993). The *shape*() function reshapes a matrix or table of columns (corresponding to an *n*-ary relation) into a single variable. Let $\mathbf{X}_{m \times n}$ be a matrix produced by concatenating the columns $(X_1,...,X_n)$. Let *i* and *j* be row and column indices respectively of the matrix $\mathbf{X}$ ($i = 1, ... , m$ and $j = 1, ... , n$). Let *k* be the row index of the variable **x** output by the *shape*() function. The *shape*() functions compute the index *k* as follows in order to reshape its input:

$$shape.rect(): \quad k = n \cdot (i - 1) + j$$
$$shape.tri(): \quad k = i \cdot (i - 1)/2 + j : (i \geq j)$$
$$shape.low(): \quad k = (i - 1) \cdot (i - 2)/2 + j : (i > j)$$
$$shape.diag(): \quad k = i : (i = j)$$

The *shape.rect*() function unwraps the rows of a rectangular matrix into a single column. The *shape.tri*() function unravels the lower triangular half (including the diagonal) of a square matrix into a single column. The *shape.low*() function does the same for the triangular half excluding the diagonal. And the *shape.diag*() function places the diagonal of a square matrix into a column.

The <statistic> argument to the *shape*() function has several alternatives:

value:	the value of the entries
rowindex:	the row index
colindex:	the column index
rowname:	the row name
colname:	the column name

The *shape*() functions leave one with the impression that a matrix algebra package could provide many (but not all) of the functions needed for structuring data at the first stage of a graphics system. Many of the graphics we draw in practice depend on a matrix data model. Notable exceptions, however, are geographic, physical, and mathematical objects that must depend on different data organizations.

The abstract functions create columns. The *iter*() function is a simple iterator for creating arithmetic series. The series *iter*(1, 10, 1) contains a sequence of the integers 1 through 10, for example. The *repeat* argument duplicates the series *repeat* times. More than one *repeat* argument may be added at the end of the list to created nested iterators. The *series*() function is a more general series generator based on a specified mathematical function. The *count*(), *proportion*(), and *percent*() functions are iterators as well. The *count*(10) function, for example, is equivalent to *iter*(1, 10, 1). A comparable *proportion*(10) iterator would be equivalent to *iter*(.1, 1.0, .1). Finally, the *constant*() and *string*() iterators supply n instances of an item and the *rand*() iterator generates independent random numbers. The *rand*() iterator has methods such as *rand.uniform*() and *rand.normal*(). If n is not specified for these functions and if the result is used in a model with empirical variables, then n is taken to be the number of rows in the dataset. I will occasionally use <string> as shorthand for the *string*("<string>") function, *e.g.*,

```
DATA: s = string("Hello world")
DATA: s = "Hello world"
```

The meta functions associate metadata with rows of datasets. I have included an atomistic example to suggest the association of a single metadata item with a row of a dataset. The <source> parameter of the *link*() function might be the index to a video image, a Web address in the form of a Universal Resource Locator (URL), or some other reference to an item of metadata.

3.2 *Empirical Data*

Empirical data arise from our observations of the world. The Greek term ʼεμπειρία , the source of the English word *empirical*, means experience or acquaintance with some thing. Among the many prevailing views of the role of empirical data in modern science, there are two opposing extremes. On the one hand, the **realist** assumes data are manifestations of latent phenomena. In this view, data are pointers to universal, underlying truths. On the other hand, the **nominalist** assumes data *are* what they describe. From this latter point of view, as the philosopher Ludwig Feuerbach noted, "you are what you eat." I use the historical realist-nominalist terminology to emphasize that these differing perspectives, in one form or another, have origins in Medieval theological controversies and their classical antecedents in Greek philosophy.

Many working scientists adopt some form of a realist position, particularly those in the natural sciences. Even social scientists, despite the myriad particulars of their field, have often endorsed a similar position. Watson (1924) and Hull (1943), for example, believed that behavioral data could be explained best through universal quantitative laws. More recently, Webb *et al.* (1981) promoted "unobtrusive" data collection methods that point to or help us triangulate on basic truths about behavior.

On the other hand, scientists like Skinner (1969) have argued that behavioral data are best understood by avoiding unobservables and inferences. Skinner even rejected statistical modeling, arguing that smoothing or aggregation obscures details that could help falsify theories. The graphics in Skinner (1961), for example, are the cumulative traces over time by a stylus connected to a lever or button pressed by a pigeon ("untouched by human hands"). Figure 3.1 shows an example of this type of graphic. The horizontal axis marks the linear movement of the stylus over time. The vertical axis marks the increment of the stylus following each bar press. The vertical trace lines are due to resetting of the stylus to keep it on a single page. Skinner argued that these graphics are sufficient representations of responses to schedules of reinforcement. He contended that smoothing, interpolation, aggregation, or model fitting only hide the associations that the scientist needs to see in order to refine theory.

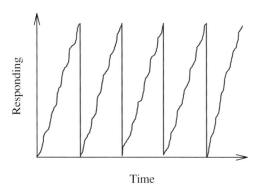

Time

Figure 3.1 *Cumulative Record*

Skinner's cumulative-record graphic would appear to short-circuit the diagram presented in Figure 2.1. It would seem that the physical production of such a graphic obviates the need for data functions, variables, indeed, a computer. In fact, however, Skinner's hard-wired device performs our data functions implicitly. Each pen movement involves a sequential indexing of the bar press events and time increments. Skinner's variables are Time and Response Count.

Computer data acquisition systems now perform the functions originally designed into mechanical lab equipment like Skinner's. In doing so, they enable alternative data organization and views not always anticipated by the scientist collecting the data. Consider Figure 3.1. It is visually indistinguishable from several of the cumulative records in Ferster and Skinner (1957). However, if we had Skinner's raw data we could use modern statistical time-series methods (unavailable to Skinner) to show that the data underlying Figure 3.1 were not produced by a real organism (human, mouse, *or* pigeon) in an operant conditioning chamber. They were generated by a computer from a stochastic equation. This detective work would involve producing a different graphic from the same data. We can sometimes image-scan older graphics to retrieve data, but there is no substitute for having the original observations and devising our own analyses.

The following examples illustrate some methods for referencing and organizing raw data to produce variables that can be graphed. The first example shows how variables are not always derived from columns in files. The second shows how they may be derived from repeated random samples.

3.2.1 *Reshaping Data*

Since any matrix is transposable, we can convert row data into column data and graph them when appropriate (*e.g.*, Jobson, 1992, p. 428). Or, as Figure 3.2 shows, we can construct a graphic based on a subset of a matrix.

A correlation matrix is a symmetric matrix of the correlations among a set of variables. If our received data are in a correlation matrix and we wish to graph the correlations, we have to restructure them into one variable that contains only correlations. We can use the data function called *shape.low()* to do this. This takes the lower-triangular elements of a symmetric matrix and strings them into one variable. Notice in the figure that we are displaying only one variable and representing it with a *point* graph (see Chapter 6).

DATA: **r** = *shape.low*(**POUNDING, SINKING, SHAKING, NAUSEOUS, STIFF, FAINT, VOMIT, BOWELS, URINE,** "value")
FRAME: **r**
GRAPH: *point(position.stack())*

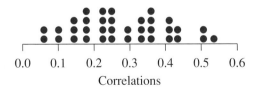

Figure 3.2 *Dot plot of correlations from correlation matrix.*

These correlations are based on recalled experiences of symptoms of combat stress (1=yes, 0=no) among soldiers who experience battle in World War II. These data fit a Guttman scale (Stouffer *et al.*, 1950). A Guttman scale is an ordinal relation that Guttman called a **simplex**. Presence of a given symptom implies presence of all milder symptoms and absence of a given symptom implies absense of all stronger symptoms. Such a relation implies that the matrix of correlations among symptoms should have all positive elements that follow a banded structure, with the largest correlations near the diagonal and the smallest near the corner opposite the diagonal.

We can display this structure by reshaping the correlation matrix in a different way. This time, I will create three variables – a row index, a column index, and the value of the correlation corresponding to each combination of these indices. Then I will plot the entire correlation matrix using color to represent the value of each correlation. This method works well in this example because all the correlations (as expected for a simplex) are positive.

Figure 3.3 reveals this structure. I have used the *shape()* data functions to derive indices for plotting the rows and columns of the correlation matrix directly and a *tile* graph (see Chapter 6) to represent the correlations through color. Notice that the colors get warmer as we approach the diagonal.

DATA: **row** = *shape.low*(**POUNDING, SINKING, SHAKING,**
        NAUSEOUS, STIFF, FAINT, VOMIT, BOWELS, URINE,
        "rowname")
DATA: **col** = *shape.low*(**POUNDING, SINKING, SHAKING,**
        NAUSEOUS, STIFF, FAINT, VOMIT, BOWELS, URINE,
        "colname")
DATA: **r** = *shape.low*(**POUNDING, SINKING, SHAKING, NAUSEOUS,**
        STIFF, FAINT, VOMIT, BOWELS, URINE, "value")
FRAME: **col*row**
GRAPH: *tile(color.hue(**r**))*

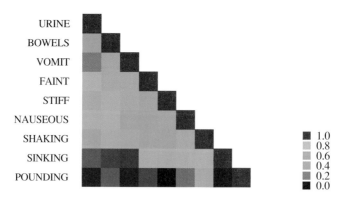

Figure 3.3 *Correlation matrix of combat symptoms.*

3.2.2 *Bootstrapping*

Efron and Tibshirani (1993) discuss a procedure for repeatedly computing a statistic using random samples (with replacement) from a dataset. This procedure, called **bootstrapping**, offers a way to compute confidence intervals when conventional methods are inefficient or unavailable. A bootstrap sample is a sample with replacement from a dataset. Usually, the size of the sample is the same size as the dataset, so that some cases are sampled more than once. Figure 3.4 shows an example of a histogram of a dataset and a histogram of means from 1000 bootstrap samples of that dataset. The variable **mean** is indexed to a set of bootstrapped means, each of which was computed from the original dataset. This operation is equivalent to computing the mean of a set of values by making a single pass through a column of a database, repeating this database query 1000 times, and then assembling all the means into a column of 1000 values. This computationally intensive operation is not one calculated to endear a user to a database administrator. Although automated boostrapping is not available in database systems, some statistical packages that have data management subsystems do perform bootstrapping.

DATA: **count** = *count*()
FRAME: **military*count**
GRAPH: *histobar*()

DATA: **mean** = *sample.boot*(**MILITARY**, 1000, "mean")
DATA: **count** = *count*()
FRAME: **mean*count**
GRAPH: *histobar*()

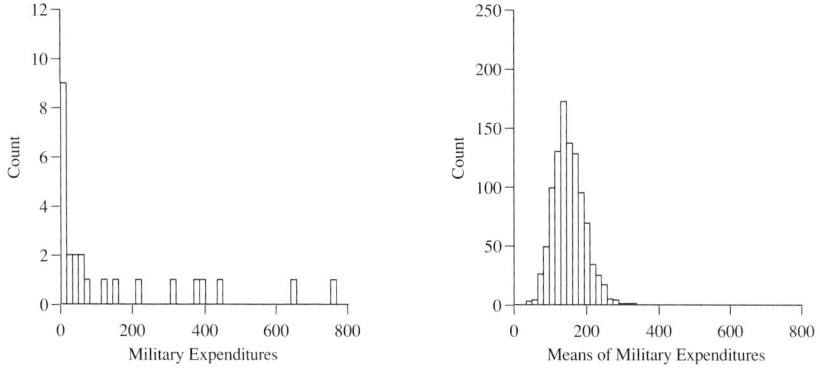

Figure 3.4 *Bootstrapped means*

Two differences between the histograms are apparent in Figure 3.4. The first is that the histogram of bootstrapped means is less positively skewed. The second is that the variation in the bootstrapped means is smaller. The standard deviation of the values in the left histogram is 214.1 and the standard deviation of the mean values in the right histogram is 42.3. These differ by a factor of

approximately 5, which is the square root of the sample size, 25. The bootstrapping results are consistent with the standard statistical theory for the sampling distribution of means. Nevertheless, the distribution of means is still
positively skewed. If the sample size were larger than 25, the means would
look more normally distributed.

3.3 Abstract Data

Abstract data functions are most often used to create variables consisting of
series, lattices, and other indexing schemes that we use to arrange observed
data values. There are many generating functions for series that could prove
useful in the data manipulation needed for statistical graphics. Knuth (1968)
discusses these functions. Sometimes we construct graphics using abstract
data that are determined by a mathematical rule or function. I will first present
some simple examples of the former and then one example of the latter.

3.3.1 Time Series

Time series datasets do not always include a column for time. Even when they
do, we sometimes wish to plot against the index of the measurement rather
than against time. Figure 3.5 contains 256 instantaneous firing rate measurements of a single cat retinal ganglion cell during a 7 second interval (Levine
et al., 1987). The points are connected with a *line* graph in series order. Most
time series packages automatically create this index variable for equally
spaced time series; some go further and code the series in calendar time. I have
chosen an aspect ratio for this plot that reveals a low-frequency component of
roughly one-and-a-half cycles over the duration of the series. This component
is due to the respiration of the cat, according to Michael Levine (personal communication). Firing rate tends to increase with more oxygen in the blood.

DATA: **case** = *series*()
FRAME: **case*****rate**
GRAPH: *line*()

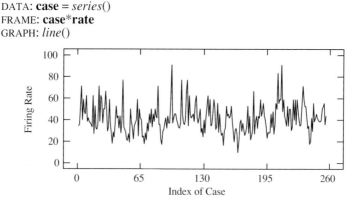

Figure 3.5 *Firing rate of cat retinal cell ganglion.*

3.3.2 Counts

Bar charts of counts often need to be constructed when there is no explicit count variable in the data. Figure 3.6 shows a count bar chart constructed from the countries data used in Chapter 6. The *count()* implicit function fills a column with counts. The *statistic.count* statistical function (see Chapter 8) tallies the counts in all combinations of **gov** and **urban** values.

DATA: **count** = *count*()
FRAME: **gov*urban*count**
GRAPH: *bar.statistic.count*()

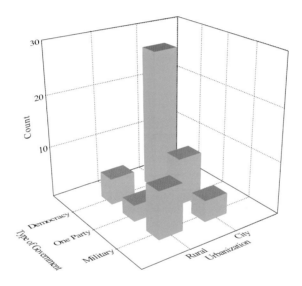

Figure 3.6 *Count bar chart*

3.3.3 Mathematical Functions

Data for a graphing system may exist only as an abstraction. This happened in a system I developed for automatically graphing interesting subsets of mathematical functions (Wilkinson, 1993a). The data for this system are expressed by an equation. The system examines the equation to determine bounded, periodic, and asymptotic behavior and then chooses a suitable range and domain for graphing the function. The system then renders the function based on its analysis. Figure 3.7 shows an example of such a plot using a polar arc-tangent function. The system determined that the behavior outside of $[-5 < x,y < +5]$ in the domain could be inferred relatively accurately by looking at the behavior in the visibly graphed domain. It scaled the range to $[0 < f(x,y) < .9]$ to encompass the interesting behavior there as well. I have plugged the domain limits into the specification for Figure 3.7 by using the *iter*() function.

DATA: **x** = *iter*(–5, 5, 0.2, 50, 1)
DATA: **y** = *iter*(–5, 5, 0.2, 1, 50)
TRANS: **z** = *atan*(**x**^2+**y**^2)/*sqrt*(**x**^2+**y**^2)
FRAME: **x*y*z**
GRAPH: *surface*()

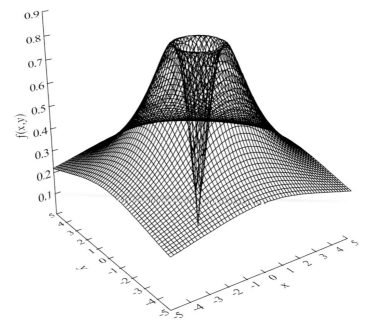

Figure 3.7 *Automated function plot.*

It is easy to miss the point in the example because of the existence of symbolic and numeric mathematics systems which plot functions by generating a regular or irregular mesh of data points within a specified range and domain. The searchable dataset in the system described here, by contrast, is theoretically infinite. It varies depending on the function being examined. For some functions, the system spends most of its time examining values densely in a local neighborhood and for others, it ranges far-and-wide looking for global behavior. Thus, abstract data are not static values generated by a theoretical function and residing in memory or a file. They are instead produced by a mathematical system or simulation algorithm that is capable of changing its search space dynamically. Abstract datasets are not massive. They are infinite.

3.4 Metadata

Because our thoughts and observations are structured by the situation in which we make them, data always include **metadata**. These are the facts about the setting and circumstances under which we made our observations. Metadata are data about data. Our countries data, for example, include information about the statistical reporting methods for each country, the reliability and biases in the reports, types of missing data, the collection of these reports through an agency of the United Nations, the encoding into a computer file, the distribution of the file via electronic and printed methods, as well as numerous other details. Metadata affect the way we select data for and interpret data in our graphics. They can influence our display formally through imputation models (Rubin, 1987) or informally through written annotations attached to the graphic.

Sometimes data structured for one purpose can serve as metadata for another. For example, we drew a pie using our ACLS data for the females in the last chapter. We could have drawn a pie using the data for the males in exactly the same way we did for the females. And we could place two pies in the same display area (see Figure 11.14) and link them so that we could compare sectors. On the other hand, we could treat the males data as metadata linked to each sector of the female pie and not display the males at all. This way, we could use the cursor in an interactive environment to click on a pie slice and get information textually (or in some other mode) on the males data relative to that slice for the females.

Thus, metadata are not distinguished from other data according to quality, but according to use. Interactive graphics systems present the opportunity to link to data sources without using aesthetic attributes in a graphic. With careful design and the use of hyperlinks (links to links), a graphic can be the gateway to a rich set of interpretable resources.

3.5 Data Mining

Recent developments in data warehousing, data mining, and knowledge discovery in databases (KDD) have blurred the distinctions between graphics, statistics, and data management. Indeed, some proponents of KDD have claimed that it will replace graphical and statistical analysis packages in the future. These claims, however extreme, must be examined in terms of models rather than commercial products. It is easy to mimic functionality and wrap old designs in new interfaces in commercial software, so product comparisons are generally not good ways to evaluate such claims.

It is difficult to discuss this field without invoking its acronyms. Perhaps the central driving slogan is OLAP, or on-line analytical processing. OLAP is intended to describe a computing environment that provides multiple views of data in real time (or, at least, responsive-to-my-needs time). These views are composites of text and graphics that can be manipulated by the user to develop alternative views. There are two main approaches to implementing an OLAP system: Multidimensional OLAP (MOLAP), and Relational OLAP (ROLAP). I will discuss these first and then conclude with a brief introduction to visual query of databases.

3.5.1 MOLAP

MOLAP depends on a basic object called a **data cube**. This object is a multidimensional array. Each dimension of this array is a set of sets representing a content domain such as time or geography. The dimensions are scaled categorically (region of country, state, quarter of year, week of quarter, etc.) so that the whole object defines a multidimensional array of cells. The cells of this array contain aggregated measures of variables such as income or gender. The data cube *is* the data for a MOLAP. In fact, this cube is usually prepared before the user begins to explore patterns in the data, sometimes in overnight processing runs on massive relational databases.

Exploring relations in the cube involves several operations. The popular names for these are **drill-down, drill-up,** and **drill-through**. Drill-down involves splitting an aggregation into subsets. For example, data for regions on a geographic dimension may be split into data for states. Drill-up is the reverse of drill-down; the user aggregates subsets on a dimension. Drill-through involves subsets of crossings of sets. The user might investigate statistics within a particular state subsetted by time, for example.

These operations work well with statistics like counts, means, proportions, and standard deviations. Simple aggregations over sub-classes can be computed by operating on sums, sums of squares, and other terms that are combined in linear functions to produce basic summary statistics. They do not work properly with statistics like the median, mode, and percentiles because the aggregate of these statistics is not the statistic of their aggregates. The median of medians is not the median of the aggregate, for example. A telling indicator of this fact is the lack of medians and modes from the menus of MOLAP front-ends.

It is unnecessary to provide examples to illustrate the importance of these alternative summary statistics. Every statistics student is introduced to the differences between the mean and median within the first few weeks of the first course in high school or college. One can find few governmental or commercial summaries based on mean income, mean housing prices, or mean cholesterol in the population. The median is used on these variables because of the extreme skewness in their distributions or because of the prevalence of outliers. And for marketing data, the mean cannot substitute for the modal choice over alternatives in a study of preferences.

Few of the graphics in this book and in other important applications can be computed from a data cube. There are several reasons for this situation. First, many of the statistics presented in Chapter 8 require raw data for their computation. These statistics give graphs the ability to represent sampling error within sub-classifications. Second, spatial and time series statistics require raw data because the distribution of errors across space and time is not independent of space and time. Third, aggregation often involves weighting of sub-classifications by measures other than sample size. This has emerged as a focal problem in the governmental deliberations over census taking versus sampling. Glymour *et al.* (1996) discuss other factors that disqualify the data cube from serious consideration as an informative database exploration model.

A recent exception to this evaluation is a model presented in Sarawagi *et al.* (1998). While the system they describe is not designed for producing general graphics, it does incorporate a statistical model at the cube-building phase that allows later exploration of the cube to be guided by robust statistical procedures. Outlier detection based on these models is used to drive the coloring of surprising cells in the cube so that ordinary users are drawn to investigate anomalies further. Their model could be used as one approach toward adapting cubes to more general graphical displays.

3.5.2 ROLAP

ROLAP places an interactive data-view at the front-end or client-side of a relational database. Some ROLAPs are based on a data cube model and can be disqualified from serious consideration for reasons similar to the ones I have given in the previous section. A more sophisticated ROLAP model has emerged recently, however. It is possible, through several technologies, to give statistical algorithms access to raw data through the relational model in real time. This is an approach I advocate in this book.

One method is to use extended Sequential Query Language (SQL) to create relations that can be presented to other language clients (Java, *C*++, etc.) for use as variables. This approach requires either storage of the data on the client side (the preferable arrangement) or slow, case-by-case processing across a communications link (network or internet). Nevertheless, this method provides access to the raw data and, if an extension to SQL is used, allows the kind of data reshapings that are featured in this and the next chapter.

Another method has become available with the advent of platform-independent languages like Java and the encapsulation offered by software **components**. These components permit remote invocation of methods that ordinarily would be an internal part of an executing program. In this way, statistical modules can be sent to servers or remote sites to process data locally and return summaries and other statistical objects. This approach is more promising than the rigid aggregations offered by structures such as data cubes. In the most elegant form of this architecture, applications can request remote components to provide information about their data-handling methods and take suitable action depending on the returned information. In this form, component architecture can achieve the real promise of distributed computing: design and execution that are independent of site, operating system, or language.

3.5.3 *Visual Query of Databases*

In a MOLAP or ROLAP, graphical displays are driven by the relational structure of a database. Queries through a language such as SQL yield tables that can be graphed. Researchers are beginning to develop approaches that reverse this dependency: they are designing search methods that are driven by visual query languages rather than relational languages. The original impetus for these methods came from Geographic Information Systems (GIS), where spatial relations rather than variable relations necessarily govern the search structure.

Papantonakis and King (1995) devised a graphical query language called GQL, which functions like SQL but operates on graphical objects rather than relational variables. Derthick, Kolojejchick, and Roth (1997) have extended this model to allow dynamic exploration rather than static queries. In their system, graphics are linked views into a database; manipulating graphical objects immediately updates data objects and updating data objects immediately updates graphical objects. Many of the graphical methods for accomplishing these actions are derived from the work of the original Bell Labs statistics group (see Cleveland and McGill, 1988).

Chi *et al.* (1997) have used a spreadsheet metaphor to organize graphical exploration. Their implementation is a prototype, but it can integrate multiple data sources in a single display. This allows exploration through dynamically linked views. This work resembles the trellis graphic of Becker and Cleveland (1996), but is designed to be a controller as well as a display.

The graphics algebra presented in this book is related to this research but comes from the opposite direction – derived from the structure of graphics rather than the structure of data. We can expect to see convergence in database query methods and graphic displays in coming years. Graphics will evolve beyond passive displays and will begin to play a role in the organization of data. This trend is driven by the need to get beyond static query to real-time interaction.

3.6 Sequel

Now that we have data assembled into a reference system, we need to link data to theoretical constructs. The next chapter covers variables and variable sets (varsets). These are the entities that graphs describe.

4

Variables

The word **variable** is derived from the Latin *variare*, to vary. A variable gives us a method for associating a concept like *income* with a set of data. Variables are used together with operators in the syntactical portion of our specification language (*e.g.*, **death*birth**).

In older statistical graphics systems, a variable refers to a column in a rectangular cases-by-variables file. Many statistical packages assume rows are cases or observations that comprise instances or samples of a variable represented by the column. There is nothing in our definition of a variable which requires it to represent a row or column, however. The only requirement is that the variable mapping function return a single value in the range for every index. This generality is especially important for graphing geometric and spatial data (Cressie, 1991). But it affects the way we approach other data as well. In a landmark book, now out of print and seldom read by statisticians, Coombs (1964) examined the relationship between structural models and patterns of data. Like Guttman (1971, 1977), Coombs believed that the prevalent practice of modeling based on cases-by-variables data layouts often prevents researchers from considering more parsimonious structural theories and keeps them from noticing meaningful patterns in their data.

In computer languages, a variable is a symbol for a data structure or container. The data contained in the structure are assumed to vary from some state of a program to another. The index function for a variable in a computer language is often called an **address**. Some computer languages type variables (logicals, strings, integers, reals, etc.) by confining their ranges to one of these or some other data types. Typing can prevent undefined or nonsensical results with some operations (adding apples and oranges), but there is nothing in our definition of a variable to require typing based on data classes. Some operations on variables do not require type compatibility. We *do* require that scales (see Chapter 9) map sets of variables to a common range, however. Otherwise, some coordinate transformations covered in Chapter 10 would not be possible.

4.1 Transforms

Transforms are transformations on variables. One purpose of transforms is to make statistical operations on variables appropriate and meaningful. Another is to create new variables, aggregates, or other type of summaries in grouped data.

Table 4.1 shows several variable transforms. This sample list is intended to cover the examples in this book and to be a template for designing the signature and behavior of new functions.

Table 4.1 **Variable Transforms**

mathematical	*statistical*	*multivariate*
$log(\mathbf{x})$	$mean(\mathbf{x})$	$sum(\mathbf{x}_1,\mathbf{x}_2,...,\mathbf{x}_n)$
$exp(\mathbf{x})$	$median(\mathbf{x})$	$diff(\mathbf{x}_1,\mathbf{x}_2)$
$sin(\mathbf{x})$	$mode(\mathbf{x})$	$prod(\mathbf{x}_1,\mathbf{x}_2)$
$cos(\mathbf{x})$	$residual(\mathbf{x},\mathbf{y})$	$quotient(\mathbf{x}_1,\mathbf{x}_2)$
$tan(\mathbf{x})$	$sort(\mathbf{x})$	$influence(\mathbf{x}_1,\mathbf{x}_2,...,\mathbf{x}_n)$
$asin(\mathbf{x})$	$rank(\mathbf{x})$	$miss(\mathbf{x}_1,\mathbf{x}_2,...,\mathbf{x}_n,"<f>")$
$acos(\mathbf{x})$	$prank(\mathbf{x})$	
$atan(\mathbf{x})$	$cut(\mathbf{x},k)$	
$atanh(\mathbf{x})$	$zinv(\mathbf{x})$	
$sign(\mathbf{x})$	$lag(\mathbf{x})$	
$pow(\mathbf{x}, p)$	$grpfun(\mathbf{x},\mathbf{g},"<f>")$	

The mathematical functions return values that are case-by-case transformations of the values in **x**, where **x** is a variable. The *log* function returns natural logarithms. The exponential and trigonometric functions are standard. The *sign()* function returns 1 if a value of **x** is positive and -1 if it is negative. The *pow()* function transforms **x** to the *p*th power of itself.

The statistical functions compute basic statistics. The *mean, median,* and *mode* fill each value in the column with the corresponding summary statistic. The *residual* function returns the residuals of a regression of **y** on **x**. It has several methods for regression type, with *linear* being the default. The *sort* function orders all variables in a variable set according to the sorted order of **x**. The *rank* function fills a column with the ranks of **x**, assigning fractional ranks when there are ties. The *prank* function fills each case in the column with the value $(i-.5)/n$ for $i = 1, ... , n$ cases assuming (as if) the column were sorted on **x**. The *cut* function cuts a sorted column into k groups, replacing the value of the argument with an integer from 1 to k. The *zinv* function replaces a value with the inverse normal cumulative distribution function value. The *lag* function replaces value x_i with x_{i-1}, setting the first value in the column to missing. It has an optional second argument, a positive or negative integer specifying the amount and direction of shifting. The *grpfn* function is a routine that evaluates the function *f* named between the quotes separately for each of the groups specified by the *g* argument in the parameter list.

The multivariate functions use more than one variable to construct a new variable. The *sum* function fills a column with the sum of values of its arguments. The *diff* function does the same for differences. The *prod* and *quotient* functions compute products and ratios. The *influence* function computes an influence function (see Figure 7.39). The *miss* function imputes missing values assuming a function named *f* (see Figure 15.1).

4.2 Examples

The following examples have been constructed to show that transforms are more powerful than simple recodings of variables. Together with data functions, transforms can help us create graphics that employ structures unavailable to ordinary graphics systems.

4.2.1 Sorting

I once met a statistician who worked for the FBI. He had helped uncover the Chicago Machine's voting fraud in the 1970's. I was curious about the methods the Federal team had used to expose the fraud, so I asked him about discriminant analysis, logistic regression, and other techniques the statisticians might have used. He replied, "We sorted the voter tape and looked for duplicate names and addresses." This statistical methodology may have been inspired by the fabled Chicago Machine slogan, "Vote early and often."

Sorting is one of the most elementary and powerful methods of statistical and graphical analyses. A sort is a one-to-one transformation. When we use position to represent the values of a variable, we are implicitly sorting those values. Sorting variables displayed by position not only reveals patterns but also makes it easier to make comparisons and locate subsets. Sorting categorical variables according to the values of associated numerical variables can itself constitute a graphical method.

Figure 4.1 shows an example. The data are numbers of arrests by sex reported to the FBI in 1985 for selected crimes. The graphic displays the differences in proportions of each crime committed by males and females. To create the graphic, we must standardize the data within crime category (dividing by the row totals). The first two TRANS statements accomplish this. The next TRANS statement creates an **mf** variable consisting of the difference in crime proportions. We sort this variable and then plot it against the crime categories. The pattern of the dots indicates that males predominate in almost every crime category except vice and runaways. The largest biases are in the violent crimes. Rape, not surprisingly, is almost exclusively male.

TRANS: **total**=*sum*(**male, female**)
TRANS: **m**=*quotient*(**male, total**)
TRANS: **f**=*quotient*(**female, total**)
TRANS: **mf**=*diff*(**m, f**)
TRANS: **mf**=*sort*(**mf**)
FRAME: **mf*crime**
GRAPH: *point*()

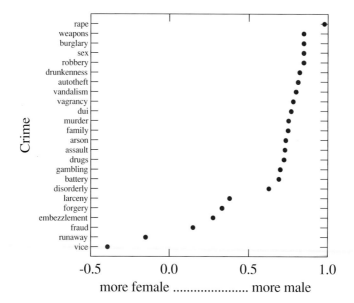

Figure 4.1 *Gender differences in crime patterns.*

4.2.2 Probability Plots

Probability plots compare the n ordered values of a variable to the n-tiles of a specified probability distribution. If we have 100 values, for example, we base a normal probability plot on the pairs $(x_1, z_{.01})$, $(x_2, z_{.02})$, ... , $(x_{99}, z_{.99})$, where x_i are the data values ordered smallest to largest and z_α is the lower 100α percentage point of the standard normal probability distribution. To fit all 100 values, we change the computation of α from $i/100$ to $(i-.5)/100$. If a probability plot follows roughly a diagonal straight line, then we infer that the shape of our sample distribution is approximately normal.

Figure 4.2 shows a probability plot of military expenditures from the countries data. Our first transformation is *prank*(), a proportional-rank that computes the value $(i-.5)/n$, $i = 1$, ... n, corresponding to the values x_i after an ascending sort. Instead of reordering the data, however, *prank*() returns the values in the original data sequence. Next, the *zinv*() function computes the values of the cumulative standard normal distribution corresponding to the points produced by *prank*(). In other words, we apply the *zinv* function to the *prank*() values to get the theoretical normal variables we plot the data against. The left panel of Figure 4.2 shows the raw **military** values and the right panel shows the plot on a log_{10} scale. Logging straightens out the plot, which is another way of saying that it transforms the distribution from a positively skewed shape to a more normal one.

A probability plot can also be produced through a probability scale transformation. I will show an example in Figure 9.12. We compute *prank*() and then rescale the α values through a probability scale transformation. The method in this chapter produces a new variable *zinv*(), while the scale method in Chapter 9 changes only the scale on which *prank*() is plotted.

```
TRANS: alpha=prank(military)
TRANS: z=zinv(alpha)
FRAME: military*z
GRAPH: point()
```

```
TRANS: alpha=prank(military)
TRANS: z=zinv(alpha)
FRAME: military*z
SCALE: log(dim1, 10)
GRAPH: point()
```

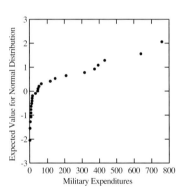 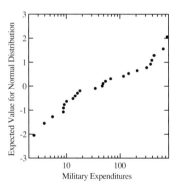

Figure 4.2 *Probability plots of military expenditures.*

4.2.3 *Aggregating Variables*

Figure 4.3 shows a **spread-level** plot (Tukey, 1977) of the birth rate data. This plot divides a variable into a set of fractiles and then displays the variation in each fractile against the median value of the variable within that fractile. It is used to determine the appropriate transformation for **heteroscedastic** data, in which the spread increases (or decreases) proportionally to some power of the

location. The figure uses a schematic plot (box plot) to represent the spread
and the median for each quartile. The *grpfun()* function computes a function
(*median*) on a variable (**birth**) within each separate group defined by a grouping variable (**quartile**). Notice that the frame crosses the same variable (**birth**)
with itself, but the *position()* function for the box graph selects the values of
birthquart to fix the location of each box.

TRANS: **quartile**=*cut*(**birth**,4)
TRANS: **birthquart**=*grpfun*(**birth**,**quartile**,"median")
FRAME: **birth*birth**
GRAPH: *schema*(*shape*("box"), *position*(**birthquart*birth**))

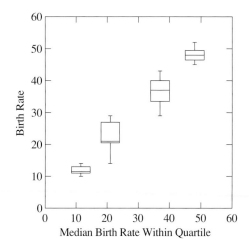

Figure 4.3 *Spread-Level plot of a variable against its quartile medians.*

4.2.4 Regression Residuals

Figure 4.4 shows a linear regression residuals plot. The independent variable
in the regression is the birth rate variable from the countries data and the dependent variable is death rate. The residuals are calculated from this regression, standardized, and then used as the dependent variable in the frame model
for Figure 4.4. The U-shaped pattern of residuals suggests that the linear model is not a good representation of the relationship between death rates and birth
rates for the countries.

   One might ask whether statistical procedures have a useful role within a
graphical system. Two alternatives are traditional graphics packages, which
receive pre-calculated data from spreadsheets and statistics packages, and traditional statistics packages, which send their calculations to basic graphics
sub-systems. Both of these are compromises, however. Obviously, a graphics
system should not incorporate the entire range of procedures within a statisti-

cal package; this would reduce its focus. On the other hand, there are analyses that can be performed only when graphics and statistics are intimately tied. Exploratory statistical packages such as Data Desk already implement such a model. Implementing basic statistical procedures such as regression and correlation in a graphics system provides functions that are unavailable in other software. In the end, the grammar of graphics has much to do with the grammar of statistics. I will discuss this further at the end of Chapter 8.

TRANS: **residual**=*residual.linear.student*(**birth, death**)
FRAME: **birth*residual**
GRAPH: *point*()

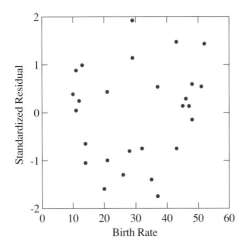

Figure 4.4 *Studentized residual plot.*

4.3 *Sequel*

Now that we have variables to describe relationships through links to data, we need a system for expressing those relationships. The next chapter covers the formal definitions for varset algebra.

5

Algebra

The word **algebra** is derived from the Arabic *al-jebr*, which means the restoring or reunion of broken parts. Its use in the West dates from the publication in the 9th century of Muhammad ibn Musa al-Khwarizmi's *Book of Restoring and Balancing*. Khwarizimi's name gave rise to the word **algorithm**. A classic discussion of the origins of algebra is given in Jourdain (1919).

This chapter deals with restoring and balancing sets of variables in order to create the specification for the frames in which graphs are embedded. The first part of a specification contains the algebraic expression relating sets of variables. I will review the rules for syntactical expressions and then present examples of typical expressions.

5.1 Syntax

5.1.1 Symbols

A symbol is used to represent an entity operated on by an algebra. The symbols in varset algebra are the names of variables. I will use capital italic letters for these names in this chapter. This notation emphasizes that we are dealing with sets when we do these operations. In examples involving algebraic specifications on variables based on real data, I will use the bold lowercase names of these variables. I will also use a special variable *1*, which represents the unity variable. Its range is one unity value. When we make a scale for this variable, no tick marks or scale values appear, but unity is located at the middle of the scale.

5.1.2 Operators

An **operator** is a method for relating symbols in an algebra. There are three operators in the graphical system. In hierarchical order (last to be evaluated through first), they are: +, *, and /. This hierarchical order may be altered through the use of parentheses.

5.1.3 Rules

The rules for these operators are as follows. Only + is commutative.

- associativity:
$$(A+B)+C = A+(B+C)$$
$$(A*B)*C = A*(B*C)$$
$$(A/B)/C = A/(B/C)$$

- distributivity:
$$A*(B+C) = A*B+A*C$$
$$(A+B)*C = A*C+B*C$$
$$A/(B+C) = A/B+A/C$$
$$(A+B)/C = A/C+B/C$$

- commutativity:
$$A+B = B+A$$

5.1.4 Expressions

An **expression** is an ordered sequence of one or more symbols with operators between each pair of adjacent symbols in the sequence. A **term** is an expression with no + operator (*e.g.*, A or $A*B$ or $A*B/C$). A **factor** is a term with no * operator (*e.g.*, A or A/B). The expression $A*B*C*D$ has one term and four factors. The expression $(A+B)/C$ has two terms; after expanding to $A/C+B/C$, we can see one factor in each term. A **monomial** is an expression with one term. A **polynomial** is an expression with more than one term. The expressions A and A/C are monomials, while the expressions $A+C$ and $A+B/C$ are polynomials.

5.1.5 Algebraic Form

An **algebraic form** is a monomial or a polynomial whose terms all have the same number of factors. The **order** of an algebraic form is the number of factors in one of its terms. The expression $A*B + C*D$ is an algebraic form of order 2, but $A*B + C$ is not an algebraic form because the first term has two factors and the second has one.

Constructing a graphic from a general algebraic specification requires a symbolic algebra machine (not a parser) that can convert general algebraic expressions into algebraic forms. Algebraic forms are then evaluated to produce graphics in this system. The first stage in normalizing an expression to algebraic form is to expand the expression into a collection of monomials. Then we determine the largest order among the monomials, say k. Finally, we augment any monomial less than order k by crossing on the right with the unity

(*1*) element enough times to make it order k. For example, we expand the expression $G+(A+B)*C/D$ to $G+A*C/D+B*C/D$ and note that $k=2$. Then we convert the expression to $G*1+A*C/D+B*C/D$.

5.1.6 *Evaluation*

Evaluating an algebraic form requires assigning symbols to sets and applying the operators to these sets to assemble a frame. In the following definitions, I have given the operators descriptive names in order to highlight the consequences of their operation on the finite ordered sets we call varsets. These names are *blend* (+), *cross* (*), and *nest* (/). In the definitions of these binary operators below, I will employ the following variables:

$A = [I_A, X_A, f_A]$, and

$B = [I_B, X_B, f_B]$, where

$I_A = \{1, ..., m_a\}$ and $I_B = \{1, ... , m_b\}$, and

$m_+ = m_A + m_B$, $I_+ = \{1, ... , m_+\}$, and

$m_- = min(m_A, m_B)$, $I_- = \{1, ... , m_-\}$.

5.1.6.1 *Blend (+)*

$A+B = [I_+, X_A \cup X_B, f_+]$, where

$f_+ : I_+ \rightarrow X_A \cup X_B$ is the function defined by

$$f_+(i) = \begin{cases} f_A(i) & \text{if } i \leq m_A \\ f_B(i - m_A) & \text{if } i > m_A \end{cases}$$

The **blend** operator involves a union ($\cup$) in the range. We often use the conjunction *and* to signify that two sets are blended into one. For example, if **diastolic** and **systolic** are measures of blood pressure among patients in various treatment conditions that we wish to see plotted on a common axis, we can plot "**diastolic** *and* **systolic**" against **treatment**. For example, if

$A = [\{1, ... , m_A\}, [0,120], \{(1, a_1), (2, a_2), ... , (m_A, a_{mA})\}]$, and

$B = [\{1, ... , m_B\}, [0,200], \{(1, b_1), (2, b_2), ... , (m_B, b_{mB})\}]$, then

$A+B=[\{1, ... , m_+\}, [0,200], \{(1,a_1), ... ,(m_+,b_{mB})\}]$

5.1.6.2 Cross (*)

$A*B = [I_-, X_A \times X_B, f_-]$, where

$f_- : I_- \to X_A \times X_B$ is the function defined by

$f_-(i) = (f_A(i),\ f_B(i))$.

The **cross** operator involves a Cartesian product ($\times$) in the range. We often use the word *by* to describe this operation. For example, if **temperature** and **pressure** are measurements of a manufacturing process, then a plot of "**temperature** *by* **pressure**" shows the combinations of measurements actually made by the experimenter. This usage derives from design-of-experiments terminology (*e.g.*, Cornell, 1990). If

$A = [\{1, \dots , m_A\}, \{\text{"blue","green"}\}, \{(1, a_1), (2, a_2), \dots , (m_A, a_{mA})\}]$, and

$B = [\{1, \dots , m_B\}, [-10,10], \{(1, b_1), (2, b_2), \dots , (m_B, b_{mB})\}]$, then

$A*B=[\{1, \dots ,m_-\},\{\text{"blue","green"}\}\times[-10,10],\{(1,(a_1,b_1)), \dots ,(m_-,(a_{m-},b_{m-}))\}]$.

If we plotted A by B in 2D with a *point* graph, we would see m_- points between -10 and 10 stacked vertically above one or both of the two color names.

5.1.6.3 Nest (/)

$A/B = [I_-, X_A^{(B)}, f_-]$, where

$X_A^{(B)} = \{X_A{:}b_1, \dots , X_A{:}b_p\}$, and

$b_j \in X_B$, $p =$ the cardinality of X_B , and

$f_- : I_- \to X_A^{(B)}$.

The **nest** operator stratifies values. On a computer, the set X_B must be finite, so B must be a categorical variable. The set $X_A^{(B)}$ contains elements of X_A tagged by the elements in X_B. For example, if A is a categorical variable with values $(1, 2)$ and B is a categorical variable with values ("blue", "red"),

$A = [\{1, \dots , m_A\}, \{1, 2\}, \{(1, a_1), (2, a_2), \dots , (m_A, a_{mA})\}]$, and

$B = [\{1, \dots , m_B\}, \{\text{"blue","red"}\}, \{(1, b_1), (2, b_2), \dots , (m_B, b_{mB})\}]$, then

$A/B=[\{1, \dots ,m_-\},\{1{:}\text{"blue"},2{:}\text{"blue"},1{:}\text{"red"}\},\{(1,a_1{:}b_j), \dots ,(m_-,a_{m-}{:}b_k)\}]$.

In this example, the elements of $X_A^{(B)}$ define the permissible values for the nesting, tagged by $b_j,\ b_k \in X_B$. There is no allowable instance of 2:"red". Also, 1:"blue" is a different value from 1:"red". The set $X_A^{(B)}$ cannot be derived from the nesting operation itself. It must be pre-defined. This definition can be made on the basis of logical or scientific information (*e.g.*, $A = pregnancy\ status$, $B = gender$), or from the patterns of coöccurrences in the data.

If A is a continuous variable and

$$A = [\{1, \ldots, m_A\}, [-273.15, 33000], \{(1, a_1), (2, a_2), \ldots, (m_A, a_{mA})\}]\ , \text{ and}$$

$$B = [\{1, \ldots, m_B\}, \{1, 2\}, \{(1, b_1), (2, b_2), \ldots, (m_B, b_{mB})\}]\ , \text{ then}$$

$$A/B = [\{1, \ldots, m_-\}, \{[-32.1, 110.2]:1, [-51.1, 130.4]:2\}, \{(1, a_1:b_j), \ldots, (m_-, a_{m_-}:b_k)\}]\ .$$

In this example, the elements of $X_A^{(B)}$ are intervals conditioned on the values of X_B. Again, the set $X_A^{(B)}$ cannot be derived from the nesting operation itself. If A represented Centigrade temperature measurements and B represented two different instruments (*e.g.*, mercury vs. bi-metallic strip), A/B would represent the values of the measurement given the instrument. The bias and error of the two instruments would be expected to differ. We cannot assume that a measurement of 20 degrees on one instrument is comparable to that on the other. The range of temperature I have chosen for X_A in this example represents roughly the extremes of absolute zero Kelvin and the temperature of the hotter stars. The range of $X_A^{(B)}$ represents the supposedly theoretical extremes of the measuring range of the two instruments. If we have no extrinsic information such as I have used to define $X_A^{(B)}$, we could use the greatest lower bound and least upper bound of the values of A within each value of B to set intervals when A is continuous.

The name **nest** comes from a design-of-experiments context. We often use the word *within* to describe its effect. For example, if **schools** and **teachers** are measured in a district, then "**teachers** *within* **schools**" specifies that teachers are nested within schools. Assuming each teacher in the district teaches at only one school, we would conclude that if our data contain two teachers with the same name at different schools, they are different people.

Those familiar with experimental design may recognize that the expression A/B is equivalent to the notation $A(B)$ in a design specification. Both expressions mean "A is nested within B." Statisticians' customary use of parentheses to denote nesting conceals the fact that nesting involves an operator, however. Because nesting is distributive over blending, I have made this operator explicit and retained the conventional mathematical use of parentheses in an algebra.

Figure 5.1 summarizes the three operators using example sets A and B shown at the top of the figure. The right hand side of the figure shows the resulting range of values for each operation on the sets. I have listed the elements in the sets in columnwise format to facilitate the visualization of the operations themselves. The row index within these columns is implied by the layout, so I have displayed only the value entry for each tuple in the column boxes. The set definitions, of course, are independent of the storage or organization of the data.

$$X_A = \{1, 2, 3\}$$
$$X_B = \{1, 3, 5\}$$
$$A = \{(1, 1), (2, 3), (3, 2), (4, 1)\}$$
$$B = \{(1, 5), (2, 1), (3, 3), (4, 5)\}$$

NAME	OPERATION	RANGE

BLEND

$$
\begin{array}{ccc}
A & B & A+B \\
\begin{bmatrix} 1 \\ 3 \\ 2 \\ 1 \end{bmatrix} +
\begin{bmatrix} 5 \\ 1 \\ 3 \\ 5 \end{bmatrix} =
\begin{bmatrix} 1 \\ 3 \\ 2 \\ 1 \\ 5 \\ 1 \\ 3 \\ 5 \end{bmatrix}
\end{array}
$$

$X_{A+B} = \{1, 2, 3, 5\}$

CROSS

$$
\begin{array}{ccc}
A & B & A*B \\
\begin{bmatrix} 1 \\ 3 \\ 2 \\ 1 \end{bmatrix} *
\begin{bmatrix} 5 \\ 1 \\ 3 \\ 5 \end{bmatrix} =
\begin{bmatrix} (1, 5) \\ (3, 1) \\ (2, 3) \\ (1, 5) \end{bmatrix}
\end{array}
$$

$X_{A*B} = \{(1, 1), (1, 3), (1, 5),$
$(2, 1), (2, 3), (2, 5),$
$(3, 1), (3, 3), (3, 5)\}$

NEST

$$
\begin{array}{ccc}
A & B & A/B \\
\begin{bmatrix} 1 \\ 3 \\ 2 \\ 1 \end{bmatrix} /
\begin{bmatrix} 5 \\ 1 \\ 3 \\ 5 \end{bmatrix} =
\begin{bmatrix} 1{:}5 \\ 3{:}1 \\ 2{:}3 \\ 1{:}5 \end{bmatrix}
\end{array}
$$

$X_{A/B} = \{1{:}5, 3{:}1, 2{:}3\}$

Figure 5.1 *Operators on two categorical variables*

5.1.7 Necessity and Sufficiency

Can we get along with only three operators or is that too many? It is not easy
to prove necessity or sufficiency for the graphical applications of the operators
in this chapter because the domain of applications is ill-defined. Nevertheless,
I claim that these three operators are necessary and sufficient for doing statistical graphics. The bases for this claim are several assertions.

First, these operators have reproduced published graphics via an automated system. They have been tested against a set of graphics I have collected over
a ten year period. The exceptions I have not addressed at this time are fractals
and parametric coordinates. Second, there were four operators in this system

before I discovered that one could be replaced with a simple combination of two others. I have not found any straightforward way to collapse the current three into two and have not found a published graphic that requires four. These claims, of course, remain to be tested.

In evaluating these assertions, one must not interpret these three operators as data transformations or as means for organizing data before plotting – as if we were rearranging cells in a spreadsheet prior to producing a graphic. We have seen those types of data operations in Chapter 3. They occur before algebraic operations on variables. If we replaced operators with *ad hoc* combinations of rows and columns of data, then we would lose the connection between variables and graphics. An automated system would not be able to respond to queries concerning variables. In a blend, for example, a legend must point to the variables that are blended – not to a synthetic variable that has no meaning apart from the blended variables. I will discuss some of these issues further at the end of this chapter when I compare graphics algebra to other algebras.

5.2 Examples

We will begin with the simplest syntax for a one-dimensional graph. Figure 5.2 is a scatterplot of the Sepal Length centimeter measurements from the Anderson Iris flower dataset analyzed by Fisher (Anderson, 1935). The first part of the specification includes the name of the variable, **sepallength**. The second part is the *point* graph. Because there is only one dimension, the *point* cloud designates points on the real number line at the values of the data.

FRAME: **sepallength**
GRAPH: *point*()

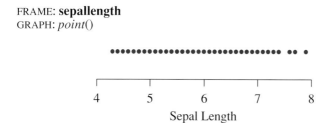

Sepal Length

Figure 5.2 *One-dimensional scatterplot.*

5.2.1 Cross

Figure 5.3 shows a two-dimensional scatterplot. The width and length of the sepals are plotted against each other. There is one frame with two dimensions represented by position.

FRAME: **sepallength*sepalwidth**
GRAPH: *point*()

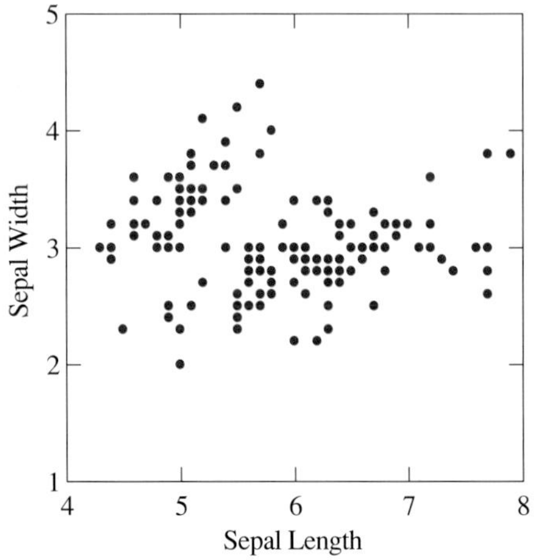

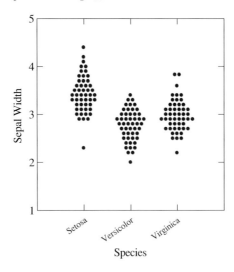

Figure 5.3 *Two-dimensional scatterplot.*

If one of the crossed variables is categorical, then it *splits* any graphs in the frame into as many categories as there are in the crossing. Figure 5.4 shows an example of this splitting. Since there are three categories for **species**, the *point* graph (see Chapter 6) is split into three objects.

FRAME: **species*sepalwidth**
GRAPH: *point(position.dodge())*

Figure 5.4 *Two-dimensional grouped dot plot.*

5.2.2 Blend

Blending increases the number of cases in a graphic. Figure 5.5 shows the simplest example of this phenomenon. We have doubled the number of cases in the graphic by using two variables on the vertical dimension. This amounts to two scatterplots overlaid on a common range and domain:

$$(A+B)*C = A*C + B*C$$

If we had put two variables on each axis, we would have produced *four* times the number of cases:

$$(A+B)*(C+D) = A*C + B*C + A*D + B*D$$

FRAME: **sepallength*(sepalwidth+petalwidth)**
GRAPH: *point*()

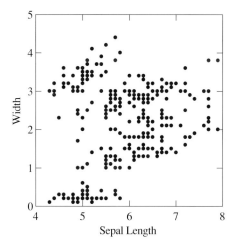

Figure 5.5 *Blended scatterplot.*

Figure 5.5 needs a legend. We will see in Chapter 7 how to use color or some other attribute to distinguish the two sets of cases that the blend operator has created. Since a variable that carries this information does not exist in the dataset, we have to create an implicit variable for the legend.

If we omitted the parentheses from the specification in Figure 5.5, we would get quite a different graphic. Because crossing takes precedence over blending, we would end up blending a crossed graph with a single dimension. Here is the algebraic form of the unparenthesized expression:

$$A+B*C = A*\mathbf{1} + B*C$$

This amounts to blending A and B on the horizontal dimension and C and the unity element on the vertical. Figure 5.6 shows the resulting graphic. It resembles two graphics pasted together. Since the unity element is by definition not in the **sepalwidth** set, it must go alongside the values of **sepalwidth** on the vertical axis. Although it creates a rather nonsensical graphic here, this syntax may not always be a mistake. It can be used for creating marginal summaries in more complex tables and graphs.

FRAME: **sepallength*sepalwidth+petalwidth**
GRAPH: *point*()

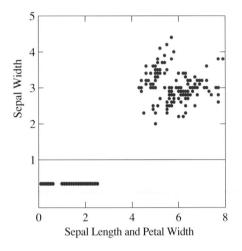

Figure 5.6 *Mixed blending and crossing.*

Blending a categorical variable combines similar categories. Only the distinct categories from the blended variable sets appear on the common scale. Figure 5.7 shows an example. The data on which this dot plot is based consist of the social status of the first two speakers in Act 1, Scene 1 of each of Shakespeare's plays. The status of the first speaker is encoded in a variable called **first**, and the second in a variable called **second**. Each of these variables has been coded into one of six possible social status categories, shown on the scale at the bottom of the plot. The Royalty category includes kings, queens, and emperors. The Nobility category includes dukes, earls, counts, countesses, princes, and marquesses. The Gentry category includes justices, tribunes, archbishops, bishops, and governors. The Citizens category includes citizens, merchants, tradesmen, and ship's masters. The Yeomanry category includes servants, boatswains, messengers, soldiers, hostesses, and porters. Finally, the Beggars category includes beggars.

FRAME: **first+second**
GRAPH: *point(position.stack())*

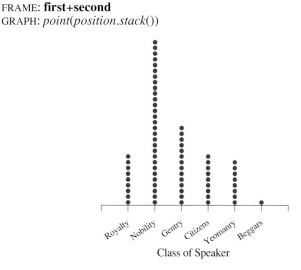

Figure 5.7 *First two speakers in Shakespeare's plays*

5.2.3 *Nest*

Nesting looks like crossing in certain respects. That is not a coincidence. In experimental design, nesting is like crossing with certain cells deleted:

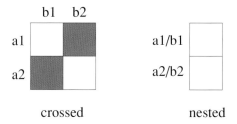

Unlike crossing, however, nesting involves tagging subsets. In Figure 5.8, **sepalwidth** is nested within **species**. This implies that each axis segment representing **sepalwidth** has a different scale. Another way to express nesting in ordinary language is to say "**sepalwidth** *given* **species**" or "**sepalwidth** *within* **species**." This phrasing expresses the conditional structure that defines nesting of **sepalwidth** under **species**. We can, of course, force the scales to have the same limits and still have a nesting. On the other hand, we may choose to *cross* **sepalwidth** with **species**, which may be more appropriate for these data. In that case, the **sepalwidth** scales would be the same.

Nesting variables are intrinsically categorical. That is, for the nesting dimension **sepalwidth/species, species** is taken to be categorical. Consequently, nesting is an operation used primarily for paneling graphs, which is discussed in Chapter 11.

FRAME: **sepallength***(**sepalwidth/species**)
GRAPH: *point*()

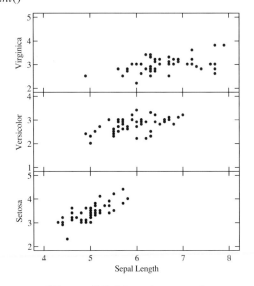

Figure 5.8 *Nested scatterplot.*

If a nested structure contains no missing cells, then it is almost indistinguishable from a linearly rearranged full-crossing. Nesting of categorical variables drawn from a true nested experimental design is a better way to illustrate the nesting operator. See Figure 7.57.

We can nest under a variable that has only one value. This is most frequently used to force separate scales when variables are blended. Figure 5.9 shows an example. The variable **s** contains the string "Sepal Width" for all cases. Similarly, **p** contains the string "Petal Width" for every case. When we blend **sepalwidth** and **petalwidth**, their values would ordinarily be pooled on a common scale. To prevent this, we blend **sepalwidth/s** and **petalwidth/p** so that 2:"Sepal Width" is a different value from 2:"Petal Width" and so on. We have forced, in effect, two panels onto our graphic. In Chapter 11, I will discuss this operation further.

We can also nest under the unity (**1**) variable. We note that **a/1** is not the same as **a**, because a tagged element is not the same as an un-tagged element. This device can be useful when we wish to concatenate two continuous scales by blending, such as **a/1 + b**. This type of expression creates two subscales under a common dimension.

DATA: **s** = "Sepal Width"
DATA: **p** = "Petal Width"
FRAME: **sepallength*(sepalwidth/s+petalwidth/p)**
GRAPH: *point*()

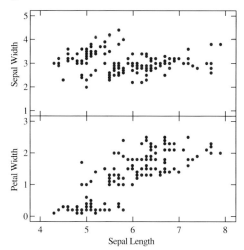

Figure 5.9 *Nesting with blending*

Figure 5.10 shows the same type of operation with the Shakespeare data, which we blended in Figure 5.7. Notice that no beggar speaks second in the plays. Beggars notwithstanding, first speakers tend to be of higher class and second lower.

DATA: **f** = "Speaker 1"
DATA: **s** = "Speaker 2"
FRAME: **first/f + second/s**
GRAPH: *point*(*position.stack*())

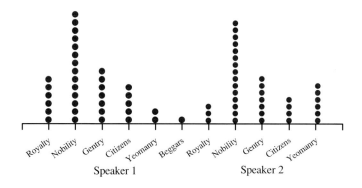

Figure 5.10 *First two speakers in Shakespeare's plays*

As Figure 5.1 shows, blending is like stacking two columns on top of each other before doing a graph. Another way to accomplish this operation is to use the data transformation called *shape.rect*() that is listed in Section 3.1. This function reshapes several columns into a single column. What would be the difference in the result if we used *shape.rect*() instead of a blend to do a graphic like Figure 5.10? Hint: would a brushing operation link Speaker 1 and Speaker 2? Hint hint: if we did a statistical test on the difference between Speaker 1 and Speaker 2, would the system recognize them as being repeated measures and therefore dependent?

5.3   Other Algebras

Several algebras developed for computer applications are related to the one I have presented in this chapter. In some cases, I need to show where I have drawn from the ideas behind these algebras, and in others, I need to show where I have not.

5.3.1   Design Algebra

An experimental design is a factorial structure that contains sets of categories embedded within other sets of categories. A design algebra operates on designs and is an application of rules derived from lattice theory and other fields of discrete mathematics. Nelder (1965) introduced a notation for implementing a computer algebra that specifies experimental designs. Wilkinson and Rogers (1973) and others have extended this notation. See Heiberger (1989) for a review.

Nelder's and more recent design algebras are intended for producing matrices of binary indicator variables that represent presence or absence of experimental treatment categories. These matrices are used in the estimation of treatment effects on outcomes for designed experiments. Nelder's work has influenced almost every subsequent statistical implementation of the general (and generalized) linear model, including GENSTAT (Alvey *et al.*, 1977), GLIM (Nelder and Wedderburn 1972; Baker and Nelder, 1978), SAS® GLM (SAS Institute, 1976), and SYSTAT® MGLH (Wilkinson, 1983a).

The cross and nest operators presented in this chapter are related to, but not the same as, the operators of the same name in Nelder's system. Where Nelder's syntax is intended to produce a correct design matrix for a particular design specification, I have been concerned to have my algebra produce a graphic or table that correctly summarizes the design. This does not mean that the two notations are syntactically compatible, however. The blend operator does not exist in Nelder's system, and application of the rules presented in Section 5.1.3 can lead to structures that are not employed in experimental design. Such structures appear in applications such as market research tables and graphical layouts not intended to be analyzed by a single statistical model.

5.3.2 *Relational Algebra*

The algebra presented in this chapter is related to, but not the same as, a **relational algebra** (Codd, 1970). For an introduction to relational algebras, see Date (1995). A relation R is defined in Section 2.1.2. A relational algebra is a set of operators together with a set of relations and rules for the operators. For our purposes, the relational operators of interest are: *union, join,* and *nest*.

The *union* relational operator (Codd, 1970) produces a union of sets (relations). Relations on identical domains are blended into a single relation and duplicate tuples are eliminated. If we create a unique tagged value for the key in each set and assign these values to a single domain, then *union* resembles *blend* in the graphics algebra.

The *join* relational operator (Codd, 1970) is an element-wise crossing of indexed sets such that tuples with a common index value are merged into new tuples. If we restrict the relational join to a common index (key) that is unique for each tuple, then a *join* of two relations is like *cross* in the graphics algebra. Such a *join* produces a relation of degree 2 (ignoring the index attribute).

The *nest* relational operator (Roth *et al.*, 1988) involves a hierarchy that was not defined in Codd's original algebra. It produces a nesting of relations under other relations and resembles the definition of *nest* in the graphics algebra.

The similarities in algebras lead one to ask whether a graphics system with the capabilities enabled by a graphics algebra could be implemented by attaching a simple viewer to a relational database. An extended Sequential Query Language (*SQL*) that implements the relational model could be used in this effort. Some of the examples in Date (1995) show how this might be done. There are several reasons why this approach would not be appropriate, however.

First, although one language can be used to imitate another, there are complexities and inefficiencies introduced when trying to adapt a system designed for a different purpose. One problem is commutativity. The *cross* and *nest* graphics algebra operators are non-commutative. The corresponding *join* and *nest* relational operators are commutative. Restrictions can be built into a specific implementation, but they would be messy side-conditions.

Second, locating the algebraic system in a database query removes knowledge in the graphics system needed for identifying and manipulating graphic objects. This would amount to a client-server model in which a graphics system is simply a viewer into a database. This system would resemble the datacube data-mining system I criticized in Chapter 3. This is *not* to say that a *SQL* client-server link is not valuable for implementing the graphics system outlined in this book. On the contrary, such a link is an essential part of its implementation (but beyond the scope of this book). Choosing the locus of the algebra, however, profoundly affects the behavior of the system.

Despite these problems, the relational model *can* play a role in a general graphics system. The graphics algebra, like relational algebra, is built on a set-theoretic approach to relations and functions that is easily packaged in objects. Embedding this algebra in an object data-model gives graphs the opportunity to view data without worrying about its structure. Graphs do not understand algebra. Algebra simply creates dimensions that govern their behavior. Consequently, a well-designed graphical system should include abstract interfaces that allow us to perform algebraic computations using functions in a relational database when they are available and appropriate. If these interfaces are designed to allow introspection or reflection (objects providing information about themselves during run-time), then we have a system that adapts to client-server and distributed environments.

5.3.3 Functional Algebra

Functional programming languages (Bird and De Moor, 1996) are based on universal algebras on abstract data classes. Functional algebras have been applied to a variety of computer geometry and graphics problems. For example, Egenhofer, Herring, Smith, and Park (1991), and Rugg, Egenhofer, and Kuhn (1995) have investigated the use of functional algebras for specifying geographic maps and navigating through spatial databases.

As with relational algebras, there are similarities between the graphics algebra operators presented in this chapter and operators in functional algebra systems. The *cross* operator produces a *product* set. The *nest* operator produces a subset of a product set called a *dependent product*. And the *blend* operator produces a *union*.

Functional algebra systems are more general than the system proposed in this chapter. While functional programming languages based on these algebras could be used for creating graph specifications, their generality exceeds the scope needed for a statistical graphics system.

5.4 Sequel

We now have an algebraic system for relating variables. Characterizing relationships requires a descriptive language of graphs. Different graphs describe different functions of variables. The next chapter will cover the different classes of graphs and how these functions produce geometrical objects that can be represented by aesthetics as perceivable things.

6

Geometry

The word **geometry** comes from the Greek $\gamma\varepsilon\omega\mu\varepsilon\tau\rho\iota\alpha$, which means land measurement. A geometer measures magnitudes in space. This chapter is about geometric functions. The Grapher object contains functions to create graphs that can be represented by magnitudes in a space. Grapher cannot make every graph in the set of all possible graphs. Grapher produces only certain graphs that can be expressed as geometric objects. I will call these **geometric graphs**.

The geometric graphs in this chapter are subsets of product sets of real numbers R^m or natural numbers N^m. We will be concerned with geometric objects for which $1 \leq m \leq 3$. These objects will be embedded in a space R^n in which $m \leq n \leq 3$. Geometric graphs are built from **bounded regions**. Bounded regions are produced by the Cartesian product of bounded intervals. The set B^m is bounded if

$$B^m \subset [a_1, b_1] \times [a_2, b_2] \times \ldots [a_m, b_m] \ .$$

These intervals define the edges of a bounding box (like the bounds of a frame) in m-dimensional space. There are two reasons we need bounded regions. First, in order to define certain useful geometric graphs, we need concepts like the *end* of a line or the *edge* of a rectangle. Second, we want to save ink and electricity. We don't want to take forever to compute and draw a line. More precisely, we need to embed geometric graphs in a frame, which is itself a bounded region (see Section 2.2.4.2). We want the image of the function that produces a geometric graph to be bounded (although a few of the transformations in Chapter 10 can produce images unbounded in R^n that we will have to clip in a renderer).

Geometric graphs are produced by graphing functions $F: B^m \rightarrow R^n$ that have geometric names like *line*() or *tile*(). A geometric graph is the image of F. And a graphic, as used in the title of this book, is the image of a graph under one or more aesthetic functions. Geometric graphs are not visible. As Bertin (1967, 1977) points out, visible elements have features not present in their geometric counterparts. The next chapter, Aesthetics, will cover methods for making graphs perceivable. Meanwhile, I will use aesthetic functions in this chapter to illustrate different types of graphs. These graphs will be displayed using position, color, size, and shape, but the same graphs could be realized using sound or even, theoretically, odors. Although this chapter is about geometry, I will discuss briefly issues in rendering these geometric objects in order to reinforce this distinction.

To maintain the distinction between a graph and its physical representation, I will call the output of a *line*() graphing function a *line* graph and I will call the output of the composite of a *line*() graphing function and its aesthetic functions (*position*(), *color*(), *size*(), ...) a *line* graphic. To distinguish geometry from function, I will use Roman type to refer to a geometric line, and Italic type to refer to the specialized *line* produced by *line*().

There are several ways to classify graphics. First, we could organize them by their appearance under standard aesthetic functions: for example, *bars* and *histobars* as opposed to *lines*. This would consolidate drawing methods and thus conserve display code. Organizing by surface appearance makes it more difficult to collect similar geometric methods in single classes, however. Although they appear similar, *bars* and *histobars* are fundamentally different geometric objects. A second approach would be to classify them by their geometric dimensionality (the *m* parameter in B^m). This would consolidate rendering methods. Organizing by dimensionality makes it difficult to consolidate data methods, however. A third approach would be to organize them by their data methods, regardless of appearance. Any method which involved computing a location estimate (mean, median, mode, etc.) could be grouped together. This approach, of course, would disperse drawing methods.

I have chosen to organize graphs by their data *and* geometry. Because this system is about statistical graphics, the most fruitful classifying scheme, I believe, is based on how graphs function in representing statistical data geometrically. Graphs that behave similarly in a variety of contexts are grouped together. This scheme results in four major categories of graphs: **relations**, **summaries**, **partitions**, and **networks**. Relations associate values in a domain with values in a range using graphs that enable one to locate one or more values in the range for any selected value in the domain. Summaries characterize a distribution of values through a collection of different geometric elements. Partitions separate a set of points into two or more subsets. Networks connect two or more points with line segments. Table 6.1 summarizes these classifications.

The remarkable feature of this table is its parsimony. An enormous number of graphical elements can be grouped into a relatively small number of graph types. Undoubtedly there are other graph types needed to reproduce some graphics not found in this book, but adding them to this system should not require altering its architecture. New graphing functions, if defined properly, should be self-contained and housebroken enough to avoid doing violence to the rest of the system. In addition, many graphics that appear radically different from the ones found in this chapter are either transformations of the geometry or functions of the data that underlie the graphs in Table 6.1. Before you wonder why a popular graphic is missing in this chapter, see Chapter 8 or Chapter 10 for how it may be derived from the base graph classes.

I have used *surface* as an alias for *line*, *volume* as an alias for *area*, and *interval* for *bar*. I could not find an ordinary word for these classes independent of dimensionality. As we shall see, a *surface* is a geometric generalization of a *line*, a *volume* is a generalization of an *area*, and an *interval* is a generalization of a *bar*.

Table 6.1 **Graphs**

Relations	**Summaries**	**Partitions**	**Networks**
point *line* (*surface*) *area* (*volume*) *bar* (*interval*) *histobar*	*schema*	*tile* *contour*	*path* *link*

6.1 *Relations*

Relation graphs associate one or more values in a domain with one or more values in a range. This is the largest super-class of graphs and one that contains most of the representation objects seen in popular charts.

6.1.1 *Point*

The *point*() graphing function produces a geometric point, which is an *n*-tuple. This function can also produce a finite set of points, called a **multi-point** or a **point cloud**. The set of points produced by *point*() is called a *point* graph.

Rendering a *point* is relatively straightforward. To visualize a *point* graph as a *point* graphic, we need a *shape* attribute that gives it the shape of a circle, a diamond, a face, or some other image. And we need a *size* attribute that makes it large enough to be discernible. We also need a *hue* attribute that makes its color different from the background color of the frame graphic in which it is displayed. If points overlap, we can use transparency to prevent occlusion.

Figure 6.1 shows examples of a *point* cloud on a categorical and continuous domain. The left panel contains three *point* graphics (one for each category) and the right panel, one. The *point* graphic can have numerous variations, produced mainly by varying the *shape* attribute of their symbols and by the aggregation function used, as we shall see in Chapter 8, where I will show examples of multivariate *icon* clouds. Otherwise, this most common of graphics is one of the simplest to visualize.

FRAME: **gov*birth**
GRAPH: *point*()

FRAME: **female*birth**
GRAPH: *point*()

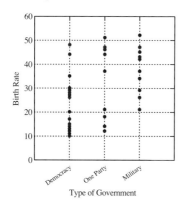 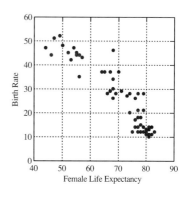

Figure 6.1 *A point cloud on categorical (left) and continuous (right) domains*

Figure 6.2 shows an example of *point* graphics in 3D. For the left panel, I have introduced another categorical variable, **urban**, which is a measure of urbanization for each country. For the right panel, the data are measurements of automobile performance in various 1996 issues of the magazine *Road & Track*. The three variables are seconds to cover a quarter mile from a standing start (**quarter**), horsepower (**hp**), and weight in pounds (**weight**).

FRAME: **urban*gov*birth**
GRAPH: *point*()

FRAME: **weight*hp*quarter**
GRAPH: *point*()

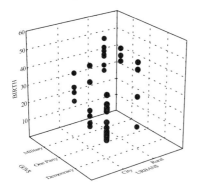 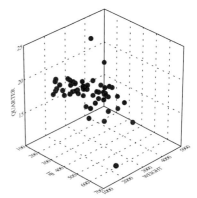

Figure 6.2 *3D points on categorical (left) and continuous (right) domains*

6.1.2 Line

Let B^m be a bounded region in $\mathbf{R}^m$. Consider the function $F: B^m \rightarrow \mathbf{R}^n$, where $n = m+1$, with the following additional properties:

    1) the image of F is bounded,

    2) $F(x) = (v, f(v))$, where $f: B^m \rightarrow \mathbf{R}$ and $v = (x_1, \ldots, x_m) \in B^m$.

If $m = 1$, this function maps an interval to a functional curve on a bounded plane. And if $m = 2$, it maps a bounded region to a functional surface in a bounded 3D space. The *line*() graphing function produces these graphs. Like *point*(), *line*() can produce a finite set of lines. A set of *lines* is called a **multi-line**. We need this capability for representing multimodal smoothers, confidence intervals on regression lines, and other multifunctional lines. An example is shown in the lower left panel of Figure 8.2.

    Rendering a *line* is not simple. The *line*() graphing function returns a value on a *line* for any tuple $(x_1, \ldots, x_m)$. We cannot compute every possible tuple in B^m in order to draw a line as a set of points, however (although some programs like MacSpin (Donoho et al., 1988) and Data Desk (Velleman, 1998) that were designed to animate point clouds do represent a line or surface by a fine mesh of points that are rendered in pixels). Instead, we must choose a few **knots** that define the ends of line segments and then interpolate between these knots. For straight lines, this is straightforward: we linearly interpolate between two endpoints. For curved lines, we may either construct many knots and use linear interpolation or make fewer knots and use a spline function to interpolate curvilinearly (Lancaster & Salkauskas, 1986; Dierckx, 1993). The advantage of splines is that some operating systems include them among their primitives, so that time and memory can be saved. For 3D surfaces, knots define a rectangular or triangular mesh that yields polygons for rendering. As with 2D, some operating systems include 3D spline functions, so we should design a renderer to take advantage of them when available.

    There are many other problems we face in rendering a *line*. We must be able to handle conditions where the slope approaches infinity. If we have missing values, we need rules to determine how a gap (or a hole in 3D) should be treated. And if we want to achieve the full range of aesthetic representations shown in Chapter 7, we have to treat a *line* as a collection of polygons or sometimes even symbols so that we can give it *size* (thickness), *shape* (symbols), and *texture* (dashing patterns). Few operating systems give us the primitives needed to draw a curved, dashed line made up of dots, for example.

    I will explore the aesthetics of lines further in Chapter 6. At this point, however, it is useful to keep in mind that the definition of a *line* as a set of points is probably the best way to approach the rendering problem. What distinguishes a *line* from a cloud of *points* is that the points comprising it are ordered. Thus, we can render a line by stamping copies of symbols in a given ordering or by connecting a set of polygons to make segments.

Figure 6.3 shows *line* graphics of average birth rates on categorical (left) and continuous (right) domains.

FRAME: **gov*birth**
GRAPH: *line*()

FRAME: **female*birth**
GRAPH: *line*()

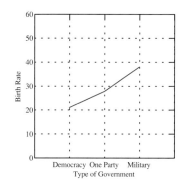 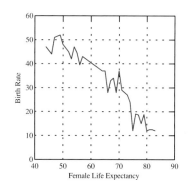

Figure 6.3　*Line on categorical (left) and continuous (right) domains*

Figure 6.4 shows 3D *line* graphics. The left panel is based on a categorical domain (**gov*birth**), so it contains a collection of *line* graphics. I have given them thickness to make them look like ribbons, a popular representation.

FRAME: **urban*gov*birth**
GRAPH: *line*()

FRAME: **x*y*z**
GRAPH: *surface*()

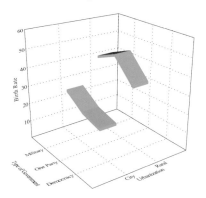 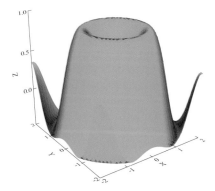

Figure 6.4　*Surface on categorical (left) and continuous (right) domain*

6.1.3 Area

The *area*() graphing function produces a graph containing all points within the region under the *line* graph. Rendering an *area* involves the same caveats as for *line*. Figure 6.5 shows *area* graphics of average birth rates. The *area* graphic looks like a *line* graphic with the area between it and the abscissa filled.

FRAME: **gov*birth**
GRAPH: *area*()

FRAME: **female*birth**
GRAPH: *area*()

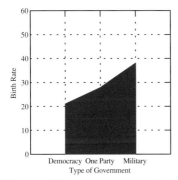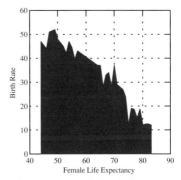

Figure 6.5 *Area on categorical (left) and continuous (right) domains*

The *area* graphic is a *volume* in 3D. Figure 6.6 shows an example.

FRAME: **urban*gov*birth**
GRAPH: *area*()

FRAME: **x*y*z**
GRAPH: *area*()

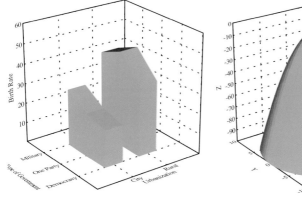

Figure 6.6 *Volume on categorical (left) and continuous (right) domain*

6.1.4 Bar

The *bar*() graphing function produces a set of closed intervals. An interval has two ends. Ordinarily, however, bars are used to denote a single value through the location of one end. The other end is anchored at a common reference point (usually zero). Figure 6.7 shows a 2D *bar* graphic.

FRAME: **gov*birth**
GRAPH: *bar*()

FRAME: **female*birth**
GRAPH: *bar*()

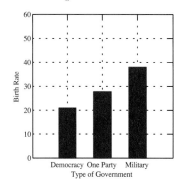 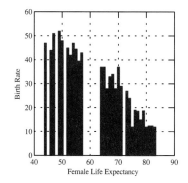

Figure 6.7 *Bar graphic on categorical (left) and continuous (right) domains*

Figure 6.8 shows a 3D *bar* graphic for the car data used in Figure 6.2.

FRAME: **urban*gov*birth**
GRAPH: *bar*()

FRAME: **weight*hp*quarter**
GRAPH: *bar*()

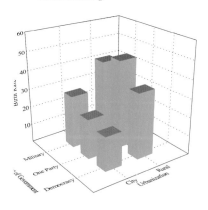 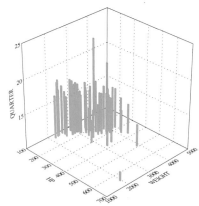

Figure 6.8 *3D bar graphic on categorical and continuous domains*

Despite appearances, there is only one *bar* graphic in each of the right panels of these two figures. The bars in the left panels, on the other hand, are split by the categorical variables. This is consistent with the behavior of *point*() (see Figure 6.1, where there are 3 clouds on the left and one on the right). The only way to sense this behavior would be to query the objects in a dynamic system by brushing or editing. In such an environment, the left panel bars would respond singly and the right ones would respond in unison.

The *bar* graphic uses a default mean aggregation function. This function returns the mean of all values in the range for a given value or tuple of values in the domain. Thus, the default *bar*() is equivalent to the expression *bar.statistic.mean*(). I will discuss aggregation functions further in Chapter 8. The top of each bar in the left panel of Figure 6.7 represents the average birth rate in each of the 3 **gov** categories and the top of each bar in the left panel of Figure 6.8 represents the average birth rate in each of the 6 combinations of **gov** and **urban**.

6.1.5 *Histobar*

The *histobar*() graphing function produces a histogram element. Figure 6.9 shows examples of 2D and 3D histograms.

DATA: **count** = *count*()
FRAME: **birth*count**
GRAPH: *histobar*()

DATA: **count** = *count*()
FRAME: **female*male*count**
GRAPH: *histobar*()

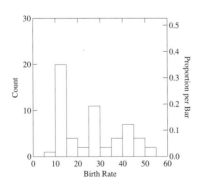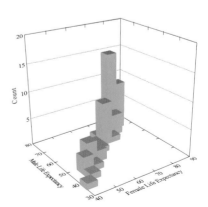

Figure 6.9 *2D and 3D histograms*

The variable **count** that is created by the DATA function *count*() is an upper bound for the number of cases in any histogram bar, since it generates the total sample size. We often want to rescale the range of this variable by using a smaller number as a parameter in the function, as in *count*(30).

The *histobar* graphic reveals some subtle characteristics when it is compared to similar-appearing graphics. Unlike the *bar* graphic, which represents intervals, the *histobar* graphic represents area. Unlike the *area* graph, which represents a single area, the *histobar* graphic is a collection of areas, one for each bar. Although most published examples show ordinary histograms with bars representing counts on equal intervals, the bars in the *histobar* graphic need not be of equal width. Some may even have zero area. Unlike the *bar* graphic, however, the bars in *histobar* must be connected. There cannot be gaps between bars unless these are due to bars with zero area.

6.2 *Summaries*

Summary graphs represent the values of a variable by three or more features. We could construct some of these graphs by combining data and drawing methods from other graphs like *bar*, *point*, and *line*. There are occasions when having a separate graph class for summaries can be useful, however.

6.2.1 *Schema*

A **schema** is a diagram that includes both general and particular features in order to represent a distribution. I have taken this usage from Tukey (1977), who invented the **schematic plot**, which has come to be known as the **box plot** because of its physical appearance. The *schema*() graphing function produces a collection of one or more points, lines, intervals, and areas.

Schema graphics can take many shapes and can be based on different statistics. Tukey's box plot is the default. This plot is based on statistics called **letter values**. The central vertical line in the box is the **median**, computed by sorting a list of values and taking the middle sorted value. If the number of cases is even, then the two middle values are averaged. The edges of the box are the **hinges**, computed from the medians of the two batches produced when the sorted values are split at the overall median. The ends of the whiskers in the box plot extend to the most extreme values inside the **inner fences**. These fences are defined as follows:

> *lower fence = lower hinge* $-1.5Hspread$
>
> *upper fence = upper hinge* $+ 1.5Hspread$, where

Hspread is the spread of the hinges, namely the *upper hinge* minus the *lower hinge*. Finally, the **outer fences** are computed using $3Hspread$ in the same formulas. Values outside the outer fences (far outside values) are plotted with a small circle and remaining values outside the inner fences are plotted with as-

terisks. This rather complicated set of definitions produces a remarkably parsimonious plot in which outlying values are immediately recognizable and the
distribution of the remaining values is schematically represented by a box and
whiskers. The general information is conveyed in the box and whiskers, and
the particular information is conveyed in the outliers.

Figure 6.10 shows a box plot of the distribution of horsepower among the
cars in the *Road & Track* dataset. Two cars are highlighted as extreme. These
are the Lamborghini Diablo (asterisk) and the Ferrarri 333 race car (circle).

FRAME: **hp**
GRAPH: *schema*()

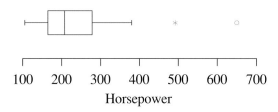

Figure 6.10 *Schematic (box) plot*

When plotted against continuous variables, boxes are usually unevenly
spaced. We compute a box where there is more than one **y** value for a given **x**.
Elsewhere, the median horizontal line marks the unique **y** value. Figure 6.11
shows an example using data on gas and electricity consumption from Tukey
(1977). The electricity values were grouped into batches before plotting.

FRAME: **electric*gas**
GRAPH: *schema*()

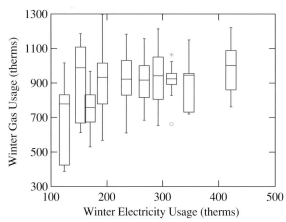

Figure 6.11 *Box plots on continuous domain*

6.3 Partitions

Partitions divide datasets into subsets. The divisions occur in two ways. One class of graphs (*tile*) separates individual data points into mutually exclusive regions (areas or volumes). One method for doing this is used in mapping, where a perimeter around a point is created by using polygon boundaries contained in associated shape files. Another method is to tile a set of points by a geometric shape or scheme, such as hexagons. The second class of partitions (*contour*) separates points into two or more regions, possibly nested.

6.3.1 Tile

A *tile*() graphing function tiles a surface or space. A *tile* graph covers and partitions the bounded region defined by a frame; there can be no gaps or overlaps between tiles. The Latinate *tessellation* (for tiling) is often used to describe the appearance of the *tile* graphic. Figure 6.12 shows a tiling based on a mathematical function. There are 10,000 tiles in the figure (a 100 by 100 rectangular grid).

DATA: $\mathbf{x} = iter(-5, 5, 0.1, 100, 1)$
DATA: $\mathbf{y} = iter(-5, 5, 0.1, 1, 100)$
TRANS: $\mathbf{z} = sin(\mathbf{x}^2) - cos(\mathbf{y}^2))^2 * \mathbf{y} * \mathbf{x}$
FRAME: $\mathbf{x} * \mathbf{y}$
GRAPH: *tile(color.hue($\mathbf{z}$))*

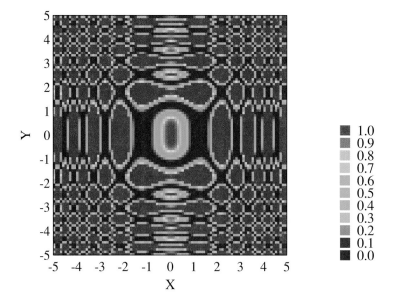

Figure 6.12 *Tiled equation*

6.3.2 Contour

A *contour*() graphing function produces contours, or level curves. A *contour* graphic is used frequently in weather and topographic maps. Contours can be used to delineate any continuous surface. Figure 6.13 shows contours for the inverse distance smoother relating average winter temperatures to latitude and longitude. I have superimposed the smoother contours on a map of the U.S. I will discuss this inverse distance smoothing method in Chapter 8.

FRAME: **longitude*latitude**
COORD: *project.stereo*()
GRAPH: *tile(shape.polygon(***state***))*
GRAPH: *contour.smooth.mean.cauchy(color.hue(***winter***)))*

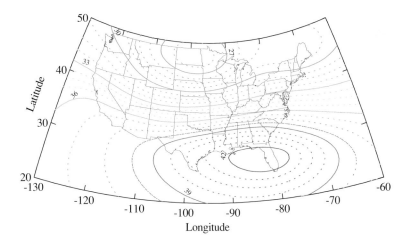

Figure 6.13 *Contour plot of smoothed winter temperatures*

6.4 Networks

Network graphs join points with line segments. Networks are representations that resemble the edges in diagrams of theoretic graphs (Harary, 1969). Although networks join points, a *point* graph is not needed in a frame in order for a network graphic to be visible.

Networks include an enormous variety of graphs, including circuits, trees, paths, graphs embedded on the plane or in three dimensions, and other structures linking points. I will cover some of these specialized graphs in Chapter 8.

6.4.1 Path

The *path*() graphing function produces a *path*. A *path* graph connects points such that each point touches no more than two line segments. Thus, a *path* visits every point in a collection of points only once. If a *path* is closed (every point touches two line segments), we call it a *circuit*.

Paths often look like *lines* (Section 6.1.2). There are several important differences between the two, however. First, *lines* are functional; there can be only one point on a *line* for any value in the domain. On the other hand, *paths* may loop, zigzag, and even cross themselves inside a frame. Second, *paths* consist of segments that correspond to edges, or links between nodes. This means that a variable may be used to determine an attribute of every segment of a *path*. For example, a line may have only a single *size*, ranging from hairline to thick. A path, on the other hand, can have a different size for each of its segments, as in Figure 15.1. Similarly, we can vary the texture, color, or other attributes of every segment of a *path* by assigning the relevant attribute to a variable. This geometric distinction between *paths* and *lines* also extends to query, brushing, and drill-down. If we click on a line segment, we can get information only about the entire line. If we click on a path segment, we can get information about that segment. Thus, in some applications, we may wish to use a *path* instead of a *line* even when we know our model is functional.

Figure 6.14 shows a price/consumption curve for cigarettes sold in the US between 1964 and 1986 (Harris, 1987). The path order, determined by time, is labeled next to each segment of the curve. Prior to 1981, the price was relatively inelastic. For other examples of paths, see theoretical Hertzsprung-Russell diagrams used by astronomers (Mihalas and Binney, 1981) or Figure 15.1.

FRAME: **price*consump**
GRAPH: *path*(*label*(**year**))

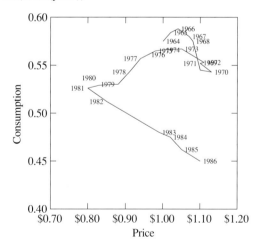

Figure 6.14 *Consumption/price curve for cigarettes*

6.4.2 Link

The *link*() graphing function produces a collection of edges. These edges are line segments joining points in a space. Two or more points are connected to one or more edges in *link* graphs. The various graphs in this class are subsets of a complete network connecting every pair of points. Figure 6.15 shows a link graph for all possible links among points at the vertices of an octagon.

FRAME: **x*y**
GRAPH: *link*()

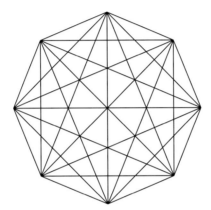

Figure 6.15 *A complete network for 8 points at the vertices of an octagon*

6.5 *Splitting vs. Shading*

As I indicated in Figure 5.4, graphs are *split* by categorical variables. The following expression is the simplest example of this behavior:

SCALE: *cat*(**species**)
FRAME: **species**
GRAPH: *point*()

Because **species** is set to be categorical, we would expect to see three dots in the graphic for the Iris data, each consisting of 50 superimposed points for each of the three **species**. Because there is no attribute other than position assigned to the splitting variable on a common axis, we would not be able to distinguish these clouds visually. In a dynamic graphics system, we could observe behavior (selection, editing, etc.) which would indicate this splitting.

Any use of a categorical variable in a specification splits graphs. Nesting splits because nesting variables are required to be categorical. A simple example would be:

FRAME: **sepalwidth/species**
GRAPH: *point*()

This would produce three *point* clouds, one for each set of 50 points derived from each of the **species**. For a multiple nesting like **a/b/c**, we must count all existing combinations of **b** and **c** to determine the number of splits. If nesting is combined with blending and/or crossing, then do this count before considering splits due to crossing and blending.

Categorical variables used for aesthetic attributes split graphs:

FRAME: **sepalwidth*sepallength**
GRAPH: *point*(*color*(**species**))

This produces three *point* clouds, one for each set of 50 points defined by **species**, and each a different color.

A continuous variable produces a similar visual result to a categorical variable but it does not split. We say that it *shades*. For many graphics, we cannot tell whether a variable splits or shades unless we know in advance whether that variable is continuous or categorical or we can explore the graphic using interactive tools that let us identify whether subgroups belong to a common class or to separate classes.

Finally, when we want to force splitting without using a variable for any other purpose, we can specify splitting explicitly by adding *split*() to the aesthetic methods, for example:

FRAME: **sepalwidth*sepallength**
GRAPH: *point*(*split*(**species**))

This method is not often used, because it leaves no aesthetic attribute to signal that splitting has happened. Figure 15.1 in the last chapter reproduces an historical graphic that requires this operation. In the original graphic, the same color was used to represent different split groups – not ordinarily a good idea.

6.6 Summary

Table 6.2 summarizes the graphs in this chapter for 1D through 3D. The pictures in the cells are graphical exemplars for the graphs shown in Table 6.1. The 1D rendering environment leaves us few opportunities to discriminate between graph types. We may use thickness in 1D when this does not measure a data attribute. For example, we can choose a symbol shape in a 1D graphic to represent some aspect of our data, but the center of all the symbols must still fall on a line and their size has no data meaning. Similarly, the thickness of *bar*, *histobar*, *schema*, and *tile* has no data meaning in 1D. The 2D graphics provide an extra degree of freedom to represent data variation. Graphics such as *area*, *contour*, *path*, and *link* require at least two dimensions to be useful. While 1D graphics are most constrained, 3D ones are least. The *line* graph becomes a *surface* and the *area* becomes a *volume*. In like manner, the *tile* graph partitions a 3D space so that each *tile* encloses a volume. The *contour* graph partitions 3D space similarly.

Table 6.2 **Geometric Graphs**

	1D	2D	3D
Relations			
Point			
Line			
Area			
Bar			
Histobar			
Summaries			
Schema			
Partitions			
Tile			
Contour			
Networks			
Path			
Link			

6.7 *Sequel*

So far, we have graphs that describe functions, but we cannot perceive them. The next chapter presents functions that link graphs to aesthetic attributes and thus make graphs perceivable as graphics.

7

Aesthetics

The term **aesthetics** derives from the Greek $\alpha \acute{\iota} \sigma \theta \eta \sigma \iota \varsigma$, which means perception. The derivative modern meanings of beauty, taste, and artistic criteria arose in the 18th century. I have chosen the name Aesthetics to describe an object in our graphical system because of its original connotations and because the modern word perception is subjective rather than objective; perception refers to the perceiver rather than the object. Aesthetics turn graphs into graphics so that they are perceivable, but they are not the perceptions themselves. A modern psychologist would most likely call aesthetics in this sense *stimuli*, *aspects*, or *features*, but these words are less precise for our purposes.

The preceding chapters have discussed the components of the system for producing graphs, but up to this point we having nothing to show. Without aesthetics, graphs are invisible, silent, indeed imperceptible. Aesthetics are functions that govern how a graph is represented as a visible or otherwise perceivable graphic.

Since this book focuses on developing statistical graphics systems that can transmit measurable multidimensional information to perceivers, the cognitive and perceptual psychological research on scaling aesthetics is relevant. The field of perception research is wide and long-standing. Its contemporary roots are in 19th century medicine and philosophy. Its recent growth has been nourished by neuroscience. For an introduction, see Shiffman (1990), Levine and Shefner (1991), or Anderson (1995).

To make a statistical graphics system, we need to map qualitative and quantitative scales to sensory aspects of physical stimuli. Each dimension of a graph must be represented by an aesthetic attribute such as color or sound. We will first examine problems in the mapping of continuous scales. Then we will examine similar issues with categorical scales. Next, we will look at problems introduced when we work with multiple dimensions. Then I will discuss the role of realism in constructing graphics.

Finally, I will discuss specific aesthetic attributes. I have extended the classification system of Bertin (1967, 1977) who, while not a psychologist, has formalized attributes in a system that can be related to psychological theories of perception. Indeed, while Bertin's work is based entirely on visual displays, his variables apply, with small modifications, to other sensory modalities. For a psychological perspective on Bertin's work, see Kosslyn (1985). For a review of cartographers' extensions of Bertin's system, see MacEachren (1995)

7.1 Continuous Scales

When we map real numbers to the intensity of a physical stimulus, how do we know that magnitude will be perceived as a linear function of the values? We know from physics, for example, that the brightness of a light source decreases as the square of its distance from a receptor. Even if we measure brightness at the retina, however, neural processes may non-linearize, truncate, or otherwise filter the signal. We will examine this problem in the next section and then consider its implication for the use of aesthetic attributes.

7.1.1 Psychophysics

Relating the magnitude of a physical stimulus to a perception comprises the field of **psychophysics** (Stevens, 1985; Falmagne, 1985). The German biologist and physicist Gustav Theodor Fechner coined this term in his *Elemente der Psychophysik* (1860). Although Fechner spent most of his career on metaphysics and religion and his psychophysical work focused on human perception, there is nothing in psychophysical theory that would limit it to humans. Psychophysics in the general sense involves mapping the intensity of a quantitative stimulus (light, sound, motion) to the response of a sensing system (human, insect, computer).

Fechner built his theory on an observation of one of his medical professors, Ernst Heinrich Weber. Weber had discovered that the change in magnitude of a stimulus needed to produce a **just-noticeable-difference** (JND) in sensation appeared to be a constant. For example, if I place a kilogram weight in each of your hands you will most likely perceive no difference in weight between the two. If I add more weight to one hand, you will just begin to notice the difference at around 1.1 vs. 1 kilograms. Similarly, if I place ten kilograms in each of your hands, I will need to add approximately one kilogram to one hand for you to begin to notice the difference. In both cases, the ratio of the difference to the magnitude is 0.1. This ratio differs for individuals and for kinds of stimuli, but the phenomenon of constancy within experiment is remarkable.

Figure 7.1 (adapted from Levine and Shefner, 1991) shows a graph of a function based on Weber's observation. Each unit increase in Sensation (δS) occurs after the stimulus Intensity increases by a JND (δI). In other words,

$$\delta S = k\left(\frac{\delta I}{I}\right)$$

The left panel of the figure shows the graph for a fixed value of δS. The units of the scales are arbitrary. It is the shape of the function that led Fechner to his formulation.

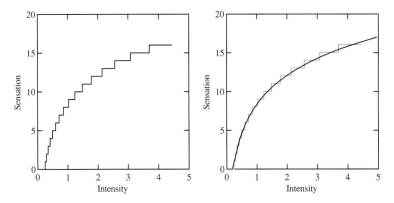

Figure 7.1 *JND's following Fechner-Weber law.*

Fechner integrated the function

$$\delta S / \delta I \,=\, k / I$$

to yield

$$S = k\, log(I) + c$$

Fechner called this Weber's law, but it really was Fechner's, based on Weber's observation. This logarithmic function is plotted in the right panel of Figure 7.1, with $c=8$ and $k=5$.

Boring (1950) discusses the assumptions Fechner made, including the potential for negative sensation, since his log function had no limits. This and other questionable assumptions caused a sensation of its own and led to controversies which have persisted for over 100 years. Nevertheless, Fechner's unique achievement was to infer from Weber's simple observation the shape of the psychophysical function without having to measure perceived intensity.

Weber's discovery and Fechner's formulation prompted other researchers to consider measuring sensation directly. Plateau (1872) had artists paint a gray patch midway between black and white under different levels of illumination. On observing that all the patches were virtually the same gray, he proposed the power function

$$S \,=\, kI^{\,p}$$

S.S. Stevens (1961) tested Plateau's function with numerous experiments employing **direct scaling**. Instead of asking subjects to report when a JND occurred, Stevens requested direct numerical estimates of the ratio of intensities of different stimuli. His model fit observed data across a wide variety of subjects, intensities, modes of stimuli, and measurement methods.

For Weber-Fechner, equal stimulus ratios produce equal sensation differences. For Plateau-Stevens, equal stimulus ratios produce equal subjective ratios. The reason for the discrepancy between their models is that they begin with a different latent variable. Both infer sensation rather than measure it directly. Because of this difference in definition and because both are based on a latent variable, scientists are still unable to reject conclusively one or the other model, despite numerous claims to have done so. In the end, neither model may be correct, or even more likely, neither may be of much use to a theory of perception (Ekman, 1964; Gregson, 1988; Lockhead, 1992).

For our purposes, these functions tell us that intensity may not be linearly related to sensation. Figure 7.2 shows power-function psychophysical curves for a variety of stimuli using data from Shiffman (1990), Stevens (1961), and other sources. Note that electric shock has an exponent greater than 3. For this and other reasons, shock would not be a good aesthetic candidate for representing a dimension in a statistical graphic.

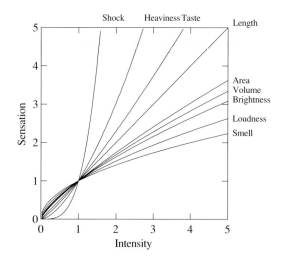

Figure 7.2 *Psychophysical functions for various stimuli.*

7.1.2 Consequences for Attributes

As we have seen, different aesthetic attributes will more or less non-linearize our signal. Should we adjust for this by including the Stevens exponents in the scaling of graphics in an automated statistical graphics system? The recommendation has been made at various times by both psychologists and statisticians, but it would be a mistake. Unfortunately, even numbers themselves behave like other stimuli in psychophysical experiments (Schneider *et al.*, 1974). So does numerosity (Krueger, 1982). If our goal for a statistical graphics system is to communicate accurately quantitative or qualitative information, should we root all our displayed numbers? This would certainly be a radical change in the output of statistical packages! Most certainly, however, the presence of bias in human information processing does not imply that we should normalize the physical world to an inferred perceptual world. As we will see in Section 7.3, nonlinearities have their uses in perceiving objects. There are ways to accommodate them.

One way is to ensure that the range of variation in an aesthetic attribute does not exceed too many orders of magnitude in intensity. If there is nonlinearity, clamping limits the psychophysical response function to a roughly linear segment. We might worry that our effect is too subtle in these circumstances, but we have to acknowledge the speed-accuracy trade-off in the perceptual process. If our goal is to emphasize differences, then we should be more willing to accept bias.

Another way is to live with the bias. With positively skewed data, we can turn a sow's ear into a silk purse. Using circle areas to represent magnitude of a third variable on a scatterplot, we will de-emphasize extremely large values because their areas will be less salient (the Stevens exponent for area is .7). If this is the effect we wish to achieve, particularly with positively skewed data, then a **bubble plot** like this might be the best representation, despite admonitions to the contrary (Cleveland, Harris, and McGill, 1981).

Finally, we can choose attributes that are closer to a Stevens exponent of 1 when we are concerned about linearity. This approach underlies Cleveland's (1985) recommended hierarchy of graphical elements. Figure 7.3 displays this hierarchy, derived from a series of graphical element perception studies by Cleveland and his associates. In most of these experiments, Cleveland used a paradigm not unlike direct scaling. He simply compared subjects' numerical judgments with the generating stimulus magnitude. The rank order of Cleveland's elements corresponds roughly to the absolute difference between their Stevens exponent (averaged across different studies) and 1. Additional variation contributing to Cleveland's results is probably due to the effects of visual illusions (especially with angular judgments).

Cleveland's hierarchy has sometimes been recommended as a general criterion for evaluating statistical graphics (*e.g.*, Wallgren *et al.*, 1996). Several researchers have found that Cleveland's results are contextual, however. Spence and Lewandowsky (1991), for example, found support for the predictions of the hierarchy only in the initial, pre-attentive stages of processing where rapid and direct evaluation of magnitude was required. Simkin and Hastie (1987) found that accuracy of comparative, magnitude, and ratio judgments depends on types of graphic elements and types of tasks. And Carswell (1992) found support for the hierarchy mainly when attention was focused on a portion of a graphic. Kosslyn (1994) discusses these and other findings concerning the hierarchy at greater length. It must be remembered, however, that Cleveland's original intention was to evaluate different elements when isolated, out of context. Furthermore, the task was deliberately restricted to magnitude and ratio comparisons. Such restriction is often desirable when attempting new research in an ill-defined field. Like all psychophysical approaches that isolate stimuli in order to examine their psychometric functions, however, the results apply only to certain restricted, indeed artificial, situations. As we shall see in Section 7.4, cognitive psychologists have recently turned away from psychophysics and toward a more integrated, ecological approach for just this reason.

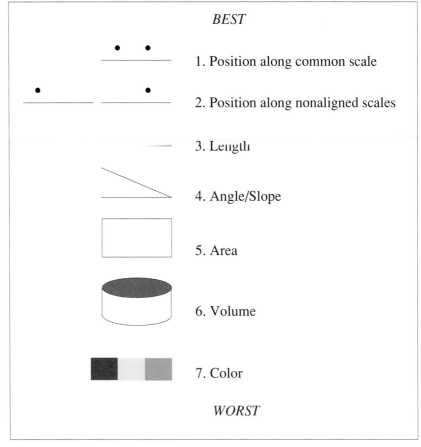

Figure 7.3 *Cleveland graphic elements hierarchy.*

7.2 *Categorical Scales*

If we assign the values of an attribute, such as color, to a set of categories, how do we know that a person will perceive categories? For example, we might assign two shades of red to a scale distinguishing males and females on a gender variable. Is it enough simply for these shades to differ by at least one JND, or will we do better assigning, say, red and green? Are there color categories at all, or is color perceived simply as a continuum in three dimensions? Indeed, does perceptual categorization itself exist, or do we simply respond to a continuum of perceived similarity among stimuli?

We take answers to many of these questions for granted when we place legends on graphics or use tick marks to separate categories on an axis. The system described in this book depends on mapping real numbers (for continuous scales) or integers (for categorical scales) to perceptual attributes. If the perceptual result is the same in both cases, then this aesthetic distinction cannot be supported. For answers, we need to consult the field of categorical perception.

Categories enable us to recognize objects in the world. Consider two berries, one black, one blue, both otherwise indistinguishable to the eye. The chokeberry is poisonous, the blueberry delicious. Color categorization allows us to distinguish them. We identify the poisonous berry as different from the tasty even though they appear identical on most available sensory attributes (size, shape, firmness, etc.). The consequences of our mistakes in categorization can be themselves categorical: we eat and die (or die and are eaten).

We should not assume that the ability to make effective categorical judgments in the world implies a categorical perceptual mechanism, however. We need instead to examine whether there is experimental evidence for categorical processing and then see if it can affect the assignment of attributes to categorical scales. First, we will review the evidence for innate categorical processing and then examine learned categories.

7.2.1 *Innate Categories*

Aristotle made categorization fundamental to his logic. His categories – substance, quantity, quality, relation, place, time, position, state, action, and affection – formed the basis of simple propositions whose truth could not be determined by logic. Although Aristotle did not claim his categories were self-evident in all cases, they were nevertheless taken to be real by most philosophers and theologians until the medieval Nominalists challenged their meaning. Categories, the Nominalists claimed, are by-products of expressions of similarity and difference between particular things, but they have no reality in themselves. There is an echo of this distinction in recent psychological theorizing on whether **prototypes** (Realist) or **exemplars** (Nominalist) underlie categorization in memory.

We can evade the philosophical question of whether categories are real and still ask if categorization can be perceptually innate. The Gestalt psychologists were driven by the belief that in perception, the whole is different from the sum of its parts (Wertheimer, 1958). Several Gestalt principles suggest an innateness to visual categorization. The **principle of proximity**, for example, states that things that are close to each other seem to belong together. The dot pattern in Figure 7.4, for example, is seen as comprising four pairs and a single rather than three triples.

Figure 7.4 *Grouping by proximity.*

Figure 7.5 shows that this principle of proximity is neurological, organized elsewhere in the visual system than in the stimulus or retinal image itself. In both halves of this figure, the dots are closer to their neighbors horizontally than vertically. Viewed separately, these figures show three rows of three dots. Viewed as a stereogram, however, three columns emerge because the differences in the perceived depths of the dots are greater than the vertical differences. Proximity applies to the perceived rather than retinal image. (Not everyone can view the stereogram easily. It requires crossing the eyes until the images blend into a third, central square. See Chapter 10)

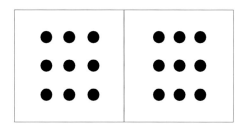

Figure 7.5 *Stereogram from Kaufman (1974).*

Developmental psychologists have uncovered evidence which suggests innate categorization (Bornstein, 1987). A categorical response to color exists in humans shortly after birth, well before language is available to name the categories (Bornstein, Kessen, and Weiskopf, 1976). This result is consistent with the findings on color categorization in the cat visual system (de Valois and Jacobs, 1968). Eimas (1974) has found similar categorical boundaries in the processing of sound. From an evolutionary perspective, pre-wired categorical perception would make sense. Some skills may be too critical for survival to leave them to learning alone.

7.2.2 Learned Categories

Categories do not have to be innate to shape perception. There is also evidence that categories learned on a dimension influence perception of stimuli invoking that dimension. Whorf (1941) is best known for inferring this phenomenon for language. Observing that Eskimos have many different words for snow, while English speakers have only one, Whorf concluded that they perceive this category differently from English speakers.

Although Whorf's hypothesis has not been widely verified by anthropologists, there is laboratory evidence for learned perceptual categorization effects (Harnad, 1987; Gibson, 1991; Goldstone, 1994). Burns and Ward (1978), for example, found that expert musicians recognized categories in pitch that novices could not detect. Categorical perception is especially pronounced in the recognition of speech. Lisker and Abramson (1970) used a computer to generate sounds continuously varying between the voiced and unvoiced phonemes [b] and [p]. English speaking listeners showed a sharp switch from recognizing one to the other. Figure 7.6 summarizes their result.

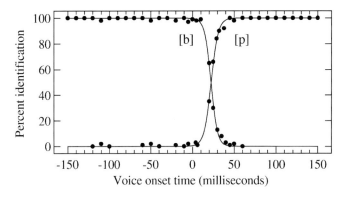

Figure 7.6 *Percentage identification of [b] vs. [p] as function of voice onset time. (adapted from Lisker and Abramson, 1970)*

7.2.3 Scaling Categories

Although it was not done in the original study, I fit logistic distributions to the two sets of data in Figure 7.6. The fit of the functions to these data is extremely good. The curves show that, although it is a discrete concept, categorization can be modeled with a continuous probability distribution. **Signal detection theory** has been used to parameterize categorical responding based on continuous probability distributions (Swets, Tanner, and Birdsall, 1961). From another perspective, Massaro (1992) has argued that the observation of sharp boundaries between categories is not sufficient evidence for concluding that categorical perception exists. He has modeled sharp identification boundaries using a Fuzzy Logical Model of Perception (FLMP).

One can always fit a continuous distribution with a steep slope parameter to model a categorical response. Nevertheless, the slopes of the curves in Figure 7.6 are substantially steeper than those for most continuously varying stimuli. As with the Weber-Fechner vs. Plateau-Stevens debate, it is not likely that the continuous-categorical scaling question will be resolved soon by mathematical modeling. What matters most for our purposes is that perceivers bring a different set of perceptual biases to categorical stimuli than they do to continuous.

7.2.4 Consequences for Attributes

That perceivers may respond to stimuli categorically creates several problems for categorical scaling of graphics. We may have the misfortune, for example, to assign two categories to two different colors that are perceived as belonging to a single color category. In general, natural category boundaries for a stimulus may interfere with the values we assign to our artificial categories. This is more likely to happen when we attempt to represent a large number of categories in a graphic. With a small number of categories, we can avoid problems by choosing as wide a range as possible for the stimulus dimension.

Even if our assignments are perceived as one-to-one, some categories may dominate our categorical scale by appearing more salient. One way this can occur is because of their perceived frequency. Tversky and Kahneman (1974) have shown that base rates can overwhelm other evidence in attributions and quantitative judgments involving categories. Rips and Collins (1993) show that category frequency can influence category judgments even more than perceived similarity. We need to be careful that this salience-bias does not conflict with the categories we are attempting to emphasize in graphing our data.

Category ideal types (prototypes) may subsume or draw other categories to themselves and thus change our intended categorization. This can occur at the earliest perceptual stages or the latest. Rosch (1975) showed, for example, that category judgments are faster for instances that are close to typical category members than atypical. Stevens and Coupe (1978) introduced nonlinear boundaries on hypothetical maps and were able to distort subjects' distance judgments and category memberships on the remembered maps. Tversky and Schiano (1989) induced a variety of similar distortions in memory for maps by manipulating categorical dimensions.

Finally, as we have seen, categories can underlie apparently continuous perceptual dimensions, through either innate or learned processes. For example, simple cells in the visual cortex are organized to detect, among other things, orientation. The most common receptive field maps of these cells involve vertical, horizontal, and diagonal patterns (Hubel and Wiesel, 1962). Stimuli presented at angles near these directions will tend to cause firing in these receptors. Thus, our best angular sensitivity is near these canonical orientations. This may account for the relatively poor performance of angle/slope in the Cleveland hierarchy (see Figure 7.3) and for why slope is most accurately judged at 45 degrees in statistical line charts (Cleveland, McGill, and McGill, 1988).

7.3 Dimensions

What happens when we combine several scales in a single display? Can we represent one quantitative dimension with color and another with orientation and expect a perceiver to respond to both dimensions? If so, how many dimensions can we represent without producing perceptual chaos? Five or six quantitative dimensions are commonplace in scientific visualization. Does this make psychological sense?

7.3.1 Integral vs. Separable Dimensions

The Gestaltists were interested primarily in **holistic perception**, in which multidimensional stimuli were perceived in an unanalyzable whole. At the other pole were classical psychophysicists, who believed that the perception of multidimensional stimuli involved a summation or aggregation of separate unidimensional percepts. While this is an oversimplification, the synthesis of these positions came from a few researchers who believed that complex stimuli could be analyzed in their parts without resorting to simple functions of dimensional attributes such as summation or weighted linear composites. Wendell Garner (Garner, 1970, 1974; Garner and Felfoldy, 1970) has been one of the pioneers in this effort.

To Garner, "A configuration has properties that have to be expressed as some form of interaction or interrelation between the components, be they features or dimensions" (Garner, 1981). The analysis of configuration implies more than paying attention to covariation, however. A configural property exists in addition to, not as a consequence of, other properties such as dimensions. Specifically, Garner distinguished **integral dimensions** – such as hue vs. brightness – from **separable dimensions** – such as size vs. texture. Integral dimensions are not as easily decomposable by perceivers as separable.

This distinction has several important practical consequences, supported by numerous studies. First, discriminations between classes defined by multiple integral stimuli are more difficult than those between classes defined by separable stimuli when the perceiver must attend to only one dimension. Selective attention to only one dimension, in other words, is more difficult with integral stimuli. Second, discrimination between classes using all dimensions together is easier for integral stimuli than for separable. Third, redundant cues in classification improve performance for integral stimuli and degrade performance for separable.

The implications of these findings for assignment of aesthetic attributes to dimensions in graphics are several. First, if we wish to facilitate comparisons among and within subgroups, it is better to assign relatively uncorrelated variables to separable aesthetic dimensions. Wainer and Francolini (1984) show, for example, that using integral dimensions in color choropleth maps makes it almost impossible to decode quantitative information separately for the color dimensions. Figure 7.7 demonstrates this phenomenon for symbols. The data are a subset of the barley yield dataset from Fisher (1935). As part of a larger experiment, three strains of barley (Manchuria, No. 475, Wisconsin) were grown at three Minnesota sites (Duluth, Crookston, Waseca). The left panel of the figure uses a double symbol to represent each of the 9 combinations of strain and site. Because the symbols are configural (the pair constitutes a "super symbol" with its own recognizable shape), distinguishing the trend in growth within site or within strain is extremely difficult.

The right panel uses symbol and size to represent strain and site, respectively. We are able to focus on symbol type to notice that growth increases across sites both years, on average, within strains as they are ordered. Similarly, we can focus on size to notice that growth increases by strains within sites, as they are ordered. There are better ways to organize a display of these data showing this additive growth increase by strain and site (*e.g.*, Cleveland, 1996), but when multiple coding of symbols is necessary, this example shows that the choice of attributes is critical.

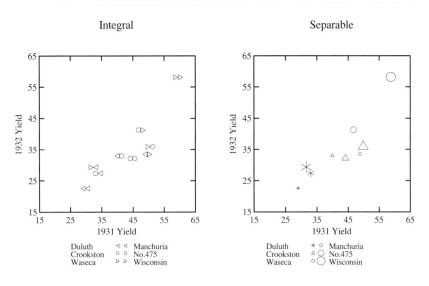

Figure 7.7 *Using separable dimensions for independent discrimination*

On the other hand, if we need to discriminate groups jointly on several variables, then integral dimensions can help us facilitate the discrimination. Figure 7.8 shows a FACES display (Chernoff, 1973) of sociometric ratings of U.S. cities (Boyer and Savageau, 1996). Each variable is assigned to a different feature of the face. The rating of a city's health-care facilities is assigned to the curvature of the mouth, for example, and pleasantness of climate is assigned to angle of the eyebrow. Section 7.6.3.4 covers the *glyph* functions needed to produce the specification. I have inserted them for reference, but you should ignore them for now.

We perceive each face as a whole. The primary component of our perception is emotional, but there are structural elements as well, such as the length and width of the nose. The face is integral because we cannot separate these components easily. A sad face with a long nose (Orlando) does not have the same emotional impact as a sad face with a short nose (Anchorage). This wholeness confounds the measured variables, but helps us to recognize the similarity between Los Angeles and San Francisco, or San Diego and Oakland. Because the dimensions are integral, there is less load on working memory for making these comparisons and recognizing clusters. In other words, the display offers us a way to do perceptual clustering (Tidmore and Turner, 1977).

Since its original presentation by Chernoff, FACES have been widely misunderstood by statisticians and data analysts. Some have dismissed them for their lack of seriousness. Based on work with Ralph Haber (Haber and Wilkinson, 1982), I proposed a real-time multivariate FACES display for command-and-control facilities where a limited number of different rapid decisions needed to be made in a multi-cue environment. The proposal received good technical ratings but was ultimately rejected for fear of it receiving a "Golden Fleece" award. Rapid, multi-attribute decision-making with a limited response repertoire is exactly where we would expect FACES to excel.

Others, particularly statisticians, consider FACES subjective, not realizing that facial perception is more consistent and innate than many other types of complex object perception. Specific neuronal responses have been found for both physical and emotional facial dimensions (Young and Yamane, 1992). The recognition of emotional expressions is well-developed in human newborns and infants (Haith, 1980; Johnson and Morton, 1991). Faces are readily categorizable into prototypes (Reed, 1972). And faces appear to be the most memorizable stimulus in psychological research. Standing (1973) has demonstrated recognition memory for up to 10,000 faces viewed in brief sessions. Bahrick *et al.* (1975) found extraordinary memory persistence for faces vs. other types of stimuli. Spoehr and Lehmkuhle (1982) summarize other studies showing the perceptual uniqueness of faces. Finally, Wilkinson (1982) showed that FACES outperform other graphical glyphs when used as cues in multivariate similarity judgments.

There are two caveats concerning FACES, however. First, FACES have little utility when decoding information for separate variables is required. This problem is shared by all graphic methods which map quantitative variables to highly integral stimuli. Second, the assignment of quantitative variables to facial features is critical (Chernoff, 1975; De Soete, 1986). This is a problem with configural stimuli in general, but especially so for FACES. Assigning variables with relatively large variance to facial features with relatively small perceptual salience (or vice versa) can result in false negative or false positive classification errors. The most successful recent automated facial recognition models (*e.g.*, Turk and Pentland, 1991) distill facial images to a relatively small number of **eigenfaces**. This research suggests that the overall facial configuration is more important to classification than isolated features. A promising approach to assignment would be to ensure that the eigenstructure of the quantitative variables matched as closely as possible the eigenstructure of the perceived set of faces.

FRAME: **col*row**
GRAPH: *point*(*shape.glyph.face*(**health..arts**), *label*(**city**))

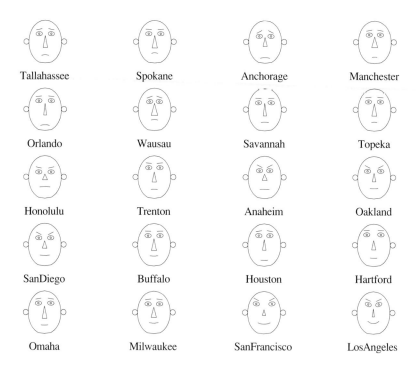

Figure 7.8 *Using integral dimensions to classify*

The fundamental misunderstanding among many critics of FACES, however, has most to do with a failure to appreciate the difference between integral and separable dimensions. To repeat, selective attention is *more* difficult with integral than separable stimuli but discrimination using all dimensions is *easier* for integral stimuli than for separable. We can see this by comparing FACES to glyphs based on more separable perceptual dimensions.

Figure 7.9 shows the same data displayed with histobar glyphs. Each city's value on each variable is now measurable by the height of each bar. The histobar glyphs make it easier to compare the health rating of Honolulu to that of Trenton, but it is more difficult to recognize that the two cities are quite different in their profile across all 9 variables. Try comparing the faces for these cities in Figure 7.8 with the histobars in Figure 7.9.

FRAME: **col*row**
GRAPH: *point*(*shape.glyph.hist*(**health..arts**), *label*(**city**))

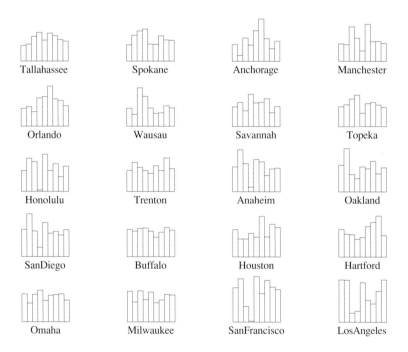

Figure 7.9 *Using separable dimensions to classify*

7.4 *Realism*

Perceptual psychology has had a long tradition of searching for principles of organization in the mind of the perceiver. In part, this has been a consequence of its phenomenological origins in Wundt's introspectionist psychology laboratory in Leipzig in the late nineteenth century. For almost a century, perceptual psychologists resisted the pressure of the behaviorists to explain perceptual constancies by looking to the regularities of the stimulus rather than those of the perceiver.

In reaction to the phenomenological tradition, James J. Gibson (Gibson, 1966, 1979) argued that the researcher must pay more attention to the perceiver interacting with a structured environment. Before imputing constancies to the perceiver, we must look for constancies in the environment. Gibson rejected the laboratory tradition of isolating stimuli to the point of making them impoverished. As an alternative, Gibson became interested in the persistent aspects of objects and their arrangements on the retina that allow us to perceive effectively and adapt to a changing world. Gibson's evolutionary perspective has influenced artificial intelligence approaches to perception, where machines must recognize and interact with their world (Marr, 1982; Winston, 1984).

Gibson helped stimulate a new trend in perceptual and cognitive psychology. Supported by new methodologies, advances in neuroscience, and the maturing of cognitive and computer science, theorists have enlarged their laboratories and turned their attention to the real world. Irving Biederman (1972, 1981) has analyzed schemas needed to comprehend creatures, objects, and their interactions in real scenes and pictures. Stephen Kosslyn (Kosslyn, 1980, 1983; Kosslyn, Ball, and Reiser, 1978) has examined the mental images used in navigating and remembering real-world situations. And Roger Shepard (Shepard and Metzler, 1971; Shepard and Cooper, 1983) has elucidated mental rotations and other cognitive operations which mirror a spatial world and derive from our need to interact with that world. Lockhead (1992) reviews this trend in perception research and Glenberg (1997) reviews recent evolutionary developments in the related field of memory.

This ecological focus offers several implications for representing multiple quantitative dimensions in graphical (aesthetic) systems. First of all, there is a new theoretical foundation for statistical graphics to achieve richer, more realistic expressions. For years, some experts on statistical graphics (*e.g.*, Tufte, 1983; Wainer, 1997) adopted Mies van der Rohe's adage, **less is more**. For Tufte, this means not wasting ink. The primary message of these writers has been that statistical graphics should be spare, abstract designs. For this formalist Bauhaus school of graphics, intent on minimizing the ink/data ratio, the major nemesis is the Rococo school of Holmes (1991), *U.S.A. Today*, and other popular pictographers. The controversy centers on **chartjunk**: 3D bar charts, pseudo-realism, and pictographs. However witty the criticisms by the formalists and however sincere their aesthetic motivations, it must be remembered that these are basically *ad hoc* and unsupported by psychological theory. Psychological research has a lot to say about the use of aesthetic/sensory features in graphic perception, but offers little support for the simple idea that less is more or that a small ink/data ratio facilitates accurate decoding.

On the contrary, there is some evidence that chartjunk is no less effective than abstract displays in conveying accurately statistical information (Lewandowsky and Myers, 1993). Pseudo 3D, drop shadows, and pictographs add redundant dimensions to multidimensional graphics. As we have seen, Garner's and others' research shows that redundant cues do not impair, and can actually improve, performance for integral dimensions. Additional dimensions degrade performance only when they are irrelevant to and vary independently of the dimensions needed for proper classification. Wilkinson and McConathy (1990) found, for example, that meaningful pictograms can contribute to memory for graphics. In short, there may be good reasons to dislike chartjunk, and Tufte's graphics are indisputably beautiful, but the crusade against chartjunk is not supported by scientific research and psychological theory.

From a somewhat different perspective, but still more Bauhaus than Rococo, Becker and Cleveland (1991) have argued that the field of scientific visualization has incorporated too much virtual reality and not enough formal structure. Making a statistical graphics scene realistic, they claim, does not improve its information processing potential or its capability to convey information accurately. In light of the psychological research, however, we should emphasize the *complement* of their statement: realism is not bad, but ignoring the constraints of realism is *really* bad. In other words, what matters in statistical graphics (or in the assignment of aesthetic features to quantitative or qualitative dimensions), is whether we construct configurations that satisfy the rules of attributes in the real world. If we violate these rules (see Biederman, 1981, for examples), our message will be distorted or meaningless.

This principle implies, for example, that we should exercise care to avoid perceptual illusions when we use cues from the 3D world to convey a 2D graphical scene to our senses. Many of the classical visual illusions are probably due to 3D cues mistakenly applied to 2D scenes (Gregory, 1978; Coren and Girgus, 1978). Huff (1954), and Kosslyn (1994) provide a variety of examples of distorted graphics which invoke these illusions. Consistent with Cleveland's hierarchy shown in Figure 7.3, most of these illusions involve angles or features related to the processing of 3D scenes. Perhaps the best (or worst) example of a graphic eliciting these illusions is the 3D pie chart, which allows perspective illusions to interfere with angular part/whole judgments.

Most of all, we should avoid representations that not only do not exist in the real world, but contradict or grossly exaggerate real-world phenomena. Figure 7.10 shows an example of this problem. In an effort to improve Chernoff's FACES, Flury and Riedwyl (1981) added an asymmetrical dimension to the glyph in order to represent paired data. Each face in Figure 7.10 represents a strain of barley in the Fisher (1935) dataset; the left half of each face represents the yields for 1931 and the right half represents the yields for 1932.

This display is simply confusing. Indeed, humans are sensitive to asymmetries in faces (Troje and Bülthoff, 1996), but this is a subtle configural phenomenon usually associated with emotions (Ekman, 1984) and the range of sensitivity is far narrower than that implemented in the asymmetrical FACES glyphs. Recognizing and recalling facial asymmetry (as evidence of lying, for example) is a skill requiring intensive training (Ekman *et al.*, 1988). More severe asymmetry is associated with paralysis, trauma, or congenital defects. In Figure 7.10, the face of No. 457 is suffering from a case of Bell's Palsy.

Asymmetrical faces present viewers with a glyph based on distracting analogues to the real world and with a perceptual task that introduces unnecessary complexity into pairwise comparisons. Half a face is no better, however. Following Flury and Riedwyl, Tufte (1983) suggested using only half of Chernoff's FACE glyph. Tufte advised that symmetries should be avoided in statistical graphics because they introduce unnecessary redundancies. While this may be true for some abstract stimuli, it makes little sense to enlist a wired-in perceptual mechanism and then defeat it by radical surgery.

FRAME: **col*row**
GRAPH: *point*(*shape.glyph.face2*(**university31**..**duluth32**), *label*(**site**))
.

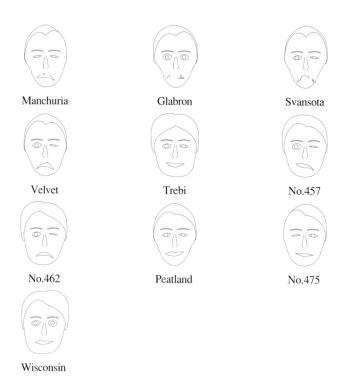

Figure 7.10 Asymmetrical FACES (1931, 1932) of Fisher barley data

Figure 7.11 shows the same barley data represented by pairs of symmetrical faces. The pairings clearly make it easier to compare faces between and within pairs. Grouping faces as siblings also allows us to consider larger families, as arise in repeated measurements. The reason comparison of siblings is easier than teasing apart halves of faces is that it resembles a real-world task. Faces are perceived as wholes. We are rarely called upon to make a second-order judgment that depends on the difference between the left and right side of a face (including its laterality). If there is asymmetry, we perceive it to have either a single emotional or congenital explanation. On the other hand, we are frequently called upon to make judgments concerning siblings and family membership. We might notice in Figure 7.11 that older (on the right) siblings tend to look unhappier or have smaller eyes. Similarly, we can easily make comparisons between families. We notice, for example, that the Trebi family is well fed and that the Svansota family is not thriving.

FRAME: **col1*row1+col2*row2**
GRAPH: *point(position(**row1*col1**),*
   *shape.glyph.face2(**university31..duluth31**), label(**site**))*
GRAPH: *point(position(**row2*col2**),*
   *shape.glyph.face2(**university32..duluth32**), label(**site**))*

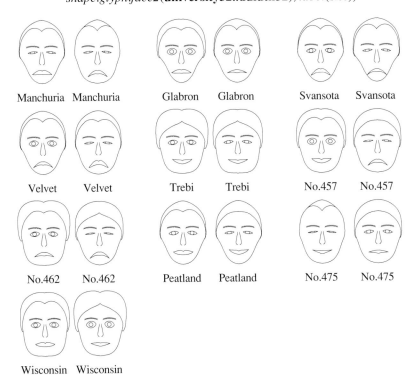

Figure 7.11 Paired (1931, 1932) symmetrical FACES of Fisher barley data

7.5 Aesthetic Attributes

The remainder of this chapter covers assignments of quantitative dimensions to aesthetic attributes. Table 7.1 summarizes these aesthetic attributes. I have grouped these attributes in five categories: form, surface, motion, sound, and text. This is not intended to be an exhaustive list; other attributes, such as odor, can be devised. Seven of these attributes are derived from the **visual variables** of Bertin (1967): position (*position*), size (*taille*), shape (*forme*), orientation (*orientation*), brightness (*valeur*), color (*couleur*), and granularity (*grain*). Bertin's *grain* is often translated as *texture*, but he really means granularity (as in the granularity of a photograph). Granularity in this sense is also related to the spatial frequency of a texture.

Some of the major attribute functions have several methods. These are indented in the table. For example, *color()* is an attribute function that normally indexes a categorical color table or scale. If one wishes to specify only hue, then one may use *color.hue()*. One can also specify only brightness by using *color.brightness()*. Custom color scales can be constructed as other named methods of the *color()* attribute function, such as *color.spectrum()*. I will not discuss these in more detail. Similarly, *shape()* specifies a table of indexed shapes (such as symbols). If one wants to reference different types of shape modification, one can use *shape.polygon()* for a general polygon, *shape.glyph()* for a multivariate glyph shape, or *shape.image()* for a general image such as a bitmap.

Aesthetic attribute functions are used in two ways. Most commonly, we specify a variable or blend of variables that constitutes a dimension, such as *size(**population**)* or *color(**trial1+trial2**)*. Or, we may assign a constant, such as *size(3)* or *color(*"red"*)*. The *position()* function cannot take constants as arguments, but it is the one attribute that can accept more than one dimension, as in *position(**x*y**)*.

Table 7.1 Aesthetic Attributes

Form	Surface	Motion	Sound	Text
position	*color*	*direction*	*tone*	*label*
stack	*hue*	*speed*	*volume*	
dodge	*brightness*	*acceleration*	*rhythm*	
jitter	*saturation*		*voice*	
size	*texture*			
shape	*pattern*			
polygon	*granularity*			
glyph	*orientation*			
image	*blur*			
rotation	*transparency*			

These aesthetic attributes do not represent the aspects of perception investigated by psychologists. This lack of fit often underlies the difficulty graphic designers and computer specialists have in understanding psychological research relevant to graphics and the corresponding difficulty psychologists have with questions asked by designers. Furthermore, these attributes are not ones customarily used in computer graphics to create realistic scenes. They are not even sufficient for a semblance of realism. Notice, for example, that pattern, granularity, and orientation are not sufficient for representing most of the textures needed for representing real objects. Instead, these attributes are chosen in a tradeoff between the psychological dimensions they elicit and the types of routines that can be implemented in a rendering system. Specifically,

- An attribute must be capable of representing both continuous and categorical variables.

- When representing a continuous variable, an attribute must vary primarily on one psychophysical dimension. In order to use multidimensional attributes such as color, we must scale them on a single dimension such as hue or brightness, or compute linear or nonlinear combinations of these components to create a unidimensional scale.

- An attribute does not imply a linear perceptual scale. As Section 7.1.2 indicates, few attributes scale linearly. In face, some attributes such as hue scale along curvilinear segments in two- or three-dimensional space. All linear scales are unidimensional but not all unidimensional scales are linear.

- A perceiver must be able to report a value of a variable relatively accurately and effortlessly when observing an instance of that attribute representing that variable.

- A perceiver must be able to report values on each of *two* variables relatively accurately upon observing a graphic instantiating two attributes. This task usually, but not necessarily, requires selective attention. This criterion probably isn't achievable for all of our attributes and may not even be achievable for any pair of them. But any attribute that is clearly non-separable with another should be rejected for our system. It is too much to expect, of course, that higher order interactions among attributes be non-existent. Much of the skill in graphic design is knowing what combinations of attributes to avoid. Kosslyn (1994) offers useful guidelines.

- Each attribute must name a distinct feature in a rendering system. We cannot implement an attribute that does not uniquely refer to a drawable (or otherwise perceivable) feature. An attribute cannot be mapped to a miscellaneous collection of widgets or controls, for example.

Bertin's books are a rich source of examples for many of these attributes and their various additive combinations. Discerning the full breadth of his classification scheme requires careful reading and testing on specific scenarios. I have made a few modifications to Bertin's scheme. These can be seen by comparing my Table 7.3 at the end of this chapter with the figure on page 230 of Bertin (1981). I have reorganized four of Bertin's graphic variables (*size, shape, orientation,* and *granularity*) into two sets of parallel components under form (*size, shape, rotation*) and texture (*granularity, pattern, orientation*).

The motivation for this separation is the following. Graphics must respond independently to messages concerning their aesthetic attributes. At the same time, these independent responses must function in concert so that the graphic produced is consistent and coherent. This requires making a few of Bertin's categories independent, by employing what computer designers call **orthogonalization**. Bertin uses *size, shape,* and *orientation* to characterize both the exterior form of objects (such as symbol shapes) and their interior texture pattern (such as cross-hatching). This appears natural and parsimonious (especially when looking at his examples) until one has to write a computer program to implement these attributes. It becomes apparent in architecting the attribute functions that Bertin has confounded form and texture attributes. Because Bertin uses *shape* to determine both the shape of an area and the pattern of a texture, it is impossible to produce a circular symbol filled with a triangular mesh pattern or a dashed line consisting of images of the French flag. Bertin has his reasons for these strictures, although they may have more to do with preventing chartjunk (making dashes out of flags) than with spanning the perceptual and representational space.

I have avoided this confounding of attributes by separating form and texture. These modifications are discussed in more detail in the sections below. None of this implies, however, that attributes orthogonalized in a design sense are not correlated in the way they are perceived by our visual system. Orthogonalization in design means making every dimension of variation that is available to one object available to another. How these variations are perceived is another matter.

Many aesthetic attributes, even ones such as size or position that are usually considered visual, need not be perceived visually. There is nothing in the definition of a graphic given in Chapter 2 to limit it to vision. Provided we use devices other than computer screens and printers, we can develop graphical environments for non-sighted people or for those unable to attend to a visual channel because, perhaps, they are busy, restrained, or multiprocessing. Touch, hearing, and other senses can be used to convey information with as much detail and sensitivity as can vision. While three sensory modalities – vision, sound, and touch – can accommodate all the attributes discussed here, taste and smell involve multidimensional processing as well (Levine and Shefner, 1991). The psychophysical components of these latter senses are not as well understood, however. Nor are they practical in current display environments. I will not discuss these specific implementations further.

7.5.1 *Position*

Spatial position refers to location in a (multi-) dimensional space. Bertin restricts his analysis to a sheet of paper or the plane (*plan*), but spatial position in a graphics system need not be restricted to even three dimensions. For example, a frame can be represented (with loss of generality) by a variety of projections into 3D, 2D, or 1D space. A positional attribute simply requires that values on a quantitative scale map to coordinates in a space.

Continuous variables map to densely distributed locations on a positional dimension. Categorical variables map to a lattice. These positions are ordered, but the ordering may or may not have meaning in terms of the scale of the measurements represented by the variable. Some projections may send two different coordinates to the same position, rendering them indistinguishable (see Chapter 10 for more information). This is commonplace in maps, where hemispheres may overlap in spherical projections, or in mixture coordinates (such as triangular), where the projection is a subspace of the data. Sometimes position is used simply to keep objects from overlapping and has no other purpose in a layout. Other times, position is used to place object near to each other. We see this in Figure 7.11.

Cleveland (1985) rates position on a common scale as the best way to represent a quantitative dimension visually. This reflects the research finding that points or line lengths placed adjacent to a common axis enable judgments with the least bias and error. This recommendation requires a major qualification, however: it depends on how far a point, line, or other graphic is from a reference axis. If a graphic is distant from an axis, the multiple steps needed to store and decode the variation can impair the judgment (Simkin and Hastie, 1987; Lohse, 1993; Kosslyn, 1994). Grid lines can reduce this problem somewhat.

Position has several children. When viewed as a transformation (see Chapter 10), *position()* is composable. That is, we may translate (move) and translate again to reach a given position. Therefore, it is useful to subdivide Bertin's attribute into several varieties, or **position methods**. The parent class *position()* sets a position within a frame. This frame is specified either in the FRAME specification or with positional parameters, as in *position(**x*y**)*. The children modify local position in various ways. One child class is *position.stack()*, which causes graphic elements to stack along a measure. Stacking works like children's blocks. This method is used to create stacked bar charts (Figure 7.32) and stacked dot plots (Figure 7.33). Another child is *position.dodge()*, which causes graphic elements to offset themselves symmetrically when they have tied values on a measure. This method is used to create clustered bar charts (Figure 7.31) and symmetric dot plots (Figure 7.33). Finally, *position.jitter()* adds a small amount of uniform random error to the position along a measure so that graphic elements are less likely to collide. This method is used to create jittered scatterplots (Figure 7.36).

7.5.2 *Size*

Bertin defines size variation in terms of length or area. The extension of this definition to three dimensions would be volume. Cleveland ranks area and volume representations among the worst attributes to use for graphing data (see Figure 7.3). Indeed, area and volume both have Stevens exponents substantially less than 1 (see Figure 7.2). Figure 7.12 reveals this clearly. The circles in the upper row have diameters proportional to the integers 1 to 5. Those in the lower row have areas proportional to the same integers. It is self-evident that the areas are not perceived in a linear relationship to the scale values.

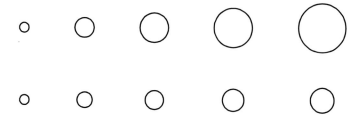

Figure 7.12 *Symbol size: diameters (upper) and areas (lower)*

Size for lines is usually equivalent to thickness. This is less likely to induce perceptual distortion than it does for symbols, although extremely thick lines present problems of their own. Thick lines must be mitred and fill patterns must be handled carefully. Size can be used to great effect with *path*, on the other hand. A notable example is the famous graphic by Minard featured in Chapter 15.

Areas can change their size only if their perimeters are unconstrained. An area is defined by a perimeter that is determined by data or by a tiling or by some other enclosure element. Thus, size for area is a data attribute, not an arbitrary value we may change for aesthetic purposes. We can modify the coarseness of a texture inside an area, however. For example, we may use *texture.granularity*() to produce Bertin's "size" effects for areas.

Surfaces can change size in a manner similar to the way lines do. That is, lines may become thicker or thinner and so may surfaces. The ribbon element used in the left panel of Figure 6.4, for example, is relatively thick. Modifying the thickness of surfaces presents problems similar to those involved in modifying thickness of lines.

Finally, solids may change size in any dimension not constrained by data or geometry. As with areas, we cannot modify size of solids to suit arbitrary aesthetic goals. Size of volumes must be driven by data. Size distortion is worse for volumes, however. Figure 7.13 shows a size series for a set of boxes. The upper row shows boxes increased in size from left to right by magnifying each dimension proportionally to the integers 1 to 5. The lower row shows increases in volume according to the same series. The size of the upper boxes increases as a cubic function while the size of the lower follows a linear function.

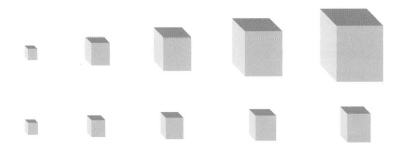

Figure 7.13 *Solid sizes: diameters (upper) and volumes (lower)*

For objects that have rotational symmetry, like circles, we can map size to the diameter rather than area (the upper rows of Figure 7.12 and Figure 7.13). The result is not always undesirable, especially for negatively skewed data or data with short upper tails. Conversely, representing size through area or volume should probably be confined to positively skewed data that can benefit from the perceptual equivalent of a root transformation. Otherwise, we might do best by following Cleveland's advice and avoiding size as an attribute.

Some designers assign size to only one dimension of an object, as in the width of a rectangle. This can confound perceptual dimensions, making selective attention to the size component difficult. Bar charts, for example, use the height of *bar* graphics to represent a variable. Their width is usually held constant. If we vary their widths according to an additional variable, we may run into trouble.

Figure 7.14 shows four different displays of the same data with various uses of size and other aesthetic attributes. The data are from Allison and Cicchetti (1976). They represent ratings of animals on a 1 to 5 scale of their exposure to predators while sleeping (**exposure**) and likelihood of being eaten by predators in their environment (**predation**). The *bar* graphic in the lower left corner uses size (bar thickness) to represent **exposure**. We might predict that since height and width are relatively more configural than separable, judgments based on a variable combining both **exposure** and **predation** (using **danger=exposure+predation**) would be easier for this graphic than for the dot plot in the upper right. The upper left graphic might do as well, since the double bars provide a rough estimate of area themselves. This graphic makes it easier to separate the **exposure** and **predation** values. The scatterplot in the lower right might also do well on this task, since clusters of animals high on both variables (*e.g.*, Goat, Pig, Kangaroo) are readily discernible. In general, however, using a variable-width bar chart is flirting with danger. As with other aesthetic attributes, it is best to let size vary on only one dimension.

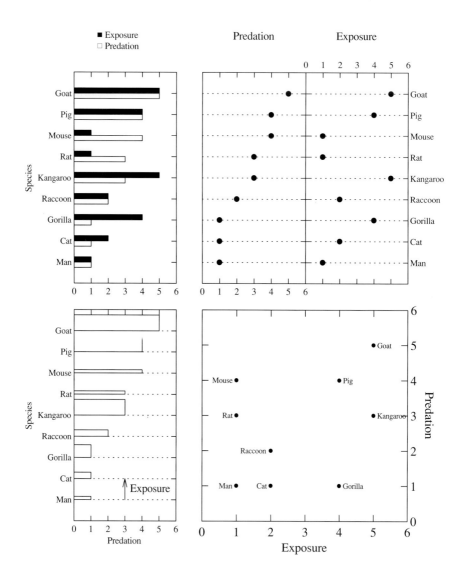

Figure 7.14 *Sized bars (lower left) vs. other representations*

7.5.3 Shape

Shape refers to the exterior shape or boundary of an object. Symbols are the most obvious example, but every graph has the potential for taking on a different shape. Figure 7.15 shows several examples of shape variation in symbols. The top row shows a **morph** of a hexagon into a circular shape. Morphing is the technique needed to vary shape along a continuous dimension. The second row shows another morph of an ellipse into another ellipse. This example is problematic, however, because it is not rotationally invariant. Shape must vary without affecting size, rotation, and other attributes. The graphics in the second row could be used for representing negative and positive variation, but it is not clear that they would work as well as sized plus and minus signs.

The bottom row shows categorical shape variation. Several researchers have investigated optimal symbol shapes for categorization (Lewandowsky and Spence, 1989; Cleveland 1993). The symbols in this row of Figure 7.15 were selected for this purpose..

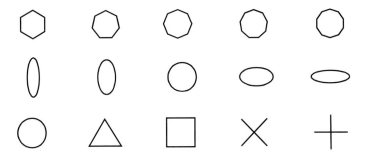

Figure 7.15 *Symbol shape: continuous (upper 2) and categorical (lower)*

Figure 7.16 shows several examples of continuous and categorical shape variation for lines. The left panel varies the roughness of the line to create a continuous shape dimension. The right modifies the outer contours of the line to create categorical shape variation.

Figure 7.16 *Line shape: continuous (left) and categorical (right)*

Areas can change shape only if their perimeters are unconstrained by a positional variable. The *tile()* graphic can be set to a hexagon, for example, in order to tile a surface or it can be set to the outline of a state in order to create a geographic map. If we want to produce some of the "shape" effects Bertin shows for areas, then we can use *texture.pattern()*.

Surfaces can change shape in a manner similar to lines (*e.g.*, bumpy surfaces), although taking advantage of this behavior is a dubious practice. Like areas, surfaces can change shape in other ways if their shape is unconstrained by positional variables.

Figure 7.17 shows continuous and categorical shape variation for solids. Some solids, like interval graphics, are constrained on one or more axes for the purpose of representing size variation. This usually leaves at least one physical dimension free to vary in shape. The solids in Figure 7.17 have constant height but vary in their shape along the other two dimensions.

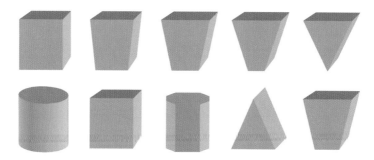

Figure 7.17 *Solid shape: continuous (upper) and categorical (lower)*

7.5.4 Rotation

The rotation of a graphic is its rotational angle. Figure 7.18 illustrates rotation variation for 2D and 3D objects. Lines, areas, and surfaces can rotate only if they are positionally unconstrained. We can produce the "orientation" effects Bertin shows in these graphics by using *texture.orientation()* instead.

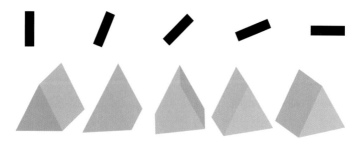

Figure 7.18 *Rotation: symbol (upper) and solid (lower)*

7.5.5 *Color*

Color is a psychological phenomenon, a fabrication of the visual system (Levine and Shefner, 1991). The physical stimulus for color is light. Light has no color; it is electromagnetic energy of different wavelengths. We see color because we have three different photoreceptors in our retinas sensitive to light of different wavelengths. Thomas Young proposed this mechanism in 1802, assuming a mixture of the output of three primary receptors for red, green, and violet would produce any visible color. Hermann von Helmholtz formalized this conjecture in 1866 by delineating hypothetical excitation curves for each of the three types of receptor fibers Young postulated.

Because our color perceptual system is three-dimensional, we can represent all visible colors with any three non-collinear axes in that space. Computer monitors and color TV's employ an RGB model, named for its use of *red, green,* and *blue* as a basis. This basis provides a wide range of color variation using comparable additive weights, and corresponds roughly to the sensitivity of the photoreceptors in the retina. Printers use a CYM model, named for *cyan, yellow,* and *magenta.* When used as pigment on an opaque surface, the colors in the CYM model absorb red, blue, and green light, respectively. This makes the CYM model *subtractive* for light, while the RGB model is *additive.* A third model called HLS refers to *hue, lightness,* and *saturation.* This model derives from Newton's analysis of the spectrum. The Munsell color solid for artists (*hue*=hue, *value*=brightness, *chroma*=saturation) is based on this system. See Travis (1991) for a review of color theory. Sacks (1995) discusses historical issues in the context of an intriguing study of a monochromatic perceiver.

Trichromatic color theory accounts for three-dimensional color perception, but it fails to accommodate some curious color phenomena. One of these is **color afterimages**. Staring at a green patch for about 30 seconds leaves us with the perception of a red patch when we look at a white background. Similarly, a red patch leaves us with green, and a blue, yellow. Another curious phenomenon involves **color naming**. When asked to give additive mixture names to spectral colors, we employ more than three primaries (Judd, 1951). To cover the spectrum, we need names such as "reddish blue" and "yellowish green." This phenomenon occurs across cultures as well (Berlin and Kay, 1969). For these and other reasons, it would appear that an **opponent process theory** is needed to account for human color perception. The modern form of this theory is integrated with trichromatic theory in a stagewise model. Trichromatic theory involves the initial integration of receptor signals, while opponent process involves later stages. The three opponent mechanisms are white-black, red-green, and blue-yellow.

Like *position*(), *shape*(), and *texture*(), *color*() has children. They are named *color.brightness, color.hue,* and *color.saturation.* Although all three attributes can be assigned simultaneously to different dimensions, they are highly configural, making this unwise for most applications. Even using two at once is dubious (see Wainer and Francolini, 1980). In general, it is safer to use a single color dimension such as *color.hue*, or the parent function *color()* to index a specific color scale (Brewer *et al.*, 1997). Travis (1991) and Brewer (1994, 1996) present strategies for effective color representation. Olson and Brewer (1997) discuss ways to construct scales for the color-vision impaired.

7.5.5.1 Brightness

Brightness is the luminance, or lightness/darkness of a patch. Figure 7.19 shows a brightness scale for five patches. Brightness can be used to represent categorical dimensions, but only with a few categories.

Figure 7.19 Brightness variation

7.5.5.2 Hue

Hue is the pure spectral component (constant intensity) of a color. Figure 7.20 shows five different hues: red, yellow, green, blue, purple. Hue is particularly suitable for representing categorical scales. Boynton (1988) names 11 basic colors: red, yellow, green, blue, white, gray, black, orange, purple, pink, and brown. These are especially suited for categorical scales, although Kosslyn (1996) advises against using all 11 at the same time.

Figure 7.20 Hue variation

7.5.5.3 Saturation

Saturation is the degree of pure color (hue) in a patch. Figure 7.21 shows five different saturation levels for a red patch, from gray (lacking any hue) to red (pure hue). The brightness of the patches should be constant. MacEachren (1992) recommends saturation for representing uncertainty in a graphic.

Figure 7.21 Saturation variation

7.5.6 *Texture*

Texture includes pattern, granularity, and orientation. Pattern is similar to **fill style** in older computer graphics systems, such as GKS (Hopgood *et al.*, 1983) or paint programs. Granularity is the repetition of a pattern per unit of area. Bertin describes it as "photographic reduction." Orientation is the angle of pattern elements. The word *orient* derives from the Latin word for *sunrise* (in the East). Conversely, the word *occident* is derived from the Latin word for *sunset* (in the West). Thus, *orientation* is alignment relative to the East.

A mathematical definition of texture is the spatial distribution of brightness values of the 2D image of an illuminated surface. This definition underlies the texture perception research of Julesz (1965, 1971, 1975). Spatial distribution can be represented in several ways. One of the most common is through the **Fourier transform,** which decomposes a grid of brightness values into sums of trigonometric components. This decomposition is orientation-dependent. Rotate the image, and another decomposition results. Another representation is the **auto-correlogram**, used by Julesz to characterize the spatial moments of a texture. The correlogram can be calculated in ways that make it orientation-independent. These and other spatial functions have been used to construct machine texture-perceivers (see Watt, 1991 for a general discussion of texture/form issues). This topic also gives me the opportunity to cite my favorite title for a statistical paper on this or any subject, Besag (1986).

Texture alone can be a basis for form perception. Two gray areas that have the same overall level of brightness can be discriminated if their texture is different. The letter R rendered in a gray sand texture is readable against a background rendered in a gray woven cloth texture. Surprisingly, this form perception occurs even when the outlines of the form itself do not exist on the retina. Julesz demonstrated this with an invention of his called the **random-dot stereogram**. This display has been popularized recently in books whose pages have paired patches of computer-generated dots that reveal hidden figures when the reader fuses both images in the mind's eye. Julesz's research shows that a form emerges when the spatial distributions of the separate retinal images are processed in the visual cortex. Papathomas and Julesz (1988) demonstrate some graphical applications of the random-dot stereogram.

Form, pattern, and granularity interact. The top row of Figure 7.22 (adapted from Julesz, 1981) shows how. In the leftmost patch, we see a backwards R embedded in a field of regular R's. English (Indo-European) readers recognize this as a shape violation. They can distinguish this on the basis of form alone without resorting to texture perception. Others can recognize the figure from a single form comparison with any adjacent letter. Still others can recognize the figure by paying attention to the texture of the whole patch. For the middle patch, either form or texture detection picks up the array of backwards R's embedded in the lower right corner. The right patch, however, invokes purely texture perception, at least if held at the proper distance from the eye.

The interaction shown in this example helps explain Bertin's use of shape and orientation to describe both form and texture. Given a continuum, Bertin's taking an opportunity to reduce the number of basic constructs makes sense. As I have explained earlier in this chapter, however, implementing a renderer requires us to keep these concepts separate but parallel.

The bottom row of Figure 7.22 shows how random orientation can defeat texture-based perception of form. Each patch is a randomly oriented version of the patch in the upper row. In the left patch, it is possible to discern the backwards R by serially scanning the forms. It is still possible to do this in the middle patch, although quite difficult. It is almost impossible to do so in the rightmost figure. The random orientation masks the spatial boundaries of the sub-patch so that it is no longer detectable as it is in the patches in the top row.

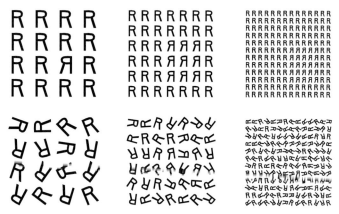

Figure 7.22 *Granularity and orientation affect perception of form*

7.5.6.1 Granularity

The top row of Figure 7.22 illustrates continuous granularity variation. Figure 7.23 shows another example. This is a grating of constant brightness that varies in spatial frequency. Optometrists use these patterns to measure resolution of the visual system. Less grainy patterns (having fewer low-frequency spatial components) are more difficult to resolve.

Figure 7.23 *One-dimensional granularity*

Figure 7.24 shows several degrees of granularity variation for lines. Notice the similarity between this example and the ones in Figure 7.23. Each row of Figure 7.24 can be considered to be a vertically compressed pattern like those in Figure 7.23. Both figures contain, in fact, 1D texture maps.

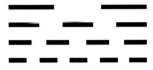

Figure 7.24 *Line granularity*

7.5.6.2 Pattern

Figure 7.25 shows continuous and categorical variation in pattern. The continuous examples (upper row) make use of increasing degrees randomness in a uniform spatial distribution. The categorical examples employ different shapes for their elements. The luminosity (brightness) of each patch is controlled by maintaining the same proportion of black pixels in each.

Figure 7.25 *Pattern: continuous (upper) and categorical (lower)*

Line patterns can be varied by filling thick lines with different patterns. A dashed line, for example, can be constructed by filling the interior of a thick line with a one-dimensional grid pattern, as in Figure 7.24. With apologies to Tufte, this is also the method we use for making lines out of flags. We fill the polygon defined by a thick line with a bitmap image of a flag. Some countries have laws against this sort of thing; check with your local authorities before using flags in graphics.

7.5.6.3 Orientation

Figure 7.26 shows several degrees of orientation variation. Orientation affects other components of texture, so it is not always a good idea to use it for representing a variable. Notice how variation in texture orientation introduces a visual illusion, making the lines seem not parallel. Tufte (1983) has excellent examples illustrating why use of orientation – whether for lines or for areas – introduces visual vibration, Moire patterns, and other undesirable effects.

Figure 7.26 *Line texture orientation*

7.5.7 Blur

Blur describes the effect of changing focal length in a display. It is implemented by filtering a bitmap. As MacEachren (1992) discusses, blur is an attribute ideally suited for representing confidence, risk, or uncertainty in a process. Wilkinson (1983b) used blur to represent sampling error in histograms. Figure 7.27 shows five different blur levels.

Figure 7.27 *Blur variation*

7.5.8 Transparency

Transparency, like blur, is an attribute suited for the display of uncertainty. It is implemented by blending layers of a color or gray-scale bitmap. Figure 7.28 shows five different transparency levels.

Figure 7.28 *Transparency variation*

7.5.9 *Motion*

Animation is discussed in Cleveland and McGill (1988) and Earnshaw and Watson (1993). It is implemented in a wide range of visualization software. For obvious reasons, a book is not the ideal format for presenting animation. For a glimpse, flip the pages and watch the page numbers in the corner change.

7.5.10 *Sound*

Sound can be used to display graphics in different ways. One approach is to use pitch, amplitude, texture, and other waveform features to represent separate quantitative dimensions (Bly, 1983; Mezrich *et al.*, 1984; Bly *et al.*, 1985, Fisher, 1994). This is the approach taken when a sound attribute is added to other dimensions in a visual graphic. The other approach is to treat every object in a graphic as a sound source and embed all objects in a virtual spatial environment (Julesz and Levitt, 1966; Blattner *et al.*, 1989; Bregman, 1990; Smith *et al.*, 1990; Hollander, 1994). In this **soundscape** approach, the metaphor of a symphony or opera performance is not inappropriate. A scatterplot cloud can be represented by a chorus of "singers" distributed appropriately in space. Thus, instead of using sound to represent a quantitative dimension, we can use sound to paint a real scene, a sonic image that realizes the graphic itself. An added benefit of this method is that motion can be represented in time without interfering with other dimensions of the signal. Sighted people must be reminded that the potential dimensionality of a sound environment is at least as large as a visual. Soundscape technology now makes this feasible, particularly for development environments like Java, where soundscape capability is built into 3D graphics foundation classes. Krygier (1994) reviews issues in the use of sound for multidimensional data representation. See also Shepard (1964), Kramer (1994), and Figure 10.55 for further information on the structure of sound perception. In the end, however, you can listen to this book for a long time before you hear any sound.

7.5.11 *Text*

Text has not generally been thought of as an aesthetic attribute. I classify it this way because reading involves perceptual and cognitive processing that helps one to decode a graphic in the same way that perceiving color or pattern does. The *label*() text attribute function allows us to associate a descriptive label with any graphic. It places text next to a point, on top of a bar, or near a line, for example. I will not present a separate example for the *label*() function in this chapter. Instead, it appears in numerous graphics throughout this book (*e.g.*, Figure 7.29, the next example). The *label*() attribute function allows us to associate with the graphic a descriptive text constant (*e.g.*, "New York") or a value that is automatically converted from numeric to text (*e.g.*, "3.14159").

7.6 Examples

The following examples illustrate selected aesthetic attributes. Each is set by using one of the attribute functions in a graphing function parameter list.

7.6.1 Position

Position is used so often as the primary attribute for a graphic that we can fail to notice the variations we can produce by altering it. One application is to embed multiple graphics in a common frame by using different positional variables. Another is to stack or place graphics side-by-side so that we can represent subcategories. This section outlines a variety of applications.

7.6.1.1 Embedding Graphics

Ordinarily, the positional attribute for a graphic is taken directly from the appropriate variables in the FRAME specification. Often we wish to embed graphics in a frame using variables that may not appear in a FRAME specification. As long as the variables we use are measurable on the dimensions produced by the FRAME specification, these embeddings can be meaningful.

As part of a study of lay self-diagnosis, Wilkinson, Gimbel, and Koepke (1982) collected co-occurrences of symptoms within disease classifications of the *Merck Manual*. We computed a multidimensional scaling of these selected symptoms in order to provide a framework for analyzing self-diagnosis from the same symptoms. Figure 7.29 shows the result of that scaling.

FRAME: **dim(1)*dim(2)**
GRAPH: *point*(*shape*(**cluster**), *label*(**symptom**))
GRAPH: *tile*(*shape.poly*("voronoi"), *position*(**mean(1)*mean(2)**)))

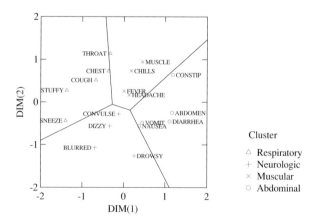

Figure 7.29 *Disease symptoms*

The coordinates of the 18 symptoms and their labels are fixed by the **dim(1)** and **dim(2)** variables in the FRAME specification. Separate ratings of the symptoms yielded four clusters: Respiratory, Neurologic, Muscular, and Abdominal. Figure 7.29 shows a Voronoi tessellation (see Section 7.6.3.6) superimposed on the graphic. This graphic was positioned by using two variables containing only the means of the four clusters on the two dimensions. The boundaries almost perfectly separate the clusters in a radial pattern that closely resembles the hand-drawn graphic in the original article.

It is important to note that the limits of the two positional scales are computed solely from **dim(1)** and **dim(2)**. If any values on **mean(1)** or **mean(2)** had exceeded these limits, then the offending cases would have been eliminated from the graph. If we want to include the means in the default scale calculations, then we must add them to the FRAME specification with a blend operator: **dim(1)*dim(2) + mean(1)*mean(2)**. We would then have to add a *position*(**dim(1)*dim(2)**) function to the *point* graphic in order to exclude the mean points from its purview.

7.6.1.2 Stacked Areas

Area graphics can be stacked to represent cumulative scales using the aesthetic function *position.stack*(). The data in Table 7.2 are from the ACLS survey used in Chapter 2. The table shows the percentage of respondents choosing one of the adverbs for how often the review process is biased in favor of males. The data are separated for male and female respondents

Table 7.2 **Responses to ACLS Survey**

Response	Female	Male
Rarely	8	30
Infrequently	11	15
Occasionally	17	10
Frequently	32	7
Not Sure	32	38

Figure 7.30 shows a stacked *area* chart on the female and male responses from the ACLS dataset. The *string*() function is used to color the profiles by gender. Because I have specified no argument, the *position.stack*() derives its splitting from the **m+f** dimension used for *color*(**m+f**).

DATA: **m** = *string*("MALE")
DATA: **f** = *string*("FEMALE")
FRAME: **response*(male+female)**
GRAPH: *area*(*color*(**m+f**), *position.stack*())

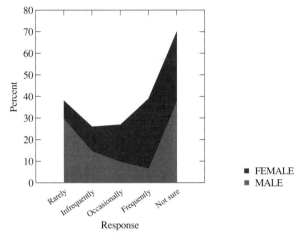

Figure 7.30 *Stacked area chart*

7.6.1.3 Clustered Bar Charts

The *position.dodge*() method is useful for creating clustered bar charts. If the *position.dodge*() function has a variable as its argument, then a separate graphic is created for each value of the variable and these sub-graphics are arranged adjacently at each location. Figure 7.31 shows an example.

FRAME: **gov*birth**
GRAPH: *bar.statistic.mean*(*position.dodge*(),*color*(**urban**))

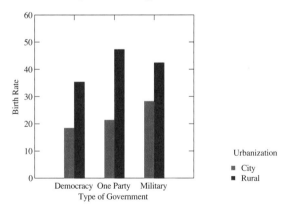

Figure 7.31 *Clustered bar chart.*

7.6.1.4 Divided (Stacked) Bar

Stacking cumulates elements. Divided bar charts, for example, consist of collections of interval-valued bars. The lower value of each bar is the previous case's value in the dataset (the first case defaults to zero) and the upper value is the current case. Figure 7.32 shows a divided bar graphic for the ACLS data used in Figure 7.30.

DATA: **m** = *string*("Male")
DATA: **f** = *string*("Female")
FRAME: **m*male+f*female**
GRAPH: *bar*(*position.stack*(), *color*(**response**))

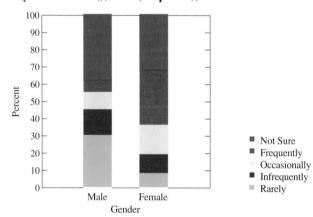

Figure 7.32 *Divided bar graphic*

7.6.1.5 Dot Plots

Figure 7.33 shows examples of dot plots on the countries dataset. The dot plot on the left looks like a tally or a histogram of dots. The dot plot on the right is used by medical researchers and other scientists to graph small batches of data. It is simply a symmetrized form of the asymmetrical dot plot.

The size of the dot determines the resolution of the graphic. One may think of the dots as a set of poker chips that must be arranged as closely as possible to their coordinate locations without overlapping. The larger the chips, the more stacking there is at common levels. The size of the dot is, in certain respects, a smoothing parameter. Wilkinson (1999) discusses the mathematical issues underlying this problem.

Just as dot plots on a single dimension require a second dimension for stacking, so do bivariate dot plots require three dimensions for their stacking. Bivariate dot plots resemble piles of cannonballs precariously stacked perpendicular to the 2D plane.

FRAME: **birth**
GRAPH: *point(position.stack())*

FRAME: **birth**
GRAPH: *point(position.dodge())*

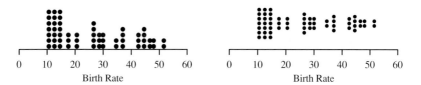

Figure 7.33 *Asymmetric dot plot (left) and symmetric dot plot (right)*

7.6.1.6 Dot-Box Plots

Figure 7.34 shows the *schema* and *point* graphics grouped by a categorical variable (**gov**) and superimposed. The information in each of these graphics enhances that of the other. This plot, suggested to me by Jerry Dallal when he superimposed separate SYSTAT graphics, resembles some variations in the box plot devised by Tukey (1977).

FRAME: **gov*birth**
GRAPH: *schema()*
GRAPH: *point(position.dodge(), color("green"))*

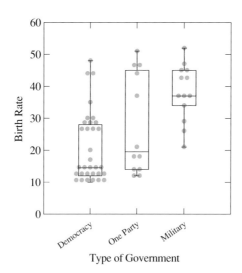

Figure 7.34 *Box and dot plots by group*

7.6.1.7 Stem-and-leaf Diagrams

Tukey (1977) discusses a variety of tallies, from the simple crossed-out groups of five marks to the stem-and-leaf diagram. This latter display adds to the simple tally a set of significant digits to convey essential numerical information. The most significant digit or digits are chosen to be the "stem" on the left of the tally. The next digit to the right of the stem in each data value is chosen for the "leaf" on the right. This digit is not rounded. The leaves are stacked in order to the right so that the entire tally resembles a histogram. Figure 7.35 shows an example for the birth rate data. I have presumed that the stems and leaves have been pre-calculated from the data. The **leaf** values are used to determine the plotting symbol for each value. Finally, the plot is transposed to take the form of Tukey's original. In other words, a stem-and-leaf diagram is a transposed, stacked dot plot in which the dots are represented by numerals.

FRAME: **birth**
GRAPH: *point(position.stack(), shape(**leaf**))*
COORD: *transpose()*

```
1   01112222222333444444
1   5788
2   011
2   6678888899
3   04
3   57777
4   23444
4   556778
5   12
```

Figure 7.35 *Stem-and-leaf diagram*

7.6.1.8 Jittering

Figure 7.36 illustrates how to jitter a plot. The data and frame are the same as for Figure 5.2.

FRAME: **sepallength**
GRAPH: *point(position.jitter())*

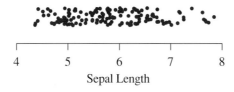

Figure 7.36 *One-dimensional jittered scatterplot.*

7.6.1.9 Bordering Frames

Position functions can be used to position graphics relative to frames. They are especially useful for representing marginal variation in rectangular plots. Figure 7.37 shows an example for a quantile plot on the same data used in Figure 5.2. I have added dot plots to the top and right borders of the plot so that we can see the skewness of the distribution.

The arguments to the *position*() functions determine the bordering. The frame is **military*rmil** and *position.stack*(**military*1**) references the first dimension (**military**) and *position.stack*(**1*rmil**) references the second (**rmil**). The unity variable (**1**) causes the graphic to shift in the same way that blending a variable with unity does (see Figure 5.6).

TRANS: **rmil** = *prank*(**military**)
FRAME: **military*rmil**
GRAPH: *point*()
GRAPH: *point*(*position.stack*(**military*1**))
GRAPH: *point*(*position.stack*(**1*rmil**))

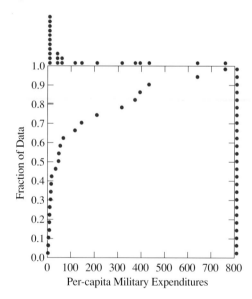

Figure 7.37 *Quantile plot of military expenditures.*

Densities (see Section 8.2.4) are especially suited for bordering. They help reveal skewness in scatterplots and can be helpful for assessing the need for power or log transformations. Bordering in three dimensions requires us to consider facets and viewing angle for displaying graphics appropriately.

7.6.2 Size

The *size()* attribute is most applicable to *point* graphics, but it has interesting applications elsewhere. Figure 15.1, for example, shows how *size()* can be used to control the segment-by-segment thickness of a path. The *size()* attribute can also be used to control the width of bars. The most popular application of *size()* is the *bubble* plot.

7.6.2.1 Bubble Plots

Figure 7.38 shows a bubble plot using symbol size to represent the reflectivity (albedo measure) of the planets in our solar system. The frame plots distance from the Sun (normalized so that the Earth–Sun distance is 1 unit) by mean temperature (in Kelvin). I have logged both scales so that the planets align roughly along the diagonal and the discrepancy of Venus is highlighted. The data are from the NASA Web site (*nssdc.gsfc.nasa.gov*).

FRAME: **distance*temperature**
SCALE: *log(dim1*, 10)
SCALE: *log(dim2*, 10)
GRAPH: *point(size(***albedo***)*, *label(***planet***))*

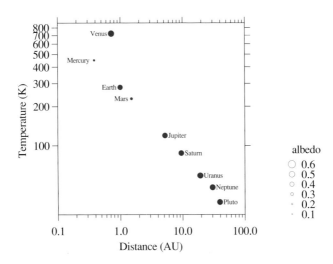

Figure 7.38 *Bubble plot of planet reflectivity (albedo)*

Another application of the *size()* attribute is in assessing statistical assumptions via graphics. The Pearson correlation coefficient, for example, measures the standardized linear association between two random variables that vary jointly. It is calculated by standardizing both variables to have zero mean and unit standard deviation and then averaging the cross-products of the standard scores. Certain extreme cases can contribute disproportionately to this computation, so it is often useful to look for such cases before trusting the correlation as a measure of association on a given set of data. One straightforward index of **influence** of a case on the computations is to compute the Pearson correlation with and without the case and examine the difference. This can be done for all cases and the influence measure used to size plotting symbols.

Figure 7.39 shows an example. I have plotted torque against horsepower for the cars dataset used in Figure 6.2. These performance statistics are usually linearly correlated among production automobile engines. One case stands out at the top of the plot, however. It is the Ferrari 333P race car. Some race car engine designers sacrifice torque for horsepower because they wish to favor top speed (at high RPM's) over acceleration. They compensate for this bias by making the car bodies as light as possible.

I have inserted two *point* clouds into the frame, one in blue to reveal each point and one in red to represent the influence function. The filled circles denote *negative* influence (correlation increased when the case was omitted) and the hollow circles denote *positive* (correlation decreased when the case was omitted). The filled circle for the Ferrari shows that it is attenuating the correlation by more than .10 even though it is in the upper right quadrant of the plot.

TRANS: **influence** = *influence.pearson*(**torque, hp**)
TRANS: **polarity** = *sign*(**influence**)
FRAME: **torque*hp**
GRAPH: *point*(*color*("blue"))
GRAPH: *point*(*size*(**influence**), *color*("red"), *texture.pattern*(**polarity**))

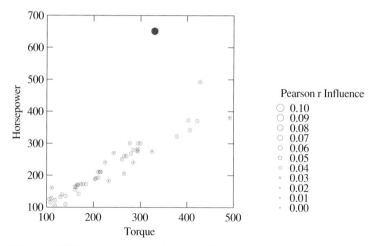

Figure 7.39 *Pearson correlation influence scatterplot*

7.6.3 Shape

The *shape()* attribute function is most often used to determine the shape of plotted symbols in *point* graphics. It also affects the shape of bars and other graphics.

7.6.3.1 Geographic Maps

The *tile* graphic is used in geographic mapping. Figure 7.40 shows a map of Europe using a *robinson* projection. Each country's *shape* polygon is derived from information in an associated polygon resource or file. The pairs of values of **longitude** and **latitude** are represented by points that lie somewhere inside the country boundaries in the figure.

The *shape* polygons determine the shape of the tiles. The same polygon file or resourse could be used to determine the shape of *points*, as in Figure 7.42. Maps and tilings are not necessarily the same. The *tile* graphic is useful for mapping political boundaries, islands, lakes, archipelagos, and any other geographic objects that tile the plane or sphere (assuming water fills its own tiles). We can use other graphics such as *point* (for towns or cities), *path* and *link* (for roads, railroads, etc.) and even images (for terrain) to create more detailed maps. Comprehensive GIS programs require more graphic representation objects in order to deal with topological data, but a statistical graphics environment can produce a substantial subset of the geographic representations needed for analysis of spatial data.

FRAME: **longitude*latitude**
COORD: *project.robinson()*
GRAPH: *tile(shape.polygon(***country***))*

Figure 7.40 *Map of Europe*

7.6.3.2 Symbol Shapes

Figure 7.42 shows a scatterplot of the distribution of king crabs captured in a 1973 survey off Kodiak Island, Alaska. The data, posted on Statlib (*www.lib.stat.cmu.edu/crab*), were provided by the Alaska Department of Fish and Game. Each symbol is located at one of the survey sites marking a string of crab pots resembling the ones used by the commercial fishing fleet. The pots were left in the water for approximately a day, removed, and the crabs counted. The symbols in Figure 7.42 are used to characterize the distribution by sex at the sites. Yields of more than 10 males at a site are marked with a vertical line, yields of more than 10 females are marked with a horizontal line, yields with more than 10 of both sexes are marked with the union of these symbols (a plus), and all other yields (including no crabs) are marked with a dot. This plot is patterned after several featured in Hill and Wilkinson (1990). Notice that the waters southwest of the island had a dearth of female crabs that year.

FRAME: **longitude*latitude**
GRAPH: *point*(*shape*(**group**))
GRAPH: *tile*(*shape*(**island**))

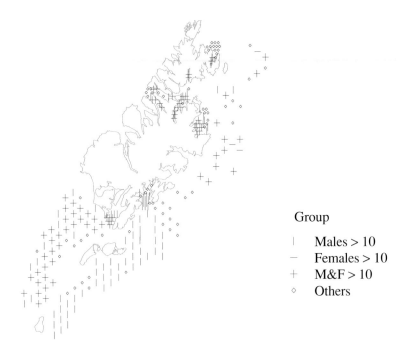

Group

| Males > 10
— Females > 10
+ M&F > 10
◊ Others

Figure 7.41 *King crabs near Kodiak Island by gender*

The choice of symbol shapes affects how distributions in a scatterplot are perceived. The obvious choice of male and female symbols (♂♀) is not a good one, because there is little perceptual contrast between the two. See Cleveland (1993) and the accompanying discussion of issues involving symbol choices. I have used vertical and horizontal line symbols in Figure 7.41 in order to maximize the orientation contrast, following a suggestion I made in a comment on Cleveland (Wilkinson, 1993b), and also to highlight the potential union of crabs at a site.

7.6.3.3 Polygon Shapes

Symbol shapes need not be determined by a fixed repertoire of symbols. They can also be set by arbitrary polygons. Figure 7.42 shows a scatterplot of winter and summer temperatures using state outlines derived from a shape file. I got the idea for this plot from Woodruff *et al.* (1998). It is a clever application, although labeling the points with the names of the states by *point*(*label*(**state**)) makes it easier to identify them, especially by those who are geographically challenged.

FRAME: **winter*summer**
GRAPH: *point*(*shape.polygon*(**state**))

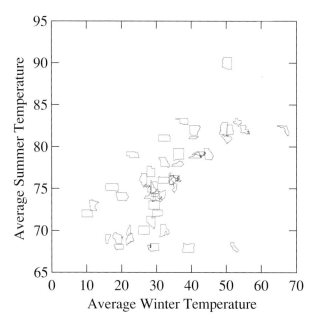

Figure 7.42 *Scatterplot of states*

7.6.3.4 Glyphs

Symbol shapes can be determined by even more complex algorithms. The following sections discuss *glyph*() functions. These are used to determine the shape of *point* graphics based on one or more variables extrinsic to the frame. Glyphs are geometric forms used to represent several variables at once (Fienberg, 1979; Carr *et al.*, 1992; Haber and McNabb, 1990).

glyph.face

Herman Chernoff (1973) invented the FACES display. Figure 7.8 shows an example of Bruckner's (1978) revision of Chernoff's FACES and Figure 7.10 shows an example of Flury and Riedwyl's (1981) version. You should consult those figures now to see how the *glyph.face* (Bruckner) and *glyph.face2* (Flury and Riedwyl) act on the *shape* attribute of *point* to produce the glyphs. Each glyph is nothing more than a plotting symbol. The figures earlier in this chapter show them plotted as a rectangular array, but some of the examples here will show how glyphs can be used in other spatial configurations.

glyph.hist

Figure 7.7 shows an example of the *glyph.hist* function. This creates a histobar profile for each row in the dataset across the specified variables.

glyph.profile

The *profile* glyph is constructed similarly to a *histobar*, except the bar heights are connected with a single profile line. Figure 7.43 shows an example.

FRAME: **col*row**
GRAPH: *point(shape.glyph.profile(***health..arts***), label(***city***))*

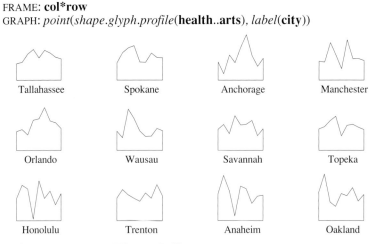

Figure 7.43 *Profile glyphs*

glyph.star

The *star* function is simply a *profile* function in polar coordinates. Figure 7.44 shows an example.

FRAME: **col*row**
GRAPH: *point*(*shape.glyph.star*(**health..arts**), *label*(**city**))

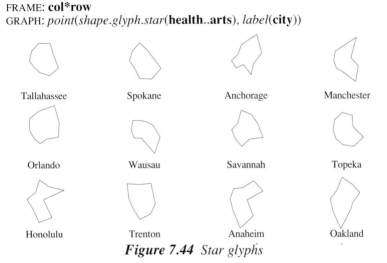

Figure 7.44 *Star glyphs*

glyph.sun

The sun glyph substitutes rays for the perimeter of a star. Figure 7.45 shows an example that uses a coordinate scaling procedure developed by Borg and Staufenbiel (1992).

FRAME: **col*row**
GRAPH: *point*(*shape.glyph.sun*(**health..arts**), *label*(**city**))

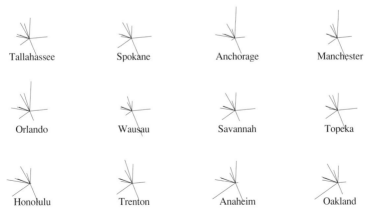

Figure 7.45 *Sun glyphs*

Instead of plotting evenly-spaced polar rays, Borg and Staufenbiel compute a set of row vectors taken from the first two columns of the matrix $\mathbf{V}$ in the singular value decomposition $\mathbf{X} = \mathbf{UDV}^T$ of the data matrix $\mathbf{X}$. These vectors are proportional to the variable coordinates of a 2D **biplot** (Gabriel, 1971, 1995; Gower, 1995). For each observation, Borg and Staufenbiel scale the length of the vectors to be proportional to the normalized values of the variables. This produces a set of stars that vary only in the length of their rays. The advantage of this procedure is that, unlike the other glyphs, it does not depend on the order of the variables in the function parameter list. Furthermore, variables that covary in the data are represented by vectors that have relatively small angles with each other. This reduces the emphasis given to redundant variables.

glyph.blob

Andrews (1972) introduced a Fourier transform on rows of a data matrix that allows one to plot a separate curve for each row. The function Andrews used is

$$f(t) \;=\; \frac{x_1}{\sqrt{2}} + x_2 \sin(t) + x_3 \cos(t) + x_4 \sin(2t) + x_5 \cos(2t) + \dots$$

where x is a p-dimensional variate and t varies continuously from $-\pi$ to π. Cases that have similar values across all variables have comparable wave forms. The *blob* glyph plots this function for each case in polar coordinates. Figure 7.46 shows an example. The shape of the blobs depends on the order variates are entered in the Fourier function.

FRAME: **col*row**
GRAPH: *point*(*shape.glyph.blob*(**health..arts**), *label*(**city**))

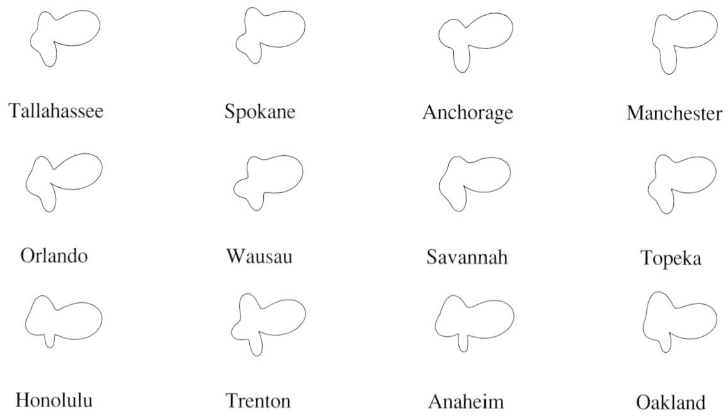

Tallahassee	Spokane	Anchorage	Manchester
Orlando	Wausau	Savannah	Topeka
Honolulu	Trenton	Anaheim	Oakland

Figure 7.46 *Fourier blobs*

glyph.therm

The *therm* glyph resembles a thermometer. Ordinarily, it is useful for representing only one variable, in a mode that resembles the mercury level in a thermometer. Cleveland and McGill (1984b) recommend it for adding a variable to scatterplots (as opposed to using *size* or *shape* attributes) because of the opportunity for accurate linear scale decoding that it offers. Dunn (1987) proposed varying the width of the *therm* to display yet another variable. Figure 7.47 shows an example. I have superimposed the *glyphs* on a map of the continental US. The width of the thermometers is proportional to winter temperatures and the filled area is proportional to rainfall. Varying width is a clever idea, but it introduces configurality into the judgment of the symbols. It needs to be used with caution.

FRAME: **longitude*latitude**
GRAPH: *tile*(*shape.polygon*(**state**), *pattern*("dash"))
GRAPH: *point*(*shape.glyph.therm*(**rain**, **winter**))

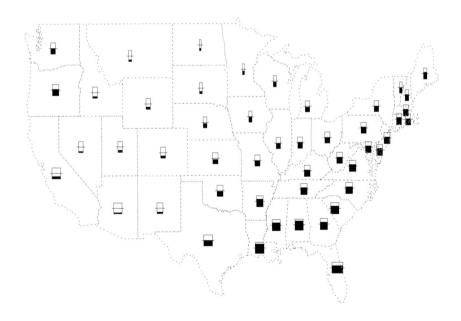

Figure 7.47 *Thermometer glyphs*

glyph.vane

The *vane* glyph uses direction and length and size of circle to represent three variables. Carr and Nicholson (1988) discuss the use of this and other "ray" representations. Many of them derive from the weather map symbols for wind vectors. These symbols resemble small flags that point in the direction of the wind.

Figure 7.48 shows an example involving continental US climate data. The size of the symbols is proportional to rainfall, the length of the vanes is proportional to summer temperatures, and the rotational angle is proportional to winter temperatures. The problem in using vanes this way is that the wind metaphor interferes with decoding values when we do not map the angles to wind direction and lengths to wind speed. See Figure 7.52 for comparison.

FRAME: **longitude*latitude**
GRAPH: *tile*(*shape.polygon*(**state**), *pattern*("dash"))
GRAPH: *point*(*shape.glyph.vane*(**rain, summer, winter**))

Figure 7.48 *Vane glyphs*

7.6.3.5 Shape set by Image

Images can be used to determine the shape of *points*, *bars*, and other graphics. Figure 7.42 shows a scatterplot of facial expressions adapted from psychometric research documented in Russell and Fernandez-Dols (1997). The configuration in this plot fits a pattern called a **circumplex** (Guttman, 1954), which is best interpreted through polar coordinates. In this example, the center of the configuration is marked by a face showing lack of emotion. Radial distance from this point in any direction represents *intensity* of emotion and polar angle represents *type* of emotion. These two polar variates can be more interpretively useful than the rectangular axis labels (sleepiness-activation and unpleasantness-pleasantness) shown here. When images have substantive meaning, as in this example, they can legend a graphic more effectively than any other type of symbol or guide.

DATA: **face** = *link*("faces")
FRAME: **pleasantness*activation**
GRAPH: *point*(*shape.image*(**face**))

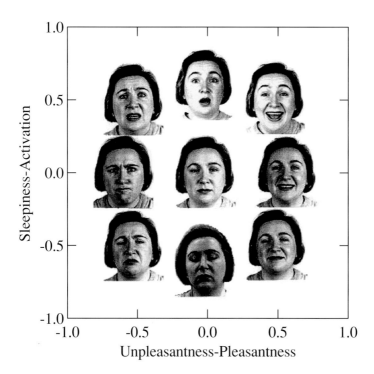

Figure 7.49 *Scatterplot of faces*

7.6.3.6 Voronoi Tessellations

The Voronoi tessellation is one of the most prevalent tilings to appear in scientific graphics. Each pair of points is separated by a boundary based on the perpendicular bisector of the line segment joining both points. Preparata and Shamos (1985) survey algorithms for computing this tiling. Stoyan *et al.* (1987), Cressie (1991), and Okabe *et al.* (1992) cover statistical and probability measures related to the Voronoi tessellation.

Figure 7.50 shows a graphic of the spatial location of fiddler crab holes in an 80 centimeter square section of the Pamet river tidal marsh in Truro, Massachusetts. I collected these data, in bare feet, at substantial personal risk. The right panel contains a sample of uniform random points distributed in the same square. Both panels contain a Voronoi tessellation. Notice the irregular structure of the polygons on the right. The contrast in tiling between the two figures suggests the territorial constraints of the real holes vs. the random grouping of the artificial.

FRAME: **crabx*craby**
GRAPH: *tile(shape.poly("voronoi"))*
GRAPH: *point()*

DATA: **uranx**=*rand.uniform*(23)
DATA: **urany**=*rand.uniform*(23)
FRAME: **uranx*urany**
GRAPH: *tile(shape.poly("voronoi"))*
GRAPH: *point()*

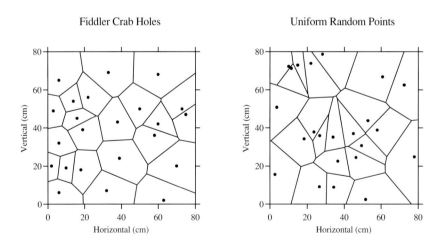

Figure 7.50 *Voronoi tessellation of fiddler crab holes*

7.6.3.7 Bar Shapes

Figure 7.51 shows a shape variation on bars using a "pyramid" shape function. This form of bars is not recommended because the slopes of the bar sides change with their height, a confusing visual illusion.

FRAME: **gov*birth**
GRAPH: *bar(shape*("pyramid"))

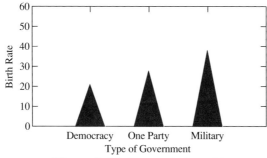

Figure 7.51 *Pyramid shaped bars*

7.6.4 Rotation

Figure 7.52 shows how to use *rotation*() and *size*() to plot velocity of winds with an arrow symbol. The data are from the Seasat-A satellite scatterometer (*podaac.jpl.nasa.gov*), reported in Chelton *et al.* (1990). We could also use *link.edge.join*() to plot with (*uwind, vwind*) coordinates (see Figure 8.26).

FRAME: **longitude*latitude**
COORD: *project.robinson*()
GRAPH: *tile(shape.polygon(***continent***), color*("green"))
GRAPH: *point(shape*("arrow"), *rotation(***direction***), size(***strength***))

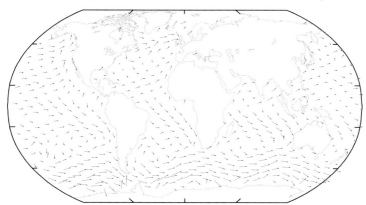

Figure 7.52 *Global prevailing winds*

7.6.5 *Color*

Color can be especially effective for categorical coding. This section also features continuous color scales.

7.6.5.1 *Shading with Color (continuous color scales)*

Figure 7.53 shows an example of shading (setting an attribute by a continuous variable) with the Iris data. The values of **petalwidth** determine the shades of color of the symbols plotted. We must use *color.hue*() instead of *color*() because we are mapping to a continuous scale rather than a table of color categories. Even though there are several species in the plot, there is only one cloud of points. No subgrouping occurs because species was not used to split this graphic. The shading shows that petal width varies more strongly with the *difference* between sepal length and sepal width than with their *sum*.

FRAME: **sepallength*sepalwidth**
GRAPH: *point*(*color.hue*(**petalwidth**))

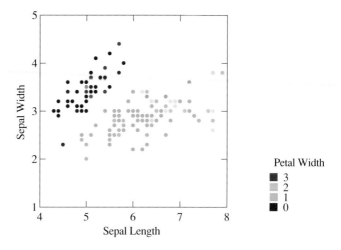

Figure 7.53 *Scatterplot shaded by color.*

7.6.5.2 *Splitting with Color (categorical color scales)*

Exchanging the continuous shading variable in Figure 7.53 for a categorical splitting variable produces the graphic in Figure 7.54. There are now three ellipses and point clouds, one for each **species**. Without the *contour* graphic, we would have no way of knowing whether there are one or three clouds. This is because we could have treated **species** as continuous (by giving it numerical values), which would yield one *point* cloud shaded with three values.

FRAME: **sepallength*sepalwidth**
GRAPH: *point(color(**species**))*
GRAPH: *contour.region.confi.mean.joint(color(**species**))*

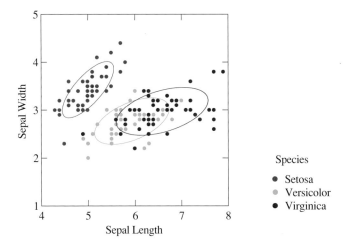

Figure 7.54 *Scatterplot split by subgroups.*

7.6.5.3 *Legending a Blend with Color*

Blends usually require legends to distinguish the variables on which the blends are based. The *string()* data function fills a column with a specified string (see Section 3.1). For example, *string()* indexes a blend of variables *A* and *B* in the following manner:

$$
\begin{array}{ccc}
A & B & (A+B) & string(\text{"a"})+string(\text{"b"}) \\
\begin{bmatrix} a_1 \\ a_2 \\ a_3 \\ a_4 \end{bmatrix} + \begin{bmatrix} b_1 \\ b_2 \\ b_3 \\ b_4 \end{bmatrix} = & \begin{bmatrix} a_1 \\ a_2 \\ a_3 \\ a_4 \\ b_1 \\ b_2 \\ b_3 \\ b_4 \end{bmatrix} \longleftrightarrow & \begin{bmatrix} a \\ a \\ a \\ a \\ b \\ b \\ b \\ b \end{bmatrix}
\end{array}
$$

The *string()* data function doesn't actually allocate storage to do this; it simply returns the appropriate string value whenever a blend is used. If there is no blend, then *string()* returns a string for as many cases as exist in the FRAME specification. We ordinarily use a *string()* variable to label, color, or otherwise describe a blend.

Figure 7.55 shows an example. Notice that the *color* attribute function operates on the *string*() function to add color to the *point* and *contour* graphics. Notice also that because *string*() creates a categorical variable, it splits the one cloud into two. Using a variable in a graphing function is like crossing with that variable.

DATA: **s**=*string*("Sepal width")
DATA: **p**=*string*("Petal width")
FRAME: **sepallength*(sepalwidth+petalwidth)**
GRAPH: *point*(*color*(**s+p**))
GRAPH: *contour.region.confi.mean.joint*(*color*(**s+p**))

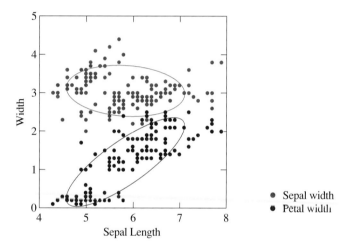

Figure 7.55 *Blended scatterplot*

For repeated measures and multivariate data, we often wish to plot values against a variable that represents the indices of the measures. For example, we might have measurements on subjects before and after an experimental treatment and we want a plot with measurements on the vertical axis and two values, *before* and *after* on the horizontal axis. Figure 7.56 shows an example of this type of design, using data from Estes (1994). The experiment involved a 320-trial learning series requiring subjects to classify artificial words as adjectives or verbs. The **exemplar** variable denotes whether words in the trials were first occurrences (new) or first repetitions (old). The trials were grouped in 4 blocks of 80 trials each.

The blend in the specification (vertical axis) is plotted against the names of the blend variables (horizontal axis). The **exemplar** variable is used to determine the hue of both graphics and the shape of the symbols in the *point* graphic.

DATA: **b1**=*string*("BLOCK(1)")
DATA: **b2**=*string*("BLOCK(2)")
DATA: **b3**=*string*("BLOCK(3)")
DATA: **b4**=*string*("BLOCK(4)")
FRAME: **b1* block1+b2*block2+ b3*block3+b4*block4**
GRAPH: *line*(*color*(**exemplar**))
GRAPH: *point*(*color*(**exemplar**), *shape*(**exemplar**))

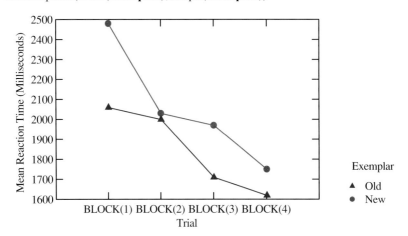

Figure 7.56 *Repeated measures experiment from Estes (1994)*

Figure 7.57 shows an application of color to distinguish groups in a nested design. The figure is based on data of Charles Darwin, reprinted in Fisher (1935). The design included 15 pairs of plants (self-fertilized and cross-fertilized) distributed across 4 pots. Plant pairs were nested within pots. Pots 1 and 2 contained 3 plant pairs each, Pot 3 contained 5, and Pot 4 contained 4.

Fisher used these data to illustrate the power of Student's *t*-test, arguing against Galton's analysis of the same data. In doing so, he noted the peculiar reversals of **plant** pair 2 in **pot** 1 and **plant** pair 4 in **pot** 4. Figure 7.57 reveals these reversals more readily than an examination of the raw numbers. The graphic is produced by the expression **plant/pot*(self+cross)**. The vertical dimension is a blend of the two fertilization variables **self** and **cross**. This blending corresponds to the repeated measure in the design. The horizontal dimension is a nested factor **plant/pot**. Notice that the tick marks are spaced categorically (on integers) and indicate **plant** within **pot**. The sections within the frame are of unequal width because there are different numbers of plants within the pots. The horizontal axis is telling us that **plant** pair 1 in **pot** 1 is not the same as **plant** pair 1 in **pot** 2. Finally, the implicit variables **s** and **c** are used to color the dots according to the measure type (**self** or **cross**). Blending these creates a categorical variable set whose value is the string "Self" or "Cross" and whose index (1 or 2) is used to determine the color from a preset color table.

DATA: **s** = *string*("Self")
DATA: **c** = *string*("Cross")
FRAME: **plant/pot***(**self**+**cross**)
GRAPH: *line*(*color*(**s**+**c**))

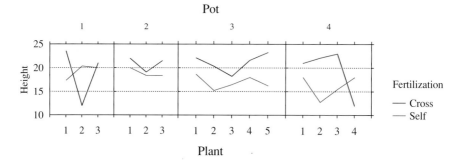

Figure 7.57 *Nested experimental design.*

Figure 7.58 shows the dot plot of the Shakespeare data featured in Figure 5.7. This time we are coloring the dots according to the name of the blended variable, which we have encoded in two data strings (**f** and **s**).

DATA: **f** = *string*("First")
DATA: **s** = *string*("Second")
FRAME: **first ı second**
GRAPH: *point*(*position.stack*(), *color*(**f**+**s**))

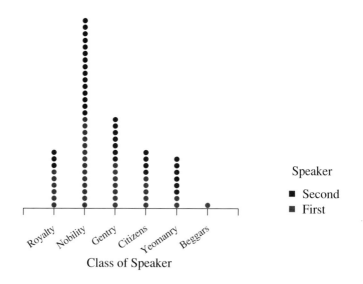

Figure 7.58 *Blended dot plot*

Several other widely used plots employ color to mark blends. Figure 7.59 shows how the *string*() function is used to create a **profile plot**. This plot has been used by individual-differences psychologists for almost a century to display profiles on psychometric tests (see Hartigan, 1975a). The vertical axis displays the subtest score and the horizontal axis shows the name of the subtest. In general, profile plots can be used to display repeated measurements of a single variable or a multivariate profile on several comparable measurements. In this example, I have used the Fisher Iris flower measurements and added color to the profiles in Figure 7.59 by referencing the **species** variable in the dataset. The three species are distinguished clearly in the plot. Compare this plot to the parallel coordinate plot shown in Figure 10.56. The difference between the two is that profile plots have a common measurement scale and parallel coordinate plots do not.

DATA: **sw**=*string*("SEPALWID")
DATA: **sl**=*string*("SEPALLEN")
DATA: **pw**=*string*("PETALWID")
DATA: **pl**=*string*("PETALLEN")
FRAME: **sw*sepalwid+sl*sepallen+ pw*petalwid+pl*petallen**
GRAPH: *line*(*color*(**species**))

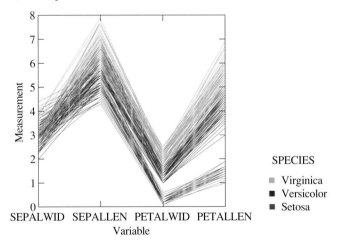

Figure 7.59 *Profile plot of Iris data.*

7.6.5.4 Using Color in Matrix Plots

Figure 7.60 shows the entire Iris dataset plotted as a matrix using the row and column data functions. The layout of the cells is determined by the index variables. The rectangular cuts between datapoints (the lattice of row and column indices) create the tiles. These tiles are colored by *color.hue*(). The same graphic can be created through the *blend* operator. Can you write a specification to do this?

DATA: **x** = *shape.rect*(SPECIES, SEPALWID, SEPALLEN, PETALWID, PETALLEN, "rowindex")
DATA: **y** = *shape.rect*(SPECIES, SEPALWID, SEPALLEN, PETALWID, PETALLEN, "colname")
DATA: **d** = *shape.rect*(SPECIES, SEPALWID, SEPALLEN, PETALWID, PETALLEN, "value")
FRAME: **x*****y**
GRAPH: *tile.density.bin.rect*(*color.hue*(**d**))

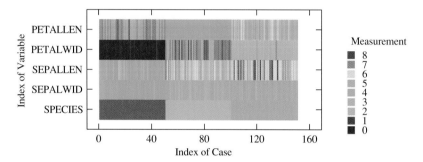

Figure 7.60 *Matrix plot of Iris data.*

7.6.5.5 Choropleth Maps

Figure 7.61 shows a **choropleth map** representing the logged population of each county in the continental US. This map is based on the Bureau of the Census Summary Tape File 3A. Geographers have traditionally disparaged the spectrum, or rainbow, color scale I have used for representing population in this choropleth map, but recent perceptual research by Brewer (1996) fails to support this conventional opinion.

It is interesting to compare this map to two others: the population density map GE-70, prepared by the Geography Division at Census (reproduced in Tufte, 1983, and available as a poster from the US Government Printing Office), and the nighttime satellite composite photo of the US, available through NASA. Not surprisingly, the distribution of artificial light emanating from cities and towns matches the Census population distribution figures almost perfectly.

I logged the population of each county because the distribution of population in the US is highly skewed. Without logging, almost every county would be blue or dark green and only a few would be orange or red. An alternative approach would be to assign population a dimension and display it on a decimal log scale. Then the legend would show population on a log scale (see Chapter 9) rather than the log values themselves.

TRANS: **lpop** = *log.10*(**population**)
FRAME: **longitude*latitude**
COORD: *project.stereo*()
GRAPH: *tile*(*shape.polygon*(**county**), *color.hue*(**lpop**))

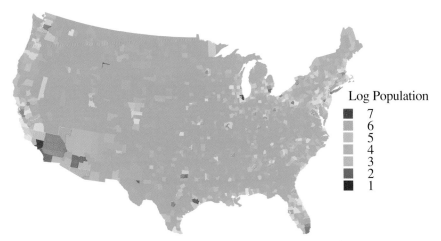

Figure 7.61 *Color map of logged county population*

7.7 Summary

The major attributes discussed in this chapter are summarized in Table 7.3. The columns represent geometric forms that are employed by different graph types: point, line, area, surface, and solid. The rows represent the attributes divided into four super-classes: form, color, texture, and optics.

Table 7.3 is relatively straightforward except for the subtable covering form attributes. In other sections of the table, we are free to vary an attribute independently of the other attributes. For example, the hue of any geometric object is free to vary independently of position, size, shape, and other attributes. With form attributes, on the other hand, we sometimes collide with the constraints of position. The size of a point is free to vary independently of its position because changing its size does not change its location. The size of a line, however, can vary only in its thickness unless its length is not constrained by a positional variable. The size of an area can be changed only if its boundary is not determined by a positional variable. The size of a *tile*(), for example, can be modified under certain circumstances, but the size of an *area*() cannot. For similar reasons, the shape of an area can be changed only if it is not constrained by a positional variable. We modify the shape of a *tile*(), for example, to do a geographic map, but we never modify the shape of an *area*(). Similar rules apply to rotation of lines, areas, surfaces, and solids. In each case, we must look for a degree-of-freedom from positional constraint.

Table 7.3 **Aesthetic Attributes by Geometry**

	Point	Line	Area	Surface	Solid
Form					
Size					
Shape					
Rotation					
Color					
Brightness					
Hue					
Saturation					
Texture					
Granularity					
Pattern					
Orientation					
Optics					
Blur					
Transparency					

A point is rendered by a symbol, polygon, or image positioned at the co-ordinates of the point. It has the most degrees-of-freedom of any object be-cause we can vary every attribute independently of position. Point objects maintain their appearance under different coordinate systems. For example, the shape of a *point* graphic does not change under a polar transformation.

A line is rendered by one or more symbols, polygons, or images posi-tioned at the coordinates of points on that line. Dashed lines, for example, are rendered by placing a small number of rectangular polygons or symbols at points along a line. We change the size of a line by increasing the size of those symbols in a direction orthogonal to the line itself. This increases the thickness of the line. The shape of a line is determined by the shape of the object used to render it – polygon, image, or symbol. Its granularity is determined by the number of symbols used to render it (if a dashed shaped is used) or by the granularity of the pattern that fills the line polygon.

An area is rendered by one or more symbols, polygons, or images posi-tioned at selected coordinates on a plane. We can vary the size of an area, its shape, or its rotation only if we have degrees-of-freedom to do so.

Surfaces are rendered by positioning one or more symbols, polygons, or images in a 3D space so that the coordinates of one of their vertices or their centroids lie on a surface. As with lines in 2D space, we vary size of surfaces by varying their thickness. For example, we could make the surfaces thicker in Figure 6.4 by adding a *size()* attribute to the graphics. We can vary shape by changing the shape of the polygons or elements used to render it. This could be used to make a surface bumpy or smooth, for example. We can vary the ex-terior shape of a surface if we have the degrees-of-freedom to do so. We can also modify the texture of a surface (independently of shape) by changing the texture map used to render it.

Solids are rendered similarly to surfaces. Depending on how they are em-ployed by a graphic, solids may have more than one degree-of-freedom avail-able for varying attributes like size, shape, and rotation. Thus, we may change the size of one or more facets of a rectangular solid and we can vary its rotation along one or more dimensions depending on which facets are positionally an-chored. I have shown this in the last column of Table 7.3. If a solid has no de-grees-of-freedom for representing an attribute such as size, then we cannot vary such an attribute.

7.8 Sequel

We now have the tools for making a wide range of basic graphics. More com-plex graphics require statistical functions. The next chapter covers the statis-tical functions that graphing functions use to create statistical graphs.

8

Statistics

Statistics state the status of the state. All four *s* words derive from the Greek σ*τάσισ* and Latin *status*, or standing. Standing (for humans) is a state of being, a condition that represents literally or figuratively the active status of an individual, group, or state. Modern statistics as a discipline arose in the early 18th century, when collection of data about the state was recognized as essential to serving the needs of its constituents. This Enlightenment perspective gave rise not only to the modern social sciences, but also to mathematical methods for analyzing data measured with error (Stigler, 1983).

In a graphical system, **statistics** are methods that alter the position of geometric graphs. We are accustomed to think of a chart as a display of a statistic or a statistical function (*e.g.*, a bar chart of budget expenditures). As such, it would seem that we should begin by aggregating data, computing statistics, and drawing a chart. This would be wrong, however. By putting statistics under control of graphing functions (rather than whole charts under the control of statistics) we accomplish several things. First, we can represent more than one statistic in a frame. One graphic can represent a mean and another a median, in the same frame. Second, making statistics into graphing methods forces them to be views or summaries of the raw data rather than data themselves. In other words, the casewise data and a graphic are inextricably bound because we never break the connection between the variables and the graphics that represent them. This allows us to drill-down, brush, and investigate values with other dynamic tools. This functions would be lost if we pre-aggregated the data. Finally, by putting statistics under the control of graphing functions, we can modularize and localize computations in a distributed system. Adding graphics to a frame is easy when we do not have to worry about the structure of the data and how aggregations were computed. I will return to this issue in Section 8.3 at the end of this chapter.

The simplest graphing method is the one students first learn for plotting algebraic functions: for every x, compute $f(x)$ so that one may draw a graph based on the tuples of the form $(x, f(x))$ that comprise the graph. Students learn to construct a list of these tuples (a finite subset of the graph of the function) in order to plot selected points in Cartesian coordinates. In the functional notation of this book, students usually draw graphs of algebraic functions using the graphing function *line.f*().

While students learn graphing methods for polynomial and other simple algebraic functions, most charts are based on statistical functions of observed values of one or more variables. In our notation, examples of statistical graphs are *point.statistic.mean* and *line.smooth.linear*, which are produced by the statistical graphing functions *point.statistic.mean*() and *line.smooth.linear*(), respectively. Statistical functions can be complicated, but their output looks the same to their geometric clients as the output of algebraic functions. A *line* does not care who produced the points it needs to plot itself.

Statistics are static (unchanging) methods that are available to all graphs. For example, we can use *bar.statistic.mean*() or *point.statistic.mean*() or *line.statistic.mean*() to produce a geometric graph of a mean. Some of the combinations of graphs and statistical methods may be degenerate or bizarre, but there is no moral reason to restrict them. Notwithstanding, graphs have default statistical methods. For example, *bar.statistic.mean*() is equivalent to *bar*() because the default statistical function for a *bar* graph is *statistic.mean*. The function *point.statistic.mean*() is not equivalent to *point*(), however, because a *point* graph plots all points. The default method for *point*() is a multifunction that returns the set of all values on y for a given x.

Statistics have the potential to alter the appearance of graphics, in some cases as radically as do coordinate transformations. It is sometimes difficult to recognize a graphic after its geometry has been altered by a statistic and, conversely, it often can be difficult to infer a statistical function from the geometry of a graphic. For example, *line.smooth.linear*() creates a single regression line, while *line.region.confi.smooth.linear*() creates a pair of lines that delineate a confidence interval on a smoother. On the other hand, *line.smooth.linear*() and *line.smooth.mean*() can both create straight lines. Sometimes we can distinguish them only if there are differences in the data on which they are based.

This chapter invokes some methods whose particulars are beyond the scope of this book. I have used these in examples to illustrate the diversity of a statistical graphing system and to alert statisticians to the design issues involved in putting statistical procedures at the service of graphics. Although the topic is graphics, the organization of this chapter, summarized in Table 8.1, gives some indication of the way I would design an object-oriented statistical package as well. If the design principles of **orthogonality** (as much as possible, everything should work everywhere and in every combination) and **hierarchy** (complicated tasks should be done by enlisting the support of simple helpers) are applied to statistical methods, a comprehensive package requires a minimum of code.

One can consult a statistics text for further information, although there are many technical issues that are not immediately apparent when looking at statistical formulas. The best sources for further information about computing and statistics are Chambers (1977), Kennedy and Gentle (1980), Maindonald (1984), and Thisted (1988).

8.1 Methods

Table 8.1 lists the most important statistical methods available to graphs. They fall under five super-classes: *statistic* (basic statistics), *region* (interval and region bounds), *smooth* (regression, smoothing, and interpolation), *density* (density estimation), and *edge* (methods for computing edges of graphs based on a set of nodes or points). The table is not exhaustive, of course. I have tried to include enough examples to make clear where new methods can be added to this system and also to cover the examples in this book

Table 8.1 **Statistical Methods**

statistic	*region*	*smooth*	*density*	*edge*
count	spread	linear	normal	mst
sum	sd	quadratic	kernel	delaunay
mean	se	cubic	ash	hull
median	range	log	quantile	tree
mode	confi	mean	bin	join
sd	mean	median	rect	tsp
se	sd	mode	gap	
range	smooth	spline	hex	

Many statistical methods rely on a scalar quantity called a **loss**, which we attempt to minimize when calculating statistics. Others rely on a scalar quantity called a **likelihood** that we attempt to maximize. We may qualify a method by appending the name of its loss or likelihood function to the method name. Ordinary least squares, called *ols*, involves a quadratic loss function of the residuals (differences between fitted and observed values). Robust estimation, on the other hand, involves a variety of loss functions that are designed to down-weight large residuals (Huber, 1972; Tukey, 1977). These weighted loss functions have names like *biweight*. We may distinguish different methods by adding the proper suffix. For example, we can specify *smooth.linear.ols* or *smooth.linear.biweight*. These examples follow the syntax *smooth.model.loss*. I will now summarize the methods in each of the super-classes.

The *statistic* class includes statistical algorithms for producing a single value (or vector value) that comprises a statistical summary. The *count* and *sum* methods return simple or weighted counts and sums. The *mean*, *median*, and *mode* methods return measures of location. The *sd*, *se*, and *range* methods return measures of dispersion. A statistician might regard these methods as disparate from a computational point of view. From a graphical point of view, however, they are all common objects; all produce a result that is graphable as a geometric point. A dot plot of standard deviations within groups, for example, would require the graphing function *point.statistic.sd()* to make a point for each standard deviation. We would examine a graphic of the *point.statistic.sd* graph to assess whether the standard deviations appeared similar across groups. We could also plot standard deviations as intervals using the function *point.region.spread.sd*(), but if our interest is only in dispersion and not location, it is easier to examine standard deviations directly than to compute them in our minds as differences between the bounds of intervals.

The *region* class includes statistical algorithms that produce two values that are graphable as two points bounding a point in one dimension, or a set of values at the vertices of a convex region bounding a point in higher dimensions. There are two ways to do this. The first method is to use a measure of spread (*sd*, *range*, etc.). This is what the *spread* method does. The *spread* method requires a suffix naming the measure of spread used to produce the interval. Examples are *region.spread.sd* and *region.spread.range*. The *sd* method is the default.

The second method for computing a *region* is to use a theoretical distribution to compute a confidence interval, not necessarily symmetric, on some statistic. This is what the *confi* method does. Unlike *spread*, which bounds only points, the *confi* method can construct regions that bound a variety of statistical objects. For example, *region.confi.mean* is a method for producing a confidence interval on a mean using a probability distribution (usually Student's *t* distribution). The method *region.confi.sd* produces a confidence interval on a standard deviation. The method *region.confi.smooth.linear* produces a confidence interval on an ordinary regression line. As this last example indicates, we can append to the *confi* method any statistical methods for which we know how to produce a valid (under appropriate assumptions) confidence interval. This can result in a rather long method function, but one that makes sense hierarchically (from left to right) and also reveals the order in which we do the computations (from right to left).

The *smooth* class includes a variety of methods for computing smoothed values. The term derives from the smoothness of a parametric function, but it covers a more general class of functions of variables that produce connected sets of values. These include ordinary linear regression, interpolators, and step functions that pass through data values. In other words, the word *smooth* should not be taken to imply that the result has many derivatives or is even continuous.

The *linear* smoothing method is perhaps the most widely used in practice. It computes the function $f(\mathbf{x}) = \mathbf{x}\mathbf{b}$ for any real-valued input vector $\mathbf{x}$. The default *linear.ols* smoother computes the vector $\mathbf{b}$ via the method of least squares on the set of pairs $\{(\mathbf{x}_i, y_i): i = 1, \dots, n\}$ taken from a set of data values. If our frame is $x*y$, then $\mathbf{x} = x$ and $y = y$. The graphic of this 2D smooth is a straight line whose intercept and slope are b_0 and b_1, respectively. If our frame is $x*y*z$, then $\mathbf{x} = (x, y)$ and $y = z$. The graphic of this 3D smooth is a plane whose intercept and slopes are b_0, b_1, and b_2, respectively.

The *quadratic* smoothing method fits a quadratic polynomial using a linear model $f(\mathbf{x}) = \mathbf{x}\mathbf{b}$. If our frame is $x*y$, then $\mathbf{x} = (x, x^2)$ and $y = y$. The graphic of this 2D smooth is a parabola. If our frame is $x*y*z$, then $\mathbf{x} = (x, y, x^2, y^2, xy)$

and $y = z$. The graphic of this 3D smooth is a parabolic surface or a saddle. The *cubic* method and higher-degree polynomial smoothers are defined similarly.

The *log* smoothing method fits the function $f(x) = log(a) + b \, log(x)$ to compute smoothed values. If our data follow the model $y = ax^b \varepsilon$, with ε representing identically distributed independent errors, then we can log transform y and x to fit this model with ordinary least squares. Estimating the coefficients of other nonlinear models usually requires iterative methods that must be carefully designed to avoid local minima and loss of accuracy (Dennis and Schnabel, 1983). Robust nonlinear methods can be implemented through the same terminology used for linear methods (*e.g., smooth.log.biweight*).

The *mean, median,* and *mode* smoothing methods produce a constant smoother. A graphic of *line.smooth.mean* in the frame **x*y** is a horizontal line whose height corresponds to the mean of **y**. In the frame **x*y*z**, a graphic of *line.smooth.mean* is a horizontal plane positioned at the mean of **z**. These constant smoothers are useful as reference objects in graphics (to mark a mean level, for example). The *smooth.median* method is useful for computing reference levels when the values to be smoothed are skewed or contain outliers. The *smooth.mode* method is useful for computing reference levels when the values to be smoothed are categorical.

So far, I have given global definitions for parametric smoothers. There is also a large literature in statistics that covers what is usually called **nonparametric smoothing**, **locally parametric smoothing**, or **kernel smoothing** (Härdle, 1990; Hastie and Tibshirani, 1990; Scott, 1992; Green and Silverman, 1994; Fan and Gijbels, 1996; Simonoff, 1996). These local smoothing methods are flexible, follow the data closely, and are especially useful for exploratory data analysis. They work by computing a weighted fit of a smoothing model inside a window containing an ordered subset of the data. The set of weights used to define the smoothing window is derived from a probability **kernel** function, which is a function on the real numbers with integral $1/n$, where n is the number of cases in the set of data to be smoothed. In 2D, the most useful window functions are the following:

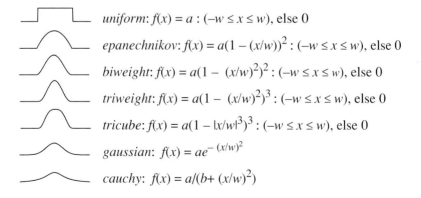

uniform: $f(x) = a : (-w \leq x \leq w)$, else 0

epanechnikov: $f(x) = a(1 - (x/w))^2 : (-w \leq x \leq w)$, else 0

biweight: $f(x) = a(1 - (x/w)^2)^2 : (-w \leq x \leq w)$, else 0

triweight: $f(x) = a(1 - (x/w)^2)^3 : (-w \leq x \leq w)$, else 0

tricube: $f(x) = a(1 - |x/w|^3)^3 : (-w \leq x \leq w)$, else 0

gaussian: $f(x) = ae^{-(x/w)^2}$

cauchy: $f(x) = a/(b + (x/w)^2)$

The constant a that scales these formulas as probability kernel functions may be set to 1 for smoothers because it cancels out in the algorithms if they are designed properly. The constant w determines the width of the window or, for kernels like *gaussian* and *cauchy* that have nonzero tails, the spread of the kernel. We can adapt these functions to 3D smoothing (assuming x and y are independent and identically distributed) by transforming them into polar coordinates. Non-circular 3D window functions are slightly more complex.

There are two simple ways, among others, that we can set the window width w for computing a smoothed value at a location x_i (not necessarily a data point). The first is to set w to be *fixed* at a chosen **bandwidth** value for all x_i. The second is to set w to be the distance from x_i to the k-th nearest neighbor in the data. This method, called *knn*, generally means that the width of a window will vary at different points x_i. The *fixed* window guarantees that smoothed values will be based on a common range and the *knn* window guarantees that they will be based on the same number of data points, namely k.

As a consequence of their evolution, nonparametric smoothers have acquired many different names, but there is a simple scheme that makes it easy to implement almost every one of them in an object-oriented system. Each of the global methods I have described (*linear, quadratic, cubic, log, mean, median*, and *mode*) can be turned into a local method by adding the name of the type of kernel weighting function used to do the smoothing. An example is *smooth.linear.epanechnikov*. For local smoothers, the default bandwidth is *fixed* and the default loss function is *ols*. If we wish to specify *knn* or other loss functions, we can use the extended syntax *smooth.model.kernel.window.loss*. An example is *smooth.mean.uniform.knn.biweight*.

This scheme yields many of the kernel and polynomial smoothers described in the literature under other names. For example, a **running-means** or **moving-averages** smoother (Makridakis and Wheelwright, 1989) is *smooth.mean.uniform*. The Nadaraya-Watson kernel smoother (Nadaraya, 1964; Watson, 1964) is *smooth.mean.epanechnikov*. Shepard's smoother (Shepard, 1965), sometimes called an **inverse-distance** smoother (McLain, 1974), is *smooth.mean.cauchy*. The **distance-weighted least squares** (DWLS) smoother (McLain, 1974) is *smooth.quadratic.gaussian*. The **step** smoother (Cleveland, 1995) is *smooth.mean.uniform.knn* with $k = 1$ (the number of nearest neighbors is set to 1). For convenience, I will name this *smooth.step* in the examples. The image-processing digital filter called a **discrete gaussian convolution** that is used to smooth black-and-white images (Gonzalez and Wintz, 1977) is *smooth.mean.gaussian.knn*. It is a *knn* method because the pixels on which it operates are evenly spaced, so it does weighted averages over a fixed number of pixels. Finally, Cleveland's LOESS smoother (Cleveland and Devlin, 1988) is *smooth.linear.tricube.knn.biweight*. Notice that Cleveland's loss function involves robust biweighting instead of ordinary least squares, which makes his smoother resistant to outliers. For convenience, I have denoted it as *smooth.loess* in the examples. The quadratic version of LOESS is *smooth.quadratic.tricube.knn.biweight*.

The local version of the *median* smoother is discussed in Tukey (1977). Tukey's smoother is equivalent to *smooth.median.uniform.knn*. The local *mode* method is based on a kernel estimate of the conditional mode, discussed in Scott (1992). The *spline* method implements cubic splines, which are piecewise cubic polynomials. These are used most frequently for smooth interpolation of a set of data points (Lancaster and Salkauskas, 1986) but also have applications in nonparametric regression (Wahba, 1990). Finally, note that all the *smooth* methods provide the possibility of computing confidence intervals when they are defined. This is done by using the *region.confi* method prefix on the smoother, as in *region.confi.smooth.linear*.

The *density* methods estimate a density using a variety of approaches. The *normal* method estimates the parameters of the normal distribution from sample data and returns the density function. Other parametric densities can be computed similarly. The *kernel* methods perform kernel density estimation using the kernels discussed under smoothing methods above. An example is: *density.kernel.epanechnikov*. Silverman (1986) and Scott (1992) discuss kernel density estimation. The *ash* method (Scott, 1992) performs an averaged-shifted-histogram, which produces a result similar to that of the *kernel* density estimation method, but is much faster. The *quantile* methods estimate a density by computing the locations of sample quantiles (such as quartiles, deciles, or percentiles). An example is *density.quantile.quartile*. Quantiles from the fractions i/n, $(i = 1, ..., n)$ can be used to construct a **sample cumulative distribution function**, on which the sample density is based. Letter values Tukey (1977), used for the box plot and stem-and-leaf plot (see Figure 6.10), are produced by *density.quantile.letter*.

The *density.bin* methods return the number of cases in each bin or the proportion of cases in each bin or the density at a given value so that clients like *histobar* or *line* can produce the histogram statistical display. The *rect* method partitions with equally spaced cutpoints on one or more dimensions. In two dimensions, the regions partitioned are rectangles. The *gap* method partitions with unequally sized cutpoints or grids. The *hex* method partitions the plane with connected hexagons. It is not used in one dimension.

Finally, the *edge* methods input tuples as nodes in a graph, and return edges according to various algorithms. The *mst* method returns the minimum spanning tree, which is the shortest set of edges (in terms of total length) connecting every node. The *delaunay* method returns the Delaunay triangulation of the nodes, which comprises the set of edges that connect every node to its nearest neighbor. The *hull* method returns the convex hull of a set of points, which is the set of edges connecting the outermost nodes in a planar graph. In three dimensions, the convex hull is made up of planar facets instead of lines. The *tree* method returns a directed tree graph. The *join* method returns edges for adjacent sets of points (serial pairs) in a list. The *tsp* method computes the traveling salesman problem, or at least an approximation. This computation involves finding the shortest path through a set of points such that every point is visited once. The lonely salesman is usually allowed to return home.

8.1.1 Conditional and Joint Methods

There are two subclasses of statistical functions: **conditional** and **joint**. The input to the conditional form of the functions is a finite set $\{(\mathbf{x}_i, y_i)\}$, where $\mathbf{x}$ is a d-dimensional vector variable and $i = 1, \ldots, n$. This set is defined by the d factors of the common term $\mathbf{x}_1^* \mathbf{x}_2^* \ldots^* \mathbf{x}_d^* \mathbf{y}$ found after expanding the FRAME specification to algebraic form using the distributivity axioms presented in Chapter 5. The input to the joint form of the functions is the finite set of data $\{\mathbf{x}_i\}$, where $\mathbf{x}$ is a d-dimensional vector variable and $i = 1, \ldots, n$. This set is defined by the d factors of the common term $\mathbf{x}_1^* \mathbf{x}_2^* \ldots^* \mathbf{x}_d$.

The conditional methods compute $f(\mathbf{x})$ from y conditioned on values of $\mathbf{x}$. These include methods like linear and nonlinear regression. The joint methods compute $f(\mathbf{x})$ from $\mathbf{x}$ alone. These include methods like principal components, orthogonal regression, minimum spanning trees, and network algorithms. In most joint methods, $f(\mathbf{x})$ is a multi-function. In the minimum spanning tree method, for example, we input a set of tuples $\{\mathbf{x}_1 \ldots \mathbf{x}_n\}$ and output a set of nodes and edges comprising a minimum spanning tree.

We designate conditional or joint methods by adding the suffix *conditional* or *joint* to statistical method functions. For example, if we have a frame consisting of $\mathbf{x}^* \mathbf{y}$, we can specify the conditional means of $\mathbf{x}$ given $\mathbf{y}$ through the graphing function *statistic.mean.conditional*() and we can specify the centroid of $\mathbf{x}$ and $\mathbf{y}$ as *statistic.mean.joint*(). The *conditional* methods are useful for displaying prediction models and the *joint* methods are useful for displaying multivariate distributions. See Table 8.2 for examples.

8.1.2 Form and Function

The consequence of distinguishing statistical methods from the graphics displaying them is to separate form from function. That is, the same statistic can be represented by different types of graphics, and the same type of graphic can be used to display two different statistics. Figure 8.1 illustrates the former and Figure 8.2 the latter. This separability of statistical and geometric objects is what gives a system a wide range of representational opportunities. Objects such as error bars, regression lines, and confidence intervals have evolved into customary forms that employ bars, lines, or other geometric objects. This makes them recognizable by viewers trained in certain disciplines, but we must understand that these representations do not necessarily reflect the deeper structure of the graphs. Stockbrokers are accustomed to high-low-close plots. Scientists are familiar with error bars. Both are using the same graphs but different statistical methods. On the other hand, we expect to see binned data displayed using histobars in a histogram, but sometimes points or lines are more useful for displaying bins.

No less important, the separation of form and function allows us to conserve computer code. The groupings in Table 8.1 are based not only on taxonomies drawn from the statistical literature, but also on shared algorithms needed to execute these functions. This saves both time and space.

Notice in Figure 8.1 that *region.confi.smooth.linear*() returns intervals ranging between upper and lower confidence bounds on a line, so that each graphic adjusts itself to an interval: *point* marks the upper and lower bound, *area* fills in the area between the bounds, *line* delineates the upper and lower bounds, and *bar* marks the bounds with a set of bars.

FRAME: **female*birth**
GRAPH: *point.region.confi.smooth.linear*()

FRAME: **female*birth**
GRAPH: *line.region.confi.smooth.linear*()

FRAME: **female*birth**
GRAPH: *area.region.confi.smooth.linear*()

FRAME: **female*birth**
GRAPH: *bar.region.confi.smooth.linear*()

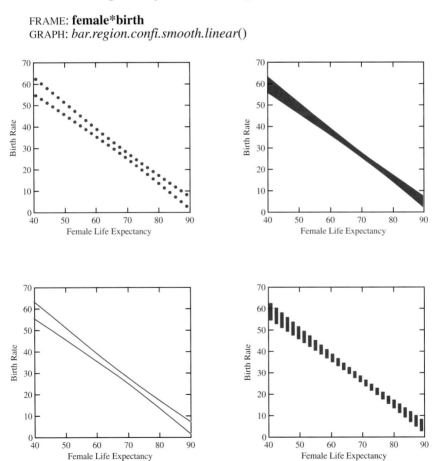

Figure 8.1 *Different graph types, same statistical method*

In Figure 8.2, *line* responds differently to functions (*statistic*, *smooth*) and multifunctions (*spread*, *confi*). For multifunctions, *line* is split into two or more segments. This is shown in the bottom two panels. The line splits in the lower left panel wherever there is more than one value on **female** for a value of **birth**, spanning the range of the data at that point.

FRAME: **female*birth**
GRAPH: *line.statistic.mean*()

FRAME: **female*birth**
GRAPH: *line.region.spread.range*()

FRAME: **female*birth**
GRAPH: *line.smooth.quadratic*()

FRAME: **female*birth**
GRAPH: *line.region.confi.smooth.linear*()

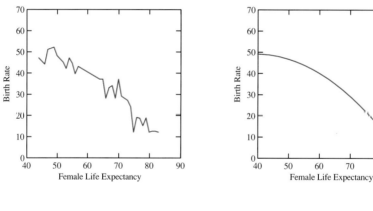

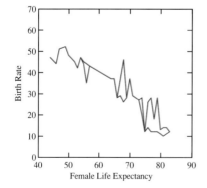
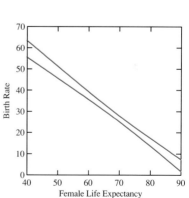

Figure 8.2 *Different statistical methods, same graph type*

8.2 Examples

Now we will proceed to explore the effects of these functional methods on each graph. The remainder of this section is organized by graph type.

8.2.1 Point

Graphs have a default statistical function. Their position is usually determined by one or more values on the domain and range. Graphs like *schema* employ a multivalued function (multifunction) that outputs values needed to determine the position of features like a midrange box, whiskers, and the outer points (outliers). For other graphs like *point*, *line*, *bar*, or *area*, position may be determined by a single-valued function (such as a mean) or a multifunction (such as a confidence interval). The type of the function determines how many shapes will be drawn for a given value in the domain.

8.2.1.1 Means in 2D

Figure 8.3 illustrates a *point* graphic on the countries data used in Chapter 1. The **gov** variable represents a classification of the type of government for each country. The **female** variable represents female life expectancy. Later graphics will also use **male**, the corresponding variable for male life expectancy. While Figure 1.1 used a subset of the countries, the full dataset of 57 countries is used in this chapter.

FRAME: *cat*(**gov**)*****birth**
GRAPH: *point.statistic.mean*()

FRAME: **female*****birth**
GRAPH: *point.statistic.mean*()

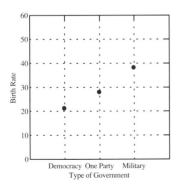 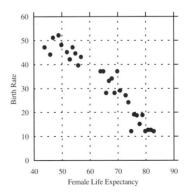

Figure 8.3 *Points on categorical (left) and continuous (right) domains*

The *point* graph can use a summary function to determine its location in the frame when there are duplicate cases in a subclass. If we use the *point.statistic.mean* method, then each point represents the mean of the **birth** values within each category of **gov** or value of **female**. Every dot represents a mean, even for continuous domains. The right graphic in Figure 8.3 looks like the cloud in the right panel of Figure 6.1 only because most of the data points are singletons (tuples with a unique first value). The mean of a singleton is the singleton's value.

8.2.1.2 Means in 3D

Figure 8.4 shows an example of *point* graphics in a 3D frame using the *point.statistic.mean* summary function. I have used a three-dimensional marker. Because of scale decoding and perspective illusion problems in 3D graphics (Cleveland, 1985; Kosslyn, 1994), it is usually better to represent summary graphics in 2D by facets (see Chapter 11). With point summary graphics, we want to be able to compare means across different groups. We need to discern the values of the means as well as their differences. The 3D environment makes this especially difficult, even when there are grid lines in the background. Our task in interpreting 3D scatterplots and surfaces, on the other hand, is quite different. With those objects, we need to discern the shape of the entire cloud or surface and make a wholistic judgment on the relations among the variables assigned to the axes. The 3D display can facilitate these tasks.

FRAME: *cat*(**urban**)*cat(**gov**)*birth
GRAPH: *point.statistic.mean*(*shape*("cube"))

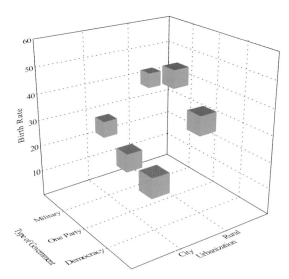

Figure 8.4 *3D point plot on categorical domain*

8.2.2 Line/Surface

Lines and surfaces are the same geometric graph type. The differences we associate with them are related to dimensionality rather than geometry. This subsection illustrates several variations in these graphs produced by different statistical methods. Some are simple functions and others are multifunctions.

8.2.2.1 Range Lines

Figure 8.5 shows a time series of the daily price of the stock of SPSS. The same series is used in Figure 8.13. Because I used the *line.region.spread.range()* graphing multifunction to position the *line* graph, we get two lines, one connecting the **low** and the other connecting the **high** values. This creates an envelope for the daily stock price.

Graphs like *point* and *line* divide into two or more instances when driven by multifunctions. Other graphs like *bar* and *area* do not divide for two-valued multifunctions because they are intrinsically interval valued. Other examples of this behavior are shown in Figure 8.1.

I plotted this series on a time scale using a monthly format. Notice that the tick marks bracketing the month of February are closer together than those bracketing other months. This means that the time scale on the horizontal axis is an interval (rather than categorical) scale. I will discuss times scales in more detail in Chapter 9.

FRAME: **date*(high+low)**
SCALE: *time(dim1,"mmm")*
GRAPH: *line.region.spread.range()*

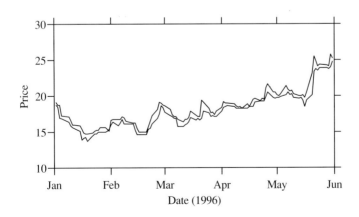

Figure 8.5 *Line plot of high-low-close*

8.2.2.2 The LOESS Smoother

The preceding graphing functions compute their summaries using data only for values in the range (y) for a given value in the domain (x_i). The *smooth* function uses other (x, y) values to compute an estimate at x_i. Parametric global smoothers do this by means of a function whose parameters are estimated from all the (x, y) values. Nonparametric smoothers do this with local functions estimated from (usually overlapping) values in the neighborhood of x_i.

Figure 8.6 shows a scatterplot of the birth rates against female life expectancy. It employs the LOESS smoother (Cleveland and Devlin, 1988), which is a locally weighted robust regression method. The smoother is specified by the *smooth.loess* function. The advantage of LOESS over other smoothers is that it employs a robust fitting method that makes it resistant to outliers in the data.

LOESS works by fitting polynomial (usually linear) regressions to fixed-size subsets of the data using a weighting function based on the distance of a data point from x_i, the location where we wish to fit $f(x)$. This fit is performed iteratively, using a *biweight* robust weighting function. The robust iterations tend to downweight large residuals, so that the final fit at x_i is more representative of the mass of the data near x_i.

The LOESS smoother indicates that the variables in Figure 8.6 are fairly linearly related to each other. We could explore a linear model to test this possibility. Local smoothers can help us in the choice of models and save us from erroneous conclusions, as the next example will show.

FRAME: **female*birth**
GRAPH: *line.smooth.loess()*
GRAPH: *point()*

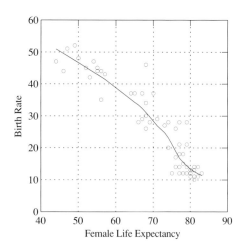

Figure 8.6 *LOESS smooth on scatterplot*

8.2.2.3 A Conditional Mode Kernel Smoother

Nonparametric smoothers can be especially useful in detecting nonlinearities before deciding to fit linear models. Figure 8.7 shows an example of an analysis whose conclusions might have been substantially different had non-parametric smoothers been used.

The data underlying the figure were digitized from a graphic in Gonnelli *et al.* (1996). Linear regressions (the green lines) were computed by the authors separately for males and females to support their conclusion that bone alkaline phosphatase increased linearly for both groups in relation to age. Figure 8.7 shows the plot for females. The curvilinear smoother is a modal kernel regression procedure (Scott, 1992) that fits an estimate of the conditional mode at points on the domain. The advantage of a modal smoother is that discontinuities are revealed when they exist in the data. When the data support it, we get two or more smoothers instead of one. Since the smoother can accommodate multimodality, it can even fit multiple estimates at given values in the domain. In other words, we can get two or more smoothers at different altitudes in the same scatterplot. No other smoothing method has this property.

The modal smoother shows that there is evidence of a discontinuity in BAP levels for females at menopause. The trend within the separate age levels is, if anything, slightly negative. Kernel smoothers are known for regressing (going flat) at their extremes. For these data, however, other local smoothers support the same conclusion. The BAP change is in level, not slope.

FRAME: **age*bone**
GRAPH: *line.smooth.mode.epanechnikov(color*("red"))
GRAPH: *line.smooth.linear(color*("green"))
GRAPH: *point*()

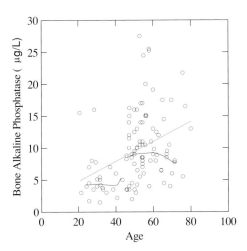

Figure 8.7 *Linear vs. modal smooth*

8.2.2.4 Joint Smoothing

Conditional smoothers minimize the sum of a function of the *vertical* distances (measured along *y*) between data values and fitted curve for all values measured on **x**. Joint smoothers generally minimize the sum of a function of the *shortest* distances between data values and fitted curve for all values measured on **x**. The joint method can be useful when there is no reason to distinguish a dependent variable from an independent variable. Hastie and Stuetzle (1989) generalize this idea to **principal curves**, which are curvilinear segments that pass through a set of points in a similar manner to the **medial axis** or **skeleton** of set of points (Preparata and Shamos, 1985).

Figure 8.8 shows a simple example of a joint linear fit to Quantitative and Verbal Graduate Record Examination scores of students in a psychology department. The conditional regression line (green) has a shallower slope than the joint regression line. The loss function for conditional linear regression is:

$$l_c = \sum_i (y_i - (b_0 + b_1 x_{1i}))^2$$

and the loss for the orthogonal regression is:

$$l_o = \sum_i \frac{(x_{1i} - (b_1 + b_2 x_{2i}))^2}{(1 + b_2^2)}$$

FRAME: **greq*grev**
GRAPH: *line.smooth.linear.conditional(color("green"))*
GRAPH: *line.smooth.linear.joint(color("red"))*
GRAPH: *point()*

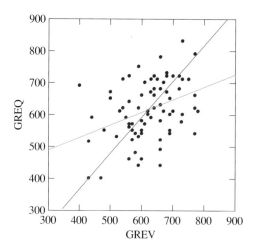

Figure 8.8 *Conditional (dashed) and joint (solid) linear smoothers*

8.2.2.5 2D Step Interpolation

Step interpolation fits points with a step function. Figure 8.9 shows a statistical plot called the Kaplan-Meier survival function. This plot displays the probability of survival from some onset time until a given time, estimated from a sample of cancer patients. The same graphic can be used on other populations subject to finite survival times, such as light bulbs, rumors, and marriages. Step interpolation is also useful for displaying empirical cumulative distribution functions (see Figure 9.2).

FRAME: **days*survive**
GRAPH: *line.smooth.step*()

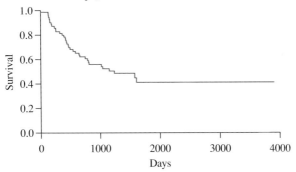

Figure 8.9 *Kaplan-Meier survival curve*

8.2.2.6 3D Step Interpolation

A 3D step smoother resembles a Voronoi tessellation (see Figure 7.50). Figure 8.10 shows a stepped surface fitted to the car data used in Figure 6.2.

FRAME: **weight*hp*quarter**
GRAPH: *surface.smooth.step*(*color*("green"))
GRAPH: *point*(*color*("blue"))

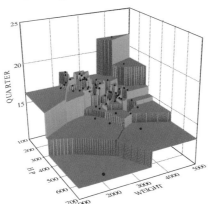

Figure 8.10 *3D Stepped Surface*

8.2.2.7 3D Inverse-Distance Smoothing

Figure 8.11 shows a 3D surface smoother on the difference between U.S. summer and winter temperatures. The specification includes a stereographic projected frame for the first two dimensions. The map is drawn within this projection via the *tile* graphic whose *position*(**longitude*latitude**) function places it on the bottom facet of the 3D frame. The temperature variation for each state is represented in the range by a *contour* graphic. The smoother for the *contour* graph is computed by the *smooth.mean.cauchy* function. The contours are colored with a *color.hue* attribute. Like the map itself, the contours are plotted on the bottom facet because only two variables are included in its *position*() attribute. Finally, the third graphic adds the surface representation of the smoother in 3D. This is accomplished by including all three variables of the specification implicitly in the *position*() attribute.

The map reveals that midwesterners are hardy folk. They are forced to tolerate fluctuations in the weather. And because of stiff airline fares (see Figure 10.36), they have difficulty fleeing to places where the weather is fair.

TRANS: **sw** = *diff*(**summer, winter**)
FRAME: **longitude*latitude*sw**
COORD: *project.stereo*(*dim1, dim2*)
GRAPH: *tile*(*shape.polygon*(**state**), *position*(**longitude*latitude**),
         color.hue(**sw**))
GRAPH: *contour.smooth.mean.cauchy*(*position*(**longitude*latitude**),
         color.hue(**sw**))
GRAPH: *surface.smooth.mean.cauchy*()

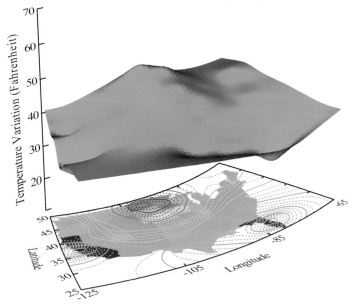

Figure 8.11 *Smooth of temperature variation in continental US*

8.2.3 Bar

Bar graphs represent interval-valued functions, or relations in which the range can have two values in the function set for a given tuple in the domain. Ordinarily, one end of an interval is fixed at the value of zero to make a bar chart. The following examples illustrate applications in which both ends are used.

8.2.3.1 Error bars

Sometimes we need to represent a range, standard deviation, confidence interval, or some other spread measure. The most common example is the ordinary error bar used in scientific graphics. Figure 8.12 shows an example for the birth rate data within different types of government.

FRAME: **gov*birth**
GRAPH: *bar.region.spread.se(shape("tick"))*
GRAPH: *point.statistic.mean()*

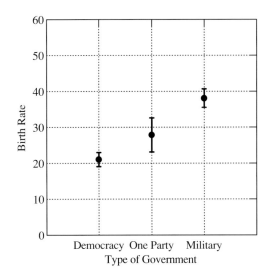

Figure 8.12 *Error bars*

The error bars in this figure are based on one standard-error in either direction from the mean estimates represented by the dots. I have used the *region.spread.se()* function to compute an interval containing the mean, plus or minus one standard error. The shape of the bars is arbitrary. The one chosen for the figure, *shape("tick")*, is the most popular, but solid bars and other graphics for representing an interval would do as well. We could use several different graphics to represent several different spread statistics at the same time (standard deviation and range, for example).

8.2.3.2 Range Bars

The high-low-close graphic used for financial trading series is a combination of a *bar* and a *point* graphic. Figure 8.13 shows a high-low-close graphic for the SPSS stock series. The shape chosen for the graphic emphasizes the closing price with a horizontal tick. Other graphic shapes are possible.

The *bar.region.spread.range()* graphing function creates the vertical lines by setting shape with the *shape*("line") aesthetic attribute function (see Figure 9.5 for range bars on this stock series using regular bars). The *range()* statistical method returns two values that define the ends of each bar. The closing price is positioned by the *point.statistic.median()* graphing function. Because there are only three *y* (**high+low+close**) values for each *x* (**date**) value, the *median()* method always returns the **close** value.

The time scale is noteworthy. I will discuss time scales in Chapter 9. Notice that the time scale spaces dates unevenly according to the lengths of different months. The interval between February and March is smaller than the other intervals because there are fewer days in February. Weekends properly appear as blank spaces because of this time scale. This scaling of time variables is especially critical for graphics based on interrupted or unevenly spaced time series data, such as financial series or clinical trials.

FRAME: **date*(high+low+close)**
SCALE: *time(dim1,"mmm")*
GRAPH: *bar.region.spread.range(shape*("line"))
GRAPH: *point.statistic.median(shape*("hyphen"))

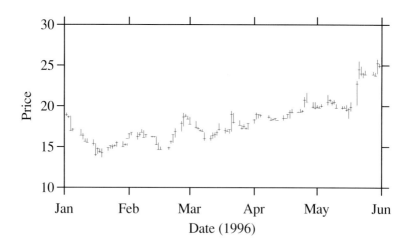

Figure 8.13 *High-low-close plot*

8.2.4 *Densities*

Densities measure the relative concentration of a sample at different values of a variable. These statistical measures range from ordinary histograms to dot plots to kernel density estimates.

8.2.4.1 *Ordinary Histogram*

The *histobar* graph creates histograms. The ordinary histogram is constructed by binning data on a uniform grid. Although this is probably the most widely used statistical graphic, it is one of the more difficult ones to compute. Several problems arise, including choosing the number of bins (bars) and deciding where to place the cutpoints between bars.

   The choice of bin width h (or its dual, k, the number of bins) has been a topic of research in the statistical community for more than 70 years. Sturges (1926) proposed that k be proportional to $log_2(n)$, where n is the sample size. He reasoned this from the approximation of the binomial by the normal distribution. For the binomial,

$$n = \sum_{m=0}^{k} \binom{k}{m} = 2^k \text{ , so}$$

$$k = log_2(n)$$

Doane (1976) showed that more bins are needed, particularly for skewed data. He included a measure of skewness into the calculation of k. If we can't read the data to calculate skewness before doing the histogram, the approximation

$$k = 3log_{10}(n)log_2(n)$$

increases k enough to cover most of the examples Doane describes.

   Working with h instead of k frames the problem in terms of density estimation. Freedman and Diaconis (1981) computed bin width from asymptotic theoretical results. For a normal distribution, Scott (1979) derived a bin width

$$h = 3.5sn^{-1/3} \text{ ,}$$

where s is the sample standard deviation.

   An additional problem arises when data are granular. The above estimates should not be used when data consist of only a few distinct values. If our data consist of the integers between 1 and 7, for example, we should pick 7 bins regardless of the sample size. It is worth a preliminary pass through the data to determine if granularity exists. A simple test is to sort the data and take differences between adjacent values. If these differences are all an integer multiple of the smallest nonzero difference, then granularity exists. In this case the bin width should be the smallest nonzero difference or the width calculated with Scott's formula, whichever is larger.

Deciding where to place the cutpoints between bars is not simple either. Generally, we want one cutpoint to be at zero, but this should not be a hard rule. Scott (1992) showed that the choice of cutpoints between bars can affect substantially the shape of the histogram. To counteract this tendency, he constructed a density estimator called the Averaged Shifted Histogram (ASH) by shifting the cutpoints while maintaining bin width and then averaging all the bins. There is a trade-off between choosing cutpoints at nice values (see Chapter 9) and choosing them to create a relatively smooth histogram.

8.2.4.2 Gap Histogram

Figure 8.14 shows an ordinary histogram of birth rate in the left panel and a gap histogram in the right. The gap binning is a partial Voronoi tessellation of the data in one dimension (see Figure 7.50 for a 2D example). The edge of each bin represents the Voronoi boundary midway between two points. Not all boundaries are computed, however; some bins are left to contain more than one data point. The area of a bar in either graphic is determined by the *count()* of the cases in the bar times its width. The gap histogram is more useful for identifying gaps in the data than for representing the density itself.

DATA: **count** = *count*(50)
FRAME: **birth*****count**
GRAPH: *histobar.density.bin.rect()*

DATA: **count** = *count*(50)
FRAME: **birth*****count**
GRAPH: *histobar.density.bin.gap()*

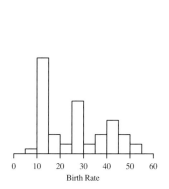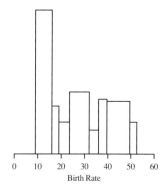

Figure 8.14 *Histogram and gap histogram of birth rates*

Figure 8.15 shows in more detail how a gap histogram works. I have superimposed a dot plot on the gap histogram to illustrate where the cuts are made. Not every adjacent pair of dots is separated by bins. The algorithm stops when it finds local clumps that are better left together than split.

DATA: **count** = *count*(50)
TRANS: **zero** = 0
FRAME: **birth*count**
GRAPH: *histobar.density.bin.gap*()
GRAPH: *point*(*position.stack*(**birth*zero**))

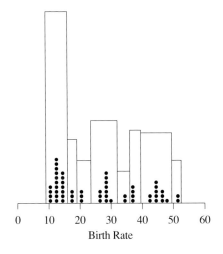

Figure 8.15 *Gap histogram with superimposed dot plot*

8.2.4.3 Dot Plots

Asymmetrical dot plots (and their close cousins, symmetrical dot plots) appear in a variety of statistical graphics packages. Almost every one of these displays is computed incorrectly. Most of these packages simply bin the data as if they were doing a regular histogram and then use dots instead of bars to represent the count in each bar. Hand-drawn dot plots, used for well over a century in medicine, economics, and other fields, place the dots where the data values actually occur so that they avoid misleadingly granularizing the data. The stacking that we see in dot plots should happen only when two or more scaled data values differ by less than some proportion of the diameter of a dot. Wilkinson (1999) discusses the details of the problem.

Figure 8.16 shows an example for the sleep dataset. I have logged the scale and used square dot shapes to emphasize the uneven spacing of the dots. For the singletons, the center of the square is placed exactly above the scale value it represents. This makes dot plots superior to histograms for recognizing and decoding outliers.

FRAME: **brainweight**
SCALE: *log*(**brainweight,** 10)
GRAPH: *point*(*position.stack*(), *shape*("square"))

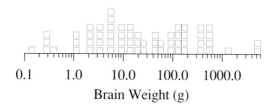

0.1   1.0   10.0   100.0   1000.0

Brain Weight (g)

Figure 8.16 *Logged dot plot*

8.2.4.4 Kernel Densities

There are many methods for estimating probability densities from sample data (Silverman, 1986; Scott, 1992). Figure 8.17 shows two popular density estimates superimposed on histograms of **brainweight** on a log scale. The *normal* method uses a parametric Gaussian distribution to produce the curve from sample estimates of its two parameters. The *kernel* method uses nonparametric kernel density estimation with an Epanechnikov kernel (Silverman, 1986).

DATA: **prop** = *proportion*()
FRAME: **brainweight*prop**
SCALE: *log*(*dim1*, 10)
GRAPH: *histobar.density.bin.rect*()
GRAPH: *line.density.normal*(*color*("red"))

DATA: **prop** = *proportion*()
FRAME: **brainweight*prop**
SCALE: *log*(*dim1*, 10)
GRAPH: *histobar.density.bin.rect*()
GRAPH: *line.density.kernel.epanechnikov*(*color*("red"))

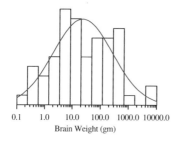
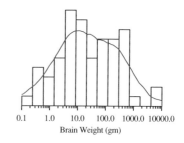

Figure 8.17 *Normal and kernel densities superimposed on histogram*

The vertical axis is not shown, but this dimension consists of the density represented by the smooths. The densities match the height of the histogram bars because we used a *proportion*() function for the vertical measure of the histogram bars. This requires an area calculation for both the histograms and the densities that sums to 1.

8.2.4.5 Bivariate Densities

Scott (1992) and Silverman (1986) discuss 2D and higher dimensional kernel density estimates. Figure 8.18 shows joint bivariate densities for the predation data. The left panel shows contours for a a normal bivariate density estimate and the right panel shows contours for a kernel density estimate. The normal density is computed from estimates of the parameters of the bivariate normal distribution and the kernel density is computed from an Epanechnikov kernel. This kernel looks like a quadratic function (parabolic solid) in two dimensions that is moved around the plane of the points and is used to compute a weighted sum of the counts of the observations within the bounds of the kernel.

```
DATA: prop = proportion()
FRAME: bodyweight*brainweight
SCALE: log(dim1, 10)
SCALE: log(dim2, 10)
GRAPH: point()
GRAPH: contour.density.normal.joint(color.hue(prop))
```

```
DATA: prop = proportion()
FRAME: bodyweight*brainweight
SCALE: log(dim1, 10)
SCALE: log(dim2, 10)
GRAPH: point()
GRAPH: contour.density.kernel.epanechnikov.joint(color.hue(prop))
```

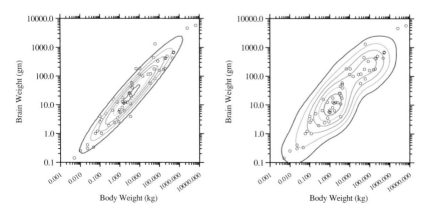

Figure 8.18 *Normal and kernel bivariate densities*

8.2.5 Multivariate Box Plots

The behavior of the box plot is different from what we saw in Figure 6.11 when we use a joint multifunction on a continuous domain. Figure 8.19 shows an example. Notice that the box plot is composed of peeled convex hulls. Tukey (1974; also see Huber, 1972) suggested this method for generalizing the box plot to more than one dimension. Each hull in this plot contains a different percentage of the total number of countries. The outermost hull contains all the countries, and each successive hull contains fewer by about 25 percent.

FRAME: **female*birth**
GRAPH: *schema.density.quantile.joint*()
GRAPH: *point.statistic.median.joint*()

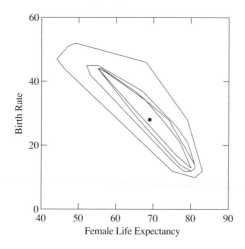

Figure 8.19 *Bivariate box plot*

8.2.6 Tile

We have seen how functions can be used to create different tilings using the same tile graph. This section shows a variety of examples.

8.2.6.1 Hexagon Binning

Figure 8.20 shows different binning methods for a two-variable histogram. The left panel shows a regular rectangular grid whose density is denoted by *color.hue*. The right panel shows hexagon binning (Carr *et al.*, 1987), where density in the bins is denoted by *color.brightness*. The *size*() of the bins is fixed by a parameter. Both graphics can be viewed as projections of 3D figures into 2D. These graphics were computed on the Allison and Cicchetti (1976) data. The variables are measured brain weight in grams and body weight in kilograms of the batch of animals. The variables are displayed on *log* scales.

DATA: **count** = *count*()
FRAME:**bodyweight*brainweight**
SCALE: *log*(*dim1*, 10)
SCALE: *log*(*dim2*, 10)
GRAPH: *tile.density.bin.rect*(*size*(.08), *color.hue*(**count**))

DATA: **count** = *count*()
FRAME:**bodyweight*brainweight**
SCALE: *log*(*dim1*, 10)
SCALE: *log*(*dim2*, 10)
GRAPH: *tile.density.bin.hex*(*size*(.08), *color.brightness*(**count**))

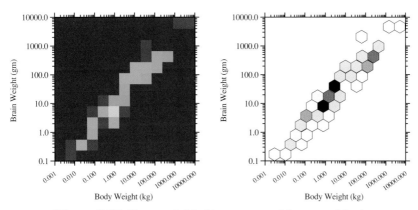

Figure 8.20 *Two variable histogram and hexagon binning*

8.2.7 *Path*

The *path*() graphing function computes a path according to the order of a set of points in a list. The order may come from the original dataset or we can sort the data. The following method computes an ordering using an algorithm.

8.2.7.1 *Traveling Salesman Problem*

Figure 8.21 shows a path that rejoins itself to make a complete circuit. The example here comprises a short path through the continental US that covers every state just once and returns to the beginning. This graphic is an approximate solution to the **traveling salesman problem** (Preparata and Shamos, 1985). Several caveats are in order, however. First, the path was computed in Euclidean 2D space after transforming with the stereographic projection. This method does not produce the shortest path on the surface of the globe. Second, the locus of the point in each state is arbitrary and was not chosen to make the path shorter. Finally, the solution itself was computed by simulated annealing (Press *et al.*, 1986), which cannot guarantee the shortest path. The advantage of this sub-optimal algorithm, however, is that Figure 8.21 can be computed in a few seconds on a desktop computer. The *edge.tsp*() function computes the path and ensures that it returns to its start in a closed loop or circuit.

FRAME: **longitude*latitude**
COORD: *project.stereo*()
GRAPH: *tile*(*shape.polygon*(**state**))
GRAPH: *path.edge.tsp*()

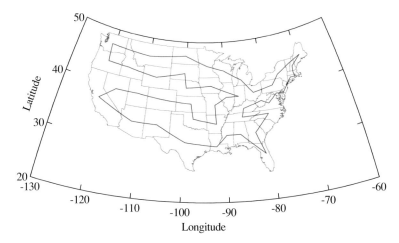

Figure 8.21 *Short path through US*

8.2.8 Link

The *link*() graphing function computes a set of links between points. The *edge*() functions offer several different methods for computing these links.

8.2.8.1 Minimum Spanning Tree

A minimum spanning tree (MST) connects points represented in a space using line segments that have minimum total length and that join all points without creating any circuits (cycles). The result is that any two nodes in an MST are connected by exactly one path. This tree has the shortest total length of all possible trees connecting the points in the plotted space. Preparata and Shamos (1985) survey algorithms for computing this tree efficiently and Hartigan (1975a) discusses its application to cluster analysis. Deleting the longest link in a minimum spanning tree results in two clusters whose total edge length is minimum among all possible two-cluster trees. Recursively deleting links follows the same computational steps (in reverse order) as the widely used **single linkage**, or **nearest neighbor** cluster analysis algorithm. The algorithm is conventionally applied to a Euclidean minimum spanning tree, but it can be adapted to other coordinates.

Figure 8.22 shows a Euclidean minimum spanning tree on the fiddler crab data. For our fiddler crabs, the solution in Figure 8.22 shows the smallest amount of wire needed to install telephones in their holes so they can communicate with each other without clicking their claws.

FRAME: **crabx*craby**
GRAPH: *point*()
GRAPH: *link.edge.mst*()

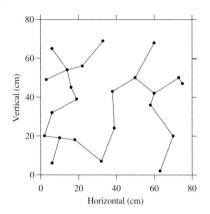

Figure 8.22 *Minimum spanning tree*

8.2.8.2 *Hull*

Figure 8.23 shows an example of a convex hull. As we shall see in Section 8.2.8.3, the convex hull is computable from the outermost segments of the Delaunay triangulation. The peeled hull (see Figure 8.19) is not a subgraph of the same triangulation, however. It makes more sense to compute hulls with routines tailored to the problem (Preparata and Shamos, 1985). Our fiddler crabs have installed a convex hull to establish a gated retirement community.

FRAME: **crabx*craby**
GRAPH: *point*()
GRAPH: *link.edge.hull*()

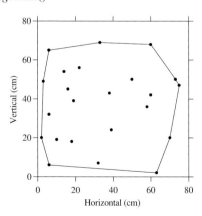

Figure 8.23 *Convex hull around crab holes*

8.2.8.3 Triangulation

A triangulation joins points with segments such that all the bounded regions
are triangles. Figure 8.24 shows a Delaunay triangulation on the crab data.

FRAME: **crabx*craby**
GRAPH: *point*()
GRAPH: *link.edge.delaunay*()

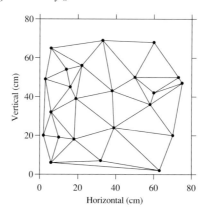

Figure 8.24 *Delaunay triangulation of crab holes*

Figure 8.25 superimposes the last three figures plus the Voronoi diagram.

FRAME: **crabx*craby**
GRAPH: *point*()
GRAPH: *tile*(*shape.poly*("voronoi"), *color*("red"))
GRAPH: *link.edge.mst*(*color*("blue"))
GRAPH: *link.edge.hull*(*color*("violet"))
GRAPH: *link.edge.delaunay*(*color*("green"))

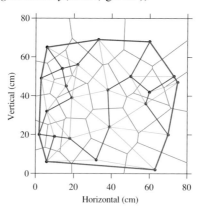

Figure 8.25 *Convex hull (purple), Voronoi tessellation (red), Delaunay
triangulation (green), and minimum spanning tree (blue)*

The Delaunay triangulation is a dual of the Voronoi tessellation (Preparata and Shamos, 1985). The computation of one implies the computation of the other. The Voronoi edges are perpendicular to the sides of the Delaunay traingles. Each Delaunay segment bisects a Voronoi edge. The convex hull is the outermost collection of line segments from the Delaunay triangulation. Many algorithms for computing the Voronoi-Delaunay problem yield the convex hull as a by-product. Finally, the minimum spanning tree is a subgraph of the Delaunay triangulation.

8.2.8.4 Building Bridges with Join

The *edge.join*() function joins sets of points from a blend. If two variables are blended, *edge.join*() joins pairs, if three are blended, *edge.join*() joins triples, and so on. A bridge is a *join* that links points from two or more sets of variables in the same graphic. It is designed to display repeated measures, migrations, flows, biplots, correspondence diagrams, and other multiple relations over time or space. Figure 8.26 illustrates an application of this graphic to **Procrustes rotation** (see Borg and Groenen, 1997).

FRAME: **caragility*carsize+dogagility*dogsize**
GRAPH: *point*(*label*(**car+dog**))
GRAPH: *link.edge.join*()

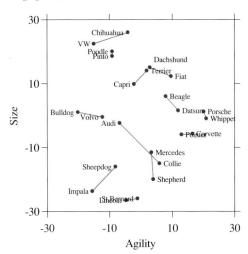

Figure 8.26 *Bridge plot*

Procrustes rotation matches two or more spatial configurations to each other using a loss function based on Euclidean distance or some other discrepancy measure between corresponding points. The data are from Wilkinson (1975). Cars and dogs were rated for similarity by dedicated (obsessed) car and dog club members. Each subject rated a set of ordinary objects known (and loved) intensely and another set known only superficially. (There were no subjects with enough time in a day to be fascinated with both.) On the basis of external measures, correspondences were inferred between pairs of cars and dogs. These links were used to establish the ordering of coordinates for the Procrustes rotation. Figure 8.26 shows the rotation of the results of two multi-dimensional scalings of the car and dog similarity ratings. The graphics offer a visual summary of the goodness of fit. The shorter the lines, the better the fit. The results of this analysis have absolutely no commercial potential.

8.2.8.5 Drawing Vectors with Join

Figure 8.27 illustrates how *join* can be used to plot vectors from an origin. The variables **factor1** and **factor2** are the first two columns of the matrix **V** in the singular value decomposition $\mathbf{X} = \mathbf{UDV}^{\mathrm{T}}$. The matrix **X** consists of scaled binary data on grounds for divorce among 50 US states in 1971. The original source is Long (1971), analyzed in Wilkinson *et al.* (1996). By constructing a new variable called **zero**, we join all the points to paired values at (0,0). In addition, we choose arrows to shape the vectors.

DATA: **zero** = *constant*(0)
FRAME: **zero*zero + factor1*factor2**
GRAPH: *link.edge.join*(*shape*("arrow"), *label*(**ground**))

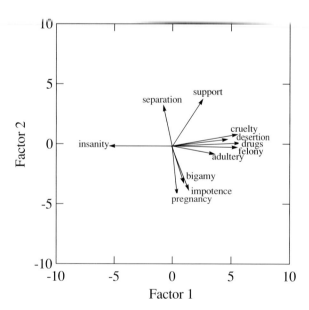

Figure 8.27 *Vector plot.*

8.2.8.6 Drawing Vectors to a Line or Surface with Join

Figure 8.27 illustrates the use of *edge.join()* for drawing vectors to a line. This method can be used to draw vectors to a curve or surface as well. The data are based on the residuals from a linear regression of **birth** on **female** for our countries dataset. In this figure, vectors are drawn from residual points to points at a zero value.

We construct this column of zero values by employing the data function *constant()* in the expression **zero** = *constant*(0). Because the frame model contains **female*(residual+zero)**, the *link.edge.join()* graphing function connects points in **female*residual** with points in **female*zero**, producing the vertical lines. We don't want two sets of *point* clouds, however. The illusory contour of the spikes is sufficient to demarcate the values at zero (Levine and Shefner, 1991). Therefore, we create another variable **miss** = *constant*(.) to use for the *point* graph. By setting *position*(**female*residual+miss*miss**) for point(), we assure that only the **female*residual** points get plotted, since missing values are ignored.

DATA: **zero** = *constant*(0)
DATA: **miss** = *constant*(.)
FRAME: **female*(residual+zero)**
GRAPH: *link.edge.join()*
GRAPH: *point(position(***female*residual+miss*miss***))*

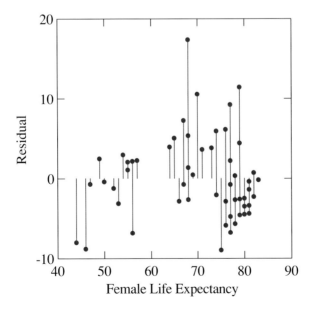

Figure 8.28 *Spikes for residuals*

8.2.8.7 Drawing Trees

Among the most widespread uses of graphical trees in statistics and data analysis are displays of the results of hierarchical cluster analysis (Hartigan, 1975a) and recursive partitioning schemes (Breiman *et al.*, 1984). These structures also appear in the directed graphs used to represent trees in computer science algorithms (Knuth, 1969).

A tree is often represented by a dataset organized as a **linked list**. The rows of this dataset contain the set of triples

$$\{(x_1, y_1, p_1), (x_2, y_2, p_2), \dots, (x_n, y_n, p_n)\}$$

The first two elements of each triple are the coordinates of the nodes. The third element in each triple is a pointer to the parent of each node. Conventionally, the root pointer is set to null and the remaining pointers contain the ordinal index of the nodes in the list. This format allows us to represent both binary trees (*btrees*) and general trees with one or more branches at different nodes.

Figure 8.29 shows a tree depicting the results of a single-linkage clustering of the cities data used in Chapter 7. The specification assumes that the clustering output yields a dataset whose data-triples in the linked list are named and organized as: (**xnode, ynode, parent**). The coordinates of the spatial tree (**xnode, ynode**) are joined by branches according to the inheritance rules given in the pointer **parent**. The distance scale (based on **xnode**) measures the closest distance between pairs of points in the two clusters joined at each node. The *edge tree*() function operates on the specified frame variables (**ynode** and **xnode**) as well as the pointer variable **parent**.

FRAME: **xnode*ynode**
GRAPH: *link.edge.tree(position(***parent***)), label(***rating***))*

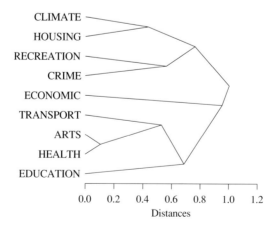

Figure 8.29 *Cluster tree*

8.3 A Statistical Scenario

In the introduction to this chapter, I gave several reasons for placing statistics under the control of graphs by making them graph methods. This is different enough from the way most statistical graphics packages work that we need to examine it further. The following example illustrates the behavior this design produces.

Most statistical graphics systems perform transformations (when requested) and pass through the data in one step to accumulate basic statistics that are used in creating a chart. In these systems, the scene assembly and rendering components are fed aggregated data to make *bars* and other graphics. The motivation for doing this is to keep the architecture simple by computing statistics before scene assembly so that different graphic elements can share common aggregated statistics. This approach severely limits the capabilities of a graphics system because it makes statistics determine functionality for graphs rather than the other way around. Ironically, limitation is not required to maintain simplicity. In a properly designed graphics system, we can employ data views and proxies to make sure that multiple graphic clients of the same statistic do not force the system to duplicate the computations.

The following scenario illustrates why graphs must control their own statistics. It is an instance of a dynamic graphical interface that is essential for exploration and data mining. Unlike other dynamic scripts, this scenario requires the recalculation of a different statistic for each separate graphical element in a common frame every time a button is pressed or a slider moved. And each recalculation requires a pass through the raw data, because a nonlinear transformation is involved. Even though such interactions are fundamental to real data mining, where MOLAPs have been heavily promoted by some, this scenario cannot be implemented by a MOLAP or data cube model (see Section 3.5.1).

This scenario is due to Sandy Weisberg (personal communication), who choreographed it using Lisp-Stat (Tierney, 1991). The application involves one of the most widely used modeling procedures: linear regression. Weisberg connected a residual plot (see Figure 8.27) to a transformation controller in order to examine dynamically the distribution of residuals under different values of a power transformation applied to the dependent variable in a linear regression. The reason for doing this is to be able to identify a proper power transformation by examining the residuals directly. Pressing a button or slider to determine the value of the power parameter (p) helps the investigator understand the behavior of the transformation over a plausible range of values. The alternative would be to run hundreds of analyses and then to examine the residuals for each analysis by plotting them separately. Although this example involves power transformations, it is only one of many similar operations that are required in a graphical system for data modeling and discovery.

8.3.1 Specification

We will use the sleep dataset in Allison and Cicchetti (1976) to predict brain weight from the average number of hours of sleep an animal takes per day (no causal relation is implied). The specification is similar to Weisberg's, but I will add a regression plot so that we can see the residuals and the regression at the same time.

FRAME: **sleep*brainweight**
SCALE: *pow*(**brainweight**, *p*)
GRAPH: *point*()
GRAPH: *line.smooth.linear*(*color*("red"))
GUIDE: *axis1*(*label*("Daily Hours of Sleep"))
GUIDE: *axis2*(*label*("Brainweight"))

DATA: **zero** = *constant*(0)
DATA: **miss** = *constant*(.)
TRANS: **bp** = *pow*(**brainweight**, *p*)
TRANS: **resid** = *residual.linear.student*(**sleep**, **bp**)
FRAME: **sleep*resid + sleep*zero**
GRAPH: *link.edge.join*()
GRAPH: *line.smooth.loess*(*position*(**sleep*resid + miss*miss**), *color*("red"))
GUIDE: *axis2*(*label*("Linear Regression Residual"))

The first specification produces the lower plot in Section Figure 8.30 and the second specification produces the upper. The lower plot includes a *point* graphic for the scatterplot cloud and a *line.smooth.linear* graphic for the regression line. The upper plot contains the residuals. The residuals are calculated with the *residual.linear.student*() function, which computes studentized residuals so that we can compare them to a *t* distribution. Instead of *point*(), I have used spikes to zero with a *link.edge.join*() in the residual plot so that we can see the distribution of the residuals more clearly. In addition, I have included a *line.smooth.loess*() smoother in order to highlight any trend in the residuals across values of the predictor (there is not supposed to be a trend). The transformations will be accomplished through the *pow*() function applied as a scale specification in the lower frame and a data transformation in the upper. Since both functions share the same parameter (*p*), the transformation will be shared by both frames.

The position function for the *line.smooth.loess*() smoother in the upper plot requires some explanation. It includes a blend of **sleep*resid** and **miss*miss**. I used the same device in Figure 8.28 to prevent points from plotting. Here, it prevents the smoother from trying to include the zero values in its computation. Since the blend operation is like stacking columns on top of each other, we use the missing values to force the graphing function to ignore the extra cases. This position function replaces the variables used in the frame model **sleep*resid + sleep*zero** so that *line.smooth.loess*() never uses them. The frame model nevertheless determines the limits of the frame, so we must be careful to assure that the frame model is large enough to contain the graphics.

8.3.2 *Assembly*

The assembly of the scene parallels the structure of the specification. First, each Frame object is constructed. This involves 1) parsing the frame model and executing the algebra, 2) linking variables to appropriate data, 3) associating the variables with the dimensions specified in the model, 4) registering the transforms, and 5) registering the scale for each dimension. Next, the graphs are set into action. Once the Frames are known, the graph computations may be done in any order, or even in parallel if the environment is **multi-threaded** (allowing separate processes to execute independently or simultaneously). The *point* graph, for example, asks its Frame for values on **brainweight** and **sleep**. Frame notices that a scale transformation is registered for **brainweight** and requests DataView to return transformed values. Since the value of the exponent is 1, no transformation is performed. The *point* graph now has data to assemble itself, so it puts together a package of tuples and attribute values (default symbol shape and color) and sends the package off to Display to render a cloud whenever it is ready.

The *line.smooth.loess()* graphing function asks its Frame to return values on **resid** and **zero** and **sleep**. Frame has a *residual()* transform registered for **resid**, so DataView must perform linear regression calculations and return studentized residuals to *line.smooth.loess()*. Because a *pow()* transformation is registered for **bp**, which is used in *residual()*, the data values must be transformed before doing the regression (although the value of the exponent is still 1 at this time). As far as the graphs are concerned, they are receiving values for their own calculations. They don't care how those values were assembled. The *line.smooth.loess()* graphing function will proceed to do *another* regression on the residuals using the LOESS locally parametric regression smoother, and *link.edge.join()* will connect the residuals to a zero level on **resid**.

A similar process is followed by the other graphs. If more than one graph requests values on the same variable, DataView can **cache** the requests (collect the requests for execution at one time) or **persist** the view (hold the values until clients stop registering requests for them) in order to make things more efficient in a client-server or Web environment. The essential thing to notice about this assembly process is that each graph must do something different with its data. Geometry drives data. However, there is no implication here that every graph must waste time reading data and doing the same work over and over again. Frame is a central clearing-house for graph activity and maintains the knowledge needed to keep graphs from thrashing.

8.3.3 *Display*

Figure 8.30 shows the graphic from this specification in the SYSTAT graphics controller window (Wilkinson, 1998). This program has a display system that implements **widgets**, or graphical toolbar controls, for dynamic graphics. The tool we will use is the *Y-Power* spinner widget, which sets p for the scale specification for **brainweight**. (The other tools are irrelevant to the scenario). The lower graphic in the window shows a regression line that does not pass through the center of the y values for most x values. This is because the brain weight data are severely skewed. The residuals plot directly above corroborates the finding; the LOESS smoother reveals a trend in the residuals due to this skewness. If our regression were appropriate, the residuals would be fairly symmetrically distributed about zero across the whole horizontal range.

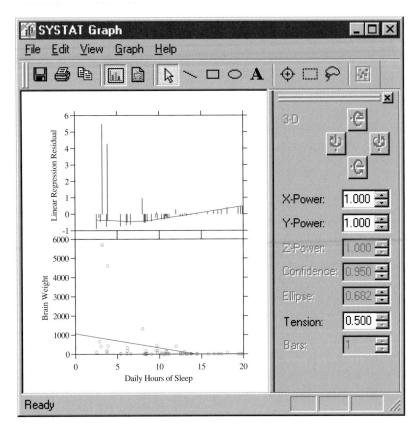

Figure 8.30 *Regression and residuals*

8.3.4 *Tap*

Now we are ready to press that *Y-Power* spinner on the controller toolbar. We want to lower the p exponent toward zero to see if transforming **brainweight** with $f: y^p$ will improve our regression fit. Figure 8.31 shows the result after we have tapped the *Y-Power* spinner to change its value to .5 (square-root). The regression now appears more reasonable. The residual plot shows less trend in the LOESS smooth and the values are more evenly spread around zero.

How did this happen? First of all, the controller for the *Y-Power* spinner sent out a ScaleChangeEvent message. Each Frame has a listener for this and other messages and orders a redraw because the graphic no longer reflects the state of the specification. All the graphs receive this redraw message and put together a new set of geometry based on the changed situation. The only difference between the ensuing events and the assembly I described in Section 8.3.2 is that the transformation is now applied to **brainweight** because $p = .5$. For example, the *line.smooth.loess*() graphing function asks its Frame to return values on **resid** and **sleep**. That Frame has a *residual*() transform registered for **resid**, so DataView will compute a linear regression and return studentized residuals to *line.smooth.loess*(). Before it can do that, however, Frame has a power transform registered on **brainweight**. So, the **brainweight** values are square-rooted before the regression is computed. At this point, *line.smooth.loess*() is looking at the residuals from a power-transformed regression. It proceeds to do its own LOESS regression smoothing on these residuals and presents the resulting geometric curve to Displayer.

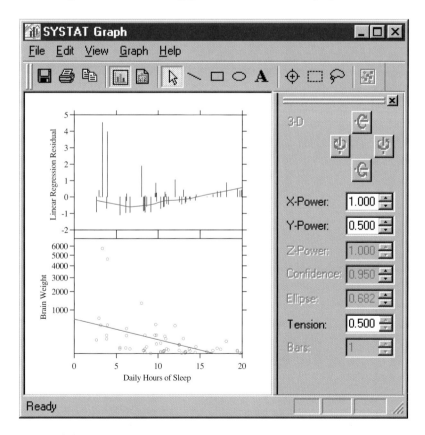

Figure 8.31 *Regression and residuals under square-root transformation*

Notice that some elements, such as *axis1*(), get values that are unchanged by the event that originally forced the redraw. They remain unchanged because there is no power transformation hooked up to their data. We can save some of this effort by having Frame keep track of regions on the Canvas where graphs are being drawn, so that unchanged areas can be left untouched. In my experience, this is not worth the extra accounting effort.

8.3.5 *Tap Tap*

We tap the *Y-power* spinner again and its value drops to zero. The display refreshes with the graphic shown in Figure 8.32. At this point, we have a fairly good model. The LOESS smoother and spikes show some irregularity in the residuals, but not enough to worry us. Incidentally, the scale numbers on the lower graphic are intended to collide at the top of the vertical axis. This signals the extent of the transformation. On the computer display, they move in real time as the button is pressed, so their behavior is smooth and predictable.

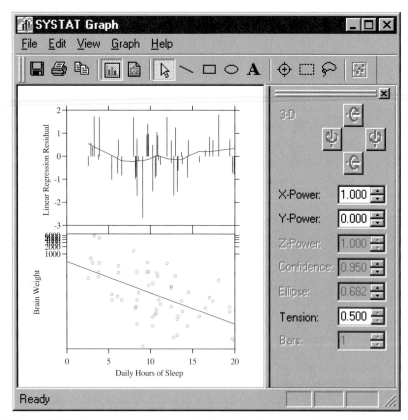

Figure 8.32 *Regression and residuals under log (pow=0) transformation*

8.3.6 *Tap Tap Tap*

Figure 8.33 shows the result of a tap on the *Tension* spinner near the bottom of the control panel. The controller for this spinner sends out a message to any smoothers or statistical procedures that have a tension parameter. This parameter governs the amount of smoothing desired: large tension values correspond to more smoothing, smaller values to less. Its default value is $t = .5$, halfway between zero and one.

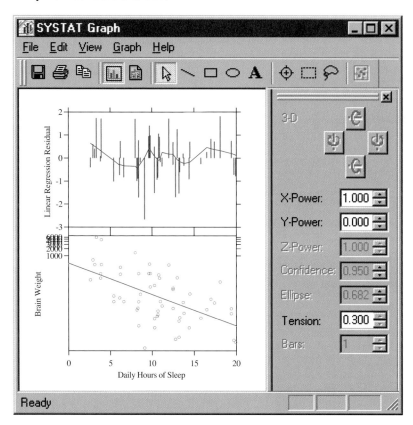

Figure 8.33 *Regression and residuals under log transformation, tension=.3*

When notified of a TensionChangeEvent, each Frame broadcasts a redraw to the graphs. This time, the *line.smooth.loess* graph relaxes a bit because the value of one of its parameters has been ordered changed through its Frame. Notice, again, that none of the other graphs are modified, because they do not have tension parameters to listen for. This type of local behavior under the control of widgets through Frame messaging can be used to produce animations over statistical parameters. We can, in effect, see a movie of the behavior of a graph like *line.smooth.loess* when tension changes in small increments over a larger range in real time. To save space, I have illustrated only one tension event over a large step. In SYSTAT, these taps change all the spinners in increments of .1 so that we can see small changes in tension or power instead of sudden jumps.

The point of this scenario is to demonstrate the value of putting statistical calculations under the control of graphs so that we can fine-tune a system and represent behavior that is far more nuanced than what we see in typical data mining displays. What our general design attempts to do is to get away from static graphic entities and instead to treat graphs and their statistical methods like little creatures that respond to different messages and do their calculations in their own peculiar ways. After all, these statistical methods evolved over centuries in the interplay between mathematics and engineering. My evolutionary perspective is not simply poetic license. I believe, following Gould (1996) and Pinker (1997), that evolutionary theory can provide clues to good design: build an ecosystem of many small organisms instead of a single dinosaur. Dinosaurs were adaptive, but nobody beats insects.

Finally, this scenario was intended to illustrate the importance of autonomy and cooperation among graphs in assembling and using statistical methods. Some contemporary graphics and statistics programs can perform part of this scenario already because they are hard-wired to animate, link, drill-down, and brush within certain widely-used graphics such as bar charts and scatterplots. The real trick, however, is to replicate this behavior for any graph, on any scale, in any coordinate system, in any ensemble of graphics. A graphics grammar gives us the means.

8.4 Summary

Table 8.2 summarizes the statistical methods discussed in this chapter. Each cell of the table shows an exemplar for the type of method in 1D, 2D, or 3D. I have included points to represent data values in the graphical exemplars; these are colored light blue. The graphics that display the results of statistical methods are colored dark blue. The conditional methods are in the upper half of the table and the joint methods are in the lower.

The conditional methods compute a unique value or unique set of values on a selected variable for every distinct value of x. For 1D, x is a constant. For 2D, x is a variable. For 3D, x is a two-dimensional vector-valued variable. If x is categorical, then the computed estimates are spaced on a lattice. If x is continuous, then these estimates are distributed in a real space. The *statistic* methods involve a single point. The *region* methods involve intervals or types of convex regions. The *smooth* methods involve connected sets of unique points for every value of x. The *density* methods involve binning or parametric smoothing for computing a density in a local region. Finally, the *edge* methods involve computations on points that are nodes in directed or general graphs.

Table 8.2 **Statistical Methods by Dimensionality**

	1D	2D	3D
	Conditional		
Statistic			
Region			
Smooth			
Density			
Edge			
	Joint		
Statistic			
Region			
Smooth			
Density			
Edge			

The joint methods compute a unique value or unique set of values on a selected set of variables. For 1D, these methods are identical to conditional methods because conditioning on a constant is equivalent to not conditioning at all. Thus, the first column of Table 8.2 is identical for conditional and joint methods. The 2D and 3D joint methods, on the other hand, differ from their conditional counterparts. The differences are most apparent when considering the geometrical features of the graphics in Table 8.2.

For example, the function *smooth.conditional*() is single-valued for y on each different value of x. The function *smooth.joint*(), on the other hand, can produce a curve that can loop back on itself in 2D or a surface that can do the same in 3D. This is because *smooth.conditional*() is based on a loss defined only on *y*, while *smooth.joint*() is based on a loss defined by *x* and *y* jointly (or **x** and *y* in 3D).

Similarly, the function *region.conditional*() is conditionally one-dimensional in 2D and 3D, while *region.joint*() is usually **convex** in 2D and 3D. (Any line connecting two points in a convex region lies entirely in that region.) Actually, *region.joint*() produces estimates that fall within a superset of the convex class, called **star convex**. (Any line connecting one central point with another point in a star convex region lie entirely in that region.) Thus, while *region.conditional*() produces an interval on *y* for any given *x*, *region.joint*() produces a region comprised of intervals in polar coordinates. To compute *region.joint*(), we look in all directions away from a centroid point and we compute bounding intervals in each of those directions. In statistical procedures based on the multivariate normal distribution, this region is calculated from a covariance matrix. The off-diagonal elements of this matrix determine the rotational angle of a joint elliptical region and the diagonal elements determine its major and minor axes. Under other distributions, however, *region.joint*() can produce a region shaped like a starfish or a daisy.

Although the image of *density.joint*() appears to be convex in Table 8.2, like *region.joint*(), it is not necessarily so. A bounded region produced from percentiles of the multivariate normal distribution is convex, but regions produced from some other distributions are not. Some are not even star convex. Scott (1992) contains color plates of non-convex multivariate density estimates displayed in 3D. Some are multi-modal and others curl around themselves in a tangle.

While statistical methods are associated with geometric regions in a space, we must remember that these regions can be represented by various geometric graphs. That is the message of Figure 8.1 at the beginning of this chapter. Some of the results may be aesthetically bizarre, but they are not ill-defined. Indeed, the power of a system that distinguishes geometric graphs and their statistical methods lies in offering a complete choice of representation methods rather than dictating a subset on the basis of custom.

8.5 Sequel

The next chapter presents scales. Scale transformations are used primarily to meet statistical assumptions or scale graphs on meaningful units such as time.

9

Scales

The word **scale** derives from the Latin *scala*, or ladder. The Latin meaning is particularly apt for graphics. The visual representation of a scale – an axis with ticks – looks like a ladder. Scales are the types of functions we use to map varsets to dimensions. At first glance, it would seem that constructing a scale is simply a matter of selecting a range for our numbers and intervals to mark ticks. There is more involved, however. Scales measure the contents of a frame. They determine how we perceive the size, shape, and location of graphics. Choosing a scale (even a default decimal interval scale) requires us to think about what we are measuring and the meaning of our measurements. Ultimately, that choice determines how we interpret a graphic.

9.1 Scaling Theory

Scaling is a field with a long history in physics and psychometrics. I will briefly cover this area. Then I will discuss a variety of measurement scales and how to construct the axes that display them.

9.1.1 Axiomatic Measurement Theory

In a landmark paper "On the theory of scales of measurement" (1946), the psychophysicist S.S. Stevens presented a theory of measurement based on the invariance of the meaning of scales under different classes of transformations. Stevens showed that measurement scales that preserve meaning under a wide variety of transformations in some sense convey less information than those whose meaning is preserved by only a restricted class of transformations.

Assume a scale s is used to assign real numbers R to the elements of a set X so that for all i and j in X, $s(i) > s(j)$ if and only if i is greater than j. That is, if we let the symbol "$\rangle$" stand for "is comparatively greater than", then

$$s: X \rightarrow R \qquad \text{such that}$$

$$i \ \rangle \ j \leftrightarrow s(i) > s(j) \qquad \text{for all } i, j \in X \ .$$

Stevens called such a scale **ordinal** if any transformation of the scale values that preserves their numerical order produces another scale that shares the same one-to-one relation between comparisons among objects (using $\rangle$) and comparisons among corresponding scale values (using $>$).

Stevens used the term **permissible** to describe the set of transformations that preserves the ordinality of this mapping. Specifically, a transformation f is permissible for an ordinal scale if and only if:

$$s(i) > s(j) \implies f(s(i)) > f(s(j)) .$$

Any monotone transformation of the values $s(i)$ and $s(j)$ is permissible for ordinal scale data. We are thus free to take logs or find square roots of the values (if they are not negative) or to perform a linear transformation, adding a constant and multiplying by another (positive) constant.

Stevens developed similar arguments for three other types of scales. **Interval** scales involve a difference ($-$) instead of order ($>$) operator, so the set of permissible transformations for interval scales preserves relative differences. Specifically, the transformation f is permissible for interval scales if and only if there is a constant c such that:

$$s(i) - s(j) = c[f(s(i)) - f(s(j))]$$

Thus, linear transformations in which we add the same constant to each value and/or multiply each value by a constant are permissible for interval scale data, but we may not, for example, take logs. This is a smaller class of permissible transformations than for ordinal data, suggesting that in some sense the data values carry more information.

Ratio scales preserve relative ratios; permissible transformations satisfy:

$$s(i)/s(j) = cf(s(i))/f(s(j))$$

for some constant c. Thus, it is permissible to multiply ratio scale data by a constant, but we may not take logs or add a constant. Ratio scale data have a defined zero, which may not be changed.

Nominal scales are at the other end of the hierarchy. They do not even require the assignment of numerical values, but only of unique identifiers (numerals, letters, colors, etc.). They are invariant under any transformation that preserves the relationship between individuals and their identifiers. Thus is it permissible to perform almost any operation on the values as long as we do not combine or confuse identities. When the data values are numeric, these operations include any functions that map one-to-one from the original set of numbers into a new set. When the data values are not numeric, permissible operations include rearranging the data values. Of course, only the weakest kind of information can survive such arbitrary transformations.

9.1.2 Applied Scaling

Since Stevens' paper, many methodologists have used his axiomatic system to prescribe, and occasionally proscribe, statistical and graphical methods. The most extreme of Steven's methodological heirs have attempted to scare researchers into using only nonparametric statistical methods. The problem with this approach, as Velleman and Wilkinson (1994) argued, is that data offer scant help in choosing a scale and the wrong choice can hinder discovery. See Hand (1996) for a response and rejoinders to our paper.

Velleman and I pointed out that scientists must rely on extrinsic information (metadata) to decide what level of measurement might be appropriate for their data. Since we are not God, the best we can do is understand the context in which the data were collected and use our intuition and substantive scientific knowledge to choose scales. Often, we need to consider several scales for the same data. As Sir Ronald Fisher (1935) noted in reaction to statisticians who (before Stevens) were promoting routine use of nonparametric statistics,

> Experimenters should remember that they and their colleagues usually know more about the kind of material they are dealing with than do the authors of text-books written without such personal experience, and that a more complex, or less intelligible, test is not likely to serve their purpose better, in any sense, than those of proved value in their own subject.

9.1.2.1 The Naive Approach

The naive approach to scaling is to decide the measurement level and then assign a variable to a scale corresponding to this measurement level. Figure 9.1 shows one way Stevens' scales might be represented in a visible graphic. The countries data from Chapter 1 are mapped to four of Stevens' scale types. They are represented visually in the figure by a set of axes. It is important to recognize that scales need not necessarily be represented by axes. Legends and other forms of guides can also represent scales.

The nominal scale is shown by ordering the country names alphabetically. Any ordering will do. All that matters for a nominal scale is that the mapping be one-to-one: that each country have a unique identifier.

The ordinal scale is represented by a rank ordering of the countries on military expenditures. The spacing of the countries on this scale is arbitrary. All that matters is that the ordering preserve the relative ranks of the countries.

The interval scale is represented by the military expenditures themselves. The spacing of the countries matters, but the origin is arbitrary. That is, the difference in spending between Iraq and Libya should be comparable to that between Canada and Italy because both pairs are spaced approximately the same distance apart on the scale. (I will discuss how to deal with the compression of the labels at the bottom of the scale later in the chapter.)

Finally, the ratio scale is represented by the count of the countries within three major types of government. On this scale, the zero tick is significant; counts are referenced by this point. We can say by looking at the graphic that the count of countries in the sample with a Military form of government is a third larger than the count of countries with One Party government.

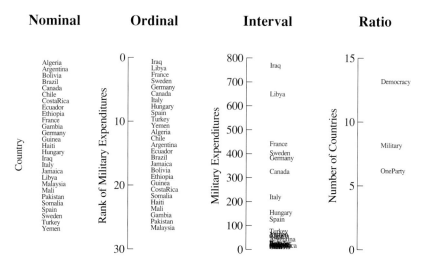

Figure 9.1 *Graphical displays of Stevens' scale types.*

9.1.2.2 Ambiguities

If we examine the data more closely, however, the neatness of these assignments breaks down. For example, we could say that normalized per-capita military expenditures map more appropriately to a ratio scale. Zero dollars seems like an absolute reference point. Spending 200 dollars per-capita seems like twice spending 100.

Money is not a physical or fundamental quantity, however. It is a measure of utility in the exchange of goods. Research by Kahneman and Tversky (1979) has shown that zero (no loss, no gain) is not an absolute anchor for monetary measurement. Individual and group indifference points can drift depending on the framing of a transaction or expenditure. This is why I classified the military expenditures as an interval rather than ratio scale.

A similar argument can be made against my classification of the country counts as a ratio scale. It would appear to make more sense to call this an **absolute scale**. While not an original Stevens scale type, it follows from his reasoning that an absolute scale has no permissible transformation other than the identity. This makes sense for counts. Ten means a count of ten – until one asks what is being counted. Counts depend on categorizations, which are not as concrete as Aristotle might have wished. The assignment of One Party, De-

mocracy, and Military as forms of government is non-overlapping in our example. It is arguable, however, that some countries might have more than one
of these types. Similar arguments can be made about most of the variables we
choose to represent in graphics. While the axioms of scaling theory are undis-
putable, there is no way to determine surely which one applies to a set of data.

9.1.2.3 Scales as Roles

Sometimes it is more useful to think of scales as roles for dimensions that help
reveal patterns in an analysis. Figure 9.2 shows that we can represent the same
data on two different scales in the same graphic. It is a quantile plot of per-
capita military expenditures. The horizontal scale is perhaps interval, based on
the numeric values themselves. What is the vertical scale? It is based on the
rank order of the data values, so it might be called ordinal. The equal spacings
are important, however, because we are using it to anchor the shape of the
curve traced by the points. Thus, it is being employed as an interval scale for
the purposes of analyzing shape. If we keep the aspect ratio 1 (a square frame),
then the shape is invariant under any interval scale transformation. The positive skewness is readily apparent in the convex shape of the curve. A unimodal
symmetric distribution would have plotted in an *S* shape. Finally, we could
call it an absolute scale because we are using it to display the **empirical cumulative distribution function** of per-capita military spending. If we are attending to the scale values rather than the shape, then we are processing
numerical information on an absolute scale between zero and one.

TRANS: **rmil** = *prank*(**military**)
FRAME: **military*rmil**
GRAPH: *point*()

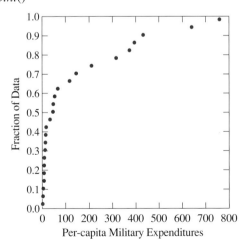

Figure 9.2 *Quantile plot of military expenditures.*

9.1.3 *Graphics and Scales*

Graphics do not care about the scales on which they are drawn. Bars, for example, do not know whether they measure counts, proportions, or other quantities. What, then, can we say about the common prescription (*e.g.*, Schmid and Schmid, 1979; Cleveland, 1985) that bars require a zero base to be meaningful? The answer is, I think, that these are statements about scales rather than graphics. Bars are multi-valued graphics. They represent two values on their range – a lower and upper point. When referenced against a ratio scale, it is most appropriate for the bottom of a bar to be at zero so that ratio comparisons can be made. Even when all the bases are at zero, however, both ends are marking an interval. There is nothing in the definition of a bar itself that requires it to have a base at the value zero.

9.2 *Scale Transformations*

In Chapter 4 we saw how to transform variables by doing such operations as logging or square-rooting. The purpose of variable transformations in a graphics system is to make statistical operations on variables appropriate and meaningful. Scales, on the other hand, operate on *sets* of variables (dimensions). The purpose of scale transformations is similar – to make statistical objects displayed on dimensions appropriate and meaningful. The next chapter will cover a third class: coordinate transformations. The purpose of those transformations is to manipulate the geometry of graphics to help us perceive relationships and find meaningful structures for representing variation. In some cases, we use scale and coordinate transformations together. And in some rare cases, we might apply transformations three times – once to a variable, once to a dimension, and once to a coordinate system.

The reason for separating transformations according to the sets on which they operate (variables, dimensions, and coordinates) is to keep clear the distinction between statistical and geometric operations. Statistical methods (*e.g.*, smoothing and aggregation) often require assumptions about the statistical distribution of the variables on which they operate. Thus, variable and scale transformations must be done *before* these statistical methods do their work. Coordinate transformations, on the other hand, change the appearance of graphics (*e.g.*, bars become pie slices) but do not alter their statistical properties. Thus, coordinate transformations must be done *after* statistical methods do their work.

The *log()* transformation may help us to see this distinction. If we log a variable, the numbers displayed on an axis will be logs (*e.g.*, 1, 2, 3) and the title of the axis should be something like "Log of Income." If we log a dimension, on the other hand, the numbers displayed will be on a log scale (*e.g.*, 10, 100, 1000) and the title of the axis should be something like "Income." Finally, if we use a log coordinate transformation, we should expect to see portions of graphics near the high end of the scale compressed more than those near the low end. The numbers on the axis should be unchanged, but their locations (and tick marks) should be compressed logarithmically.

Table 9.1 shows several scale transformation functions. This sample list is intended to cover the examples in this book and to be a template for designing the signature and behavior of new functions. All the functions have a standard form that includes a dimension name followed by other optional parameters. Examples are: *interval(dim1*,0,1000), and *time(dim2*,"mmm dd, yyyy"). The number and order of the optional parameters are peculiar to each function. Because the parameters are positional, a missing value (. or " ") may be used to leave a parameter in the middle of a list unspecified.

Table 9.1 Scales

categorical	*interval*	*time*	*one-bend*	*two-bend*	*probability*
cat()	*interval*()	*time*()	*log*() *pow*()	*asn*() *logit*() *probit*() *atanh*()	*prob*()

The categorical scale demarcates k points for locating k categories in a serial ordering. The interval scale has the property that any two equal-length intervals on the scale have the same measure. For example, if an interval from 0 to 2 on an axis measures two inches, then an interval from 4 to 6 must measure two inches. The time scale measures time. The one-bend functions are increasing or decreasing concave or convex. The *log* scale returns logs. The *pow*() transformation computes $f:x^p$. However, $pow(\mathbf{x},0)=log(\mathbf{x})$. The two-bend functions are ogive shaped. The *asn*(), *logit*(), *probit*(), and *atanh*() scales are arcsine, logit, probit, and Fisher's z statistical transformations. The probability scales implement various probability distributions.

9.2.1 Categorical Scales

The syntax for *cat*() is

$$cat(dim\#,"string1","string2", ...) \quad \text{or}$$

$$cat(dim\#, val1, val2, ...)$$

The extra parameters after *dim#* are optional. Categorical scales index categories. Because scales must order categories by design, there is no visible difference between a nominal and an ordinal scale in a graphic. String variables are by definition categorical, so we need not use a *cat*() scale to ensure that they are mapped to categories. The optional parameters for a categorical scale determine the choice and ordering of the categories and their format, *e.g.*, *cat(dim1*,"Jane","Jean","June"). The system searches all values available in the data, does a string match to determine the unique assignments, and then uses the strings in the *cat*() list to label the scale.

Picking numbers for numerical categorical scales is easy. Simply choose the natural numbers, since categories are best displayed evenly spaced. Figure 9.3 shows three examples of categorical scales. Notice that the endpoints of the scale are not mapped to categories. This makes it easy to distinguish a categorical scale with numerals from a numerical scale with the same numerals. It also keeps graphics (such as bars) from colliding with the edges of the frame.

I have chosen three categorical representations of hue in Figure 9.3: nanometer wavelength, color name, and a color index. Provided the values are mapped properly to the scales, all three representations would produce the same graphic for a particular graph.

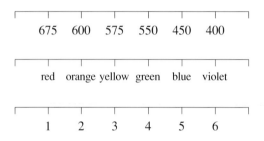

Figure 9.3 *Categorical scales*

9.2.2 Interval Scales

The syntax for *interval*() is

$$interval(dim\#, min, max, base, ticks, delta, cycle, "format")$$

The extra parameters after *dim#* are optional. The *min* and *max* parameters set minimum and maximum scale values. The *base* parameter (default is 10) sets the number base. The *ticks* parameter sets the number of tick marks (default is determined by program). The *delta* parameter sets the interval between ticks (default is determined by program). The *cycle* parameter is an integer specifying how many cycles there are to be between *min* and *max*. The default is 1. This is useful for specifying more than one revolution on polar plots, but it can be used on rectangular coordinates to overlay subsections of a time series. The optional *format* parameter can be used for scientific notation and other formats.

Constructing axes for default interval scales requires us to choose minimum and maximum values, the number of tick marks, and numbers to go with the tick marks. Most people prefer to see nice numbers on these scales so that they can use them like rulers to measure graphics. There are several approaches to this problem. I will begin with numbers in base 10.

9.2.2.1 Nice Numbers

Nice numbers include the numbers we preferred as children when we learned arithmetic. These numbers persist in our habits and preferences when we label and view decimal scales on graphics. Although there might be some disagreement (perhaps cultural) over definition, nice numbers are members of an infinite subset of the real numbers, *e.g.*, $R_N = \{... , .1, .2, .5, 1, 2, 5, ...\}$. A **nice scale** is an interval scale marked with an ordered sequence of numbers whose first differences are nice numbers. The following sequences all have this property for the set R_N given above.

> ..., 1, 2, 3, 4, 5, ...
> ..., 2, 4, 6, 8, 10, ...
> ..., 0, 50, 100, 150, 200, ...
> ..., .001, .003, .005, .007, .009, ...

Really nice scales have an additional property: they include zero. The first three series above have this property, but the last does not. Nice scales can also be defined for some nonlinear scales. For scales like log and power, nice scales can be chosen in the transformed metric and inverse transformed to the original. For example, if we choose the nice scale $[-1, 0, 1, 2, 3]$ in logarithms, then our log scale will be $[.1, 1, 10, 100, 1000]$.

Nelder (1976), Stirling (1981), and Heckbert(1990) discuss nice numbers and provide algorithms for producing them when we are given a range of data values. These simple algorithms work well for a variety of instances. When they fail, we end up with too few or too many tick marks or a scale that does not fit closely the range of the data.

A more effective method is to compute scales using a multi-parameter search algorithm. First of all, we need to expand our set of nice numbers a bit in order to improve our chances of an attractive solution. We begin with the finite, ordered set $Q = \{1, 5, 2, 25, 3\}$. We may reorder, expand or contract this set to suit our tastes, although I have found this set works well in practice. Then our set of nice numbers is $R_N = \{q \times 10^z : q \in Q, z \in \mathbf{Z}\}$, where $\mathbf{Z}$ is the set of integers.

Let n be the cardinality of the set Q ($n=5$ in this case). Let $i = 1, ... , n$ be the index of an element of Q. Let k be the number of ticks on a scale. Let r_d be the range of the data and r_s be the range of the scale (we assume $r_s \geq r_d$). Let S be a finite, ordered solution set of k numbers for our nice scale. (Note that usually $S \not\subset R_N$.) Let $v = 1$ if S contains zero, otherwise, let $v = 0$. Finally, let *m* be an ideal number of tick marks for a scale. This may depend on the physical size of a graphic and the size of fonts used for scale numbers, although the choice $m = 5$ usually suffices. Now we can construct a scale goodness index from the following components, each of which varies between 0 and 1:

simplicity: $s = 1 - i/n + v/n$

granularity: $g = \begin{cases} 1 - |k - m|/m , & 0 < k < 2m \\ 0 & , \quad \text{otherwise} \end{cases}$

coverage: $c = r_d / r_s$

For a given scale S, the simplicity value is based mainly on the index i of the element chosen from Q that determines the set R_N that includes the first differences among the ordered elements of S. This simplicity value is incremented by $1/n$ if the set S contains zero. The granularity value reflects closeness to an ideal number of tick marks. Too few tick marks hamper scale lookup and too many clutter the display. The coverage measure rewards solutions that leave less white space around the data. Cleveland, Diaconis, and McGill (1982) have shown, for example, that this white space can bias judgments of correlation in scatterplots. I prefer to set a floor on coverage, say .75, so that we will never automatically select a data range that fills less than 3/4 of a scale.

I claim that $w = (s + g + c)/3$ is an indicator ($0 \le w \le 1$) of the goodness of a scale. There might be other functions of s, g, and c that do better for this purpose, but in my experience, this simple composite works well. Optimizing w can be done by direct search through the whole parameter space or, if we want to consider more values, by using algorithms such as O'Neill (1971). An advantage of the optimization approach is that any parameter can be constrained. This is especially important when users choose to fix the number of ticks, the minimum or maximum scale value, data coverage, or some combination of these and other parameters.

I tend to prefer restricting the search so that extreme ticks and numbers coincide with the ends of the scale, as opposed to allowing the tick marks to float elsewhere along the scale. The examples in this book generally have justified scales like this. When data cover intervals like [0,1] or [0,100], we may want to relax this restriction by indenting the tick marks to allow some empty space at both ends.

Nice numbers are not particularly interesting; they're just nice. If we are willing to relax the requirement that tick marks be evenly spaced on a scale, we can pick other number sequences that might be useful for emphasizing features of our data. For example, it may be useful to have more tick marks in the center of a scale than at the edges, depending on the distribution of data ruled by the scale. Knuth (1969) and Conway and Guy (1996) discuss a variety of interesting number sequences and algorithms for generating them. Tufte (1983) discusses scales that have ticks at significant data landmarks.

9.2.2.2 Number Bases

Different number bases affect the choice of nice numbers but not the treatment of tick marks. The methods I outlined in Section 9.2.2.1 can be modified easily for other number bases. We modify R_N to be $R_N = \{q \times b^z: q \in Q, z \in \mathbf{Z}\}$, where b is the number base (2, 8, 10, 16, etc.). We also need to modify Q to contain nice numbers in the chosen base.

9.2.3 Time Scales

The syntax for *time*() is

$$time(dim\#, "format", "min", "max", "origin", cycle)$$

The extra parameters after *dim#* are optional. The *format* parameter uses a picture format to specify dates. The symbol set "YMDhms" is used to denote year, month, day, hour, minute, second. When there is no ambiguity between month and minute, case may be ignored. All other characters in a format are used literally. Examples are "mmm dd, yyyy", "mm/dd/yy", "dd-mm-yy". When fewer than two characters are available for month, numerals are used. The *min* and *max* parameters set minimum and maximum scale values in formatted time. Examples are "Jan 1, 1956" or " 6/ 1/ 95". The *origin* parameter (default is January 1, 1900) sets the time origin for the numerical scale. The *cycle* parameter is an integer specifying how many cycles there are to be between *min* and *max*. The default is 1.

As Einstein famously established, time is the fourth dimension of our physical world. In Western and most other cultures, time is measured in lunar and solar astronomical cycles: days, months, and years. Other units have obscure etiologies. Seconds, minutes, and hours probably derive from the Sumerian practice of sexagesimal (base 60) arithmetic (Conway and Guy, 1996). Weeks, on the other hand, may have their origin in the Babylonian sacred number 7 (Ronan, 1991).

The annual circuit of the earth around the sun presents an arithmetic problem. It occurs in approximately 365.242 days. In 46 BCE, the Julian calendar added an extra day every four years to adjust for the roughly quarter-day-per-year gain. The difference between .242 and .250 is enough to have caused significant accumulation over centuries, however, so the Gregorian calendar introduced a new calculation in 1582. This calendar, now prevalent, specifies a leap year every four years except for centuries not divisible exactly by 400. Thus 2000 is a leap year, but 1900 is not.

Setting an origin for time requires relative precision (apologies to Einstein). If we want to measure and record century time to the resolution of mean solar seconds (based on a mean solar day of 86,400 seconds), we need a long number (more than 10 decimal digits) to span several centuries in daily units. With that precision, we can place our origin at 1582 if we are historically inclined or at 1900 if we are more financially motivated. The latter scale is used by modern spreadsheets and accounting packages, with positive units denoting day of the century. Negative numbers record time before 1900. Thus, my birthday (November 5, 1944) is the 16380th day of the 20th century. Apparently the developers of the most widely used spreadsheets did not consult an encyclopedia to learn that 1900 is not a leap year, so their dates are off by one day after February 28, 1900. This error has consequences when data from spreadsheets are imported into other database, statistical, and accounting packages that compute time correctly.

The Year 2000 or Y2K problem, as it is popularly called, may arise in software for a variety of reasons. The most common problem is that some computer programs encode years as two-character strings or two-digit integers. This causes problems when they compute time spans or make comparisons. Truncating years is not the only way to make a program vulnerable to the advent of a millenium, however. If software employs a real-valued variable for storing time, careless programmers may fail to use sufficient numerical precision to store day-of-the-century. Finally, as I have noted, some programmers may not know how to compute leap years correctly. Having failed to note that 1900 was not a leap year, they may not realize that 2000 is.

Contemporary popular discussions concerning what an operating system is supposed to be and do often ignore the most important basics like dealing with time correctly. International date formats, time zones, and correct calculation of leap years is a critical function that an operating system should provide so that programmers are freed from having to think about the numerous details involved in calculations. Java performs these tasks correctly and conveniently because it has an object DateFormat that uses a long signed integer for recording absolute time in milliseconds, with an origin at Jan 1, 1970. With wisdom beyond its years, Java also seems to understand leap years backwards and forwards for many centuries.

In a nice time scale, tick numbers are separated by intervals contained in the set $T_N = \{ \dots, second, minute, hour, day, week, month, year, \dots \}$, where the words I have used in the braces denote numerical time values anchored at some origin such as the first second of January 1, 1900. While niceness for numbers depends on numerals, niceness for time depends on calendar notation. Thus, an algorithm for nice time scales requires an understanding of Julian or other calendars used to display continuous time. Calendars differ across cultures, so the task can be quite complex when we intend to develop international software.

Figure 9.4 shows examples of several different time scales. Daily and weekly scales have evenly spaced ticks, but monthly and yearly scales do not. Notice that the gap between February and March is less than that between any other two months because February has the fewest days. The same irregularity can occur for years. The yearly scale in this example would have slightly irregular ticks if it included a leap year.

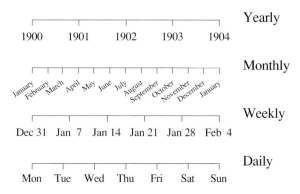

Figure 9.4 *Time scales*

Using time scales allows us to display graphics at the points on the scale that correspond to real dates. Figure 8.5 and Figure 8.13 illustrate this principle. Figure 9.5 shows a selection from the SPSS stock price series that shows specific dates formatted in slash notation. The major tick marks are set to Sundays, so the weekday trades occur between the weekend gaps. We are accustomed to seeing equally-spaced bars in printed charts and computer software. Time series data show us how restrictive this limitation can be.

FRAME: **date***(**high+low**)
SCALE: *time(dim1,*"mm/dd/yy")
GRAPH: *bar.region.spread.range*()

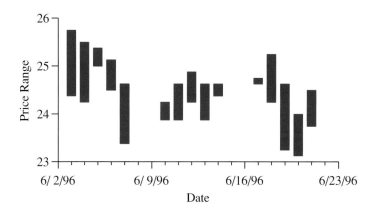

Figure 9.5 *Stock price ranges*

9.2.4 One-bend Scales

One-bend scales are convex (concave) upward or concave (convex) downward in their mapping functions. They include a variety of logarithmic, power, and probability scales.

9.2.4.1 Logarithmic Scales

The syntax for *log()* is

$$log(dim\#, base, min, max, ticks, cycle)$$

The extra parameters after *dim#* are optional. The *base* parameter (default is *e*, or natural logarithm) sets the log base. The *min* and *max* parameters set minimum and maximum scale values. The *ticks* parameter determines the number of ticks. The *cycle* parameter is an integer specifying how many cycles there are to be between *min* and *max*. The default is 1.

The logarithmic scale is usually computed on base 10, although other bases are possible and many are useful. The log base has no effect on the visual appearance of the plot; only the labeling of the tick marks on axes is affected. The same is true for most statistical tests of significance on logged data. This equivalence follows from $log_b(x) = ln(x)/ln(b)$, where $ln()$ is the natural logarithm and $b>1$.

Figure 9.6 shows examples of log scales to several bases. Base 2 is useful when it makes sense to represent doublings. Base 3 is for triplings. Base 7 is for biblical time. (Logging time is an eschatological transformation, or perhaps a sign of old age!) The upper limit of the log septenary scale in Figure 9.6 comes just before Pentecost or Jubilee, depending on whether we count days or years. Base 10, of course, is most often used in our decimal society.

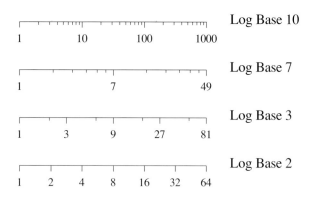

Figure 9.6 *Log base scales*

One detail is often overlooked by programmers when they implement a log scale. If a user requests, say, a minimum value of 3 and a maximum of 105 on a decimal log scale, a well-designed scale algorithm ought to position the minor tick marks at exactly those values and display two major tick marks at 10 and 100. This requires somewhat more computation but is worth the effort for saving white space inside the borders of the frame. See Figure 8.16 for an example.

Figure 9.7 shows a log scale for the predation data used in Figure 8.20. The variable **brainweight** is the weight in grams of the brains of the animals surveyed. The variable **exposure** is a rating of the degree an animal is exposed to predators while sleeping (1=sheltered, 5=exposed).

FRAME: **exposure*brainweight**
SCALE: *cat(dim1)*
SCALE: *log(dim2, 10)*
GRAPH: *point.statistic.mean()*
GRAPH: *bar.spread.sd(color("red"))*

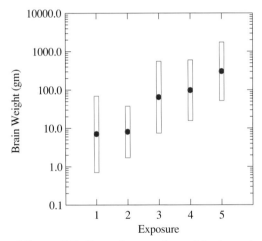

Figure 9.7 *Error bars on logarithmic scale*

9.2.4.2 Power Scales

The syntax for *pow()* is

$$pow(dim\#, exponent, min, max, ticks, cycle)$$

The extra parameters after *dim#* are optional. The *exponent* parameter (default is .5, or square-root) sets the exponent. The *min* and *max* parameters set minimum and maximum scale values. The *ticks* parameter determines the number of ticks. The *cycle* parameter is an integer specifying how many cycles there are to be between *min* and *max*. The default is 1.

Figure 9.8 shows examples of power scales to several powers. For the inverse transformation ($p = -1$), I have reflected the scale to keep the polarity consistent. Reflecting the scale for negative powers makes it easier to compare the effects of different power transformations on graphics. Tukey (1977) discusses the "ladder of powers" that the general power transformation $pow: x^p$ encompasses. Tukey also shows that for p in the neighborhood of zero, pow approximates the *log* transformation if the scale is shifted appropriately.

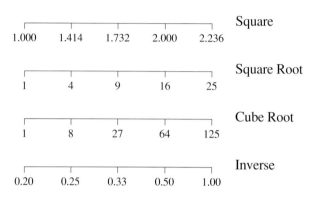

Figure 9.8 *Power scales*

As Figure 9.8 reveals, it is difficult to find equally spaced nice numbers for power scales, except for reciprocals of positive integers (*e.g.*, square or cube roots). Consequently, it is easier to move the tick marks than to search for nice numbers on power scales. There is an added benefit to this method. If we inverse transform our tick-moved scale with the appropriate coordinate power transformation (see Chapter 10), the ticks and scale values will return to their original locations. To gain the same duality with logs, we implement the natural log scale by moving ticks and retaining the original scale values. Then the exponential coordinate transformation *exp*() will return the ticks to their original positions (see Figure 10.31).

Figure 9.9 illustrates three examples of tick-moving for power scales on the brain weight data for $p=1$ (bottom), $p=.5$ (middle) and $p=.01$ (top). Although the scale values are different, the top plot is visually indistinguishable from a dot plot of the log-transformed values. Notice that the ticks and scale values move to the right as the exponent of the power transformation decreases. On a dynamic display system, this movement provides an additional cue to the change in shape of the distribution itself. Almost all the shape information revealed by the equivalent of the log transformation is contained in the interval below the first tick mark (0 to 1000).

FRAME: **brainweight**
SCALE: *pow(dim1, .01)*
GRAPH: *point(position.stack())*

FRAME: **brainweight**
SCALE: *pow(dim1, .5)*
GRAPH: *point(position.stack())*

FRAME: **brainweight**
SCALE: *pow(dim1, 1.0)*
GRAPH: *point(position.stack())*

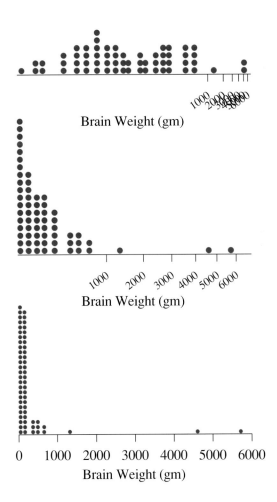

Figure 9.9 *Power transformations*

9.2.5 Two-bend Scales

The syntax for the two-bend scale transformations is, in general

function(dim#, parameter, ...)

The extra parameters after *dim#* are optional. These are usually the parameters from related probability distributions. Two-bend scales are ogival (S shaped) in their mapping functions. They include several statistical scales used to normalize data.

9.2.5.1 Arcsine Scales

Proportions fall in the closed interval [0,1]. The binomial proportion $p = x/n$ (*e.g.*, x heads in n coin tosses) has mean π and variance $\pi(1 - \pi)/n$, where π is the population proportion estimated by p. This statistic thus has its variance dependent on its mean. The left panel of Figure 9.10 shows this behavior for 1000 replications of 25 tosses of a coin. On the lower level is a dot plot of the sample distribution of the proportion of heads in 25 tosses when the coin is biased to come up heads only 10 percent of the time. On the middle level is the dot plot for a fair coin. And the top level shows the dot plot for a coin biased to yield heads 90 percent of the time.

We can derive a transformation of π such that the variance of the transformed variate is constant across its range. Following the inverse weighting approach for stabilizing variance in Section 10.1.4, and assuming that n is fixed, we can integrate the reciprocal function of this variance to get the standardized arcsine transformation

$$asn\!: \pi \to 2\,asin\sqrt{\pi}\ .$$

In other words, since the derivative of this transformation:

$$1/\sqrt{\pi(1 - \pi)}\ ,$$

is proportional to the reciprocal of the standard deviation, we end up holding the standard deviation relatively constant for different location values of the transformed variate (Rao, 1973).

The right panel of Figure 9.10 illustrates this transformation on the coin toss data. Notice that the values near the bounds of the [0,1] interval are stretched compared to those in the middle. The only difference in the specifications between the left and right panels is the addition of the *asn()* function to the TRANS specification. As with power scales, it is easier to move tick marks than to search for round numbers in the inverse domain.

FRAME: **p1**
GRAPH: *point(position.stack())*

FRAME: **p1**
SCALE: *asn(dim1)*
GRAPH: *point(position.stack())*

FRAME: **p5**
GRAPH: *point(position.stack())*

FRAME: **p5**
SCALE: *asn(dim1)*
GRAPH: *point(position.stack())*

FRAME: **p9**
GRAPH: *point(position.stack())*

FRAME: **p9**
SCALE: *asn(dim1)*
GRAPH: *point(position.stack())*

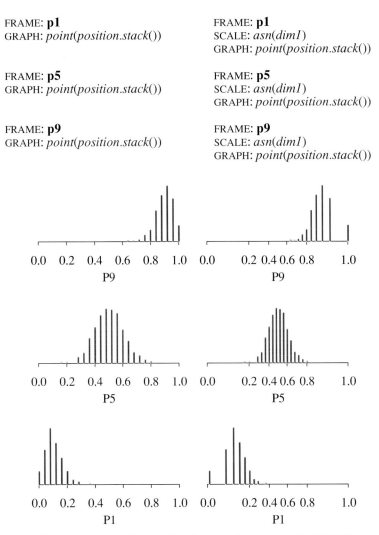

Figure 9.10 *Proportion of heads in 25 tosses for* π = .1, .5, .9 *(1000 samples)*

9.2.5.2 Logit and Probit Scales

The *logit* and *probit* transformations are based on probability frames. When *p* is assumed to be a probability measure on the interval (0,1), we can use the inverse probability function to transform *p* into a distribution. When probability density functions are symmetric and unimodal, these transformations have an ogive shape similar to the arcsine transformation. The lower panel of Figure 9.11 shows two of these functions, the *probit*, based on the standard normal distribution:

$$p = \Phi(x) = \int_{-\infty}^{x} \frac{1}{\sqrt{2\pi}} e^{-\frac{1}{2}z^2} dz$$

and the *logit*, based on the logistic distribution:

$$p = L(x) = \int_{-\infty}^{x} \frac{e^{-z}}{(1 + e^{-z})^2} dz = \frac{e^x}{1 + e^x}$$

DATA: **x**=*iter*(0., 1., 0.1)
TRANS: **y**=*asn*(**x**)
FRAME: **x*y**
GRAPH: *line*()

DATA: **x**=*iter*(−1., 1., 0.1)
TRANS: **y**=*ath*(**x**)
FRAME: **x*y**
GRAPH: *line*()

DATA: **x**=*iter*(0., 1., 0.1)
TRANS: **y**=*probit*(**x**)
FRAME: **x*y**
GRAPH: *line*()

DATA: **x**=*iter*(0., 1., 0.1)
TRANS: **y**=*logit*(**x**)
FRAME: **x*y**
GRAPH: *line*()

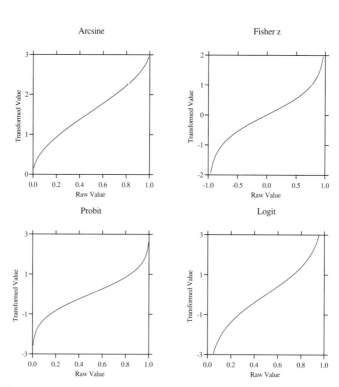

Figure 9.11 *Probit, logit, arcsine, and Fisher's z transformations*

I have drawn the functions in the lower two panels of Figure 9.11 as $\Phi^{-1}(p)$ and $L^{-1}(p)$, respectively, in order to match them to the orientation of the other panels in the figure. Inverse probability functions are usually an-cillary to formal statistical modeling using these distributions. Sometimes we need to use them directly, however. One example is probability plotting (*e.g.*, Chambers *et al.*, 1983), in which we plot ordered data values against the in-verse probability values of their fractiles, assuming a particular distribution. We also use these transformations occasionally in statistical modeling where the data are probabilities, such as in meta-analysis (Hedges and Olkin, 1985).

9.2.5.3 Fisher's z Scale

Fisher (1915; see also 1925) developed a transformation to stabilize the vari-ance and skewness of the Pearson correlation coefficient:

$$z = \frac{1}{2}\log\left(\frac{1+r}{1-r}\right) = \operatorname{atanh} r$$

Fisher's transformation can be understood with the same logic that we used for the arcsine transformation. In this case, the derivative of the transformation is $1/(1-r^2)$, which is proportional to the reciprocal of the standard devia-tion of r. Figure 9.11 shows this transformation in the upper right panel. The range of the correlation is $(-1, 1)$ but the shape of the transformation closely resembles the others for proportions and probabilities.

9.2.6 Probability Scales

The syntax for *prob*() is

> *prob(dim#, "distribution", parameter, ...)*

The extra parameters vary by type of distribution. The default is the normal probability distribution, which yields the same result as *probit*().

We have already seen the logit and probit scale types under Section 9.2.5. Other probability distribution functions can be used for a variety of purposes. Figure 9.12 shows a gamma probability plot of the firing rate variable in the cat dataset used in Figure 3.5. I have square-rooted the firing rate scale and ap-plied a gamma probability scale with parameter 40 to the fractiles. This joint rescaling straightens out the cumulative distribution function shown in the right panel of the figure. The compression of the tick marks at the center of the vertical scale is the same phenomenon we see with the transformations in Fig-ure 9.11. Since the gamma probability density is not symmetric, however, the tick marks do not compress the same amount at each end.

We might want to follow the enumeration strategy used for log scales in order to enhance the detail at the ends of the probability scale. That is, we have room to add tick marks on the lower end at .01, .001, .0001, and so on. Similarly, we could add marks at .99, .999, .9999 at the higher end. Grid lines at these major tick marks could help in decoding information.

Compare this result with Figure 4.2. What is the difference between using a variable transformation and a scale transformation to produce a probability plot? Does this difference affect real-time events such as brushing, linking, and metadata access? The linearized probability plot is based on the idea that it is easier to perceive straight lines than to evaluate curvilinear cumulative distribution functions in the mind's eye. Are there other graphical applications where a probability scale would be useful? If so, is there any 3D application?

TRANS: **p**=*prank*(**rate**)
FRAME: **rate*p**
SCALE: *pow*(*dim1*,.5)
SCALE: *prob*(*dim2*,"gamma", 40)
GRAPH: *point*()

TRANS: **p**=*prank*(**rate**)
FRAME: **rate*p**
GRAPH: *point*()

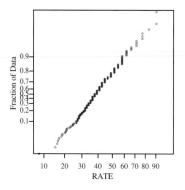 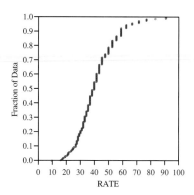

Figure 9.12 Gamma probability scale

9.3 *Sequel*

Most business and scientific graphics are displayed in rectangular coordinates. The next chapter covers coordinate systems that alter the appearance of graphics. Some of these coordinate transformations are so radical that we may fail to recognize the same geometric object embedded in different coordinate systems.

10

Coordinates

The word **coordinate** derives from the Latin *ordinare*, which means to order or arrange. Coordinates are sets that locate points in space. These sets are usually numbers grouped in tuples, one tuple for each point. Because spaces can be defined as sets of geometric objects plus axioms defining their behavior, coordinates can be thought of more generally as schemes for mapping elements of sets to geometric objects.

The most familiar coordinates are Cartesian. A point is located on a Cartesian plane, for example, by its distances from two intersecting straight lines. The distance from one line is measured along a parallel to the other line. Usually, the reference lines (axes) are perpendicular. Most popular graphics, such as line or bar charts, are drawn using Cartesian coordinates. The same real numbers behind these graphics can be mapped to points along circles, curves, and other objects, however. This chapter examines functions that transform a set of coordinates to another set of coordinates.

There are many reasons for displaying graphics in different coordinate systems. One reason is to simplify. For example, coordinate transformations can change some curvilinear graphics to linear. Another reason is to reshape graphics so that important variation or covariation is more salient or accurately perceived. For example, a pie chart is generally better for judging proportions of wholes than is a bar chart (Simkin and Hastie, 1987). Yet another reason is to match the form of a graphic to theory or reality. For example, we might map a variable to the left-closed and right-open interval $[0,1)$ on a line or to the interval $[0,2\pi)$ on the circumference of a circle. If our variable measures defects within a track of a computer disk drive in terms of rotational angle, it is usually better to stay within the domain of a circle for our graphic. Another reason is to make detail visible. For example, we may have a cloud with many points in a local region. Viewing those points may be facilitated by zooming in (enlarging a region of the graphic) or smoothly distorting the local area so that the points are more separated in the local region.

In the figures in this chapter, axes often become curves or change their orientation or scaling or direction after a change of coordinates. This is an important consequence of coordinate transformations. Axes, or guides, share geometry with graphics and are therefore subject to the same transforming effects as *bars*, *boxes*, and other graphics. Not everything in a guide changes, however. In particular, text may rotate or move in other ways, but the placement and orientation of text is a special problem created by some coordinate systems. We must be able to read text. Because of this constraint, we cannot draw an image of a graphic and its text and then transform the entire image. The technical problem of text placement is not trivial and may account for why so few graphics and geometry programs handle text well.

There are many ways to organize this material, because coordinates are basic to analysis, geometry, algebra, and other areas of mathematics. In applying these concepts to graphics, however, we are most interested in the appearance of a result and its effect on the perception of variation being represented in a graphic. Therefore, I will tend to organize concepts by geometry.

Most of this chapter concerns continuous transformations, but I will cover discrete examples briefly. I will begin with the classic transformation groups involved in mapping the plane to itself. Then I will discuss polar and other general planar transformations. Next, I will cover projections to the plane, including global map projections. I will conclude with triangular, spherical, cylindrical, and parallel coordinates. I will omit detail in some of the specifications when it is not needed to make clear the geometry.

None of these treatments pretends to be comprehensive or abstract. The focus here is on practical methods for representation and organization of this material in a form that lends itself to efficient computer code for the task. Introductory core and tangential references for some of the topics discussed in this chapter are Preparata and Shamos (1985), Rogers and Adams (1990), Foley *et al.* (1993), Emmer (1995), Banchoff (1996), and Gomes and Costa (1998).

10.1 Transformations of the Plane

If (x, y) and (u, v) are elements respectively of two sets S_1 and S_2 respectively, then the set of equations

$$\begin{cases} u = g(x, y) \\ v = h(x, y) \end{cases},$$

where g and h are functions, transforms (x, y) to (u, v). As with all functions, we call (u, v) the **image** of (x, y) and $T(x,y)=(g(x, y), h(x, y))$ a **mapping** of S_1 to S_2. Ordinary graphics such as *bars* and *tiles* take on radically different appearances under different planar transformations. Furthermore, if we don't recognize this visually profound effect of shape transformations, we are likely to think a particular chart involves a new type of graphic or a different source of variation when, in fact, it is a simple coordinate transformation of a popular rectangular graphic.

The first part of this section is organized in terms of the class hierarchy of planar transformations in Figure 10.1. The CLASS column shows each class of transformation inheriting from its more general parent. For example, an isometry is a similarity, but a similarity is not an isometry. The TRANSFOR-MATION column indicates the methods within the transformation class. The INVARIANCE column indicates the feature of graphical objects unchanged after transformation. Finally, the IMAGE column shows the effect of each transformation on a *dino* graphic (you didn't see one in Chapter 6?).

The **isometry** group is the set of transformations that preserve distance between points. These operations obey the axioms of Euclidean geometry. The three isometric transformations are the **rigid transformations**: translation, rotation, and reflection. Translation moves an object vertically or horizontally without changing its shape, size or orientation. Rotation rotates an object around a point (usually its center) without changing shape or size. Reflection inverts an object horizontally or vertically without changing its size or shape, like looking in a mirror.

The **similarity** group is the set of transformations that change the size of an object. The transformation name, dilatation, suggests enlargement. Nevertheless, dilatation includes both shrinking and enlargement. The word dilation is sometimes used for this transformation when only enlargement is involved. The name similarity implies that two objects of the same shape but of different sizes and at different locations nevertheless are similar.

The **affinity** group is the set of transformations that cause a dimension to stretch independently of the other. It also includes a shear, which is like turning Roman into Italic letters. The word affinity implies that linearly stretched and sheared objects, regardless of their size and location, share an affinity of form. We call stretch and shear *affine* transformations.

The **projectivity** group is the set of transformations that is most easily visualized by thinking of a light source shining on graphics drawn on a transparent plane and projecting an image on another plane. This transformation preserves straight lines but can modify angles. The best physical model for imagining this group of transformations is a slide projector that we can move to any angle and location relative to a white wall. A picture projected on the wall from an oblique or acute angle will fan out across the wall; straight lines in the picture (sidewalks, buildings, etc.) will remain remain straight on the wall.

The **conformality** class covers conformal mappings. Conformal mappings preserve local angles in graphics, but may distort global shape considerably. The conformality class, like the affinity class, is a parent of the similarity class. The conformality class is not a parent of the affinity class, however, because affine transformations do not preserve angles. Similarity transformations (unlike affine transformations) are angle preserving. In fact, a conformal map looks like a similarity map at the local level. "Small" objects maintain their shape under a conformal transformation. "Big" objects are bent, sometimes considerably, so that straight lines become curves.

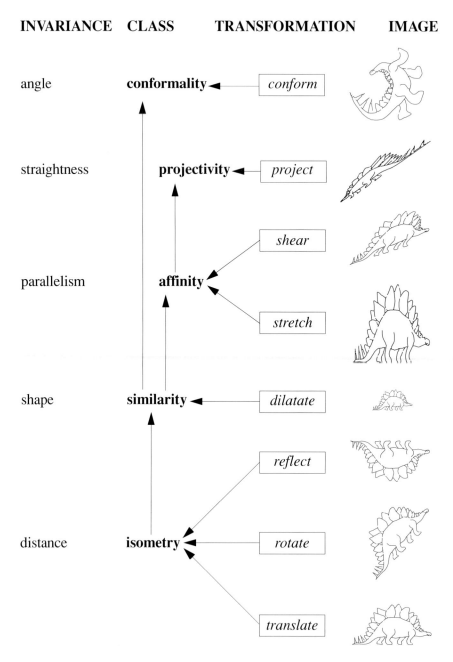

INVARIANCE   CLASS   TRANSFORMATION   IMAGE

angle   **conformality** ◄─── *conform*

straightness **projectivity** ◄─── *project*

                                     shear

parallelism   **affinity**

                                     stretch

shape   **similarity** ◄─── *dilatate*

                                     reflect

distance   **isometry** ◄─── *rotate*

                                     translate

Figure 10.1 *Hierarchy of planar transformations*

10.1.1 Isometric Transformations

A **metric space** is a set S together with a function

$$\delta: S \times S \to [0, \infty) \text{ , where}$$

$$\delta(x, y) = 0 \iff x = y$$
$$\delta(x, y) = \delta(y, x)$$
$$\delta(x, z) \le \delta(x, y) + \delta(y, z)$$

Although this definition is general enough to be applied to objects other than real numbers, we will assume δ is a distance measure and x, y, z are points in a space defined on the real numbers. Thus, 1) zero distance between two points implies that the points are the same, and if two points are the same, the distance between them is zero, 2) the distance between the point x and the point y is the same as the distance between the point y and the point x, and 3) a **triangle inequality** among distances exists for any three points x, y, and z.

An instance of a metric space is the n-dimensional Euclidean space consisting of n-tuples $(x_1, \ldots, x_n)$ of real numbers x_i, with distance metric

$$\delta = \left(\sum_{i=1}^{n} x_i^2 \right)^{1/2}$$

If S_1 and S_2 are metric spaces with distance functions δ_1 and δ_2, then a function $g: S_1 \to S_2$ is an **isometry** transformation if and only if

$$\delta_2((g(x)), g(y)) = \delta_1(x, y) \text{ for all } x, y \in S_1$$

Isometries on the plane involve translation, rotation, and reflection. All of these preserve distance. While there are formal proofs for this assertion, the simplest thing is to look at the pictures.

10.1.1.1 Translation

Translation sends the coordinates (x,y) to $(x+a, y+b)$. I will not show a figure for this, because translation is nothing more than moving a graphic right or left, up or down, or a combination of both, without changing its orientation. The dinosaur in Figure 10.1 has been translated from somewhere off the page (in space, not time), perhaps from Philadelphia.

The most frequent use for translation is in paneled graphics. As I will show in Chapter 11, we use translation to arrange a set of frames in a table of graphics. By composing translations with other coordinate transformations, we can produce even more unusual arrangements of multigraphics.

10.1.1.2 Rotation

Rotation sends the polar coordinates (r,θ) to $(r,\theta+c)$. This is equivalent to sending (x,y) to $(cos(\theta)x–sin(\theta)y,\ sin(\theta)x+cos(\theta)y)$. The dinosaur in Figure 10.1 is rotated 45 degrees. Figure 10.2 shows a bar graphic rotated $\theta=270$ degrees counter-clockwise. This is the coordinate transformation most commonly done to produce horizontal bar graphics. Notice that not everything is rotated in the graphic, however. Because the *rotate*() function operates on the view instead of the frame, the location of text rotates to follow the location of associated elements (axes in this case), but its orientation can be governed by other aesthetic considerations or constraints.

FRAME: **gov*birth**
GRAPH: *bar*()

FRAME: **gov*birth**
COORD: *rotate*(270.)
GRAPH: *bar*()

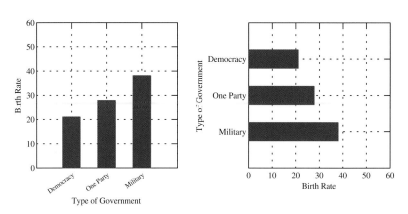

Figure 10.2 *270 degree orthogonal rotation*

Figure 10.3 shows an unusual graphical application of the rotation transformation. This example is taken from Tukey (1977). Tukey devised this graphic to represent simple additive models involving effects computed from a row-by-column two-way table. The model he graphs is

$$fit = row + column$$

where *fit* is the predicted value for a cell in the table. Tukey plots *fit* against a "forget it" dimension (*row – column*) through the transformation:

$$(row, column) \rightarrow ((row + column), (row - column))$$

This is proportional to the rotation $(cos(\theta)x–sin(\theta)y,\ sin(\theta)x+cos(\theta)y)$, where θ is -45 degrees, x is the *column* and y is the *row*.

The data are mean monthly temperatures for three places in Arizona. Tukey's fitted values that determine the raw coordinates in Figure 10.3 are based on row and column medians of the means. The motivation for these calculations is to enable both simple paper-and-pencil methods and robustness of the fit. The size of the plotting symbols is proportional to the residuals of the fit. Crosses (+) indicate positive residuals and circles (o) indicate negative.

Tukey calls the horizontal direction of the rotated graphic a "forget-it" dimension. The vertical dimension that shows the fitted average temperatures across locations and months defines the principal variation of interest. Tukey has produced a scale of temperature based on joint variation among places and months. I will present in Chapter 11 another example of this approach in the context of a procedure that Duncan Luce and Tukey developed, called **conjoint measurement** (Luce and Tukey, 1964).

To keep this example simple, I omitted from the specification the overlay to produce the vertical temperature scale on the right. I also omitted a dilatation constant of $1/\sqrt{2}$ (due to using cosines and sines). Related applications motivated by Tukey's graphic can be found in numerous sources, including Velleman and Hoaglin (1981) and Hsu (1996). Tukey's graphic reminds us to turn our heads occasionally so that we can see hidden relationships.

FRAME: **month*city**
COORD: *rotate(-45.)*
GRAPH: *point(size(abs(***residual***)), shape(sign(***residual***)))*

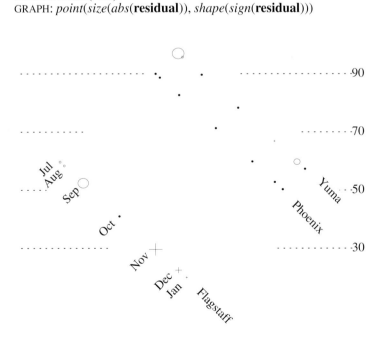

Figure 10.3 *Tukey additive two-way plot*

10.1.1.3 Reflection

Reflection sends (x, y) to $(-x, y)$ or to $(x, -y)$. This operation reverses the vertical or horizontal orientation of a graphic. The dinosaur in Figure 10.1 is up-ended by negating the second coordinate. In Figure 10.4, I have used the *reflect*() method to accomplish a vertical reflection. The last argument (2) ties the reflection to the second dimension.

Vertical reflection produces stalactites from stalagmites. To switch similes, reflection is a way to make icicles out of trees. When the tree display used in cluster analysis is turned upside-down so that the leaves are at the bottom and the root is at the top, it is called an **icicle plot**.

FRAME: **gov*birth**
GRAPH: *bar*()

FRAME: **gov*birth**
COORD: *reflect*(*dim2*)
GRAPH: *bar*()

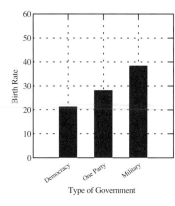
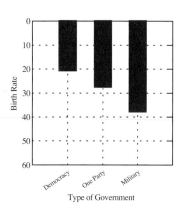

Figure 10.4 *Vertical reflection*

Figure 10.5 illustrates the composite transformation of *reflect* followed by *rotate*. This composite transformation is useful enough to merit its own function, *transpose*(). A transposition is a flip of a graphic around its northeast-southwest diagonal, similar to a matrix transpose, but on the other diagonal.

A reflection followed by a rotation is still an isometry. Indeed, any sequence of $T_1(T_2(T_3(...)))$ is still an isometry if each T_i is a *reflect*(), *translate*() or *rotate*(). However, the result of the sequence *rotate*(*reflect*()) is not equivalent to that of the sequence *reflect*(*rotate*()). Even within their own class (*e.g.*, isometry) planar transformations are not commutative. As we shall see, these transformations are equivalent to matrix products and matrices are not commutative under multiplication. Compare Figure 10.5 to Figure 10.6.

FRAME: **gov*birth**
GRAPH: *bar*()

FRAME: **gov*birth**
COORD: *reflect*(*dim1*)
COORD: *rotate*(270.)
GRAPH: *bar*()

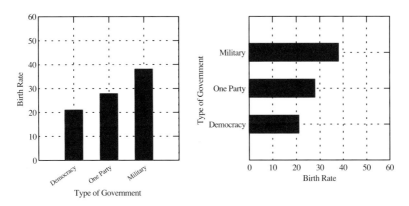

Figure 10.5 *Reflection followed by rotation*

FRAME: **gov*birth**
GRAPH: *bar*()

FRAME: **gov*birth**
COORD: *rotate*(270.)
COORD: *reflect*(*dim1*)
GRAPH: *bar*()

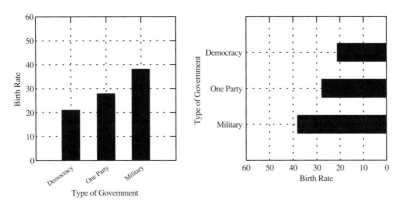

Figure 10.6 *Rotation followed by reflection*

As we have seen, the *transpose* transformation is easily mistaken for a rotation, but there is an even more subtle consequence that is easily overlooked. This involves the role of the range and domain in a graph. In Figure 10.5, **birth** is assigned to the range and **gov** is assigned to the domain. That is, the graph and its resulting graphic are designed to treat birth rates as a function of type of government. Whether or not this is true in real life is another matter.

What if we decided to reverse these roles? Figure 10.7 shows the difference. This operation is a *pivot* of the frame. I have reassigned the range to **gov** and the domain to **birth** in the specification. The resulting graphic expresses type of government as a function of birth rates. Note that the range need not be continuous. In this case a categorical range works fine. If we wanted a summary measure (instead of one bar for every value), we could use the mode. In any case, the graphics and summary measures inside a frame do not change the following fundamental rules of a specification:

$$\mathbf{x}^*\mathbf{y} \neq \mathbf{y}^*\mathbf{x}$$

$$\mathbf{x}^*\mathbf{y} \neq transpose(\mathbf{y}^*\mathbf{x})$$

$$\mathbf{x}^*\mathbf{y} = pivot(\mathbf{y}^*\mathbf{x})$$

Figure 10.7 shows that careless use of pivoting may have unintended consequences. To get what we want, we need to pay attention to the model rather than to the appearance of the graphic.

FRAME: **birth*gov**
GRAPH: *bar*()

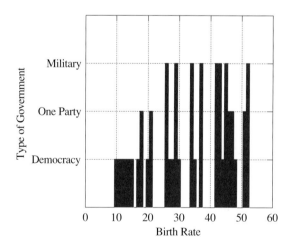

Figure 10.7 *Pivot of* **gov*birth**

I have purloined the name *pivot* from tables and database terminology. A *pivot* of a two-way table in spreadsheets and other computer software is an exchange of rows and columns. Tables aren't ordinarily thought of as having a range and domain, but statisticians who have developed models for analyzing variation in tables know well the difference between a log-linear model and a logistic regression model. The former model adopts the cell entries for the range and the cell margins (averages or other functions of rows and averages or other functions of columns) for the domain. The latter model adopts one margin for the range and the other for the domain. Sharing terminology between tables and graphs is not motivated by convenience or analogy, however. Tables *are* graphs. I will discuss in Chapter 11 the isomorphism between tables and graphs that makes clearer why pivoting a graph is the same operation as pivoting a table. This has important implications for spreadsheet technology, particularly those spreadsheets that produce graphics. Graphics algebra takes the guesswork out of producing a pivoted graphic from a pivoted table.

Figure 10.8 illustrates these important points in a pair of graphics that differ only subtly. In both graphics, the clouds look identical because *point* graphics look the same across range-domain exchanges. In the left plot, however, I have embedded a logarithmic regression smoother

$$E[y] = a + b\log(x)$$

where y is assigned to **data** and x is assigned to **dist**. In the right plot, I have embedded the same smoother except y is assigned to **dist** and x to **data** because of the pivot. The differences between the two curves are due to the different regression models. On the left, estimates for **data** are conditioned on **dist** and on the right, estimates for **dist** are conditioned on **data**. In the left plot, residuals (differences between the points and the regression line) are calculated vertically and in the right, horizontally. In the left plot, the range is on the vertical axis and domain on the horizontal. In the right plot, the range is on the horizontal and the domain on the vertical.

The graphic consequences of these specification rules are more than aesthetic. Figure 10.8 comprises a Shepard diagram from a multidimensional scaling (MDS) of Morse Code confusion data in Rothkopf (1957). The variable **data** contains the confusions (similarities) among the 26 Morse Codes for the letters of the alphabet (numbers have been omitted here). The variable **dist** contains corresponding distances between points in the MDS configuration representing the letters. The smaller the residuals in the Shepard diagram, the better the fit of the MDS configuration to the original data.

Roger Shepard, the inventor of nonmetric multidimensional scaling and the person after whom this plot was named, oriented the plot as in the left panel of Figure 10.8 because the problem had been posed in the classical framework of fitting a theoretical configuration of points to a set of observed data values (Shepard, 1962). Subsequently, Kruskal (1964) and others formulated the problem as a multidimensional minimization of a loss function defined on the distances instead of the data. Rather than change the orientation of the Shepard diagram, Kruskal changed the assignments of the range and domain and represented his residuals horizontally. Later computer programs finally transposed the plot, presumably to reduce confusion over this matter.

This example is related to the statistical procedure known as **inverse regression** (Brown, 1986). In linear inverse regression, we employ the linear model $X = \alpha_0 + \alpha_1 Y$ to predict X, as opposed to the model $Y = \beta_0 + \beta_1 X$ to predict Y. If the ordinary least squares estimates of the parameters of these models are a_0, a_1, b_0, and b_1 then the prediction for a value of X at a given value y_h is $\hat{X} = a_0 + a_1 y_h$ for inverse regression and $\hat{X} = (y_h - b_0)/b_1$ for ordinary regression. This model was originally proposed for machine calibration problems and is now chiefly of historical interest.

> FRAME: **dist*data**
> GRAPH: *point()*
> GRAPH: *line.smooth.log(color("red"))*

> ·FRAME: **dist*data**
> COORD: *pivot()*
> COORD: *transpose()*
> GRAPH: *point()*
> GRAPH: *line.smooth.log(color("red"))*

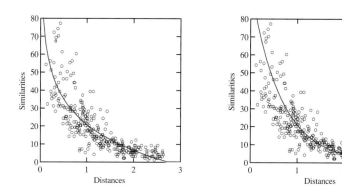

Figure 10.8 *Reflection and rotation exchanges range and domain*

10.1.2 *Similarity Transformations*

A transformation g is a **similarity** if and only if there is a positive number r such that

$$\delta_2((g(x)), g(y)) = r\delta_1(x, y) \text{ for all } x, y \in S_1$$

Similarities on the plane involve isometries as well as dilatation.

10.1.2.1 Dilatation

Dilatation sends polar coordinates (ρ, θ) to $(c\rho, \theta)$ or rectangular coordinates (x, y) to (cx, cy). The dinosaur in Figure 10.1 is shrunk by 50 percent. Figure 10.9 illustrates a dilatation for the countries data. The dilatation works like a photo magnifier or reducer. The multigraphics found in Chapter 11 require dilatation transformations in order to size frames properly within an array of graphics.

Another application of dilatation is for zooming in to reveal detail or zooming out to expose global structure. It is important to distinguish this **graphical zoom** from a **data zoom**. In a graphical zoom, we enlarge or reduce everything, including the axes and text. This operation is achieved through the dilatation transformation. The graphical zoom is best thought of as an optical manipulation. It enables us to examine small areas of a graphic to analyze detailed structure. In a data zoom, on the other hand, we reduce or enlarge a frame by adjusting its bounds in data units. The physical size of the frame graphic (the box demarcated by the axes) and the size of the other graphics inside the frame (points, lines, bars) do not change. Instead, a data zoom-in subsets the data and a data zoom-out embeds the data in a wider range than usual. This data zoom operation has consequences for embedded graphics; they must be recalculated based on the subset of the data in the frame. A graphical zoom, on the other hand, requires no recalculations; only the image is transformed. I will discuss the subtleties of this problem at length in Section 10.1.8.1 later in this chapter.

FRAME: **gov*birth**
GRAPH: *bar*()

FRAME: **gov*birth**
COORD: *dilatate*(.5)
GRAPH: *bar*()

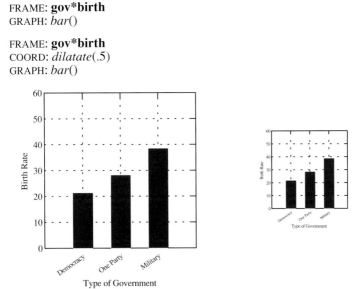

Figure 10.9 *Dilatation transformation*

10.1.3 *Affine Transformations*

The n-tuple coordinate for a point in a space can be represented by the vector $\mathbf{x} = (x_1, \dots, x_n)$. Vector notation allows us to express simply the affine class of transformations:

$$\mathbf{x}^* = \mathbf{x}\mathbf{T} + \mathbf{c} ,$$

where $\mathbf{x}^*$, $\mathbf{x}$, and $\mathbf{c}$ are row vectors and $\mathbf{T}$ is an n by n transformation matrix. In this notation, $\mathbf{x}\mathbf{T}$ is the image of $\mathbf{x}$. If $\mathbf{c} = \mathbf{0}$, we call this a **linear mapping**. The linear subset of the affine class includes rotation, reflection, and dilatation, as well as stretch and shear. If $\mathbf{c} \neq \mathbf{0}$, we call it an **affine mapping**. This adds translation to these operations.

Let's first review the matrix form of the isometric and similarity transformations we have seen so far. Beginning with $\mathbf{T}$, we can see that an identity transformation results from making $\mathbf{T}$ an identity matrix:

$$\mathbf{T} = \begin{bmatrix} 1 & 0 \\ 0 & 1 \end{bmatrix}$$

Rotation involves the more general matrix

$$\mathbf{T} = \begin{bmatrix} \cos\theta & \sin\theta \\ -\sin\theta & \cos\theta \end{bmatrix}$$

where θ is the angle of rotation.

Reflection involves an identity matrix with one or more diagonal elements signed negative, *e.g.*:

$$\mathbf{T} = \begin{bmatrix} -1 & 0 \\ 0 & -1 \end{bmatrix}$$

Any negative diagonal element will reflect the corresponding dimension of $\mathbf{x}$. This particular $\mathbf{T}$ matrix reflects both dimensions.

Dilatation involves a matrix of the form:

$$\mathbf{T} = \begin{bmatrix} a & 0 \\ 0 & a \end{bmatrix}$$

where a is a real number.

Finally, translation involves a row vector of the form:

$$\mathbf{c} = \begin{bmatrix} u & v \end{bmatrix}$$

where u and v are real numbers.

The affine class permits **T** to be a real matrix of the form:

$$\mathbf{T} = \begin{bmatrix} a & b \\ c & d \end{bmatrix}$$

where a, b, c, and d are real numbers. Stretch and shear are produced by two types of this matrix.

10.1.3.1 *Stretch*

Stretch is the transformation that sends (x,y) to (ax, dy), so

$$\mathbf{T} = \begin{bmatrix} a & 0 \\ 0 & d \end{bmatrix} .$$

The dinosaur in Figure 10.1 is stretched by a factor of 2 on the second coordinate (vertical axis).

The stretch transformation varies the **aspect ratio** of a graphic. This is the ratio of the physical height to the physical width of the frame graphic. Often this ratio is chosen to make a graphic fit in a page layout or on a computer screen. This practice of convenience more often degrades than improves the accuracy of the perception of the information underlying the graphic. As Cleveland, McGill, and McGill (1988) have shown, many conventional prescriptions for aspect ratios in a plot ("make it square," "make it a Greek golden rectangle," etc.) have no empirical or theoretical justification. Instead, aspect ratios should be determined by the perceptual considerations of the content in the frame, namely, the shape of the graphics. Cleveland has shown that for line plots, perception of *relative* changes in slope is most accurate near a 45 degree orientation. (Sensitivity to *absolute* slope differences near threshold is highest near verticals or horizontals, but this is not relevant to this context.)

Figure 10.10 shows a stretch transformation of a time series graphic. The two graphics in this figure are rescalings of the sunspot data from Andrews and Herzberg (1985). The aspect ratio on the left makes a global absolute slope component approximately 45 degrees. The extreme shear transformation on the right highlights local, high-frequency detail in the plot. It was computed by setting the median absolute slope of the line segments (approximately 500 in number) to unity, following a procedure outlined in Cleveland, McGill, and McGill (1988). The choice of aspect ratio must be guided by the information we wish to communicate. Sometimes more than one graphic is needed to highlight the important frequency components. In a dynamic graphics system, we could connect aspect ratio to a controller so that the user could explore these variations in real time. The simplest implementation of such a controller would be on the frame itself, so that we could resize by dragging vertically or horizontally.

FRAME: **year*spots**
GRAPH: *line*()

FRAME: **year*spots**
COORD: *stretch*(2.0, 0.111)
GRAPH: *line*()

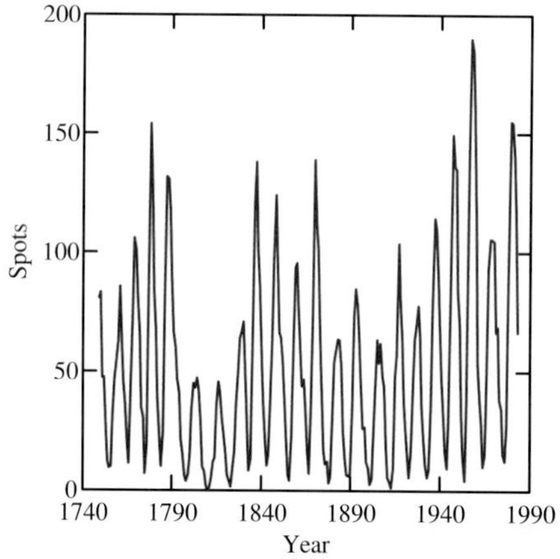

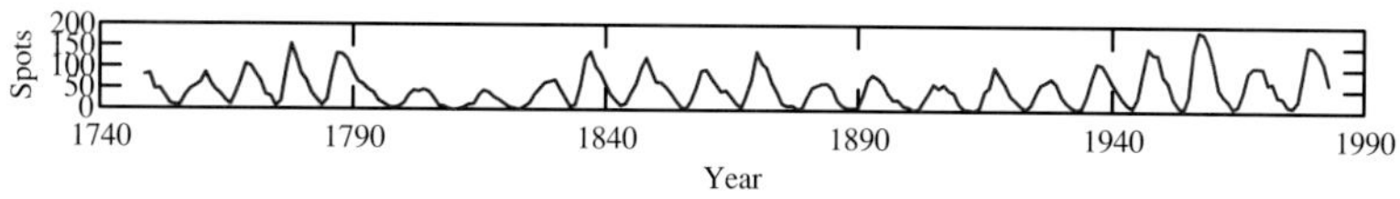

Figure 10.10 *Stretch transformation*

10.1.3.2 Shear

Shear is the transformation that sends (x, y) to $((ax+cy), (bx+dy))$, so

$$\mathbf{T} = \begin{bmatrix} a & b \\ c & d \end{bmatrix}.$$

The dinosaur in Figure 10.1 was produced by the matrix whose elements are $a=.96$, $b=.3$, $c=.3$, $d=.96$. Figure 10.11 shows the same shear transformation on a data graphic. The data are principal components of the sociometric ratings of U.S. cities (Boyer and Savageau, 1996). The components have been rotated using an oblique rotation method called **oblimin** (Harman, 1976; Clarkson and Jennrich, 1988). This rotation fits basis vectors through bundles of component vectors without a restriction that the basis vectors be orthogonal. Computer packages typically graph oblique rotations in the manner of the left panel of Figure 10.11. Making the basis orthogonal helps us to see the separation between components, but conceals the dependency among oblique factors. The right panel shows a shear transformation applied to the graphic underlying the left pane. It makes clear the dependency between factors and thus encourages us not to make independent unitary interpretations.

Applications of oblique transformations in factor analysis sometimes show oblique axes running through the center of the vectors in an oblique cross. This graphic can be helpful for thinking of an oblique rotation as a fitting of a non-orthogonal basis under some loss function. As the right panel of Figure 10.11 shows, however, it can be helpful sometimes to place the axes at the edge of the plot to keep clutter outside the center of the frame, especially when there are many vectors,

DATA: **zero** = *constant*(0)
FRAME: **factor1*factor2 + zero*zero**
GRAPH: *link.edge.join*(*label*(**name**))

DATA: **zero** = *constant*(0)
FRAME: **factor1*factor2 + zero*zero**
COORD: *shear*(0.96, 0.3, 0.3, 0.96)
GRAPH: *link.edge.join*(*label*(**name**))

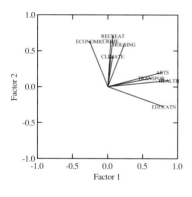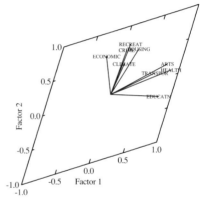

Figure 10.11 *Oblique factor rotation (shear)*

10.1.4 *Planar Projections*

A planar projection is the mapping of one plane to another by perspective projection from any point not lying on either. Figure 10.12 illustrates this mapping spatially. For every point in the image on the lower plane in the figure, there is a single corresponding point in the domain on the upper plane.

As the figure suggests, we may use a similar model to produce a perspective projection that creates 2D perspective views of 3D objects in computer graphics. Planar projections are more restrictive than 3D-to-2D projections, however. They share the *composition* behavior of other planar transformations. We can, in other words, project a projection and stay within the projectivity class. In the 3D-to-2D projection, it is possible to have more than one point in the domain for a single point in the image.

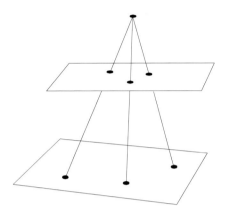

Figure 10.12 *Projection of one plane on another*

To notate projections, it is helpful to adopt **homogeneous coordinates**. We combine the **T** and **c** matrices into one general square matrix **A**:

$$\mathbf{A} = \begin{bmatrix} a & b & p \\ c & d & q \\ u & v & s \end{bmatrix}.$$

The elements $a, b, c,$ and d are from the **T** matrix and u and v are from the **c** vector that we used for affine transformations. The elements $p, q,$ and s are for projection. To make this system work, we need to express **x** in homogeneous coordinates by augmenting our coordinate vector by one element:

$$\mathbf{x} = (x, y, h)$$

If $h = 1$, then our Cartesian coordinates are simply $x = x/h$ and $y = y/h$. This re-parameterization makes the general projective transformation

$$\mathbf{x}^* = \mathbf{xA}$$

This matrix equation produces the following homogeneous coordinates:

$$\mathbf{x}^* = ((ax + cy + u), (bx + dy + v), (px + qy + s))$$

If we renormalize after the transformation so that the third coordinate is unity, we can retrieve (x^*, y^*) as the Cartesian coordinates from the projection. To see what projection adds to the affine class, we should notice that the third column of **A** produces a different scaling of x and y depending on their values. And because all the transformations are linear, the straightness of lines is preserved in the class.

10.1.4.1 Project

The projected dinosaur in Figure 10.1 was produced by the coordinate transformation

$$(x, y) \rightarrow (1/x, y/x) .$$

This projection involves a transformation used in the statistical technique called **weighted least squares**. I will present an example.

Figure 10.13 shows a scatterplot relating diastolic blood pressure to age. Neter, Wasserman, and Kutner (1990) devised this dataset to illustrate a popular technique for dealing with unequal variances (**heteroscedasticity**) in linear regression. As the left panel of the figure shows, the variation around the fitted line is larger for older people than for younger. This violates an assumption of equal variances (**homoscedasticity**) needed for conventional tests of hypotheses involving the regression coefficient relating blood pressure and age. The panel on the right of the figure shows the distribution of data we would like to see for testing these hypotheses appropriately.

One simple approach statisticians have used to ameliorate this problem is to transform the data before fitting the line. This transformation involves weighting the values of age and blood pressure according to the corresponding blood pressure value. We start by noticing that the envelope of the variation about the line in the left panel is like a fan with straight sides. Assuming we have a random sample of values, this pattern suggests that the population variance of blood pressure at a given level of age increases linearly with age:

$$\sigma_i^2 = \sigma^2 x_i .$$

Neter, Wasserman, and Kutner illustrate some statistical and graphical approaches to confirming this supposition by examining the distribution of the data. If we believe the data fit this model, then we can attempt to equalize the conditional variances by dividing both variables by the value of age for each pair. In other words, we transform a model we are almost certain is false to one that appears to be true:

$$y_i = \beta_0 + \beta_1 x_i + \varepsilon_i \quad \rightarrow \quad \frac{y_i}{x_i} = \beta_0' + \frac{\beta_1'}{x_i} + \varepsilon_i'$$

The graphic in the right panel of Figure 10.13 is a fit of this latter model. It is plotted using the transformed data (**age/bp** and **1/bp**). The result resembles the classic textbook example of linear regression. The fan shape has been transformed into a stripe; the variance of y appears to be constant across all values of x. The regression line runs through the center of this stripe, as it should.

FRAME: **age*bp**
GRAPH: *line.smooth.linear()*
GRAPH: *point()*

TRANS: **iage** = *inverse*(**age**)
TRANS: **rage** = *ratio*(**bp,age**)
FRAME: **iage*rage**
GRAPH: *line.smooth.linear()*
GRAPH: *point()*

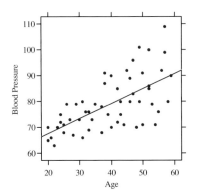 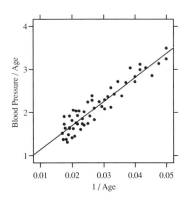

Figure 10.13 *Weighted least squares via transformation of variables*

A problem students often have with this approach is understanding what was done to the data. It is difficult to relate the plot in the right panel to the one in the left. The cloud is reversed horizontally and the scale values are not in the original metric. If we parameterize this model as a projection, however, we can produce a graphic in the original metric transformed. Note that the weighted model can be viewed as the coordinate transformation

$$(x, y) \rightarrow (1/x, y/x) \ .$$

The projection matrix for expressing this transformation is:

$$\mathbf{A} = \begin{bmatrix} 0 & 0 & 1 \\ 0 & 1 & 0 \\ 1 & 0 & 0 \end{bmatrix} \ .$$

This takes **x** in homogeneous coordinates to **x*** = (1, y, x) which produces the result we want in Cartesian coordinates after dividing through by x. Figure 10.14 shows the result. I have included the **A** matrix in the parameter list as the array a[]. Now we see explicitly that the transformation reflects the x axis because of inversion and fans out blood pressure for younger ages. Notice that the regression line passes through the same observations in all these plots. The ordinary fit of the line under heteroscedasticity is unbiased. It is the *variances* we have adjusted.

Data-modeling statisticians have devised more elaborate methods to deal with these problems, including iterative reweighting, maximum likelihood, and generalized least squares. While Figure 10.14 may look unfamiliar even to some experts at first glance, however, it is no different in spirit from polar coordinates, log scales, and other coordinate transformations we routinely use to produce more familiar scientific graphics. Coordinate transformations allow us to see what was done to our data.

FRAME: **age*bp**
COORD: *project(a[])*
GRAPH: *line.smooth.linear()*
GRAPH: *point()*

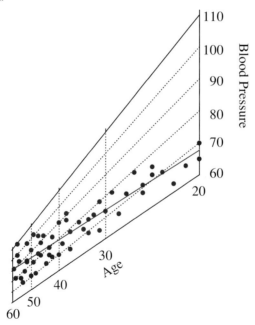

Figure 10.14 *Projection*

Figure 10.14 highlights an interpretive problem with transformations. Statistical modeling via transformation or weighting is a widely used method for dealing with unusual distributions. The problem is that we most often want to state our conclusions in terms of the original variables. Sometimes we can escape the problem by keeping the transformation and not inverting it to explain our result. Miles-per-gallon, for example, can be transformed to gallons-per-mile in order to make it more normally distributed. This form of the index may be more useful anyway. Paul Velleman (Velleman and Wilkinson, 1994) has suggested this transformation for routine use and has noted that Europeans use this form (liters-per-kilometer) presumably because it enables travelers to compute more easily their gas needs on a trip. If we transform, do statistics, and invert our transformation, however, we must be extremely careful in our interpretations of the result, particularly when random error is included in our models. I will examine this problem further in Section 10.1.8.

10.1.5 Conformal Mappings

We need to generalize our coordinates once more in order to move to the next level of the planar transformation hierarchy. By working on the complex plane, we can define functions that would be messy or difficult to understand in the real domain. A complex number $z = x + iy$ may be represented by a vector $\mathbf{z}$ on the complex plane whose coordinates are $Re(z) = x$ and $Im(z) = y$. Coordinate transformations on (x, y) can then be expressed in the form

$$w = f(z) = u(z) + iv(z) ,$$

where $u(z)$ and $v(z)$ are real functions of z and w is the image point of z under f.

First, as I did with the affine and projective classes, let us dress the child of the conformal class in the clothes of this new notation. Similarity transformations can be expressed in the complex formula

$$w - az + b$$

where w, a, b, and z are all complex. We can see this by noting that

$$(a_1 + ia_2)(x + iy) = (a_1x - a_2y) + i(a_2x + a_1y) + (b_1 + ib_2)$$

which is the same set of operations involved in the similarity subclass of the projective transformation

$$\mathbf{xA} = (x, y, 1) \cdot \begin{bmatrix} a_1 & a_2 & 0 \\ -a_2 & a_1 & 0 \\ b_1 & b_2 & 1 \end{bmatrix}$$

The projective matrix notation tells us that the complex constant b is involved in translation and the complex constant a is involved in rotation and dilatation of the plane represented in z, since the submatrix

$$\begin{bmatrix} a_1 & a_2 \\ -a_2 & a_1 \end{bmatrix} = r \begin{bmatrix} \cos\theta & \sin\theta \\ -\sin\theta & \cos\theta \end{bmatrix} ,$$

where r is a real number. There is another way to show the rotational role of the complex constant a. Euler's formula

$$e^{i\theta} = \cos\theta + i\sin\theta$$

locates a point on the unit circle at angle θ on the complex plane. It tells us that any complex number can be expressed as

$$z = re^{i\theta} .$$

We can thus re-express the complex constant a and define a similarity transformation as

$$w = re^{i\theta}z + b ,$$

which rotates z by θ and dilatates it by r.

A conformal mapping adds a peculiar geometric characteristic to a similarity transformation: local angles (at the intersection of two curves) are preserved, but straight lines may become curves. A planar mapping is conformal if every point on the plane is transformed so that all possible infinitesimal vectors emanating from that point are rotated and dilatated by the same amount in the image. This local rotation and dilatation means that very small squares remain squares in the image, but large squares can be distorted considerably. The paradoxical beauty of this transformation is that locally it looks like a similarity but globally it looks like a nonlinear warping.

The conformal dinosaur in Figure 1 was produced by the transformation

$$w = \frac{1-z}{1+z}$$

Figure 10.15 shows several examples of conformal mappings of a chessboard pattern. I have set the domain of these mappings to the interval $[-\pi,+\pi]$ on both x and y. Several of these transformations are a subclass of the Möbius transformation

$$w = \frac{az+b}{cz+d} ,$$

where all the constants and variables are complex. This transformation has inspired a variety of basic applications in physics, fluid dynamics, electromagnetic fields, and other areas. Needham (1997) offers a glimpse into this world from a geometric perspective and illustrates its application to vector flows and other graphics in physics. Running graphics through variations of this transformation to see what they look like can be addictive.

FRAME: **x*y**
COORD: *conform(w[])*
GRAPH: *tile()*

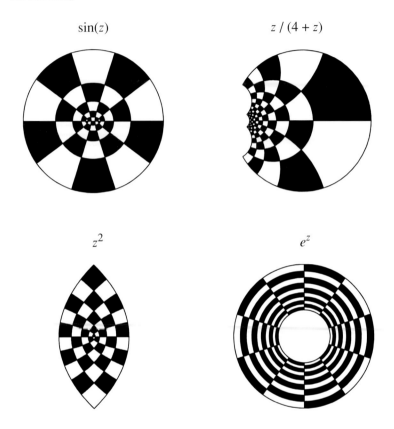

$$\sin(z) \qquad\qquad z/(4+z)$$

$$z^2 \qquad\qquad e^z$$

Figure 10.15 *Conformal mappings of a chess board*

10.1.5.1 Conform

Figure 10.15 may seem a looking-glass world for most of the graphics in Chapter 6, but there are practical applications of planar conformal maps. I will omit the vector flow diagrams used in physics and instead show a simple graphic from the field of meteorology. Figure 10.16 is a graphic relating humidity to wind direction for a ground-level site. The data comprise hourly meteorological measurements over a year at the Greenland Humboldt automatic weather station operated by NASA and NSF. These measurements are part of the Greenland Climate Network (GC-Net) sponsored by these federal agencies. Data like these are available at numerous sites on the World Wide Web.

FRAME: **direction*humidity**
COORD: *conform(w[])*
GRAPH: *line.smooth.loess()*
GRAPH: *point()*

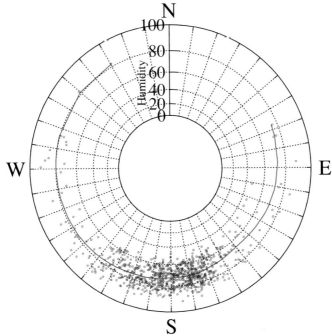

Figure 10.16 *Conformal mapping*

On first glance, Figure 10.16 resembles a polar wind chart with a LOESS smoother. The wind direction is represented by a polar angle from 0 to 360 degrees and humidity is represented by the outer section of the radius. The conformal mapping (e^z) underlying the graphic is not a polar transformation, however. Notice that the radial dimension (**humidity**) is exponentially spaced. High humidities are spaced farther apart than low. This nonlinear scale transforms the negatively skewed distribution of **humidity** to a more normal one. The other feature distinguishing this from a polar chart is that zero humidity is not mapped to the center of the circle. In the complex exponential transformation, the center of the circle corresponds to negative infinity. This graphic is not a pie. Its center is a black hole.

The LOESS robust smooth shows that humidities tend to be lower for winds coming from a south-easterly direction. The highest humidities prevail in the west. The cloud reveals that there are few wind measurements over the year in the northerly sectors.

10.1.6 Polar Coordinates

If (u, v) represents the polar coordinates (ρ, θ) of a point, then the polar coordinate function $P(u, v) \rightarrow (x, y)$ corresponds to the case $u = \rho$, $v = \theta$, where $x = \rho \cos\theta$ and $y = \rho \sin\theta$. There are numerous important applications of the polar transformation in graphics. Mathematicians and scientists usually deal with polar coordinates measured on the real numbers such that one revolution corresponds to an interval of 2π radians.

Figure 10.17 shows an example for the cosine function with period $\pi/3$. The range of this graph is on the interval $[-1, +1]$ and the domain is on the interval $(-\infty, \infty)$. Our graphic shows a domain only on the interval $[0, 2\pi)$. This means that we can see only one cosine curve at each petal even though there would be an infinite number of these curves at each petal if we allowed the domain to cycle more than once around the circle (see the *cycle* parameter in Section 9.2.2). There are not many good ways to fix this representation problem. We could plot the function in cylindrical coordinates (see Section 10.3.3) with the cylindrical axis assigned to the same variable as θ.

We could treat polar coordinates as an exception to the way all other scales are handled in this system. That is, we could interpret angular values absolutely as radians. This would make sense if all our graphics were mathematical or engineering applications involving radians. I have chosen not to do this, however, so that we can hide scaling details when doing coordinate conversions. This makes it easy, for example, to represent yearly time in polar coordinates. In the polar coordinate conversion, therefore, I align 0 radians with the minimum scale value in data units (degrees, radians, proportions, etc.) and 2π radians with the maximum. The *cycle* parameter, together with *min* and *max* parameters in the scale functions allows us to create polar graphs with more than one revolution if we wish.

A note about the *polar*() function in the COORD specification: the arguments are reversed from the order given for $P(u,v)$ above. That is, the first dimension is taken to be the domain, which is assigned to θ. The second dimension is taken to be the range, which is assigned to ρ. This is in keeping with the general order of algebraic specifications within a frame: the factors are ordered as *domain₁, domain₂, ... , range*.

As I will show in this section, applications of polar coordinates range far beyond technical and mathematical graphics. The polar transformation is useful whenever data lend themselves to circular arrangements. This includes directional data (vector wind, compass bearings), rotational data (defects on disk drives), astronomical time (daily, monthly, annual), periodic waveforms (radio signals), and proportions (the humble pie chart). Sometimes, circular arrangements offer simpler parameterizations or structures for making sense of a phenomenon. Polar models of facial expressions, for example, provide the most parsimonious summaries of behavioral observations (see Figure 7.49).

DATA: **x** = *iter*(0, 6.28, 0.01)
TRANS: **y** = *cos*(6***x**)
SCALE: *interval*(*dim1*, 0, 6.28, . , . , "pi")
FRAME: **x*****y**
COORD: *polar*()
GRAPH: *line*()

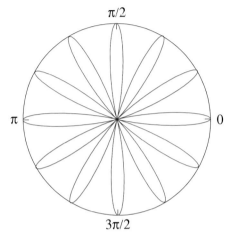

Figure 10.17 *Polar cosine*

Polar plots are often a means to a geometric end. In these cases, we are happy to limit our domain to one revolution because our goal is to represent objects in a circular arrangement. Figure 10.18 shows a polar dinosaur.

FRAME: **x*****y**
COORD: *polar*()
COORD: *transpose*()
GRAPH: *link.edge.mst*()

Figure 10.18 *Polar dinosaur*

The coordinates for the tail-to-head dimension have been scaled to vary between 0 and 2π and I have oriented the graphic to make 0 at the top by transposing it after the polar transformation. This dinosaur is hibernating.

The specification for the graphic reveals how I created these dinosaur transformations. Instead of working with bitmaps, I digitized the outlines into (x, y) coordinates computed at closely spaced intervals. Then I added the minimum spanning tree (MST) version of the *link* graph to "connect the dots." Occasional irregularities and gaps are due to the resolution of the dot spacing I chose and the MST algorithm's compulsion to go to the nearest adjacent dot.

Any circular directional variable is an obvious candidate for polar representation. Compass direction, for example, varies between 0 and 360 degrees. There are other reasons to send graphics through a polar transformation, however. The most popular application in graphics is the pie chart, which I will discuss first. Pies lend themselves to proportion-of-whole representations for valid visual-processing reasons. Polar coordinates also provide a useful medium for fitting a lot of information in a small space. Polar trees allow the highest resolution in the area of their leaves, which makes them popular among geneticists and others who must cluster large sets of objects.

There are several different *polar* coordinate methods needed for statistical graphics. The conventional *polar* function requires two arguments. We use this one for embedding graphics in two-dimensional frames, such as in scatterplots and mathematical graphs of polar functions. The other polar functions take only one argument. The *polar.theta* function assigns its argument to θ and sets ρ to unity. The *polar.rho* function assigns its argument to ρ and sets θ to unity. The *polar.rho.plus* function works like *polar.rho* except 1 is added to ρ before the transformation. This pushes the range outside the unit circle. This function is used for producing rose diagrams (see Section 10.1.6.3).

10.1.6.1 Polar.theta

As we have seen in Chapter 2, a pie chart is a stacked bar in polar coordinates. The *polar.theta* function assigns its only argument (the position attribute) to θ, and assigns the radius (ρ) to a constant that determines the size of the pie.

Figure 10.19 shows a pie chart. Notice that the only difference from the stacked bar specification in Figure 7.32 is in the *polar.theta* transformation. Notice also that the labels for the slices are not part of an axis, scale, or other guide. They are attached to each slice through the *label*() aesthetic function. I will discuss this further in Chapter 12, where I will cover guides. The appearance of a graphic can sometimes deceive us. We must analyze text carefully to determine whether it is part of a guide or part of a graphic.

It seems odd to go through a function to produce the most popular chart of all. Simplicity is in the eye of the beholder, however. Once we learn to bake pies in round and square pans, we can graduate to other shapes, as the next example will show.

FRAME: **female**
COORD: *polar.theta()*
GRAPH: *bar(label(**response**), color(**response**), position.stack())*

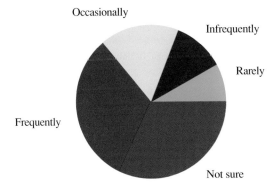

Figure 10.19 *Pie chart*

10.1.6.2 Polar.rho

A circular pie chart is a variation on the divided bar in polar coordinates. It bakes a pie in a bundt cake pan. The *polar.rho* projection assigns the position attribute to ρ and wraps θ around the circle.

Figure 10.20 shows an example for the bias data. This graphic is occasionally used by newspaper and magazine marketing departments to represent spheres of circulation among different readerships. The perceptual problem with the graphic is that areas are confounded with the radial variable.

FRAME: **female**
COORD: *polar.rho()*
GRAPH: *bar(label(**response**), color(**response**), position.stack())*

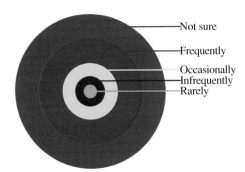

Figure 10.20 *Circular pie chart*

10.1.6.3 Polar.plus

The *polar.plus* and *polar.rho.plus* functions are for rendering graphs along the circumference of a circle. This is needed when essential features of graphics get jammed together near the center of the polar domain. Graphics in this form are seen most frequently in ecology and spatial statistics applications, where circular distributions are analyzed (*e.g.*, Upton & Fingleton, 1989). Figure 10.21 shows a polar dot plot and rose histogram for the wind direction data used in Figure 10.16.

FRAME: **direction**
COORD: *polar.rho.plus()*
GRAPH: *point(position.stack())*

DATA: **count** = *count()*
FRAME: **direction*count**
COORD: *polar.rho.plus()*
GRAPH: *histobar()*

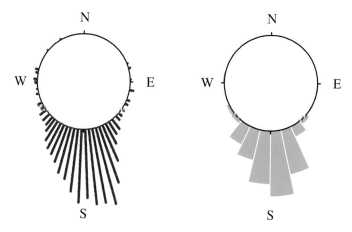

Figure 10.21 *Polar dot plot and histogram*

    The wind rose (*rosa ventorum*) has been drawn for centuries by cartographers. Predating the compass rose, it appeared on navigational charts as early as the 13th century. Wainer (1995) shows an example by Léon Lalanne from 1830. Lalanne drew by hand his estimates of prevailing ocean wind strength and direction.

    We can construct a similar graphic by computer today. Figure 10.22 shows a statistically based smoothing of the Greenland wind direction data. I have drawn the axes to resemble Lalanne's chart. This rose results from embedding a kernel smoother *density* graphic in a polar frame. Because I used the *polar* function in this figure, much of the detail near the center is lost. This graphic would benefit from a nonlinear transformation of the radial scale. Nevertheless, it is interesting that coordinate-based applications of relatively recent technology (kernel smoothing) can benefit from clever cartographic insights of the past. One thing to note: the radial distance from the center represents the proportion of measured times that the wind was blowing in a given direction, not the strength of the wind itself.

DATA: **prop** = *proportion*()
FRAME: **direction*prop**
COORD: *polar*()
COORD: *transpose*()
GRAPH: *line.density.kernel.epanechnikov*()

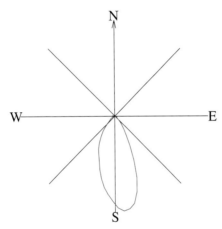

Figure 10.22 Rose kernel density

10.1.6.4 Polar

The standard *polar* two-argument function has numerous applications. Figure 10.23 shows a Nightingale rose chart and the bars from which it is constructed. I have used the ACLS data from Chapter 2. The left panel shows the rectangular coordinate graphic as an ordinary bar chart. The bar thicknesses are set to full width so that the bars touch each other. This makes the segments in the polar graphic in the right panel span the entire circle. Notice that, unlike Figure 10.19, the polar angles are constant for every bar. While this figure seems to be a type of pie chart, it is in fact a fundamentally different graphic based on a *bar* instead of a slice. This chart derives its name from a graphic devised by Florence Nightingale (Wainer, 1995). Attractive as it may be, the polar bar chart confounds area with radius. Square rooting the radii only partly ameliorates this confounding.

FRAME: **response*female**
GRAPH: *bar*(*color*(**response**))

FRAME: **response*female**
COORD: *polar*()
GRAPH: *bar*(*color*(**response**))

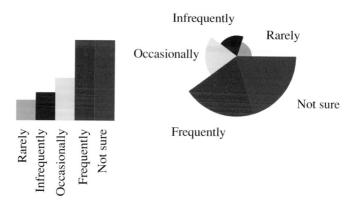

Figure 10.23 *Bar graphic and Nightingale rose*

Figure 10.24 shows a reflection of the Nightingale rose. I have included this rather atrocious chart to illustrate further the composition of coordinate functions. Notice that the **female** variable is assigned to the range, so the *reflect* function reverses the range scale before mapping to polar coordinates.

FRAME: **response*female**
COORD: *reflect*(*dim2*)
COORD: *polar*()
GRAPH: *bar*(*color*(**response**))

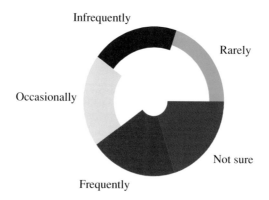

Figure 10.24 *Reflected Nightingale rose*

Figure 10.25 shows a polar transformation of a dual stacked bar. As in the previous example, polar coordinates do not help to elucidate the structure, but this example illustrates the roles the dimensions play in the coordinate transformation. Compare these results to the un-transposed version in Figure 7.32. What would the right panel look like if we did not use *transpose()*?

DATA: **m** = *string*("Male")
DATA: **f** = *string*("Female")
FRAME: **m*male+f*female**
COORD: *transpose*()
GRAPH: *bar*(*position.stack*(), *color*(**response**), *label*(**response**))

DATA: **m** = *string*("Male")
DATA: **f** = *string*("Female")
FRAME: **m*male+f*female**
COORD: *transpose*()
COORD: *polar*()
GRAPH: *bar*(*position.stack*(), *color*(**response**), *label*(**response**))

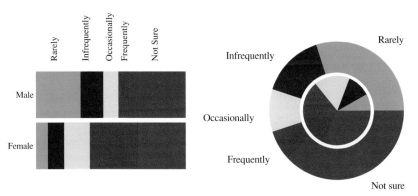

Figure 10.25 *Polar divided bar of ACLS data*

Polar coordinates can be used to enhance detail in areas where it is important. When there are many leaves, or terminal nodes, a cluster tree becomes unwieldy. Placing the tree in polar coordinates leaves room for displaying more leaves. Figure 10.26 shows a polar tree on the cities data. Notice that straight lines become curves in the polar representation, although we could take special steps to prevent this behavior if we wished to design the software that way.

Polar trees are often used by biologists to display results of cluster analyses or large genetic trees. Recently, computer scientists have taken an interest in similar layouts for displaying large trees in browsers and other windows. The fish-eye coordinate transformation (see Section 10.1.8) can be used to show more detail in a region of the tree. Munzner (1997) describes a hyperbolic tree that has been used in several commercial applications.

FRAME: **xnode*ynode**
COORD: *polar*()
GRAPH: *link.edge.tree*(*position*(**parent**),*label*(**city**)))

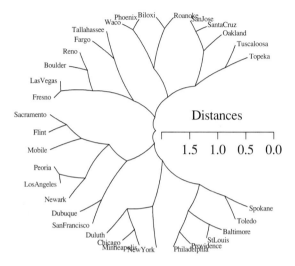

Figure 10.26 *Polar cluster tree*

Polar coordinates have many uses for displaying seasonal data. Time series are usually displayed linearly. This is the format in which we are accustomed to viewing stock market data, for example. This format facilitates scale look-up and decoding of prices. When seasonal characteristics are of interest, however, strip charts of annual time series are less effective as a display. Figure 10.27 shows a three-year time series of the daily closing price of the stock of SPSS. I have omitted the stock price scale because the focus of interest here is the trend. I have also specified a three-year cycle for the time scale; see Chapter 9 for information on the format of the *time*() scale function. Polar coordinates make it easy to compare local features across seasons, especially at the end/beginning of years. Moreover, the plot enables a global assessment not possible with strip charts of time series: if the stock is everywhere increasing over its previous season's price, the *line* graphic will appear as a spiral. Seasonal comparison is most prevalent in the language of companies when they present quarterly results to the brokers who set earnings numbers. Wadsworth *et al.* (1986) have made this same observation in the context of process control monitoring.

Carlis and Konstan (1998) propose polar visualizations for periodic series, although they employ a spiral for anchoring the data (see Figure 10.30). This method can be effective for series where the inspection of trend components is less critical than seasonal. Stock series would not be appropriate for their method, but they present other series for which it makes sense. Tufte (1983) shows historical examples.

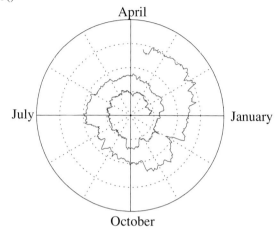

FRAME: **date*price**
SCALE: *time(dim1,"month", " ", " ", " ", 3)*
COORD: *polar()*
GRAPH: *line()*

Figure 10.27 *Polar time series (SPSS stock)*

A favorite graphic among quality control engineers, particularly in Japan, is the **radar plot**. Like the spiral time series, this display facilitates rapid discrimination of a single important feature: is an ordered set of numbers pairwise larger than another ordered set of the same size? The radar plot makes this relation easy to detect because the convex hull of the larger set completely contains the hull of the smaller. This display generalizes easily to more than two sets of numbers. General Motors used this graphic in 1997 advertising to demonstrate that the envelope of performance features for its C5 Corvette – handling, economy, acceleration, safety, etc. – substantially exceeded the numbers for its previous model. Figure 10.28 shows this type of plot for weather data. The two polar profiles show average summer and winter temperatures for eight regions of the US. Not surprisingly, average summer temperatures are higher than winter in all regions. Some radar plots involve different scales for each variable in the plot. These are instances of polar parallel coordinate plots rather than polar profiles. See Figure 10.57 for an example.

There is one technical detail you may have noticed. Why is the outer edge of the *area* graphic a straight line instead of a circular arc? There is no mathematical reason to make it so, but some statistical justification for it to remain straight. Since **region** is a categorical variable, the line segments linking regions are not in a metric region of the graph. That is, the segments of the domain between regions are not measurable and thus the straight lines or edges linking them are arbitrary and perhaps not subject to geometric transformation. This is a detail where mathematical purity collides with statistical and graphical goals. The appearance of the graphic has been dictated by custom rather than geometry.

DATA: **s** = *string*("Summer")
DATA: **w** = *string*("Winter")
FRAME: **region*****(summer+winter)**
COORD: *polar*()
GRAPH: *area*(*color*(**s+w**))

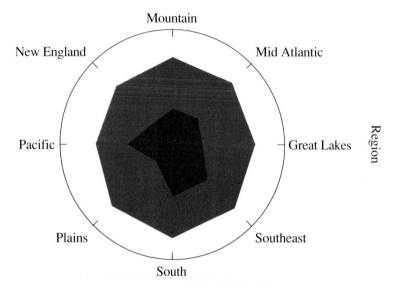

Figure 10.28 *Radar plot*

The polar domain offers numerous opportunities for contouring and other graphs that represent additional dimensions. Figure 10.29 shows a transposed polar plot of barometric pressure by wind speed by wind direction. The pressure values have been smoothed by distance-weighted least squares onto the surface represented by wind speed and direction. The contours have been colored by level of barometric pressure. Lower pressures (blue) correspond to southeasterly high speed winds while higher pressures (red) correspond to westerly low-speed winds. The plotted speeds are the highest gust recorded each hour, so they have a ceiling, as evidenced by the uniform boundary of values in the cloud near 11 meters per second at the bottom of the circle.

When contouring in the polar domain, we must be careful in the way we compute contours. If we contour in rectangular coordinates and then transform the contours, there will be discontinuities at the boundaries, especially with polynomial and related smoothers. A similar problem exists when contouring on the sphere. To solve the problem, we must do our calculations in the transformed metric.

FRAME: **direction*speed**
COORD: *polar()*
COORD: *transpose()*
GRAPH: *point()*
GRAPH: *contour.smooth.quadratic.cauchy(color.hue(**pressure**))*

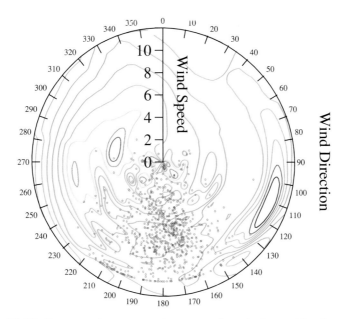

Figure 10.29 *Barometric pressure (contours) by wind speed by direction*

10.1.7 Inversion

Complex inversion is a turning inside-out of the plane. It is most easily understood by considering the transformation $(\rho, \theta) \rightarrow (1/\rho, \theta)$ in polar coordinates, where radii are converted to their reciprocals. More generally, we define
the **complex conjugate** of $z = x + iy$ to be $\bar{z} = x - iy$. Then the transformation of the complex plane $z \rightarrow 1/\bar{z}$ is a geometric inversion. The invariance of this transformation is that circles remain circles (notice that θ is
unchanged and ρ is simply inverted in the polar representation of the transformation).

Figure 10.30 shows an inversion of a spiral. Notice that the points outside
the unit circle are turned in and the points inside are turned out. This coordinate transformation would be useful for highly skewed data or whenever we
wish to expose the detail in the center of the polar coordinate world. Inverting
an image suggests some interesting possibilities. Inverting a face is best re-
served for Halloween.

DATA: $\mathbf{x} = iter(0., 18.86, 1000)$
TRANS: $\mathbf{y} = \mathbf{x}/8 - .2$
SCALE: $interval(dim1, 0, 18.86, 10, 3)$
COORD: $polar()$
GRAPH: $point(color.hue(\mathbf{x}))$

DATA: $\mathbf{x} = iter(0., 18.86, 1000)$
TRANS: $\mathbf{y} = \mathbf{x}/8 - .2$
SCALE: $interval(dim1, 0, 18.86, 10, 3)$
COORD: $polar()$
COORD: $inverse()$
GRAPH: $point(color.hue(\mathbf{x}))$

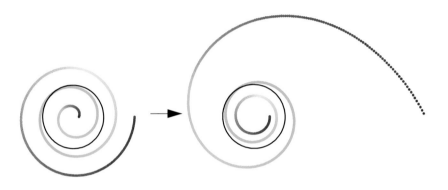

Figure 10.30 *Inversion of a spiral*

10.1.8 *Bendings*

This section covers coordinate transformations that bend the plane like a sheet of plastic. Bendings stretch the plane along *x* or *y* or in both directions. I will first discuss single bending, most frequently used to straighten curves and linearize scales. Then I will discuss double bends, used to compress or dilate sections of the plane. Bendings involve the continuous planar transformation:

$$(x, y) \rightarrow (f(x), g(y)) = (u, v) .$$

One way to visualize this class of transformations is to think of a frame graphic with axes and grid lines and note that the grid lines remain parallel after transformation and the axes remain perpendicular. Bendings involve no shear. This is because *u* and *v* depend only on *x* and *y* respectively.

10.1.8.1 Inverting a Scale Transformation

The logarithmic planar transformation is

$$(x, y) \rightarrow (log(x), y) \text{ , or}$$

$$(x, y) \rightarrow (x, log(y)) \text{ , or}$$

$$(x, y) \rightarrow (log(x), log(y)) \text{ ,}$$

where the log function is

$$log: x \rightarrow ln(x)/ln(k) \text{ , } k>0 \text{ , } x>0.$$

Many graphs use aggregation functions in their position computations. However, the *mean* of the *log* is not the *log* of the *mean*. Nor is the *sd* of the *log* the *log* of the *sd*. In general, any aggregation must be computed *after* nonlinear transformations in order for the results to be statistically correct. Thus, we should not use a log coordinate transformation to deal with skewness in our data. Instead, we should use a log scale (see Figure 9.7) to address this problem. We may *anti-log* our results, however, if we wish to view them in the original metric. Figure 10.31 shows how this works.

FRAME: **exposure*brainweight**
SCALE: *log(dim2, . , 0, 2000)*
COORD: *exp(dim2)*
GRAPH: *point.statistic.mean()*
GRAPH: *bar.spread.sd(color("red"))*

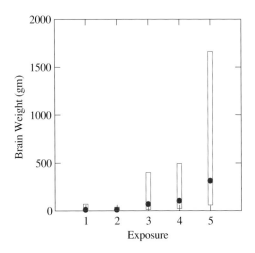

Figure 10.31 *Log error bars on raw scale*

In Figure 10.31 I have inverse-transformed the *log* scale to the raw metric by exponentiating the graphic in Figure 9.7. I have restricted the range to 2000 by leaving the log *base* parameter to missing (default natural log) and setting the *min* to 0 and *max* to 2000. Now the standard deviation bars are asymmetrical because they have been computed on the logged data. This may seem odd until we consider that the raw distributions are asymmetric, so conventional *mean* and *sd* calculations make sense only after *log* transformation of the brain weight values. Computing this way, and assuming the logged values are normally distributed, we would expect the bars to cover approximately 68 percent of the values (the central two-standard deviation spread for a normal distribution). That would not be true if the calculations were done on the raw data.

Figure 10.31 is misleading. The two largest brain weights in the dataset (5712, 4603) belong to elephants, yet the vertical scale suggests that the data range between 0 and 2000 grams. One might argue that we are faithfully representing the standard deviations and means, but I would reply that this misrepresents the data. It also violates my fundamental rule for a statistical graphics system: the frame should always cover the data on which the graphs are based. The range of any dimension should not depend on the graphs that live in the frame. Graph dependence is dangerous.

Defining the range independently of summary functions means that the displayed range covers *all* the data included in the calculation of *all* the means. If the data are positively skewed, as in this example, the points will tend to congregate at the bottom of the display unless the data are transformed to be roughly symmetric about the means. Figure 10.32 shows the same data on the proper scale. The cloud graphic in the left panel shows why Figure 10.31 is misleading.

Statisticians are accustomed to doing these transformations before plotting and analysis because statistics like means are otherwise unrepresentative of their data batches. That is why I logged the data before plotting. If the data were not logged, and if we restricted the range to less than 1000, say, then the dot summaries would have excluded humans as well as elephants and their locations would have been different. This can be disconcerting to those users who might want to place the points to conserve white space or to make them look pretty. The only possible answer to this desire is to point out that the summary would be misleading. It is a fundamental principle (some would call it a drawback) of the system presented here that displayed ranges and domains define the behavior of graphics, not the other way around. If a graph summarizes data in this system (*e.g.*, regression lines, confidence intervals, etc.) this summary is based on data within the bounds of the frame only. I would claim that the alternative – clipping white space around a summary graphic for aesthetic purposes – is a form of lying with graphics (Huff, 1954). I have spent some time on this issue because it is so widely misunderstood. After designing this behavior for SYSTAT's graphics, I heard from some users who thought this was a bug. I began to realize that this preference for the geometry of summaries over the geometry of data may be a worrisome and pervasive problem in scientific practice. Some scientists are publishing graphics that conceal the range and variability of their data. Graphics programs that encourage them to do this thoughtlessly are promoting scientific malpractice. There are exceptions to this statement, as there are to all generalizations. But I believe we are usually better served by showing, rather than hiding, our data.

FRAME: **exposure*brainweight**
GRAPH: *point*()

FRAME: **exposure*brainweight**
SCALE: *log*(*dim2*)
COORD: *exp*(*dim2*)
GRAPH: *point.statistic.mean*()
GRAPH: *bar.spread.sd*(*color*("red"))

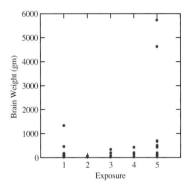 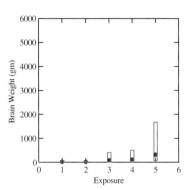

Figure 10.32 *Cloud and error bars on raw scale*

After looking at Figure 10.32, a persistent sceptic might argue that elephants and humans are outliers in this dataset, so we might as well exclude them and *then* restrict our range. This would solve our data-clipping problem in Figure 10.31 but would also be wrong. Figure 10.33 shows normal curves superimposed on dot plots of these data in the logged metric. The value most outlying from its group is the brain weight of the *smallest* animal (.14gm); the lesser short-tailed shrew sits at the far left end of the dot density for the group corresponding to a value of **exposure** equal to 2. The brain weights of the elephants (at the right end of the scale in the group with an **exposure** value equal to 5) are *not* remarkable relative to their **exposure** cohorts. Logging often has this effect. Values that we suspect are outliers in the raw metric are not necessarily outliers in the transformed metric. The problem is not with our measurements; it is with the way we think about scales.

FRAME: **exposure*brainweight**
SCALE: *log*(*dim2*, 10)
COORD: *transpose*()
GRAPH: *point*(*position.stack*())
GRAPH: *line.density.normal*()

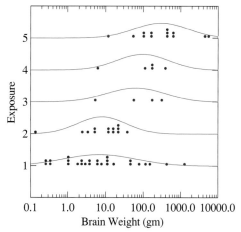

Figure 10.33 *Transformed densities*

10.1.8.2 *Lensing and Fisheye Transformations*

The *fish* transformation expands a graphic away from an arbitrary locus, usually the center of the frame or viewing area. This class of transformations has received a lot of attention from computer interface designers because of the need to make the best use of limited screen "real estate" when navigating through dense networks and graphical browsers (Furnas, 1986; Sarkar and Brown, 1994; Leung and Apperly, 1994). Smooth versions of fisheye functions look like the transpose of the graphics in Figure 9.11. This is because we wish to perform the opposite of those transformations: instead of lengthening the periphery and shortening the center so as not to be distracted by extreme variation, we wish to push the center toward the periphery in order to see more variation in the center. A broad class of functions will serve; one example is the logit cumulative distribution function $f(x) = e^x / (1 + e^x)$. We can improve speed by using the function

$$\textit{fish:}\ \ x \rightarrow 2^x / (1 + 2^x)\ ,$$

which allows us to use bit-shifts in integer arithmetic instead of exponentiating floating-point numbers.

Figure 10.34 shows how to make our dinosaur put on weight by a simple transformation. The important feature to notice is the independence of the transformation on x and y. The center of the dinosaur is pushed to the edges of a square, not a circle.

FRAME: **x*y**
COORD: *fish*()
GRAPH: *link.edge.mst*()

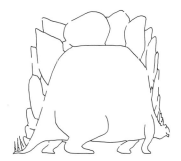

Figure 10.34 *Fisheye dinosaur*

Figure 10.35 shows a fisheye transformation of a circular Gaussian scatterplot cloud with a message embedded in the center (patterned after a dataset constructed by David Coleman). This transformation is especially suited for dynamic displays where the center of magnification (a constant subtracted from *x* before the transformation) can be moved with a mouse or joystick. Carpendale, Cowperthwaite, and Fracchia (1997) discuss applications for 3D graphics.

FRAME: **x*y**
GRAPH: *point*()

FRAME: **x*y**
COORD: *fish*()
GRAPH: *point*()

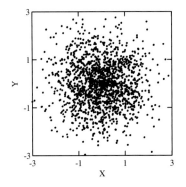 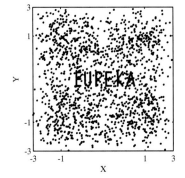

Figure 10.35 *Fisheye transformation*

10.1.9 *Warpings*

Warpings involve the continuous planar transformation:

$$(x, y) \to (f(x, y), g(x, y)) = (u, v) .$$

This introduces shear into the general bending transformation, because u and v both depend on x and y. Many global and local transformations fit this model, but I will focus on a locally parametric example. This transformation amounts to stretching a plane over a set of irregularly distributed bumps, a procedure called **rubber sheeting** by cartographers.

10.1.9.1 *Locally Parametric Warping*

Because of terrain, congestion, road conditions, and other factors, the set of all points at the end of one hour's travel time from a point located on a road map does not lie on a circle centered at that point on the map. Tobler (1993, 1997) proposed to analyze travel-time geometry as a two-manifold of variable curvature. From this analysis, one could construct polar geodesic maps showing **isochrones** (contours of equal travel time) centered on a selected location.

Tobler collected data on a number of measures for this type of spatial modeling, including road travel times, airline travel costs, parcel shipment costs, and estimates of distances by individuals. Tobler's non-Euclidean spatial methodology brings to mind Saul Steinberg's famous *New Yorker* cover that shows a native New Yorker's parochial view of the United States. Steinberg's map compresses almost all of the country west of the Hudson river.

Figure 10.36 contains a map for airline travel costs using a similar concept but different methodology from Tobler's. This map is not centered at any location, but instead reflects the distortion of the plane due to variations in fares within all pairs of cities. It is designed so that the airline fare can be approximated by computing a straight-line distance between any two points.

To make this graphic, I began by visiting several travel sites on the Internet to collect the cheapest round-trip airline fares on September 1, 1998 for all pairs of 36 continental US cities. I then used nonmetric multidimensional scaling to compute a configuration of cities embedded in a two-dimensional Euclidean space. The stress for this solution was .19 and the Shepard diagram revealed a roughly linear relation between prices in dollars and distances between cities in the *MDS* solution. If the airline fares had been perfectly proportional to distances between cities, then the stress would have been zero and the *MDS* solution would have been similarity transformable (see Figure 10.1) to a map of the US on the Euclidean plane.

Next, I used Procrustes rotation (Borg and Groenen, 1997) to align the *MDS* configuration as closely as possible with the geographic map. The Procrustes rotation produces a similarity transformation (translation, rotation, reflection, dilatation) that minimizes the sum of the squared differences between the transformed source and target coordinates. This computation produced a set of airline-fare-spaced city "knots" that I could use to pin down the distortions in a map. The following equation shows the transformation I used. Let θ_i be the longitude of the ith city ($i = 1, \dots , 36$) and let ϕ_i be its latitude. Let r_i be the coordinate of the ith city on the first rotated *MDS* dimension and let s_i be its coordinate on the second rotated *MDS* dimension. For any point at coordinates (x, y) on the geographic plane, I computed new coordinates (u, v) with an inverse distance-weighted average of the displacements of the cities:

$$\begin{cases} u = x + \Sigma w_i(\theta_i - r_i)/\Sigma w_i \\ v = y + \Sigma w_i(\phi_i - s_i)/\Sigma w_i \end{cases}, \text{ where}$$

$$w_i = 1/((x - \theta_i)^2 + (y - \phi_i)^2 + \alpha) \ .$$

The summation is taken over the 36 cities. The parameter α is a small value chosen to prevent division by zero when a point is located at one of the cities.

FRAME: **longitude*latitude**
COORD: *warp(r[], s[])*
GRAPH: *tile(shape.polygon(***state***))*

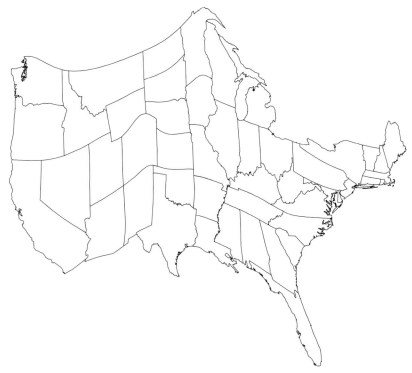

Figure 10.36 *US Airline Pricing Map*

The map reveals that Midwesterners pay relatively higher fares to get out of town. The "distance" from New York to Los Angeles is roughly the same as that from Duluth to Los Angeles. And, cruel fate, Midwesterners have to sacrifice their first-born (relatively speaking) to get to Florida!

10.1.10 *Permutations on the Plane*

A permutation transformation of the plane sends every point to another point in a one-to-one mapping. Permuting a row-column lattice of points within rows and columns to reveal patterns of association is not a new idea (Bertin, 1967; Hartigan, 1972; Ling, 1973; Lenstra, 1974; Slagel *et al.*, 1975; Wilkinson, 1979). With modern computing power and display technology, permutation of large matrices of values is feasible. Figure 10.37 shows an example of permuting a small matrix whose values are represented by colored tiles.

DATA: **x** = *shape.rect*(CLIMATE, ECONOMIC, RECREATION, TRANSPORT, ARTS, HEALTH, EDUCATION, CRIME, HOUSING, "colname")
DATA: **y** = *shape.rect*(CLIMATE, ECONOMIC, RECREATION, TRANSPORT, ARTS, HEALTH, EDUCATION, CRIME, HOUSING, "rowname")
DATA: **d** = *shape.rect*(CLIMATE, ECONOMIC, RECREATION, TRANSPORT, ARTS, HEALTH, EDUCATION, CRIME, HOUSING, "value")
FRAME: **x*y**
COORD: *permute*(*r*[], *c*[])
GRAPH: *tile.density.rect*(*color.hue*(**d**))

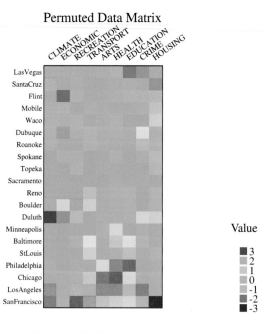

Figure 10.37 *Permuted tiling*

10.2 Projections onto the Plane

So far, we have examined coordinate transformations that help to enhance the perception of patterns and structures in two dimensions. Now we are going to look at transformations that allow us to explore 3D and higher dimensional worlds through a 2D window. This enterprise is doomed from the start. If we attempt to view pairs of dimensions separately, we will have trouble detecting second-order or higher relations between pairs not in the same view. If we try to find linear combinations of dimensions that reveal structures, we will have difficulty orienting ourselves in the full dimensional space. And, if we use some nonlinear projection or compression method to characterize an entire structure, we risk distorting our view enough to prevent accurate interpretation. In short, 2D windows into higher dimensional spaces can give us a glimpse into another world but may either confuse us with apparent complexity so that we overlook global coherence or mislead us with apparent simplicity that leads us to incorrect global inferences. Statisticians call this general problem the "curse of dimensionality." It does not prevent them from devising methods for circumventing it in specific instances, however. I will begin with the 3D issues and then move to higher dimensions.

10.2.1 Perspective Projections

We saw in Figure 10.12 how planar linear projection works. Figure 10.38 illustrates linear projection of a 3D object onto a plane. Rogers and Adams (1990) show how to construct the projection matrix from the coordinates of the projection point, projection plane, and object. This is the perspective planar projection used in computer graphics libraries. It is not exactly the model for realizing an image on our retina and definitely not the model for how images are processed in our visual cortex. But it does provide a result good enough to allow our visual system to use its tricks to reconstruct a 3D scene from a picture. Pinker (1997) explains these tricks to non-psychologists in a beautiful work of general science writing.

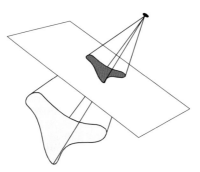

Figure 10.38 Perspective projection onto plane

Figure 10.39 contains a perspective projection of a 3D compound object. The points, axes, grid lines, and text are all put through the same projection. These are the countries data I used in Chapter 1. I have plotted annual per-capita health care expenditures in adjusted US dollars against death and birth rates for selected countries. The heaviest investment in health care is in those countries with low birth and death rates. In general, countries with lower death rates (except for the lowest) tend to have heavier investments in health care. As birth rates increase, however, per-capita investment declines.

FRAME: **birth*death*health**
COORD: *project(a[])*
GRAPH: *point(shape("cube"))*

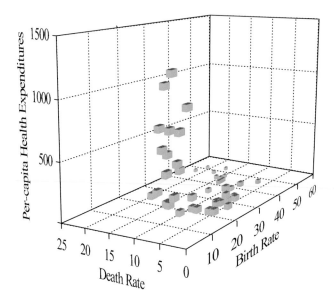

Figure 10.39 *Health expenditures by birth and death rates (enhanced)*

Why do we display data in 3D? As I have argued in Chapter 7, there is often an effective 2D alternative to a specific 3D display. Unfortunately, 3D graphics often elicit more perceptual illusions and make it difficult to use scale look-up in perspective to recover data values. Nevertheless, 3D graphics can be useful when we encounter **configurality** among variables (Meehl, 1950). While it is possible to define configurality for some functions using partial derivatives or parallelism of level-curves, it is perhaps simpler and more general to describe it in ordinary language and to illustrate it with these data. For three variables x, y, and z, configurality occurs when the way z changes across values of y at some level of x is different from the way z changes across values of

y at some other level of x. There is a duality in this definition. Configurality also implies that the way z changes across values of x at some level of y is different from the way z changes across values of x at some other level of y. Statisticians often describe this condition as an **interaction** between y and x with respect to z, but I mean something more general (which is why I used the more general word "way" rather than "rate"). My definition of configurality assumes that an interaction cannot be removed by the coordinate transformations in this chapter; if it could, we could do a transformation and resort to a 2D plot instead (see Abelson, 1995).

Consider Figure 10.40. If there were no configurality among health expenditures (z), death rates (y), and birth rates (x), then this figure would be an adequate representation of the relation between health expenditures and death and birth rates. We could look at the left panel, for example, and conclude that health expenditures decline precipitously with increasing birth rate regardless of death rate. Similarly, we could conclude that health expenditures hit a peak for death rates slightly less than 10 per 100,000 regardless of birth rates. Comparing Figure 10.39 to Figure 10.40 reveals that these descriptions are misleading, however. The high health expenditures for low death rate countries are spread across a large range of birth rates, for example.

DATA: **b** = "Birth Rate"
DATA: **d** = "Death Rate"
FRAME: (**birth/b + death/d**)*health
COORD: *rect*()
GRAPH: *point*()

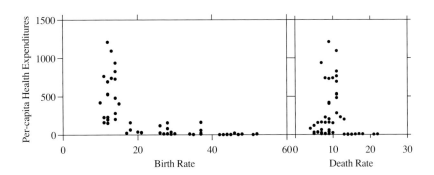

Figure 10.40 *Health expenditures by birth and death rates*

We can graphically model configurality by **blocking** (or **stratifying**) on the x or y variables so that we can see the z variable at various levels of one or the other. This is shown in Figure 10.41. I cut the distribution on birth rate into three equal intervals and then plotted health expenditures against death rate within each interval. Now the change in the relationship is clearly apparent. We could construct a similar plot by stratifying on death rate and plotting health expenditures against birth rate. Becker, Cleveland, and Shyu (1996) developed the **trellis display** to produce such plots automatically.

TRANS: **birthgroup** = *cut*(**birth**,3)
FRAME: **death*health*birthgroup**
COORD: *rect*(*dim1*,*dim2*)
GRAPH: *point*()

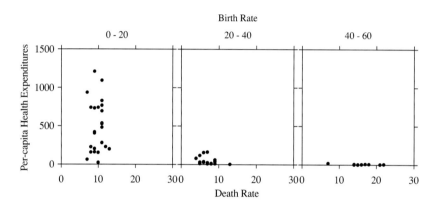

Figure 10.41 *Health expenditures jointly by birth and death rate*

I will discuss faceted displays like Figure 10.40 and Figure 10.41 in Chapter 11. These can be effective for dealing with configurality. And they facilitate scale look-up to help recover data values. There is some price we pay for this stratification, however. First of all, we may have too few cases left in some of the strata, particularly if we stratify on more than one variable. Cleveland (1995) has a clever way of dealing with this problem. He calls it **shingling**, which is cutting the distribution into overlapping groups. This provides more cases in each cell and provides more continuity in the changes across cells.

We are left with a second, more difficult problem, however. Faceted displays are designed to answer one type of question, and 3D displays another. To illustrate this problem, I need to distinguish **variable world** from **object world**. (I might say dimension world rather than variable world, but I will assume that there is one variable per dimension in this discussion). Variable world requires variable descriptions, *e.g.*, "health expenditures tend to decrease with increasing birth rate." Object world requires object descriptions, *e.g.*, "the points spiral in a ram's horn pattern from low and thin in the rear of the plot to high and thick in the foreground." Engineers alternate between these two worlds when they speak of rotating an object or rotating axes. Mathematicians alternate between these two worlds when they describe a function either as $z = x^2 - y^2$ or as a saddle.

I believe that if we have a three-variable system, we are better served by displaying the data in 3D when we are interested in object world and we do better with facets when we are interested in variable world. The ram's horn that we see in Figure 10.39 is not readily discernible in any faceted plot of these data. Furthermore, this ram's horn is memorable as a single object. I would expect that, following results in Wilkinson & McConathy (1990), we would recognize and recall configural relationships in 3D plots better than we would in faceted displays because they more closely fit the way we deal with objects in the physical world. On the other hand, we would decode values more accurately when presented with a faceted graphic. There are limits, however. Cleveland (personal communication) has stated that effective 3D graphics require **coherence**. If a geometric graphic does not cohere in a single recognizable thing, 3D representation won't help us much. There are enough problems when parts of objects remain hidden behind other parts in a 3D plot. If points, lines, and other primitives do not cohere, we are better served by a faceted display.

Other questions: How are trellis displays related to linear projections? Would it make sense to facet a display with nonorthogonal or nonlinear projections? There is one sleight-of-hand I played in Figure 10.39. What did I do and does it help or hurt our perception of the structure? Hint: look at the size of the boxes.

10.2.2 Stereo Pairs

Our minds perceive depth through a variety of strategies. Illumination, texture, occlusion, contiguity, surface color, and other features of a scene all provide clues to the 3D orientation of objects in that scene. One important optical mechanism for depth measurement is called **parallax**. If we observe an object in space from two different points of view, then we have a triangle whose base lies between the observation points and whose apex lies at the object. Figure 10.42 shows two examples. The baseline distance and the angles at each end of the baseline are sufficient information to compute the dotted line perpendicular to the baseline in the figure. This technique has been used in astronomy and surveying for centuries, and it is not surprising that it should play a role in the visual system through the physical separation and orientation of the eyes.

In order to use parallax to elicit a sense of depth from a 2D scene, we have to present a different perspective projection to each eye separately so that the parallax effect will resemble that found in viewing a real 3D scene. In other words, the same object must be projected to different coordinates on each retina as it is in Figure 10.42. Sir Charles Wheatstone, the English physicist, found a way to do this in 1938. His **stereoscope** projected a separate image to each eye through the use of mirrors. Each image was produced from a photograph taken with a camera located at one of two different positions in front of a scene. The stereoscope artificially reproduced the optical projection that takes place when we view a natural scene. The inexpensive contemporary equivalent of Wheatstone's stereoscope is the plastic ViewMaster stereo slide viewer. ISSCO, a mainframe technical graphics company, used ViewMasters to present some spectacular visualizations in the early 1980's before virtual reality technology was generally available.

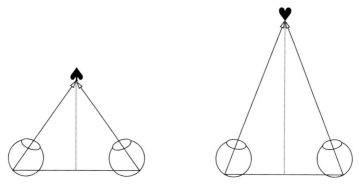

Figure 10.42 *Parallax*

If we do not have a stereoscope, we can project a separate 2D image on each retina by crossing our eyes. To see how this works, we begin with Figure 10.43. The left panel shows two eyes aimed at a common focal point represented by a red dot. I have drawn an arrow from the center of the retina to the focal point. Two objects, a spade and a heart, are viewed by the eyes. I have drawn dotted lines from these objects to the retinas in order to indicate where they are projected onto the retinal surface.

The blue eye in the middle represents the **cyclopean eye** (named after Ulysses' one-eyed nemesis). This is not a real eye, but instead a schematic representation of the result of the visual system's merging separate patterns of retinal stimulation into a common perceptual image. Because spade and heart are projected to similar coordinates on each separate retina, they coalesce in the cyclopean image and we see them as single objects. The arrows below the eyes show how the spade and heart are merged.

The right panel of Figure 10.43 shows the same eyes presented with a single heart closer than the point of focus. This time, the object projects to a different part of each separate retina. The visual system cannot merge the sources of stimulation into a single cyclopean image, so we see double in this circumstance. You can verify this by focusing on your right index finger held at arm's length while you hold your left index finger at half the distance. The left finger doubles. If you switch your gaze to the foreground, the finger in the background doubles.

If we do the same thing with a double graphic that looks like Figure 10.44, then we get a double of doubles. If we focus our gaze at the correct distance, and hold the page at half that distance, then the doubling of doubles overlaps in the center and we see a single middle composite image and two surrounding separate images. This means that the central overlapping image is compiled from both graphics, mimicking the result that happens when we look at a real scene at the focused depth. By plotting each graphic from a different perspective (by a few degrees), we trick our visual system into blending them stereoscopically, as if they were real projections on each eye.

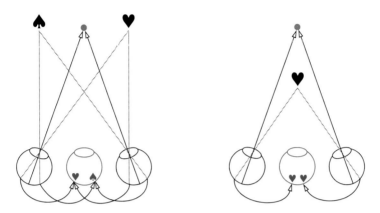

Figure 10.43 Cyclopean vision

Not everyone can view these graphics without mechanical assistance. I find it easiest to place the page two feet from my eyes (not two eyes from my feet), and force the image to double by focusing on my index finger held about 8 inches from my eyes. Then I move the index finger away while carefully transferring my concentration to the central composite image. Remember to do this only with Figure 10.44. If you focus on Figure 10.43 by mistake, you will permanently cross your eyes and lose your driving privileges (except in Boston). Actually, the eye-crossing lockup is a myth, but if you gaze too long on Figure 10.43, you may turn into a post-modernist.

3D virtual reality systems use mechanical stereoscopic devices based on cathode-ray tubes or liquid-crystal displays to present a separate image to each retina. Goggles with separate displays for each eye can present images controlled by separate processors. The most intense psychological experience, however, is offered by the CAVE immersive environment (Cruz-Neira, Sandin, and DeFanti, 1993). This apparatus consists of separate color projectors aimed at the walls of a room large enough to hold three or four people. Each person wears polarizing glasses controlled by the same computers running the projectors. The perspective images are switched at a high enough rate to blend in a single perception, like a movie. Because the environment is immersive, allowing other people to move about the room, it provides the highest level of virtual reality currently obtainable. Recent advances in desktop computers and LCD color projector technology are bringing this capability that once cost over a million dollars to smaller laboratories and homes.

FRAME: **birth*death*health**
COORD: *project(dim1,dim2,dim3,a[])*
GRAPH: *point(shape("cube"))*

FRAME: **birth*death*health**
COORD: *project(dim1,dim2,dim3,a[])*
GRAPH: *point(shape("cube"))*

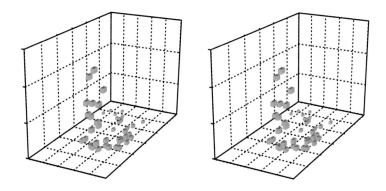

Figure 10.44 *Stereo pair*

10.2.3 *Triangular (Barycentric) Coordinates*

If three variables are constrained to sum to a constant, the set of all possible values they may take lies on a plane. If all these values are constrained to be positive, they are bounded by a triangle. Figure 10.45 shows an example of this triangle. Triangular coordinates are especially useful for representing mixtures of three variables. Perhaps the best known application is the *CIE* color diagram which shows perceptible mixtures of the three color primaries red, green, and blue (Levine and Shefner, 1991).

A formula for computing this projection is:

$$\begin{cases} u = \left(2\tan\left(\dfrac{\pi}{3}\right)x + \tan\left(\dfrac{\pi}{3}\right)y\right)/(x+y+z) \\ v = y/(x+y+z) \end{cases}$$

The tangent function is on 60 degrees, the angle of the vertices of an equilateral triangle. This triangle is shown tilted in Figure 10.45. The denominator of the expression $(x + y + z)$ controls the scaling of the triangle.

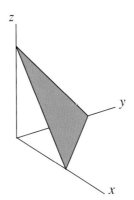

Figure 10.45 *Triangular coordinate plane*

Nielsen *et al.* (1973), cited in Andrews and Herzberg (1985), reported percentages of three components – sand, silt, and clay – in core borings from 20 different plots in a soil field. Figure 10.46 shows a triangular coordinate plot of
their data. To read the values on a given axis, choose the grid lines that are parallel to the axis that shares an apex at the zero end of the axis. For example,
the **silt** axis grid lines are horizontal and the **clay** grid lines tilt 30 degrees to
the right.

FRAME: **sand*silt*clay**
COORD: *triangular*()
GRAPH: *point(color.hue(**plot**))*

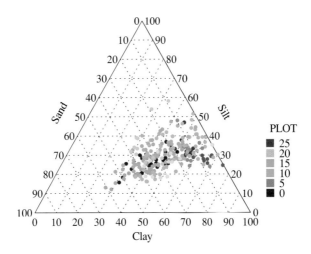

Figure 10.46 *Triangular coordinates plot of soil samples*

We can see that most of the samples contain fairly high percentages of clay and lower percentages of silt and sand. Furthermore, the plots with lower index numbers tend to have higher concentrations of clay and somewhat lower percentages of sand.

Triangular coordinates are especially important for displaying the results of mixtures experiments. When engineers seek to find optimal combinations of three ingredients (on some price, quality, or performance criterion), a triangular coordinate plot provides a convenient summary of the model they fit to predict the criterion. Cornell (1990) presents the results of an experiment designed to measure the suppression of the population of mites on strawberry plants after spraying with a mixture of three different pesticides. The surface plotted with contours represents the seasonal average mite population per leaf after a period of spraying. Cornell fit these numbers with a variety of parametric models, all of which fairly closely resemble the nonparametric fit in Figure 10.47.

Notice that the data points were chosen to provide support for estimating parameter values of the fitted function. The contours of the fitted function follow a valley running from the lower right apex to the middle of the **x1** axis. Cornell selected more data points along this valley in anticipation of finding a surface roughly resembling this form. Since collecting data at each mixture point can be costly, careful planning and iterated experimentation is needed to converge on a model that identifies the optimal combination of ingredients.

FRAME: **x1*x2*x3**
COORD: *triangular()*
GRAPH: *point()*
GRAPH: *contour.smooth.quadratic.cauchy(color.hue(**mites**))*

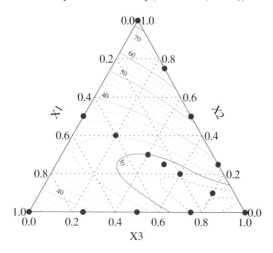

Figure 10.47 *Contours in triangular coordinates*

10.2.4 Map Projections

This class of mappings involves the continuous transformation:

$$(x, y, z, ...) \rightarrow (f(x, y, z,...), g(x, y, z,...)) = (u, v) .$$

It includes everything from linear projections of the hemisphere onto the plane to nonlinear and piecewise projections of the whole globe onto the plane.

Map projections have a long history in cartography, beyond the scope of this book (see Maling, 1992; Snyder, 1989). Spherical projections are basic to non-Euclidean geometry, another area beyond the scope of this book. Mapping the sphere to the plane has graphical applications beyond representing the earth in a 2D map. Map projections are useful for representing graphically any statistical distribution on the sphere.

Most cartographic projections can be classified according to their projective surface: planes, cylinders, or cones. Figure 10.48 shows three normal planar projections of the Eastern hemisphere. I have projected latitudes between −75 and 75 degrees and longitudes from 0 to 180 degrees. The light-ray model is realistic, but there is one small anomaly that you should be able to detect even if you are not a geographer. Hint: Wrong Way Corrigan would have liked my map. Double hint: Australians are used to being down-under, but not backwards. I needed to do this to maintain the physical model.

The Gnomonic projection assumes a light source located at the center of the sphere and a projection plane tangent to the surface (or parallel to this plane) at a selected point on the sphere. It can project only a hemisphere. As the figure shows, area distortions are severe at the poles. Longitudes project to straight lines and latitudes (except the Equator) to curves. The Stereographic projection places the light source on the surface of the globe and the projection plane tangent to the point on the opposite side of the globe. This important geometric projection maps the whole sphere (except for one point) to the plane. It figures in geometric theory as well as geography (Stillwell, 1992). The Orthographic projection places the light source at infinity. This projection produces a result that resembles the view of the Earth from the moon. All three of these planar projections are a form of perspective projection (see Section 10.2.1).

Figure 10.49 shows cylindrical and conical projections. By bending the plane, these methods help to represent more of the global surface and, in some cases, distort area less. Normal cylindrical methods project longitudes and latitudes to straight lines. The classic Mercator cylindrical projection is especially useful for navigation because compass bearings plot as straight line segments on the plane. Standard nautical maps still use the Mercator projection. The conical methods are most suited for regional maps. In the normal conical projections, longitudes plot as oblique lines and latitudes as straight lines or curves.

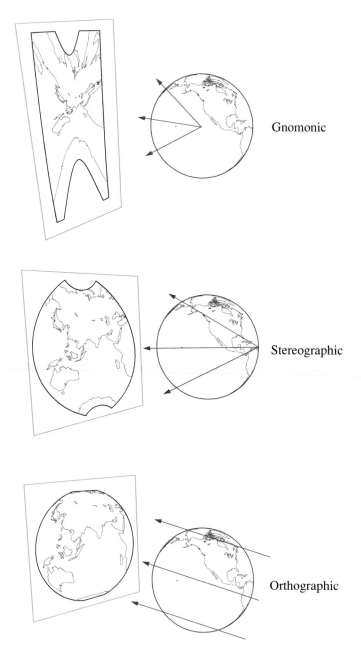

Figure 10.48 *Planar map projections*

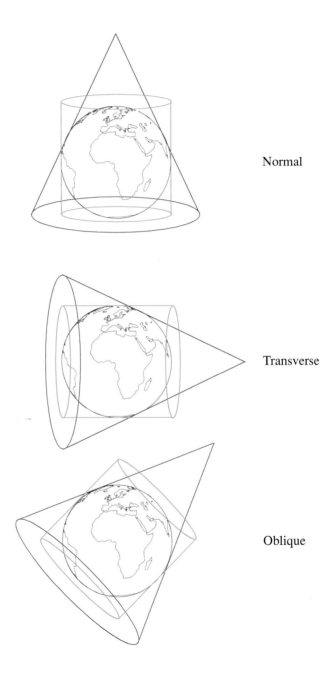

Normal

Transverse

Oblique

Figure 10.49 *Cylindrical and conical map projections*

10.2.4.1 Global Maps

Figure 10.50 shows several global map projections. The Peters, Miller, and Mercator are recognizable as cylindrical because the longitudes are parallel. The Peters projection favors the southern hemisphere in a politically motivated attempt to counter the influence of centuries of maps positioned transversely on the northern hemisphere. The Robinson projection (Robinson, 1974) achieves more balance. Unlike the others, the Robinson projection is not the result of a single trigonometric function; it is a smooth piecewise blending. Robinson has been a projection used by *The National Geographic* in many of its maps because it favors the temperate zones without discriminating against the southern hemisphere. Unfortunately, the Robinson projection discriminates against penguins.

I have included axes on all the maps to reveal global distortions. Instead of repeating the specification four times, I have substituted "*xxx*" for the projection name in the specification.

FRAME: **longitude*latitude**
COORD: *project.xxx*()
GRAPH: *tile*(*shape.polygon*(**continent**))

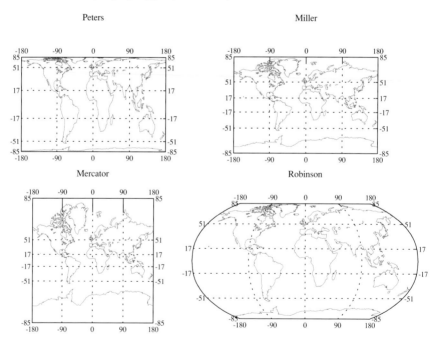

Figure 10.50 *Global map projections*

10.2.4.2 Local Maps

Local maps suffer less from global distortion. Figure 10.51 illustrates several.

FRAME: **longitude*latitude**
COORD: *project.xxx*()
GRAPH: *tile*(*shape.polygon*(**state**))

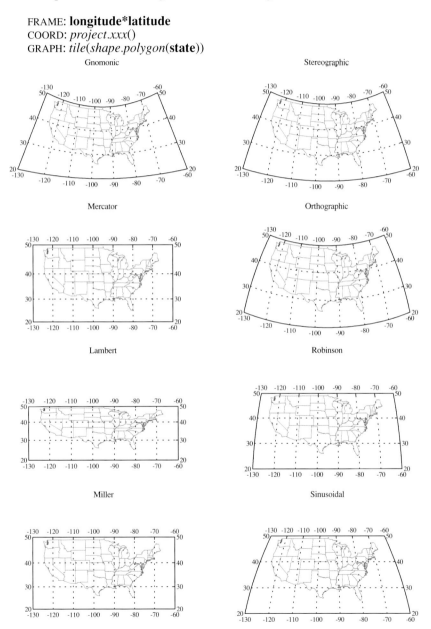

Figure 10.51 *Map projections of US*

Map projections transform the geometry of graphics. Except for symbols, which maintain their shape regardless of coordinate systems, graphic shapes are modified by coordinate transformations. Figure 10.52 shows an example. The data were taken from a compilation of worldwide carbon and nitrogen soil levels for more than 3500 scattered sites. These data were compiled by P.J. Zinke and A.G. Stangenberger of the Department of Forestry and Resource Management at the University of California, Berkeley. The full dataset is available at the US Carbon Dioxide Information Analysis Center (CDIAC) site on the World Wide Web (*cdiac.esd.ornl.gov*)

The sampling grid for these data was not uniform. I have used *tile* graphics to represent the carbon levels in bins delineated by latitude and longitude boundaries. The Stereographic spherical projection changes the shapes of these bins from spherical rectangles to planar arcs. This is not a cartographic map. It is a statistical distribution measured in geographic coordinates. Unfortunately, rectangular bins do not represent equal sampling areas on the surface of a sphere. Carr *et al.* (1992) comment on the usefulness of hexagonal bins for this purpose.

FRAME: **lon*lat**
COORD: *project.stereo*()
GRAPH: *tiledensity.rect*(*color.hue*(**carbon**))

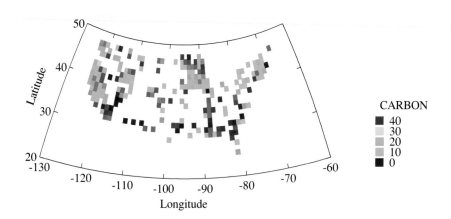

Figure 10.52 *Tiles of soil samples*

10.2.5 *Higher Dimensions*

Projections to the plane in higher dimensions present more severe problems than we have already encountered. We tend to encounter both fragmentation (inability to keep adjacent objects near each other on the plane) and distortion (preserving lines, circles, angles, etc.). Two approaches to solving these problems have been taken. The first is to relax global structure in order to reveal local. Banchoff (1996) summarizes a variety of applications involving the visualization of higher dimensional geometric objects. Shepard and Carroll (1966) present a numerical relaxation method for representing on the plane configurations of points in higher dimensions. The second method is to compute interesting 2D projections and present them singly or in concert. Friedman and Stuetzle (1981) and Friedman (1987) developed loss functions for such problems and a method for minimizing them called **projection pursuit**. Their algorithm has been used, for example, to locate configurations of points bounded by a triangle when projected to a plane. Asimov (1985) and Buja and Asimov (1986) developed a method for computing a series of 2D projections that follow a continuous path through a higher dimensional space. Animating these projections with a video player in a **Grand Tour** allows a viewer to perceive aspects of higher dimensional structure.

10.3 *3D Coordinate Systems*

So far, we have considered 2D, 3D, and higher-dimensional objects. We have visualized all these objects through the plane, sometimes directly and sometimes through projections. Some higher dimensional coordinate systems are interesting in themselves, apart from their projected representations. We have already seen some of these – for example, the spherical coordinates used for mapping the globe.

The coordinate systems in this section resemble polar and other nonrectangular 2D coordinates. In order for us to visualize objects in these systems, I will have to use 2D perspective projections, but this is only because they are presented in a book. Virtual reality systems – especially immersive environments – could be used to represent these structures in a 3D setting.

The focus of our interest in this section is thus on non-rectangular 3D coordinates, including spherical, triangular, and cylindrical. As the examples will show, these coordinates are useful for applications that involve both spatial and non-spatial statistics. While geography has motivated the most popular applications, other theoretical structures are best represented in these nonrectangular coordinate systems.

10.3.1 *Spherical Coordinates*

If (u, v, w) represents the spherical coordinates (ρ, θ, ϕ) of a point, then a spherical coordinate function $S(u, v, w) \rightarrow (x, y, z)$ corresponds to the case $u = \rho$, $v = \theta$, $w = \phi$ where $x = \rho \sin\phi \cos\theta$, $y = \rho \sin\phi \sin\theta$, and $z = \rho \cos\phi$. Spherical coordinates are useful for representing points on a sphere when ρ is a constant, and bundles of vectors at a common origin when it is not.

Contouring on sphere presents special problems because distances must be calculated on the surface rather than in rectangular coordinates. There are technical problems with the drawing of other graphics as well. Figure 10.53 shows an example of tiling the sphere using geographic data. McNish (1948) reports magnetic declinations for 22 locations on the globe. I have used inverse distance smoothing on the surface of the sphere to represent the average declination at different areas on the globe. The *spherical.phitheta*() coordinate function takes two arguments only: ϕ and θ. The radius is assumed to be constant. This function is similar to the way I handled polar coordinates in Section 10.1.6.1 when only one argument is used to make a pie chart. Spherical coordinates for three arguments are handled with *spherical*().

FRAME: **lon*lat+longitude*latitude**
COORD: *spherical.phitheta(p[], t[])*
GRAPH: *tile.smooth.mean.cauchy(position(**lon*lat**), color.hue(**declination**))*
GRAPH: *tile(shape.polygon(**continent**), position(**longitude*latitude**))*

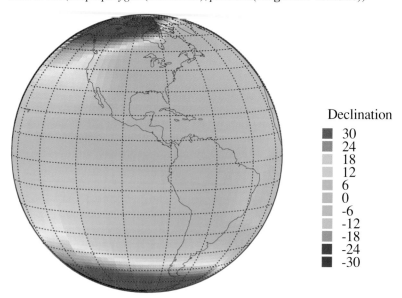

Declination

  30
  24
  18
  12
   6
   0
  -6
 -12
 -18
 -24
 -30

Figure 10.53 *Spherical distribution of magnetic declination*

10.3.2 Triangular-Rectangular Coordinates

Figure 10.54 shows a 3D triangular coordinate plot whose first three dimensions are embedded in 2D triangular coordinates and whose fourth dimension (the vertical axis) is represented by a rectangular coordinate system. This representation allows us to show a surface as a function of mixtures of three ingredients. This type of surface was represented by contours in Figure 10.47.

We need a different coordinate function here, however, because the graphic involves a projection from a 4D space to a 3D. The *tri4*() function computes this projection by computing triangular coordinates on the first 3 dimensions and rectangular on the fourth. I have used the soil data from Figure 10.46 and let the fourth axis represent the depth of the core samples. The plot shows that there is a higher percentage of silt and lower percentage of sand toward the surface, and there is a higher percentage of sand and lower percentage of silt deeper down.

FRAME: **sand*silt*clay*depth**
COORD: *tri4*()
GRAPH: *point(color.hue(**plot**))*
GRAPH: *surface.smooth.mean.cauchy*()

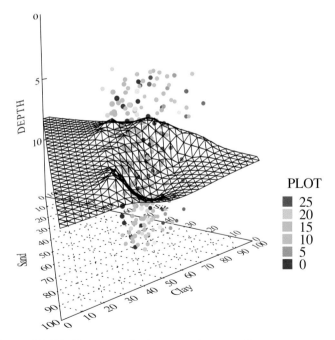

Figure 10.54 *3D triangular/rectangular coordinates*

10.3.3 *Cylindrical Coordinates*

If (u,v,w) represents the cylindrical coordinates (ρ, θ, ζ) of a point, then a spherical coordinate function $S(u, v, w) \rightarrow (x, y, z)$ corresponds to the case $u = \rho$, $v = \theta$, $w = z$, where $x = \rho\cos\theta$, $y = \rho\sin\theta$, and $z = \zeta$. Cylindrical coordinates are useful for representing cylinders, spirals, and cones.

Krumhansel (1979) analyzed the perception of musical pitch in a tonal context. She presented her multidimensional scaling results in a 3D graphic showing the configuration of musical tones lying on the surface of a cone. Figure 10.55 shows the specification and graphic based on her model.

FRAME: **pitch*tone*chroma**
COORD: *cylindrical*()
GRAPH: *point*(*label*(**note**), *shape*("sphere"), *color*("silver"))
GRAPH: *surface.smooth.linear*(*transparency*(.8), *color*("mauve"))

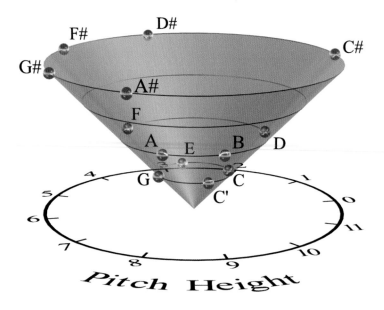

Figure 10.55 *Cylindrical plot of musical pitch perception*

I have used Krumhansel's data to illustrate the usefulness of a cylindrical coordinate representation for certain configurations. The linear smooth based on a single parameter predicts her results quite well. An equivalent parameterization would be to think of her tone-pitch model as a **modular surface**. The modulus of a complex number is $r = |z|$, the length of z in its vector representation. In this form, her surface is simply $f(z) = |z|$.

Krumhansel's original article contains a simple line drawing that I think is superior to the representation in Figure 10.55. The original figure shows a black-and-white line drawing outline of the cone with a vertical cut (like an open shirt collar) to highlight the depth of the cone and the fact that the notes do not span a full 360 degrees in one octave. This is probably a case where realism in scientific visualization contributes little to the comprehension of the graphical information, as Becker and Cleveland (1991) have argued.

10.4 Parallel Coordinates

Inselberg (1984) proposed a coordinate system for displaying high-dimensional objects through connected points on axes drawn parallel on a plane. These coordinates have become popular in statistical and graphics packages.

10.4.1 Rectangular Parallel

The **parallel coordinates plot** (Inselberg, 1984; Wegman, 1990) assigns a separate, parallel real number axis to each dimension. Figure 10.56 illustrates this plot on the world countries data. The *line* graphic is one of the few that is of any use in this coordinate system. Most other graphics go to points on each line. Even if we colored them, they would be difficult to recognize.

FRAME: **birth*death*education*health*military**
COORD: *parallel*()
GRAPH: *line*(*color*(**gov**))

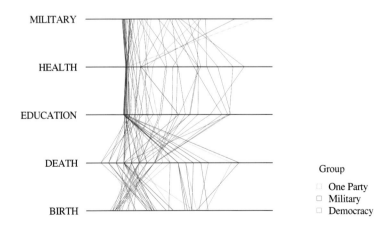

Figure 10.56 Parallel coordinates

10.4.2 Polar Parallel

We can send parallel coordinates through a polar transformation to produce something called a **spider web** or **star plot**. Figure 10.57 shows an example using the data from the previous Figure 10.56. This plot is analogous to the radar plot shown in Figure 10.28.

FRAME: **birth*death*education*health*military**
COORD: *parallel*()
COORD: *polar*()
GRAPH: *line(color(**gov**))*

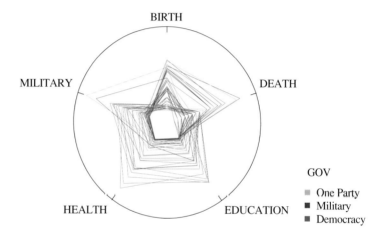

Figure 10.57 *Parallel coordinates in polar form*

10.5 Tools and Coordinates

A **brush** is a bounded region inside a frame that is movable via a translation controller such that all points inside it are highlighted in other graphics based on the same data (Cleveland and McGill, 1988). This linking is accomplished through the relational key index (case number) associated with a variable set as defined in Chapter 2. This tool allows a user to select points in one plot, for example, and see them highlighted in another. In a continuous mapping, we would expect to see points that are close together in one graphic (inside the brush region) close in the other, but this is not generally the case with statistical graphics. Two cars may have similar acceleration but differ in weight or fuel economy. A brush helps us to perceive these second-order relationships.

In a rectangular coordinate scatterplot, a brush is usually a square. It demarcates intervals on two orthogonal scales. What shape would this brush assume in triangular coordinates? Did you guess triangle? What shape would this brush have in polar coordinates? Hint: it's not a circle. A brush does not change size or shape when moved in rectangular coordinate space. It is translated. What happens in polar coordinates? What is the polar equivalent of movement along the vertical rectangular axis? Horizontal? Diagonal? Try sending a square brush through the various other coordinate transformations in this chapter.

Some writers have suggested that circular brushes would be more appropriate than square ones for rectangular coordinates; a circle is the iso-distance contour on the Euclidean plane. How would a circular brush behave in polar coordinates? Would this make more sense than the transformed square? Finally, how do coordinate transformations affect the behavior of other selection tools? Some software implements a lasso tool that allows the user to select points within any closed region, for example. Would that require any special programming attention under coordinate transformations?

10.6 Sequel

We have so far concentrated on single graphics. Often, we want to create tables and other structures of graphics. The next chapter covers facets, which create such multiplicities.

11

Facets

The English word **facet** is derived from the Latin *facies*, which means face. A facet implies a little face, such as one of the sides of an object (*e.g.*, a cut diamond) that has many faces. This word is useful for describing an object that creates many little graphics that are variations of a single graphic. In a graphical system, facets are frames of frames. Because of this recursion, facets make frames behave like points in the sense that the center of a frame can be located by coordinates derived from a facet. Thus, we can use facets to make graphs of graphs or tables of graphs. Indeed, tables *are* graphs. This general conception allows us to create structures of graphs that are more general than the specific examples of multigraphics such as scatterplot matrices (Chambers *et al.*, 1983), row-plots (Carr, 1994), or trellises (Becker and Cleveland, 1996). We can also construct trees and other networks of graphs because we can link together graphic frames in the same way we link points in a network. And we can transform facets as well as frames to make, for example, rectangular arrays of polar graphics or polar arrangements of rectangular graphics. For a similar concept in the field of visualization, see Beshers and Feiner (1993).

All the machinery to make a faceted graphic can be derived from the definition of a frame itself in Chapter 2. In other words, a facet is simply another frame extended from the frame class. Its name denotes its role as a pattern maker for other frames. How patterns of frames are produced, organized, and displayed is a matter of attaching various schemes to their drawing methods. These schemes may be driven by explicit data (as in most of the examples in this chapter) or by implicit methods that involve simple iterations.

11.1 *Facet Specification*

Facets are embeddings. A facet of a facet specifies a frame embedded within a frame. A facet of a facet of a facet specifies a frame embedded within a frame embedded within a frame. Each frame is a bounded set which is assigned to its own coordinate system. To make this explicit, facets are notated through the COORD specification. The *facet()* coordinate transformation determines a separate facet.

For example, the three-dimensional frame

FRAME: **a*b*c**
COORD: *rect(dim1,dim2,dim3)*

consists of a 3D frame represented by the variables **a**, **b**, and **c**. The *rect()* function denotes rectangular coordinates. Adding graphics to this specification produces a single 3D plot. On the other hand, the three-dimensional frame

FRAME: **a*b*c**
COORD: *facet(dim1, dim2)*
COORD: *rect(dim3)*

consists of a 2D frame represented by the variables **a** and **b** embedded in the 1D facet frame represented by the variable **c**. Adding graphics to this specification would produce a row of 2D plots. The second COORD specification is optional because there is only one dimension left to use in the specification after the first two are given in the first frame.

More complex facet structures follow the same model. That is, a four-dimensional graph can be realized in four 1D frames, a 1D frame embedded in a 2D frame embedded in a 1D frame, two 2D frames, a 3D frame embedded in a 1D frame, and so on. A chain of COORD specifications is a tree of facets, with the first child of the second, the second child of the third, and so on.

11.2 Algebra of Facets

Trees and tables are alternate ways to represent facets. Table 11.2 lists a variety of facets sharing a common COORD specification. I have omitted the first variable set (say, **x**) associated with the first dimension in order to show the remaining terms in the frame that produce a table in each case. You may think of these examples as involving a dot plot of **x** for each combination of the facets determined by the variables in Table 11.1.

Table 11.1 contains the data on which Table 11.2 is based.

Table 11.1 **Data for Table 11.2**

a	b	c	d
Barb	Jean	Young	Short
Jean	Jean	Young	Short
Barb	Mark	Young	Short
Jean	Jean	Old	Short
Jean	Jean	Old	Tall
Jean	Jean	Old	Tall

The first row of Table 11.2 shows the simple expression **a**, which yields a tree with two branches and a table with two cells, one for each value of **a**. I have used a dot in each cell to represent the presence of a graphic within the cell. We could put a one-dimensional graphic in each of the two cells of this table with the expression **x*a**. The full specification for a one-dimensional scatterplot split into these two cells would therefore be:

FRAME: **x*a**
COORD: *facet(dim1)*
COORD: *rect(dim2)*
GRAPH: *point()*

Again, the second COORD specification is optional. I will omit optional COORD specifications from now on. The specification for a two-dimensional scatterplot split into these two cells would be:

FRAME: **x*y*a**
COORD: *facet(dim1, dim2)*
GRAPH: *point()*

The second row of Table 11.2 shows a crossing **a*b**, which produces a 2x2 table in this case. We should not assume this operator always implies a cross-tabulation structure, however. As I will show in row 5 of Table 11.2, a crossing can look superficially like a nesting. Market-research, data-mining, and statistical tabulation packages fail to make this distinction and thus miss the fact that crossing is an aspect of a frame, not a layout. A frame and a view must be carefully distinguished. Notice that only three of the four cells are filled. The fourth cell has no dot, but there remains the possibility that data may be encountered that fits this combination of categories.

The third row shows the nested expression **a/b**. As the definition of nesting in Chapter 2 reveals, the term **a*b** is two-dimensional, while the term **a/b** is one-dimensional. In other words, there is only one scale of values above the three cells in row 3 of Table 11.2. I have made these reference values italic to indicate that they are nesting rather than crossing categories.

The distinction between row 2 and row 3 may appear subtle and of only surface importance. Imagine, however, the difference between the following two associations. The first to consider is the crossing of gender with marital status. The possible combinations are married men, married women, single men, and single women. The second is the nesting of pregnancy status under gender. The possible combinations are pregnant women, non-pregnant women, and non-pregnant men. Non-pregnancy has a different meaning for men than for women. Marital status by gender is two-dimensional because all possible combinations of the values are possible. Pregnancy status by gender is one-dimensional because only three combinations are possible and the values of status are not comparable across the gender variable. We could design a variety of physical layouts to convey the difference between nesting and cross-ing, but any layout for nesting must clearly show only the possible combinations. If a cell is left empty, we might imagine that it could be filled by an observation. This must never occur for a physical representation of an impossible category in a nested structure.

Row 4 shows a blending. A blending is a one-dimensional operation that collapses tied categories. We see only three cells because the name Jean within variable **a** is taken to be the same value as the name Jean within variable **b**.

Row 5 illustrates the subtlety with crossing that I mentioned in discussing row 2. It also illustrates the use of a constant value (**1**) as a place-holder. The **a** variable set is crossed with **1** to yield one row of two values. This set, in turn, is split into two by the values of **b**. The placement of the **1** is critical. The sequence of orientations in the faceted coordinate system is $h, v, h, v, \ldots$, where v is vertical and h is horizontal. The lattice on which this coordinate system is based has no limit. Remember, also, that the cross operator is not commutative.

Row 6 shows a tree and table for the expression $(\mathbf{a} + \mathbf{b}) * \mathbf{c}$, which is equivalent to $\mathbf{a}*\mathbf{c} + \mathbf{b}*\mathbf{c}$. Notice, as in row 4, that there are only three levels for the blended dimension because of the presumed tie in data values.

Row 7 shows a tree and table for the expression $(\mathbf{a} + \mathbf{b})/\mathbf{c}$, which is equivalent to $\mathbf{a}/\mathbf{c} + \mathbf{b}/\mathbf{c}$. This operation blends two trees like the one in row 3.

Row 8 illustrates the expression $\mathbf{a}*\mathbf{b} + \mathbf{c}*\mathbf{1}$. There is no row label for the two columns Y and O because the crossing set for this group is unity. Using a nesting operator in combination with crossing may produce row or column labels in the middle of the aggregated table, however (see row 12).

Table 11.2 **Tables and Trees**

Expression	Tree	Table
1 **a**		
2 **a * b**		

Table 11.2 Tables and Trees

Expression	Tree	Table
3 **a/b**		
4 **a + b**		
5 **a*1*b**		
6 **(a + b) * c**		
7 **(a + b)/c**		
8 **a*b + c*1**		

Table 11.2 **Tables and Trees**

Expression	Tree	Table
9 **a * b * c**		
10 **a / b / c**		
11 **a * b/c**		
12 **(a * b)/c**		
13 **a/(b*c)**		

Table 11.2 Tables and Trees

Expression	Tree	Table
14 **a/(b*1*c)**		
15 **a * b * 1 * c**		
16 **a * b * c * d**		
17 **a/c * b/d**		

Table 11.2 Tables and Trees

Expression	Tree	Table
18 (a*b)/(c*d)		

Row 9 illustrates a three-way crossing **a*b*c**. Because the COORD specification for Table 11.2 is 2D, we end up with two groups of 2x2 cross-tabulations. Many of the cells are empty, but the layout of the table signals that these combinations are theoretically possible.

Row 10 illustrates a three-way nesting **a/b/c**. Only combinations existing in the data appear in the tree and table.

Row 11 illustrates the expression **a * b/c**, which is a crossing with a nested factor. The layout therefore shows a full crossing, but the vertical table axis contains italic labels to indicated that the cells fall under a nesting of **b** within **c**.

Row 12 shows a tree and table for the expression **(a * b)/c**. This example has an unusual structure that shares a number of subtleties with the example in row 8. We are nesting a crossing under variable **c**. To do this, we must examine each separate value of the nesting variable **c** for all combinations of the crossing variables **a** and **b**. As the tree and table show, there are two values of **a** and **b** available to cross under **c** = "Young", but only one value of **a** and **b** under **c** = "Old". Consequently, we produce a 2x2 and 1x1 table to nest under **c**.

Row 13 shows a tree and table for the expression **a/(b*c)**. The **b*c** part of the term determines a two-way table under which the levels of **a** are nested.

Row 14 shows a tree and table for the expression **a/(b*1*c)**. This time, the **b*1*c** part of the term determines a crossing aligned in a row because of the unity operator taking place for a crossed variable. The levels of **a** are nested within each of these levels of crossing.

Row 15 shows a table that, on the surface, appears to be a crossing of a nested variable with another. The corresponding expression **a * b * 1 * c** shows, however, that this is a three-dimensional rather two-dimensional table. Reinforcing this in the view is the lack of italics that would denote nesting.

Row 16 shows a simple four-way table. The expression **a * b * c * d** produces a table with many empty cells, but is fully crossed.

Row 17 shows a two-dimensional table produced by the nested expression **a/c * b/d**. This expression is a simple crossing of two nested variables.

Finally, row 18 shows a nesting of two crossings. Producing this table requires us to compute the crossing **c*d** and then examine every possible crossing
a*b nested within each of the resulting combinations. The layout seems to violate
the rule that a nesting cannot be represented as a crossing. There are no data under
the combination T by Y. Nevertheless, the expression tells us that this is a meaningful combination even if there are no values for it in the data set. Therefore, a
crossed layout is required. There are two dimensions in the resulting graph.

11.3 Examples

Multiplots are graphics faceted on extrinsic variables. For example, we might
want to plot heart rate against blood pressure for different clinical populations
or for males and females separately. These would be categorical multiplots.
We could also make scatterplots of scatterplots, employing continuous variables to lay out the graphics. These would be continuous multiplots. The following sections show examples of both kinds

11.3.1 One-way Tables of Graphics

11.3.1.1 Tables of Scatterplots

Figure 11.1 shows a table of ordered categories. The data are from the predation dataset. Each scatterplot of body weight against sleep is ordered by the
danger-of-being-killed index. This enables us to discern a trend in the orientation and position of the scatterplot cloud. The animals most in danger tend to
have the lowest levels of sleep and highest body weights.

FRAME: **bodyweight*sleep*danger**
SCALE: *log(dim1, 10)*
COORD: *facet(dim1, dim2)*
GRAPH: *point()*
GRAPH: *contour.region.confi.mean.joint())*

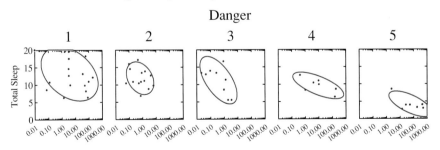

Figure 11.1 *Table of scatterplots*

11.3.1.2 Tables of 3D Plots

Figure 11.1 shows a table of 3D *bar* graphics. The data are from the king crab dataset used in Figure 7.41. Each bar measures the yield of crabs per pot at the sampled location. The plots are ordered by year, revealing the decline in yield over a six year period.

FRAME: **longitude*latitude*yield*1*year**
COORD: *facet(dim1, dim2, dim3)*
GRAPH: *tile(shape.polygon(**island**), color("green"))*
GRAPH: *bar(color("blue"))*

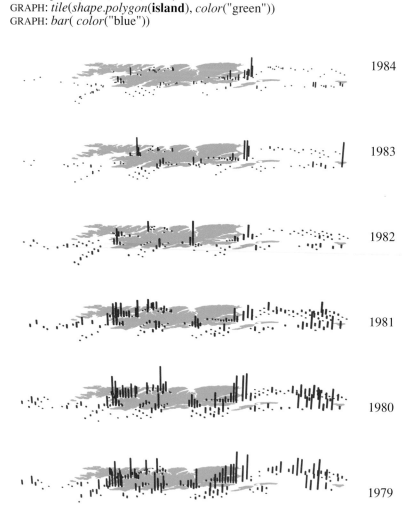

Figure 11.2 shows a table of 3D *bar* graphics.

Figure 11.2 Table of 3D bars

11.3.2 Multi-way Tables

Multi-way tables are produced by categorical facet variables. The popular word for this is **cross-tabs**. The following examples show how to embed a variety of graphics within multi-way tables.

11.3.2.1 Simple Crossing

Figure 11.3 shows a two-way table of line plots using the barley dataset from Chapter 7. The barley yields by variety have been plotted in an array of site by year. The average yields have been ordered from left to right. This table follows a general layout that I prefer for tables of graphics. The top and left axes are devoted to the table variables and the bottom and right for the scale variables. The table values are ordered from top to bottom and left to right. This fits the format table viewers are accustomed to seeing. The scale variables are ordered according to the usual layout for a single graphic. If higher-way tables of graphics are needed, then the scale variables are always moved to the bottom and right sides of the tables. This makes table look-up a left-top scan for categorical information and a bottom-right scan for scale information. The regularity of this layout generalizes nicely to any number of facets.

The problem with this layout for this particular graphic is that the lengthy string values for **variety** on the horizontal axis are unreadable. Ordinarily, this scale would be numerical and there would be only a few tick marks. With a categorical variable, however, we need one tick per category. Thus, when we have a categorical variable on an inner frame, we often need to change the layout. We will fix this problem in the next figure.

FRAME: **variety*yield*site*year**
COORD: *facet(dim1, dim2)*
GRAPH: *line()*

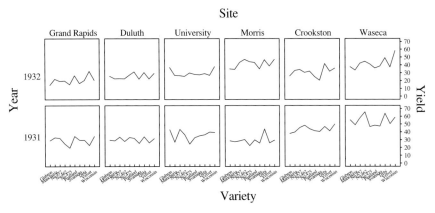

Figure 11.3 *Two-way Table of Graphics*

11.3.2.2 Transposed Tables

Figure 11.4 transposes the table in Figure 11.3 to provide more readable labeling, following a layout in Cleveland (1995). This makes the range of the inner frames (**yield**) horizontal and the domain (**variety**) vertical.

FRAME: **variety*yield*site*year**
COORD: *facet(dim1,dim2)*
COORD: *transpose(dim1,dim2)*
COORD: *transpose(dim3,dim4)*
GRAPH: *line()*

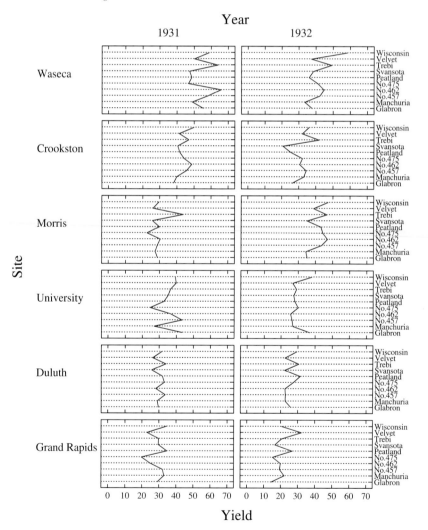

Figure 11.4 *Transposed barley data*

11.3.2.3 Blended Facets

Figure 7.57 showed a nested design based on the data from Darwin used in Chapter 7. We can rearrange the nested factor to produce another tabular display of the same data. Figure 11.5 shows an example. This time, we use the nested variable set **plant/pot** to determine the pattern used for the *line* graphic. This causes *line* to split into a different number of graphics in each panel.

The first facet consists of the blend s***self** + c***cross**. This is plotted in rectangular coordinates. The second frame consists of **1*pot**, which makes the panels stack vertically. The expanded expression is equivalent to the blend of s***self*1*pot** + c***cross*1*pot.**

DATA: **s** = *string*("SELF")
DATA: **c** = *string*("CROSS")
FRAME: (**s*self+c*cross)*1*pot**
COORD: *facet*(*dim1*,*dim2*)
GRAPH: *line*(*pattern*(**plant/pot**))

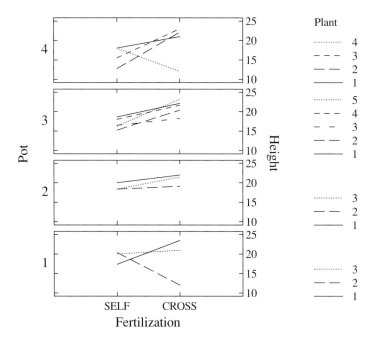

Figure 11.5 *Darwin data.*

11.3.2.4 Tables of Mathematical Functions

Tables of graphics are often useful for visualizing different slices through higher-dimensional objects. Figure 11.6 shows an example of a 3D object we can tabulate. It is a beta density function (*bdf*) for parameters p and p. The *iter*() function is used to create a series on the domain.

DATA: $\mathbf{x}$ = *iter*(0, 1, 0.1, 25, 1)
DATA: $\mathbf{p}$ = *iter*(0.1, 9, 0.1, 1, 25)
TRANS: $\mathbf{z}$ = *bdf*($\mathbf{x,p,p}$)
FRAME: $\mathbf{x*p*z}$
GRAPH: *surface*(*color.hue*($\mathbf{z}$))

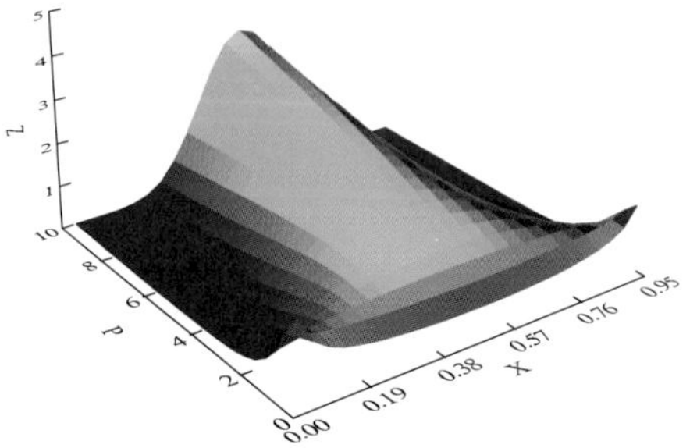

Figure 11.6 *Beta density.*

Figure 11.7 shows a table of slices through this density for different parameter values. We are allowing the two beta parameters to vary independently rather than linking them to the same value. The values of the p and q parameters determine the orientation of the outer frame. Cross-slices of Figure 11.6 can be seen on the diagonal of the table from the lower left to the upper right.

DATA: $\mathbf{x}$ = *iter*(0, 1, 0.1, 16, 1)
DATA: $\mathbf{p}$ = *iter*(0.1, 6.1, 2.0, 1, 4)
DATA: $\mathbf{q}$ = *iter*(0.1, 6.1, 2.0, 4, 1)
TRANS: $\mathbf{z}$ = *bdf*($\mathbf{x,p,q}$)
FRAME: $\mathbf{z*x*p*q}$
COORD: *facet*(*dim1,dim2*)
GRAPH: *line*()

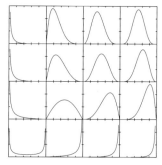

Figure 11.7 *Table of beta densities*

11.3.2.5 Nesting under Crossed Tables

Figure 11.8 shows a graphic nested within a crossed table. The data are from Lewis *et al.* (1982). This was a study of the fixation of six different types of tibial prosthetic components used in total knee operations. The authors used finite-element analysis to determine the maximum stress at several locations around the prostheses. The variables were **configuration** (type of prosthesis component), **material** (metal or polyethylene), **mode** (location and type of stress), and **stress** (meganewtons per square meter under 2000-newton total load).

DATA: **configuration** = *link*("prostheses")
FRAME: **stress** / (**mode*material/configuration**)
COORD: *facet(dim1)*
COORD: *transpose(dim1)*
GRAPH: *bar()*

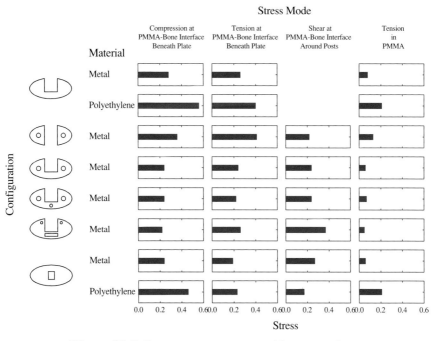

Figure 11.8 *Stress measures on total knee prostheses*

The **material** is nested under **configuration** because not all designs are available in both plastic and metal. To produce the outer crossing, the stress **mode** is crossed with **material/configuration**. To make the left margin more readable, the values of **configuration** are associated via metadata links with images of the prostheses. There are 32 potential graphics in the crossing (4 stress modes and 8 materials given configuration). The **stress** is not measurable at the "Shear at PMMA-Bone Interface Around Posts" value of **mode**, however. This is because the first configuration (top left in the figure) has no posts (represented in the other images by small circles to the right and left of the central notch). Consequently, there can be no bar graphic and no frame for two of the combinations. This situation is *not* like having missing **stress** data or zero values, however. The nesting tells us that the combination is not defined for **stress**.

This may seem to be a small point, but it is important. The original graphic in Figure 5 of Lewis *et al.* (1982) places all the bars in a regular grid of 32 frames and leaves these two cells empty, assuming the readers will realize that the measurement of **stress** under this combination makes no sense. This is confusing. To see why, we can draw an analogy from survey research. Pollsters are careful to distinguish several types of missing values for a response: "refuse to answer" vs. "no opinion" vs. "not asked" and so on. Their care shows that it is important to understand whether lack of information is due to a structural condition or to a failure to measure.

One remedy for the original journal graphic layout would be to place the words "Not Measurable" in these two empty cells. That would substitute for the two missing inner frames in the layout of Figure 11.8. This strategy would be satisfactory for a printed graphic, but it would not satisfy the structural problem in a live display system. The reason we need the nesting operator is so that a query to an area containing a missing frame yields a different response (concerning metadata, links to other graphics, etc.) than a query to an area containing an empty frame.

There is another consequence of nesting that profoundly affects the functioning of a graphics system involving tables. Some market-research programs compute statistical tests such as chi-square tests and *t*-tests on tables that violate basic assumptions needed for inference. This happens because these programs have no concept of statistical independence when they are given data to tabulate. A system that correctly implements the cross and nest operators can be designed to prevent these situations. The details of this implementation are beyond the scope of this book, but solving these problems can yield for the first time a system that is at once capable of producing complex tables and appropriate statistical tests.

One final point. With the crossing of **mode*material/configuration**, we are assuming that some possible variable (not **stress**) *could* be measured under all the combinations. This assumption is implicit in the layout of Lewis *et al.*'s Figure 5. It could be argued, however, that **mode** is not crossed but is instead nested under **material/configuration** because no measurement of any kind could be made around non-existing posts. This argument highlights the role of algebra versus display. An automated system cannot tell us how to structure displays if extrinsic knowledge is required. Making specifications explicit, however, is the only way to insure that we will recognize the difference between two graphics that are visually similar but structurally different.

11.3.3 *Continuous Multiplots*

Continuous multiplots are rare, but have their uses. Scatterplots can be positioned on a map, for example, to show the relations among variables at different geographical locations. Scatterplots of scatterplots can sometimes reveal second-order relations among non-spatial variables as well.

11.3.3.1 *Scatterplots of Scatterplots*

Figure 11.9 shows a scatterplot of scatterplots. The spacing of the plots is determined by an additive linear model based on the means of beginning and current salary at a Chicago bank sued for discrimination (SPSS, 1996). I used the CONJOINT procedure in SYSTAT to compute the marginal scales. The unity constant (**1**) insures that the **gender** variable plots in a vertical orientation. The last facet is thus **1*gender**. The salary spacing makes sense for **education** but is harder to defend for the other variables.

FRAME: **salbeg*salnow*education*race*1*gender**
COORD: *facet(dim1,dim2)*
COORD: *facet(dim3,dim4)*
GRAPH: *point()*

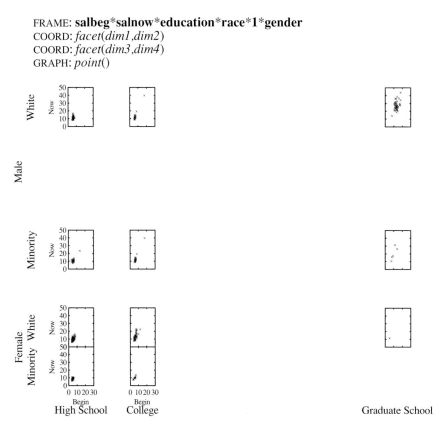

Figure 11.9 *Bank salaries.*

11.3.4 Scatterplot Matrices (SPLOMs)

The **scatterplot matrix** (SPLOM) was invented by John Hartigan (1975b). The idea has been rediscovered several times since and has been most extensively developed by the research group originally at Bell Labs (Chambers *et al.*, 1983; Cleveland, 1985). The SPLOM replaces the numbers in a covariance or correlation matrix with the scatterplots of the data on which they were computed. Most SPLOM's are symmetric, but they can be constructed from rectangular sub-matrices as well. Hartigan included scatterplots in off-diagonal cells and histograms in the diagonal cells, but other graphics may be used.

11.3.4.1 Symmetric SPLOM

Figure 11.10 is a SPLOM of the 1997 EPA emissions data for cars sold in the US. The variables are horsepower (HP), miles-per-gallon (MPG), hydrocarbons (HC), carbon monoxide (CO), and carbon dioxide (CO2). The emission of pollutants are measured in per-mile weight.

DATA: **s1** = "HP"
DATA: **s2** = "MPG"
DATA: **s3** = "HC"
DATA: **s4** = "CO"
DATA: **s5** = "CO2"
FRAME: (**hp/s1**+ **mpg/s2**+**hc/s3**+**co/s4**+**co2/s5**)*
       (**hp/s1**+ **mpg/s2**+**hc/s3**+**co/s4**+**co2/s5**)
GRAPH: *point(select(dim1!=dim2))*
GRAPH: *histobar(select(dim1==dim2))*

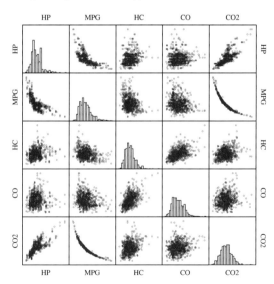

Figure 11.10 *Scatterplot matrix.*

The most striking feature of this SPLOM is the almost perfect inverse relationship between miles-per-gallon and carbon dioxide emissions. We have reached a point in Federal regulations where the emissions of other potentially harmful gases in new vehicles is almost negligible, but the production of carbon dioxide is increasingly worrisome for its potential effects on global warming. The gasoline engine, governed by computers, has become a fairly efficient and clean converter of gasoline to heat and carbon dioxide.

11.3.4.2 SPLOM with a Grouping Variable

Figure 11.11 shows a SPLOM with a grouping variable. Notice that this addition causes the graphics in each cell to split in three, because **species** has three categories. If we had not declared **species** to be categorical, this would not have happened. There would have been different symbols for shading by **species**, but only one point cloud and kernel per cell.

DATA: **sw** = "SEPALWID"
DATA: **sl** = "SEPALLEN"
DATA: **pw** = "PETALWID"
DATA: **pl** = "PETALLEN"
FRAME: (**sepalwidth/sw+sepallength/sl+petalwidth/pw+petallength/pl**) *
      (**sepalwidth/sw+sepallength/sl+petalwidth/pw+petallength/pl**)
GRAPH: *point*(*shape*(**species**), *color*(**species**), *select*(*dim1!=dim2*))
GRAPH: *line.density.kernel.epanechnikov*(*color*(**species**))

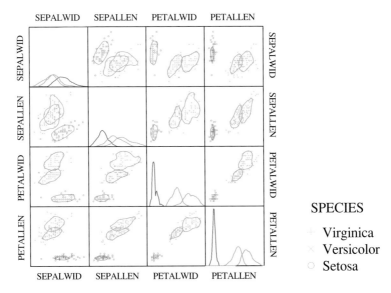

Figure 11.11 *Scatterplot matrix split by categorical variable.*

11.3.5 Facet Graphs

Facets can be proxies for graphs themselves. By structuring the organization
of a facet through a function, we can orient graphics in more complex or customized structures. See Butler and Pendley (1989) for an example.

Facet graphs extend graphing functions such as *link()*. They require data
to construct graphs of graphs. Like maps, facet graphs use sets of variables (relational tables) that are linked through common keys or functions. For example, to make a tree of scatterplots, we need triples (*e.g.*, **xnode**, **ynode**, **parent**)
for the tree and tuples (*e.g.*, **x**, **y**) for the scatterplot. The following examples
illustrate how this works.

11.3.5.1 Trees

Organizational charts, clustering trees, prediction trees, and other directed
graphs offer a superstructure for embedding graphics. Figure 11.12 shows a
regression tree (Breiman *et al.*, 1984) for predicting accident rates from sociometric variables aggregated by states in the continental US.

FRAME: **accident*xnode*ynode**
COORD: *facet*(*dim1*)
COORD: *link.edge.tree*(**xnode**, **ynode**, **parent**)
GRAPH: *point*(*position.stack*(**accident**), *color*(**tnode**))

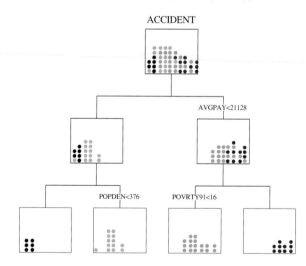

Figure 11.12 *Regression tree predicting accident rates.*

This tree is called a *mobile* (Wilkinson, 1997). This display format gets its
name from the hanging sculptures created by Calder and other artists. If the
rectangles were boxes, the dots marbles, the horizontal branches metal rods,
and the vertical lines wires, the physical model would hang in a plane as

shown in the figure. Each box contains a dot density based on a proper subset of its parent's collection of dots. The scale at the bottom of each box runs from low accident rates on the left to high on the right. The dots are color coded according to which terminal (red) box they fall in. There are 46 dots altogether because two states have missing data.

11.3.6 Facet Coordinates

Facets can be embedded in different coordinate systems. This section shows examples.

11.3.6.1 Reflection: Dual Histograms and Pyramids

Reflecting facets enables us to take advantage of symmetry to contrast paired graphics. The most popular application of this method is a favorite plot of demographers, called a **population pyramid** (Cox, 1986). This plot places age histograms back-to-back, one for males and the other for females. Dallal and Finseth (1977) extend this idea to general dual histograms. Figure 11.13 shows an age-sex pyramid for the United States, based on the 1980 Census. The coordinate function *mirror()* implements a composite transformation consisting of reflection and translation. For an even number of categories on a facet (usually two), it reflects half of the graphics contained in the facet.

FRAME: **age*pop*sex**
COORD: *facet(dim1,dim2)*
COORD: *transpose(dim1,dim2)*
COORD: *mirror(dim3)*
GRAPH: *histobar(color(**sex**))*

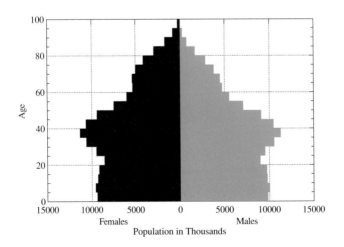

Figure 11.13 *Age-sex pyramid of 1980 US population*

11.3.6.2 Tables of Pies

Figure 11.14 shows a table of pie charts. This figure includes both females and males from the ACLS dataset used in Figure 7.30. The *string()* function is used to create a new variable on which the second dimension is based. This defines the facet on which we stratify the pies.

DATA: **m**=*string*("Male")
DATA: **f**=*string*("Female")
FRAME: **male*m+female*f**
COORD: *facet(dim1)*
COORD: *polar.theta(dim1)*
GRAPH: *bar(label(***response***), color(***response***), position.stack())*

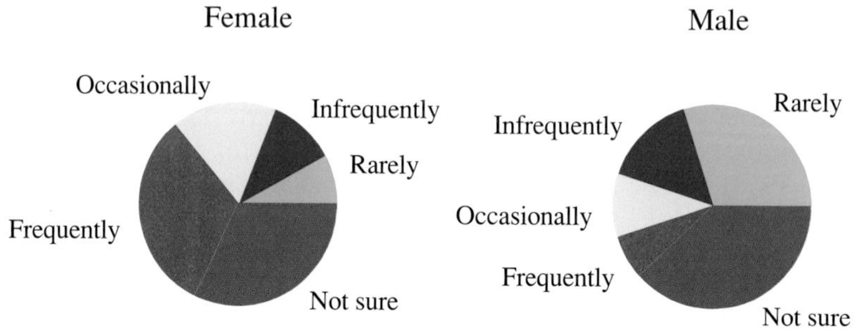

Female   Male

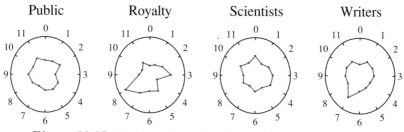

Occasionally   Rarely
     Infrequently Infrequently
       Rarely
Frequently   Occasionally
           Frequently
     Not sure   Not sure

Figure 11.14 *Table of pie charts*

11.3.6.3 Tables of Polar Plots

Figure 11.15 shows a table of polar graphics of death-month by social group. The data are from Andrews and Herzberg (1985), contributed by C. O'Brien. The polar arrangement makes sense for years because it allows us to examine relations across the annual boundary.

FRAME: **month*death*group**
COORD: *facet(dim1,dim2)*
COORD: *polar(dim1,dim2)*
GRAPH: *point()*
GRAPH: *line()*

Public   Royalty   Scientists   Writers

Figure 11.15 *Deaths as function of months from last birthday*

11.3.6.4 Polar Array of Polar Plots

Figure 11.16 shows a polar plot of polar plots of the Greenland wind data. This arrangement is particularly appropriate because wind direction and astronomical time (month of year) are intrinsically polar. The plot reveals cyclic trends that would be difficult to discern in a rectangular time-series plot. Changing the coordinate transformations from polar to rectangular would turn this into a trellis plot.

```
DATA: count = count()
FRAME: direction*count*month
COORD: facet(dim1,dim2)
COORD: polar(dim1,dim2)
COORD: polar.theta(dim3)
GRAPH: histobar()
```

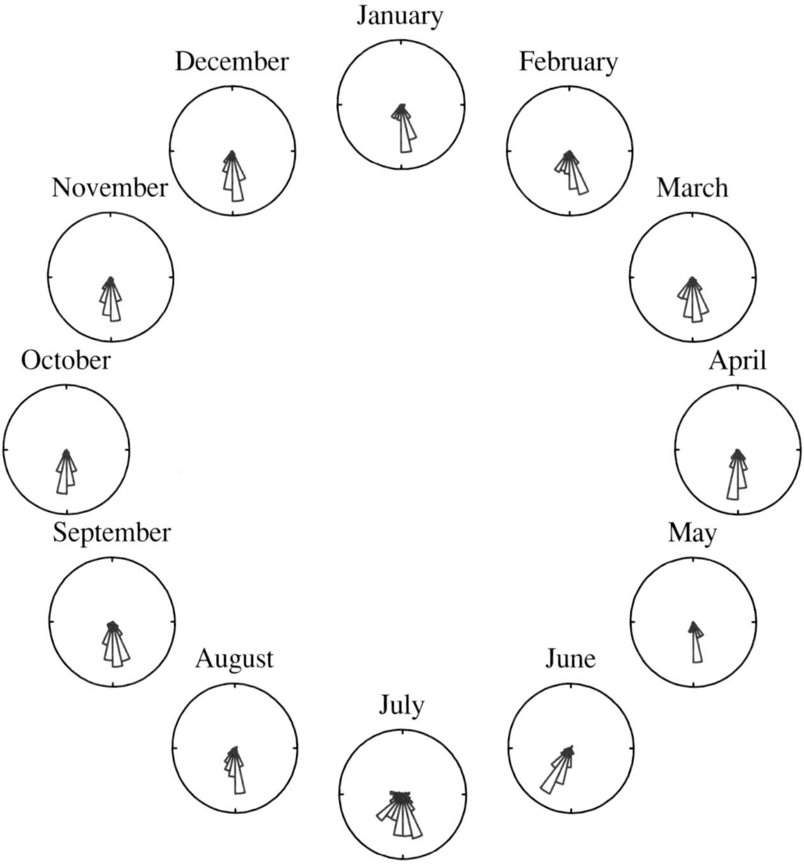

Figure 11.16 One year of wind data

11.3.6.5 Mosaics

The **mosaic** plot is a method for displaying categorical data in a contingency table whose cell areas are proportional to counts (Hartigan and Kleiner, 1981, 1984). It is a type of tiling. Friendly (1994) presented a generalization of the mosaic that is equivalent to a set of crossed frames (see also Theus, 1998). I will use a famous dataset to illustrate how the mosaic and its generalization works.

Figure 11.17 shows a 3D bar graphic representing proportions of survivors of the Titanic sinking, categorized by **age**, social **class**, and **sex**. The data are from (Dawson, 1995), who discusses various versions and their history. Simonoff (1997) fits a logistic regression model to these data that predicts survival from **class**, **sex**, and the interaction of **class** by **sex**. The two bar graphics were produced by a facet on **sex**, which aligns each on a horizontal facet dimension.

FRAME: **class*age*survived*sex**
COORD: *facet(dim1, dim2, dim3)*
GRAPH: *bar.statistic.mean()*

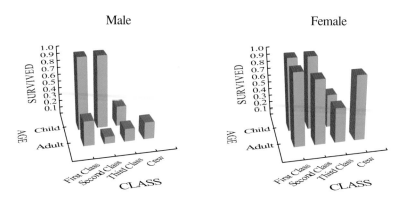

Figure 11.17 *3D bar graphic of Titanic survivor data*

Figure 11.18 shows a tiling of these data with the same faceting on **sex**. In this graphic, **survived** is used to determine the color of the tiles instead of the heights of bars. This graphic shows more clearly that there were no registered children among the crew. It also reveals the poignant fact that a relatively small proportion of the third-class passengers (even children) survived. Although color is not always suited for representing continuous variables (see Chapter 7), Figure 11.18 is preferable to Figure 11.17 because 3D bars tend to hide each other and the 3D display angle makes it difficult to decode the height of the bars.

FRAME: **class*age*sex**
COORD: *facet(dim1, dim2)*
GRAPH: *tile.density.rect(color.hue(***survived***))*

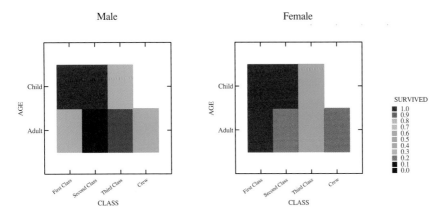

Figure 11.18 *Tiled graphic of Titanic survivor data*

The mosaic plot varies the area of each tile according to another variable, usually the count of the cases represented by that tile. Figure 11.19 shows a two-way mosaic plot for the Titanic data. I have omitted axes (see more about guides in Chapter 12) to make the figure resemble a mosaic more closely.

FRAME: **class*age*sex**
COORD: *facet(dim1,dim2)*
COORD: *mosaic(dim1, dim2)*
GRAPH: *tile.density.rect(color.hue(***survived***))*
GUIDE: *axis.none(position(***class***))*
GUIDE: *axis.none(position(***age***))*

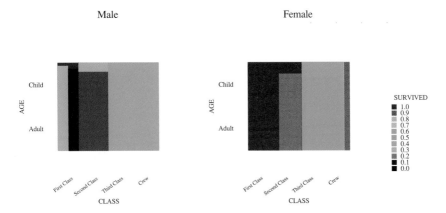

Figure 11.19 *Two-way mosaic plot of Titanic survivor data*

In a mosaic plot, the widths of the tiles are proportional to the column counts and the heights are proportional to the row counts within each column. We accomplish this with a coordinate transformation called *mosaic()*. I did not present this in Chapter 10 because I want to discuss the full generalization of the *mosaic()* transformation here. The *mosaic()* coordinate transformation is best understood as a discrete local warping. I presented an example of a continuous local warping in Section 10.1.9. A discrete local warping performs piecewise coordinate transformations. It resizes the height and width of each tile and glues them together to fill the plane.

Figure 11.19 is unsatisfactory for several reasons. Gluing the tiles together makes it difficult to perceive the areas, particularly when colors are similar. Also, this method does not work for more than two categorical variables. We must make several mosaics to accommodate additional variables. To remedy this, we can use the *mosaic()* transformation on facet coordinates. Figure 11.20 shows how this works for the Titanic data. The innermost frame (**1*1**) holds one *tile* graphic colored by **survived**. The remaining facet variables define coordinates that are modified by the *mosaic()* transformation. Eliminating axes leaves gaps between the tiles.

FRAME: **1*1*age*1*1*sex*class**
COORD: *facet(dim1, dim2)*
COORD: *mosaic(dim3, dim4, dim5)*
GRAPH: *tile.density.rect(color.hue(**survived**))*

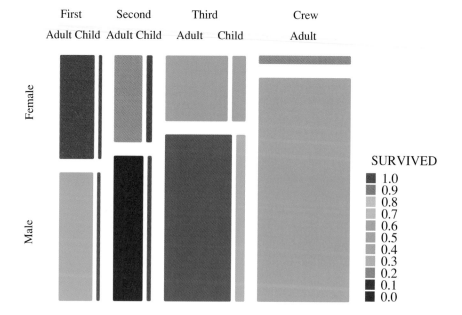

Figure 11.20 *General mosaic plot of Titanic survivor data*

11.3.7 Multiple Frame Models

For some tables of graphics, we have no choice but to set up multiple frames. Carr *et al.* (1998) present a paneled graphic called a Linked Micromap Plot that is designed for displaying spatially indexed statistical summaries. Figure 11.21 shows a variety of this plot.

TRANS: **octile** = *cut*(**popden**, 8)
FRAME: **longitude*latitude*1*octile**
COORD: *facet*(*dim1*,*dim2*)
GRAPH: *tile*(*position*(**longitude*latitude**), *shape.polygon*(**state**), *color.hue*(**popden**))
FRAME: **state/octile*popden**
COORD: *transpose*(*dim1*,*dim2*)
GRAPH: *point*(*position*(**state*popden**), *color.hue*(**popden**))
GRAPH: *line*(*position*(**state*popden**))

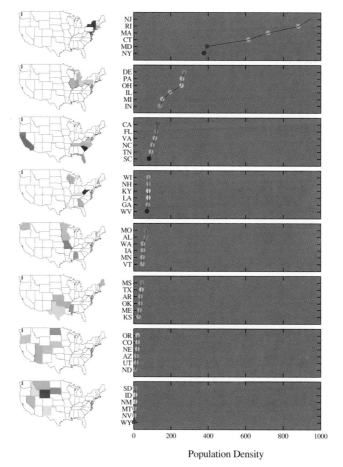

Figure 11.21 *Linked micromap plot of US population density*

The reason we need two frame models in this specification is that we cannot blend **state** and **latitude**. One is categorical and the other continuous, so the two cannot overlap on a common scale. Because we want to position the maps to align with the plot frames, we must make two separate graphics and align them using **octile** (the 8 fractiles of **popden**). Facets allow us to construct a tremendous variety of tabled graphics in a single frame specification, but there are limits. Some tabled graphics are really two or more graphics glued together. Because common variables are defined through a single DataView, however, all such graphics are linked for the purposes of brushing, drill-down, and other operations.

I have taken one liberty with Carr's graphic (apart from minor differences in layout). Carr uses the same categorical color palette within each map block. This facilitates look-up and comparisons with the maps. I have instead represented each value with its appropriate color on a continuous scale within blocks. This reinforces the anchoring in the data values but makes look-up more difficult. Either method is preferable to using a single color scale across blocks. That would make the colors within most maps almost identical, particularly for a variable with a skewed distribution like **popden**'s.

11.4 Sequel

So far, we have taken axes and legends for granted. The next chapter covers guides, such as axes and legends and titles, which help us to decode graphics.

12

Guides

Guides show us the way. They give us absolute directions in a relative world. We need guides in graphics to help us associate categories or quantities with aesthetics. Position, for example, allows us to compare magnitudes among graphics in a frame, but we need a positional guide to help us to relate magnitudes to non-graphical information. Color can help us discriminate categories, but we cannot associate colors with specific categories without a color guide.

Table 12.1 contains a list of standard graphical guides. Scale guides include *legend* and *axis*. These guides help us to decode continuous and categorical scales. Annotation guides include *text* and *form*, and *picture*. These guides link a graphic to extrinsic metadata. Guide functions work like graphing functions (see Chapter 6). Their syntax is *guide.method(position(), size(), ...)*. An example is *form.line(position((0,0),(30,30)), label("Zero Population Growth"))*, used in Figure 1.1.

Table 12.1 Guides

Scales	Annotations
legend	*text*
none	*title*
vertical	*footnote*
horizontal	*form*
interior	*line*
axis	*rectangle*
none	*ellipse*
cross	*arrow*
single	*tag*
double	*image*

In thinking about guides, we must keep in mind a built-in guide that all graphics share: the *label()* aesthetic attribute. This attribute associates a text string with each instance of a graphic. Because text can represent categorical or continuous values, the *label*() attribute can serve as a guide. It can be used to attach numerals to the tops of bar graphics, for example, or category names next to line graphics. Labeling of graphic elements is sometimes preferable to axes or separate legends because it allows local look-up without changing our focus and it can provide exact values without requiring comparative judgments. Kosslyn (1994) surveys some of the literature showing the superiority of labeling to legends. We also need to keep in mind that *label*() is an available attribute for guides themselves. It provides, in essence, a guide to a guide. The example from Figure 1.1 cited above shows a label attached to a reference line guide. Labels are also used to annotate axes and legends.

12.1 Scale Guides

Chapter 9 covers continuous and categorical scales. Scale guides help us to decode specific scale values, translating them to numerical or string values that help us access metadata (in our memory or through hyper-links). Pinker (1990) and Simkin and Hastie (1987) discuss the perceptual issues and Cleveland (1993) addresses statistical issues in this process.

Scale guides are so ubiquitous and necessary that they should appear by default. Axes, for example, routinely define the position of a frame. Legends regularly appear when *size*(), *color*(), or other attributes are specified. It is easier to turn off guides than to require them in the specification every time an aesthetic attribute is used. To suppress the horizontal axis in Figure 5.3, for example, we add GUIDE: *axis1*.*none*(*position*(**sepallength**)) to the specification.

12.1.1 Legend

The *legend*() guide function produces a legend. Legends serve as guides for all aesthetics except *position* (although an axis, we shall see, is best thought of as a positional legend). Table 12.2 shows some examples of *size*, *shape*, *brightness*, and *hue* legends. A legend contains a **scale**, a **label**, and a **rule**. In the left panel of Table 12.2, the scale consists of the numbers 0 through 9. The label consists of the string "X" at the top of the legends. The rule consists of the linear arrangement of symbols or colors used to represent the attribute for the legend. The English word "rule" stems from the Latin *regula*, a straightedge. Rules help us measure lines, which is the role they play in an axis guide. Rules also give us formal methods for making associations, which is the role they play in a legend. On an axis, the rule spans the frame dimension referenced by the *position* attribute and, through the placement of tick marks, allows us to measure location and decode it through the adjacent scale. On a legend, the rule spans the dimension referenced by *size*, *shape*, and other attributes by instantiating reference values on that attribute. Tick marks, usually absent in legends because they are redundant, connect the points on the rule with the values on the adjacent scale so that we can decode the attribute.

Continuous legends have a continuous rule and categorical legends have a categorical rule. Some continuous legends blend hues to create a linear spectrum, marking the scale values with ticks. I have chosen to keep a slight space between the values, which obviates the need for tick marks and makes color attributes behave like other attributes such as *size* and *shape*. For categorical legends, I have chosen a wide spacing to differentiate the rule and scale from continuous legends. See Brewer *et al.* (1997) for further information on legending color.

There are many styles for legends. I have listed a few in Table 12.1. The legends in Table 12.2 are produced by *legend.vertical()*, the default. Horizontal legends, produced by *legend.horizontal()*, are useful when located underneath or above a frame graphic. Legends inside a frame graphic are produced by *legend.interior()*. These are used when there is available blank space inside a frame graphic.

Table 12.2 **Size, Shape, Brightness, and Hue Legends**

Continuous				Categorical			
X	X	X	X	Y	Y	Y	Y
○ 9	○ 9	■ 9	■ 9	○ A	○ A	■ A	▪ A
○ 8	○ 8	■ 8	▨ 8	○ B	× B	■ B	▪ B
○ 7	○ 7	■ 7	▢ 7	○ C	+ C	■ C	▪ C
○ 6	○ 6	■ 6	▨ 6	• D	△ D	□ D	D
○ 5	○ 5	■ 5	▨ 5				
○ 4	○ 4	■ 4	▨ 4				
○ 3	○ 3	■ 3	▨ 3				
○ 2	⬠ 2	■ 2	▨ 2				
° 1	□ 1	■ 1	▨ 1				
· 0	△ 0	□ 0	■ 0				

Figure 12.1 shows an example of a double legend. It is not generally a good practice to legend more than one attribute in a graphic, although it works in this example because similar symbols and colors are contiguous. Multiple legends raise configural/separable issues in perception and often make decoding difficult. See Chapter 7 for more information.

I have included the two *legend()* functions in the specification, although these are automatically created by the use of the attributes in the *point()* function. Including them explicitly allows us to add a *label()* aesthetic attribute to each legend that we would customarily call a legend title. In this case, each label serves as a guide to a guide. I have also included the default axes, each with its own label.

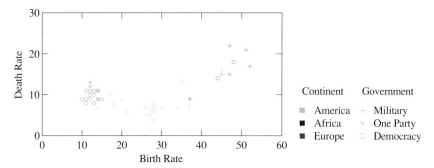

FRAME: **birth*death**
GRAPH: *point*(*shape*(**government**), *color*(**continent**))
GUIDE: *legend*(*color*(**continent**), *label*("Continent"))
GUIDE: *legend*(*shape*(**government**), *label*("Government"))
GUIDE: *axis1*(*position*(**birth**), *label*("Birth Rate"))
GUIDE: *axis2*(*position*(**death**), *label*("Death Rate"))

Figure 12.1 *Double legend*

12.1.2 *Axis*

The *axis*() guide function produces an axis. Axes are positional legends. As a legend, an axis contains a **scale**, a **label**, and a **rule**. The rule includes associated tick marks. As with legends, there are several styles for axes. Table 12.1 shows a few. The *cross*() method crosses all axes (in 2D or 3D at their zero values. The *single*() method produces a single axis. The *double*() method (the default) produces a single axis plus a parallel rule at another side of the frame. This default option produces squares in 2D and cubes in 3D. The *axis*() function is numbered by the dimension number it represents, *e.g.*, *axis2*().

The pains we take to devise uniform terminology for the components of axes and legends are not driven solely by semantics. We group components like scales, labels, and rules together so that the drawing methods to produce them are programmed only once. There is no reason to have one routine to draw a legend and another to draw an axis. Both should extend naturally from the architecture of a guide. Even if we are not programming, however, we can avoid confusion by learning why axes and legends are members of the same species.

There *is* one fundamental difference between an axis and a legend, however. Axes are transformable and legends are not. As numerous examples in this book show, especially in Chapter 10, axes can be bent all sorts of ways by coordinate transformations. Legends cannot, because the relative positions of their rules, scales and labels is governed by readability and not by frame coordinates. This is a simple distinction to implement. We simply transform the location of a legend into other coordinate systems, but not its components.

Figure 12.2 shows the super-smooth function $y = exp(-1/x^2)$ plotted on crossed axes. Because the y axis has its zero value at one end, the axes form an inverted T rather than a cross. This function, with its infinite number of derivatives, should be used in designing roller coasters for senior citizens.

DATA: **x** = *iter*(-2, 2, 0.04, 100, 1)
DATA: **y** = *iter*(0, 1, 0.01, 1, 100)
TRANS: **y** = *exp*(-1/ **x**^2)
FRAME: **x*y**
GRAPH: *line*()
GUIDE: *axis1.cross(position(**y**),label("Y"))*
GUIDE: *axis2.cross(position(**x**),label("X"))*

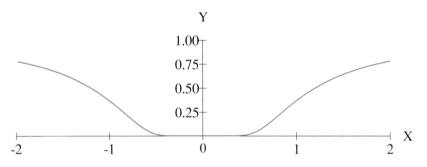

Figure 12.2 *Crossed axes*

12.1.3 *Scale Breaks*

In Section 10.1.8.1, I discussed the behavior of graphs when data exceed the bounds of frames. I indicated that nonlinear transformations can help this problem and simultaneously remedy some violations of statistical assumptions. I also questioned the wisdom of allowing data outside the bounds of a frame to determine the geometry of a graph inside a frame and claimed that this was a form of lying with graphics.

Sometimes graphic designers encounter the opposite problem. They have a graphic located far from the value of zero inside a frame spanning positive numbers. In a desire to include zero on the scale, these designers add a scale break that looks like this ——⋀—— or this ——⫽—— to the axis. This device allows them to indicate zero without representing its value – to seem to use *position*() but not to invoke it. Curiously, this device appears to be favored by scientists, although it occasionally appears in business graphics as well.

If zero really is important, then it should be part of a scale. If it is not, then it should be omitted. Some would say scale breaks are confusing. If we think about what they are intended to do, we must conclude they are meaningless. They really signal the need for two frames. If this still seems unclear, review the definition of a frame in Section 2.2.4.2.

12.1.4 Double Axes

Some scientific and business graphics have double axes. These usually appear as right and left vertical axes with different scales in 2D graphics. Double axes can serve two different purposes. The first is to represent two different scales for the same variable. For example, we might wish to present US dollars on the left vertical scale and the Euro on the right. The second purpose is to index different graphical elements inside the frame against different variables. For example, we might wish to align two different *line* graphics – one for educational spending and another for students' test scores – so that we can compare trends across time. Wainer (1997) comments on this questionable practice. Multiple axes with multiple graphics gives the designer extraordinary license to manipulate conclusions.

In either case, double axes imply double, superimposed frames. This is easy to implement with two FRAME specifications. Recognizing this geometrical fact should alert us to the danger of hiding it from the viewer. Double (or multiple) axes generally should be avoided.

12.2 Annotation Guides

Annotations become guides when they are driven by data. Otherwise, they are scribbles or doodles. Being driven by data means that the aesthetics of an annotation object are linked to variables in a dataset in a similar manner to that for a graphic. A text annotation, for example, might be positioned according to a value of a variable, or its color might be determined by a variable value, or its content might be determined by statistical parameters. There are many consequences to this data linking. For example, annotations that are anchored in a 3D frame rotate and stay frontally visible in 3D when the view is changed. Other linked annotation attributes, such as color, change when databases or other data sources are updated. This section offers a few examples to indicate how these graphical objects can function in a system.

12.2.1 Text

The *text*() guide function produces a text string. There are many types of strings that can be attached to graphics. I have included only two in Table 12.1: *title*() and *footnote*(). Ordinarily, we devise annotation from our own subject knowledge and embed it in a graphic as a simple string, for example, GUIDE: *text.title*(*label*("This is a title")). The other aesthetic attributes of text (*e.g., color* or *size*) can be determined by a constant or a variable.

Figure 12.3 shows an example of text determined by a statistical model. The data are taken from the car performance dataset used in Figure 6.2. I have fitted a quadratic regression predicting the acceleration of the cars from horsepower and vehicle weight. The title is determined by the parameters from the

smooth through the *smooth.quadratic()* function that is passed to *label()*. This
device assumes that statistical procedures have interfaces for reporting their
parameter estimates as strings and that *label()* is written to know how to ask
for such strings. The coefficients for WEIGHT*WEIGHT and HP*WEIGHT
have been deleted from the string because they were zero (to printed precision). I have added SCALE: *interval(dim3, 0, 25)* to the specification to avoid truncating the surface; this gives a larger range than used in Figure 6.2.

FRAME: **weight*hp*quarter**
SCALE: *interval(dim3, 0, 25)*
GRAPH:*surface.smooth.quadratic()*
GUIDE: *axis1.single(position(**weight**), label("WEIGHT"))*
GUIDE: *axis2.single(position(**hp**), label("HP"))*
GUIDE: *axis3.single(position(**quarter**), label("QUARTER"))*
GUIDE: *text.title(label(smooth.quadratic()))*

QUARTER = 17.81841 − .04681*HP + .00178*WEIGHT + .00005*HP*HP

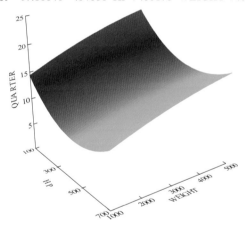

Figure 12.3 *Title text determined by parameters*

This example gives me the opportunity for a brief statistical digression.
The model in Figure 12.3 is nonsensical. It implies that increasing horsepower
above 500 retards quarter-mile acceleration. Dragsters are an existence proof
against such a model. On the other hand, the fit of this quadratic model to the
car data is quite good. The squared multiple correlation is above .9 and residuals are reasonably distributed. Unfortunately, some researchers who use statistical methods pay more attention to goodness of fit than to the meaning of a
model. It is not always convenient to remember that the right model for a population can fit a sample of data *worse* than a wrong model – even a wrong
model with fewer parameters. We cannot rely on statistical diagnostics to save
us, especially with small samples. We must think about what our models
mean, regardless of fit, or we will promulgate nonsense.

12.2.2 Form

The *form*() guide function produces a geometric primitive form such as a line, rectangle, or ellipse. I have included only a few form methods in Table 12.1. A well-designed graphics system will have a set of drawing and text tools in its user interface. These tools will operate on the display surface in inch or centimeter coordinates referenced by a 2D or 3D grid system. Nevertheless, it is useful to include primitive objects that live in variable coordinate space so that we can drive them with data or direct value references.

Figure 12.4 shows an example of a *form.tag*() object. This allows us to annotate points or other elements in a frame by providing their coordinates. Through a constraint system, the software can determine where to place tags so that they do not collide with themselves or other graphic objects. Figure 12.4 annotates two unusual cases – a race car and a utility van – for the scatterplot introduced in Figure 6.2. Another example of a *form* object is the *form.line*() in Figure 1.1.

As I mentioned at the beginning of this chapter, the *label*() aesthetic attribute function can provide similar identification to the *form.tag*() and other annotations. The difference is that a *form* is a single object and must be specified repeatedly for more than one instance. Also, a *form* is not necessarily bound to a graphic such as a *point* cloud. We could attach a *form.tag*() to the edge of a frame, for example, or even to a title in a graphic. If we wished to label all points in a cloud, then using *form.tag*() would be inefficient.

FRAME: **weight*hp*quarter**
GRAPH: *point*()
GUIDE: *axis1.single*(*position*(**weight**), *label*("WEIGHT"))
GUIDE: *axis2.single*(*position*(**hp**), *label*("HP"))
GUIDE: *axis3.single*(*position*(**quarter**), *label*("QUARTER"))
GUIDE: *form.tag*(*position*(4245, 109, 21.6), *label*("VW Van"))
GUIDE: *form.tag*(*position*(1950, 650, 11.3), *label*("Ferrari 333SP"))

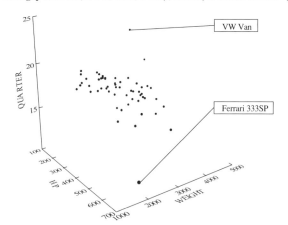

Figure 12.4 *Tag annotations*

12.2.3 *Image*

The *image*() guide function attaches an image to a frame. Figure 12.5 shows an example. This figure is adapted from a portion of a graphic in Shepard and Cooper (1982). The data are from a perceptual experiment in which subjects viewed pairs of objects differing only by rotational angle. Three different objects are represented in the panels of the figure. The **rt** variable is reaction time (delay in saying "same" for a pair). The **depth** variable marks the type of rotation used in the pair. Circles stand for picture-plane (2D) rotated pairs and squares stand for depth (3D) rotated pairs. Shepard's remarkable discovery in this and other experiments was that rotational angle is linearly related to reaction time. The February 19, 1971 cover of *Science* magazine displayed five of Shepard's computer-generated images under various rotations. This research has been replicated by psychologists and neuroscientists studying spatial processing in humans and other primates. Shepard received the National Medal of Science for this and other work in cognitive psychology.

DATA: **s1** = *link*("figure1")
DATA: **s2** = *link*("figure2")
DATA: **s3** = *link*("figure3")
FRAME: **angle*rt*object**
COORD: *facet*(*dim1*, *dim2*)
GRAPH: *point*(*shape*(**depth**))
GRAPH: *line.smooth.linear*()
GUIDE: *image*(*position*(60, 6, 1), *shape*(**s1**))
GUIDE: *image*(*position*(60, 6, 2), *shape*(**s2**))
GUIDE: *image*(*position*(60, 6, 3), *shape*(**s3**))
GUIDE: *legend*(*shape*(**depth**), *label*("Rotation"))
GUIDE: *axis1*(*position*(**angle**), *label*("Angle of Rotation (degrees)"))
GUIDE: *axis2*(*position*(**rt**), *label*("Mean Reaction Time for ""same"" Pairs (seconds)"))

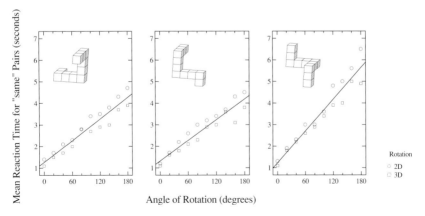

Figure 12.5 *An image annotation*

As with *form.tag*(), the *image*() guide shares functionality with the *label*() aesthetic attribute function and even with legends. We could construct a legend, for example, by associating the three images in Shepard's graphic with the values of **object**. They could then appear as axis scale values (see Figure 11.8) or as legend scale values. I used the *image*() guide function in this example in order to place the images inside the frames where Shepard did.

This usage annotates the entire frame, but we can imagine other applications where a one-to-one relationship between an *image*() and a frame would not exist. For example, we could use *image*() to place images along various parts of a curve in a 2D plot to signify another dimension. Imagine, for example, pictures of cigarette packs along various sections of the path in Figure 6.14.

12.3 Sequel

We have completed our survey of the world of graphics. The remaining chapters demonstrate the consequences of our new world-view. The next chapter introduces the graphboard, which is a user interface for implementing graphics algebra.

13

Graphboard

The word **graphboard** is a neologism. It serves my purposes to describe a device that looks like a whiteboard but implements visually the grammar of graphics. In a well-designed object system, basic components are independent of the interface needed to access them. This principle benefits not only the developer, who must be able to speak an abstract language based on a content domain, but also the end-user, who must be able to able to handle concrete tools that behave as much as possible like real objects in the physical world. More importantly, individual differences in abilities, expertise, aesthetic preferences, and cognitive styles require that interfaces be designed to be flexible and modifiable by the user.

This chapter presents one interface designed to produce and modify the graph specifications described in this book. This interface is only one of many possible ways to interact with a graphics system. It is meant to illustrate principles rather than to implement a specific commercial operating system, toolkit, or browser. I call this user interface a **graphboard**, a surface for creating and modifying graphics. Its name suggests a whiteboard, but it also incorporates rules that make objects written on it behave in a predictable manner. The graphboard is a whiteboard with a grammar.

The following sections are organized by stages of interaction with the system. The first section, *Learning*, describes available help and basic navigation. The second, *Playing*, describes the process of graph creation and exploration. These are not serial stages of interaction. One may play before learning or learn before playing. I have made efforts throughout the design of this interface to eliminate dialogs, wizards, and other order-dependent devices so that both novices and experts can explore, backtrack, and modify without being forced through steps someone else imagined to be helpful.

The style of these sections is motivated by user scenarios rather than theoretical issues. As much as possible, I will present issues within the flow of actual user interactions in a session. This requires more figures, but is closer to the experience of using the real system. Macintosh users should substitute "command-click" for the term "right-button mouse click" in the following descriptions.

13.1 Learning

Figure 13.1 shows a basic graphboard. It is split into two regions: a **control panel** and a **whiteboard**. The whiteboard in Figure 13.1 contains the help screen a user sees after pressing the help (?) button in the control panel when the screen is empty (although it can be pressed at any time). The help screen contains a lot of information, but it has a transparent typeface that overlays existing graphics without obscuring them. This help overlay obviates the need for a separate hierarchical help system that requires multiple user-interactions before offering the desired assistance. And unlike some context-sensitive help, this system facilitates browsing in a single screen. This is not the only help available within the system, of course. Other help is offered after significant user delays in responding or in specific contexts where the system recognizes the need for support or as pop-up tips. This text in the basic help screen reveals the fundamental characteristics of the graphboard.

First, most user interactions with the system are based on the graphics themselves, not on dialogs. The English word *dialogue* comes from the Greek $\delta\iota\alpha\lambda\delta\gamma o\sigma$, which means alternating speech, as in a conversation. This mode of interaction, whether implemented with *wizards* or with *dialog boxes*, can frustrate experienced users or even some novices who are impatient. Dialogs are best for those who prefer to do tasks serially rather than in parallel. (The use of the term *dialog* to describe menus, panels of check boxes, tool bars, and other miscellaneous collections of visual controls is a misnomer. Controls involve dialogs only when they force the user to interact sequentially.)

Second, all actions in the graphboard are reversible, so it is straightforward to return to where one was several steps back. There is no need for UNDO. This characteristic is due partly to the grammar underlying the board and partly to the design of the controls themselves.

Third, the order of operations needed to reach a goal is usually not significant. There are often several paths to reaching the same goal. This characteristic reflects the way we draw many complex figures. We can assemble components in any order as long as the result contains all the needed components.

13.1.1 Controls

The control panel contains the basic tools needed to create graphics. At the top is a **scroll-list** of variable names in the data source. These are draggable objects that represent variables in the graph specification. When we wish to include a variable in a graph, we place our cursor arrow on the name and hold down our mouse button and drag a copy of the variable name into the whiteboard. To remove a variable from a graph, we do the reverse: drag the copy of the name back into the scroll-list. Some applications use a double click to signal this kind of reversal. I prefer to use the drag-out-of-frame operation to reinforce the idea that gestures are invertible.

At the bottom of the list are italicized names of synthetic variables. These names do not exist in the data source. They are needed whenever we wish to construct a dimension from functions of the data, as with histograms or bar graphs of counts. See Figure 3.6 for examples.

The section below the scroll-list is a **glyph tray**. Dragging an image of a graphic into the whiteboard specifies that a graph is to be represented with this object. We may drag one or more of any of these into the whiteboard in any order, before or after we have dragged variable names into this area.

The design and behavior of this tray is meant to convey to the user that it is not a list of chart types. Some graphics programs have buttons with lines, bars, and other images that enable users to choose a type of chart. The glyph tray works instead by dragging, so that a user is encouraged to try more than one graphic in a frame. I have made two conspicuous concessions to user preconceptions, however. One is the pie icon at the bottom of the tray. As we have seen in Chapter 2, a pie is a stacked *bar* in polar coordinates. This insight is too much to expect of non-technical users, however. Dragging a pie icon is therefore equivalent to dragging a *bar* icon and setting the coordinates of the frame to polar. Similarly, the smoother icon (to the left of the pie) is designed to be equivalent to dragging a *line* and setting the statistical method to a smoother. Other icons could be added to this tray for similar purposes. It is designed to grow to accommodate them. There is always a tension, however, between keeping an interface simple versus making it look like the cockpit of a fighter jet in order to impress technical users or to expose rarely used options. These decisions must be made carefully and with accompanying user testing. Finally, the numerical icon (123) is for using numerals instead of other graphics to represent quantity.

Below the glyph tray is a set of **annotation** tools. These tools are for drawing forms on a graphic, such as lines, rectangles, ellipses, or text. They are not intended to replace or duplicate paint programs. Instead, annotations are intended to link meaningfully to objects in a frame. The leftmost arrow-button is for restoring the cursor to the standard pick-arrow after drawing with a tool.

At the bottom of the control panel are two exploration tools. The one on the left is a **rotation pad** for orienting 3D images. Its central *home* button restores the orientation to the default view and the other buttons control two degrees-of-freedom of rotation. On the right is a **pan-and-zoom** controller. The central, darker square can be resized to demarcate the subset of the graphic shown in the whiteboard. For tables of graphics, this controller can be used to show anything from a single frame up to the entire table.

Finally, the **help button** (?) controls the help system. Help is always given in the whiteboard and is contingent on the material displayed. At times, this material may obscure the material in the whiteboard, but only when necessary to avoid clutter.

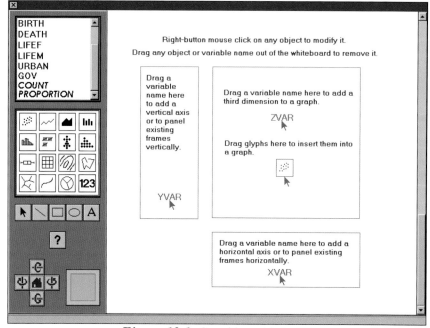

Figure 13.1 *Graphboard help (?)*

As we shall see, the graphboard offers additional capabilities for interacting with the system, but these are not implemented with visible controls. There are several means for accomplishing this. First, as the help screen shows, dragging operations are defined by their target area in the whiteboard. Dragging variable names into the **vertical target area** at the left of the whiteboard assigns them to a vertical (y) dimension. If there are any variables already assigned to this vertical dimension, then dragging a variable name to this area panels the frames according to the values of the variable being dragged. We will see this operation in Section 13.2. Dragging variable names into the **horizontal target are**a at the bottom of the whiteboard assigns them to a horizontal (x) dimension in the same manner as the vertical. Dragging variable names to the **frame target area** adds a third (z) dimension to the graph. Finally, dragging variable names on top of other variable names *blends* the two variables (see Section 5.1.6.1 for the definition of a blend).

The second method for implementing other controls is the use of delay. After 1500 milliseconds, the system responds with prompts. These may be help messages or modal choice options presented to qualify the meaning of a gesture. This time-dependent modality, such as a delayed interruption requiring a choice between *cross* and *nest*, is employed when one option (in this case, *cross*) overwhelmingly predominates in ordinary applications. Expert users can turn off this delay feature.

The next section will illustrate some of these features by following a simple user scenario of interactions with the system.

13.2 *Playing*

We begin with the countries data used in Chapter 1. The variables in that
dataset are listed in the variable scroll-list of Figure 13.2. In each figure of this
section, I will represent the user action by a strobed arrow (pale blue) next to
the thing being dragged (pink). The consequence of the action is what shows
in the figure. In Figure 13.2, dragging a variable name (LIFEM) into the horizontal target area of the whiteboard creates a horizontal (*x*) axis with scale
values produced from the data. If we placed our cursor arrow on the axis label
(LIFEM) in the whitboard and dragged it back to the scroll-list, we would return to our previous state, an empty whiteboard. If, on the other hand, we
dragged the axis label to the vertical target area at the left edge of the whiteboard, we would have created a vertical axis. The specification produced by
the action shown in the figure is:

MODEL: **lifem**

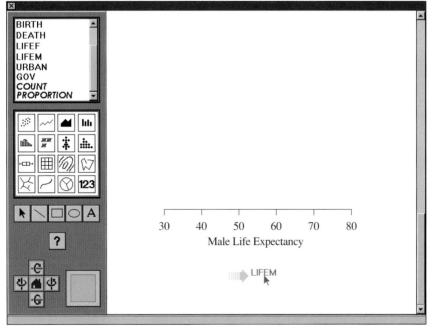

Figure 13.2 *Adding a variable to create a dimension*

Figure 13.3 shows the result of adding a *point* graphic to the frame. We have dragged the *point* icon from the glyph tray into the central frame target area. The result is a one-dimensional scatterplot. The specification produced by this action is:

MODEL: **lifem**
GRAPH: *point*()

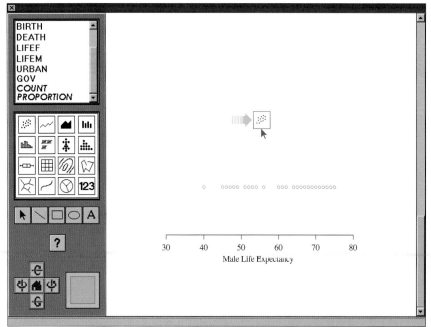

Figure 13.3 *Adding a point graphic to a frame*

Notice that the result looks like the one-dimensional scatterplot in Figure 5.2. If we had originally dragged LIFEM to the left-most area controlling the vertical axis, then the gesture in Figure 13.3 would have resulted in a one-dimensional vertical scatterplot. If we had wanted to put in two axes before dragging in a *point*, then we could have dragged a second variable to the other axis box, viewed two empty axes, dragged in *point*, and viewed a 2D scatterplot. This latter series of gestures is probably closer to the graph-construction script most users would expect. On the other hand, few non-technical users are aware that a one-dimensional scatterplot exists at all. Exposing users to new creatures is part of the purpose of creating a zoo-like environment that allows them to visit cages without a prior appointment. Or, even better: select the right animals and environment so that we can do away with cages.

Figure 13.4 shows the result of dragging a second variable from the scroll-list to the vertical target area. This adds a second dimension to the frame. Now we see two axes, and the point cloud expands to become a 2D scatterplot. The specification produced by this action is:

MODEL: **lifem*lifef**
GRAPH: *point*()

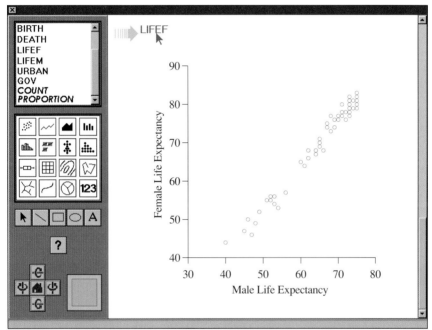

Figure 13.4 *Adding a second dimension to a frame.*

At this point, we could reverse any of the actions we have taken by dragging from the whiteboard back to the control panel. For example, we could remove the *point* graphic and leave ourselves with an empty frame. Or, we could drag the horizontal axis variable LIFEM back to the scroll list and leave ourselves with a one-dimensional scatterplot on LIFEF (Female Life Expectancy). We will move forward, however.

Figure 13.5 adds a smoother to the scatterplot. We have dragged the *smoother* icon from the glyph tray to the frame target area. As I mentioned in Section 13.1, this single action is equivalent to dragging a *line* graphic icon into the frame and then right-button mouse clicking on the line to change its statistical method to a smoother. Figure 13.7 shows an example of this right-button gesture. The specification produced by this action is:

MODEL: **lifem*lifef**
GRAPH: *point*()
GRAPH: *line.smooth*()

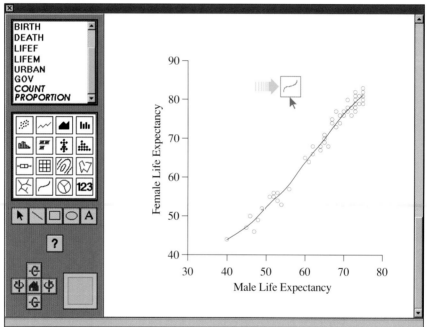

Figure 13.5 *Adding a second graphic to a frame*

So far, we have two variables in our graphical frame model. How do we add more variables? Getting a user to think about dimensions versus variables is a difficult problem. Specifically, we could represent a third variable in this graphic by using *position*() in the frame model to go to 3D, using *position*() with faceting to panel the graphic, or using some other aesthetic attribute such as *color*() to modify the *point* graph. In the graphboard, the 3D world is signalled by dragging a variable into the center of a frame. Paneling through facets is signalled by dragging a variable to one of the edges of a frame. And adding a variable to aesthetic attributes is accomplished by right-button clicking the graphic itself. By applying these rules consistently, we can add more dimensions to simple graphics, paneled graphics, and 3D graphics. We will continue this example by going to 3D first. Then we will backtrack and try attributes. Finally, we will try paneling.

Figure 13.6 shows the result of adding a third dimension to the frame by dragging **birth** from the scroll-list to the inside of the frame target area. This creates a 3D scatterplot with a surface smoother. The specification produced by this action is:

MODEL: **lifem*lifef*birth**
GRAPH: *point*()
GRAPH: *line.smooth*()

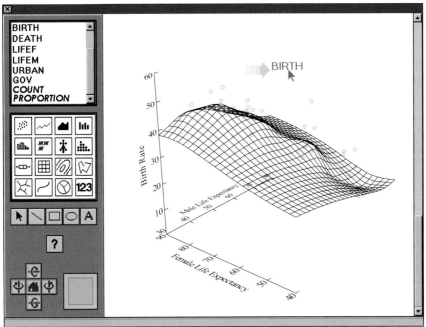

Figure 13.6 *Adding a third dimension to a frame*

Figure 13.7 shows how to remove the third dimension by dragging the **birth** variable name off the vertical axis and back to the scroll-list. I have also highlighted three other gestures that reveal how to change properties of graphics, frames, and variables. The **graph drop-down list** in the middle of the frame was created by pointing to the smoother in the frame area and clicking with the right mouse button. This list contains three modifiable domains: attributes (*hue, size, orientation*, etc.), statistical methods (*smooth.linear, smooth.loess*, etc.), and properties (associated metadata, annotations, etc.). The content of these domains is documented in Chapter 7 and Chapter 8.

An example of a **scale drop-down list** is shown at the bottom of the frame. It is produced by right-button mouse clicking on a variable label for the desired dimension. The modifiable entries in the list are transformations (list-ed in Table 8.1), categorization (making a scale categorical or continuous), and properties (metadata and other annotations). These actions affect the SCALE paragraph of the specification.

Finally, the figure shows an example of a **frame drop-down list** accessed by right-button mouse clicking in the frame target area (but not on a graphic itself). The coordinates listing directs the user to the coordinate transforma-tions available in the system. And the properties listing points to frame-level properties.

All of these directives arise from right-button mouse operations. In gener-al, right-button (command-click) mousing is a *modify* operation in the white-board. It is always relevant to the particular object being pointed to. The right-button is never used for miscellaneous short-cuts or other operations. The specification represented in this figure is the same as for Figure 13.5:

MODEL: **lifem*lifef**
GRAPH: *point*()
GRAPH: *line.smooth*()

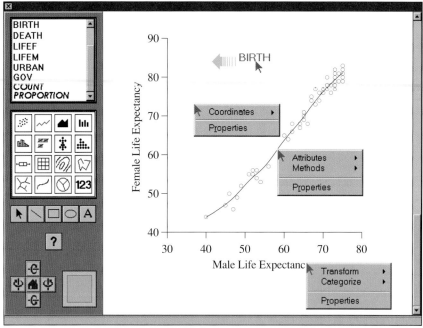

Figure 13.7 *Right button mouse clicks*

Figure 13.8 shows how to panel graphics. We have dragged a variable (**gov**) into the horizontal target area. This action creates three graphics, one for each value of the **gov** variable. The specification produced by this action is:

MODEL: **lifem*lifef*gov**
COORD: *facet(dim1,dim2)*
GRAPH: *point()*
GRAPH: *line.smooth()*

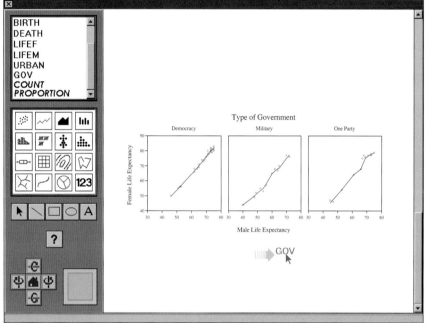

Figure 13.8 *Paneling*

This paneling operation can be carried on indefinitely. We simply drag new paneling variables to either of the margins of the current frame. This implies a structural model for tables of graphics that is documeted at the beginning of Chapter 11. That is, we create frames of frames by working from the inside out, like the layers of an onion. The graphboard displays these faceted graphics as larger tables of frames. It would not be difficult to add layout templates to allow layers, or pages of tables. Layout, it must be remembered, is an aspect of the view, not the model.

Figure 13.9 shows how to panel with two variables. We have dragged a second variable (**urban**) into the vertical target area. This produces two rows of paneled graphics, one for each level of the urbanization variable. The specification produced by this action is:

MODEL: **lifem*lifef*gov*urban**
COORD: *facet(dim1,dim2)*
GRAPH: *point()*
GRAPH: *line.smooth()*

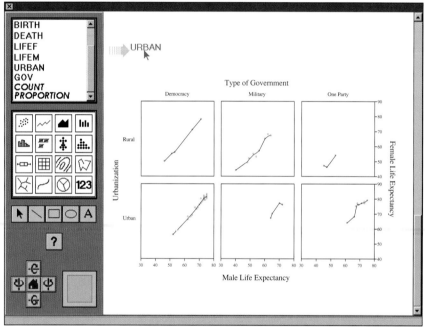

Figure 13.9 *Two-way paneling*

Although layout is an attribute of views, not models, there are some operations that change appearance through modifying a model. As I explained in Chapter 10, *pivoting* is an operation that exchanges the domain and range of a graph. The following example shows how this operation can be accomplished in the graphboard. This pivoting is performed by drag-and-drop of a variable name (instantiated as an axis label) onto another (on a different axis). The graphboard does not limit this operation to outer variables. Any two axes can be exchanged, thereby modifying the model.

Figure 13.10 shows how to pivot a panel. We have dragged a variable name from one paneling dimension to another paneling dimension. This flips the graphic. The specification produced by this action is:

MODEL: **lifem*lifef*urban*gov**
COORD: *facet(dim1,dim2)*
GRAPH: *point()*
GRAPH: *line.smooth()*

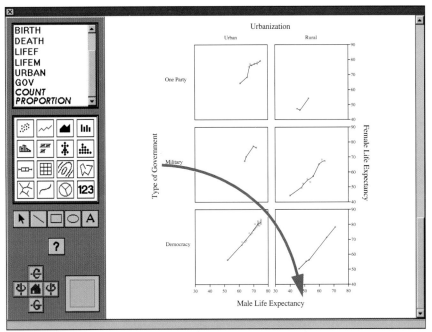

Figure 13.10 *Basic graphboard*

13.3 *Principles of Operation*

The title of this section brings to mind the nickname of one of the (ancient) IBM 360 mainframe manuals, *POOP*. A principle of operation is something less than a theory, something more than a feature. This section explores some principles of operation through questions.

In order to maintain a simple drag-and-drop environment, we have constrained the graphics algebra to models that expand alternatively in vertical and horizontal directions, *e.g.*, **a*b*c*d** is mapped to $h*v*h*v$. Are there any expressions in Table 11.2 that cannot be created by the graphboard GUI? Can this interface be adapted to work in all the coordinate systems described in Chapter 10? You may find some clues to this coordinate problem in the next chapter. Are there any drag-and-drop gestures available between the control panel and whiteboard that would not be reversible because of the result of a transformation or its non-invertibility? Again, there may be some clues in the next chapter. Finally, what special problems does a 3D coordinate system present to this GUI?

13.4 Sequel

The next chapter turns everything inside-out. We will learn how to produce data from graphics.

14

Reader

The word **read**, according to the *Oxford English Dictionary*, has obscure origins in Old English, French, and other Indo-European languages. Its earlier meanings have mostly to do with giving counsel, considering, expounding, or explaining something obscure. Its modern association with text derives from the older sense of understanding, rather than just looking. This interpretation suits our purposes, because a **reader** in this sense is someone who can parse and understand a graphic, including *both* text and image. This chapter introduces the design of a graphics reader.

This task is formidable. As Pinker (1997) says,

> A seeing machine must solve a problem called inverse optics. Ordinary optics is the branch of physics that allows one to predict how an object with a certain shape, material, and illumination projects the mosaic of colors we call the retinal image. Optics is a well-understood subject, put to use in drawing, photography, television engineering, and more recently, computer graphics and virtual reality. But the brain must solve the *opposite* problem. The input is the retinal image, and the output is a specification of the objects in the world and what they are made of – that is, what we know we are seeing. And there's the rub. Inverse optics is what engineers call an "ill-posed problem." It literally has no solution. (p. 28)

In designing a graphics reader, my goals are less ambitious. First, I will limit the problem to a particular decoding task. Then I will leverage what we have learned so far about the organization of objects in **graphics world**. Specifically, I will *invert* the functions we have already used to create graphics. Because I designed these functions to be invertible, this becomes a "well-posed problem." We have been making graphics from data. Now we are going to examine how to make data from graphics.

The function

$$f: S \rightarrow T$$

is invertible if there exists a function

$$g: T \rightarrow S$$

such that for every x in S, $g(f(x)) = x$ and for every y in T, $f(g(y)) = y$. We call g the *inverse* of f and denote it as f^{-1}. In a sense, inversion is how to get from there to here assuming we know how to get from here to there. Not every function is invertible. And not every system or composition of functions is invertible. If all the functions in a chain of functions are invertible, however, then the chain itself is invertible by executing the inverse functions in reverse order.

In the development of this system, I have been concerned about invertibility because it keeps objects clean and domesticates their behavior in an interactive environment where we often need to know where we came from. Sometimes it is not easy to invert a function without doing a lot of extra work or carrying along extra information (as with 3D to 2D perspective projections), but this should not deter us from pursuing the goal wherever we can.

In the next section, I will present the problem. Then, I will summarize Steven Pinker's propositional model of graphics reading to provide psychological background. Finally, I will outline the approach to a solution through a graphics grammar.

14.1 The Problem

Suppose we have the graphic shown in Figure 14.1. Our problem is how to derive the table at the bottom of this figure by scanning the graphic. We may bring to the task prior knowledge about what graphs and graphics are, but not knowledge about this specific graphic.

There are several constraints we must place on the problem. First of all, we accept as a solution any table whose organization allows us to decode the data correctly. For example, if **summer** and **winter** were stacked in a single column called **temperature** and we had an extra index column called **season**, this would be a feasible solution. Without metadata, we have no way to determine whether **summer/winter** denotes independent groups or repeated measures. In other words, this graphic could have been produced by either

DATA: **s** = *string*("SUMMER")
DATA: **w** = *string*("WINTER")
FRAME: **region***(**summer**+**winter**)
GRAPH: *bar*(*color*(**s**+**w**))

or

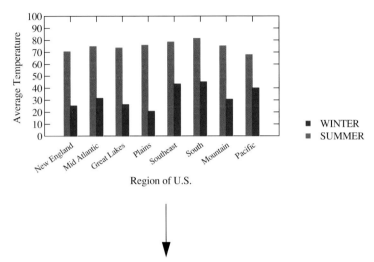

region	summer	winter
New England	71	25
Mid Atlantic	75	32
Great Lakes	74	26
Plains	76	21
Southeast	79	44
South	82	45
Mountain	75	31
Pacific	68	40

Figure 14.1 *From graphic to data*

Second, we expect rounding error. But we assume this error is uniform over the field of the graphic if we are working in rectangular coordinates. If a scale or coordinate transformation is involved, then we expect error to be transformed in the process.

Third, we are not concerned with general understanding. The problems Pinker addresses – detecting relationships, reasoning about trends, proportions, and so on – are not part of our problem domain. Of course, if we produce a graphics reader capable of decoding data, then we can feed the data mining and statistical engines already designed to address these more general problems in an automated system. People are better than computers when finding patterns in images, but computers are better than people when finding patterns in numbers.

14.2 A Psychological Reader Model

Bertin (1967), Simkin and Hastie (1987), Kosslyn (1989), Pinker (1990), Cleveland (1993), and MacEachren (1995) have all developed models to explain how people decode graphics. Pinker's model goes farthest toward solving the specific decoding problem I have posed. Pinker's model also resembles in many respects the object-oriented approach I have taken later in this chapter. This is not surprising, because Pinker used a propositional system developed by mathematical logicians (see Copi, 1967; Epp, 1990) and implemented by cognitive psychologists for modeling memory (see Rumelhart, 1977; Anderson, 1983) that influenced the development of object-oriented design itself.

A **propositional calculus** is a system that involves

1) a set of variables whose truth or falsity is assumed,
2) symbolic operators, and
3) syntactical rules for producing expressions.

Expressions consisting of variables and operators following proper syntactical rules are called *well-formed formulas* (*wff*). A *wff* produces a truth table that can be used for a variety of purposes ranging from testing a logical argument to producing an electronic circuit. A **predicate calculus**, on the other hand, is a propositional system that involves variables whose truth or falsity is *not* assumed. A predicate calculus consists of a set of *objects* (variables) and *predicates* (functions). The predicate functions operate on variables. These functions are unary, binary, or *n*-ary. Some examples are *circle*(x), *part*(x, y), and *parallel*(x, y). If x = '*body*' and y = '*head*', then *part*(x, y) is true, but *part*(y, x) is false.

It is often convenient to represent object-predicate relationships in a graph consisting of a network of labeled nodes and edges. Nodes are labeled with object names and edges are labeled according to predicates. Figure 14.2 shows Pinker's general graph schema based on a predicate calculus system. Pinker has omitted variable names inside the nodes (except for iterators, which I will discuss later) and has labeled the graph with predicate function names. I will use the name of the unary predicate function operating on a node to describe the node itself. The node at the top of the graph, for example, represents *scene_graph*(x). This entity stands in a part/whole relationship with everything below it. The *framework*() node stands in relation to *scene_graph*() via the function *part*(*scene_graph*(), *framework*()). There is a formal duality between the graph and the predicate calculus. This formalism distinguishes Figure 14.2 from the loosely-drawn network diagrams that people use to make *ad hoc* collections of objects look like information processing systems.

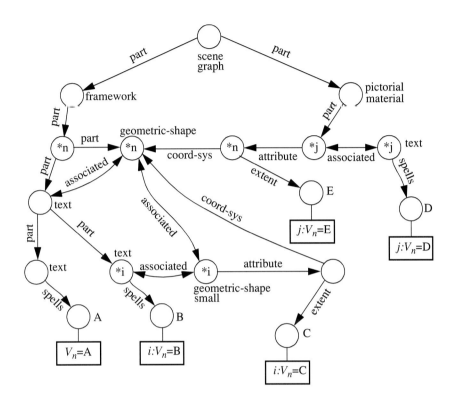

Figure 14.2 *Propositional reader model (adapted from Pinker, 1990)*

Some of the nodes in Figure 14.2 contain iterator variable names, which are denoted by an asterisk. The *n iterator, for example, specifies an iterated replication of the node plus all its predicate relationships. Because the iterators are variables, their values are known to other functions linked to them. For example, each iteration of the *geometric_shape(*n)* node is associated with a result value V_n at the bottom of the graph.

Another notation peculiar to Figure 14.2 is the capital letter designation for predicate functions at the bottom of the figure. These are *unknown predicates*, which are functions that are instantiated at "run-time" when specific values of the variables are available.

The output of this system is defined in the bold outlined boxes below the unknown predicates at the bottom of the figure. The two extent measures $C()$ and $E()$ are for comparisons of size or intensity that are used by graph readers to answer questions like "Is the third bar taller than the second?". The $A()$, $B()$ and $D()$ predicates yield the numbers or strings that we need to enter into our data table of Figure 14.1.

Let's focus on the problem of decoding the leftmost red bar in Figure 14.1. In the following explanation, I will supply the predicate function names specific to a bar graph schema that are missing in the general graph schema of Figure 14.2. I will try to do this in a series of sentences. First of all, the *j* node directly below and to the left of *pictorial_material*() would be *bar*(*j) in a bar graph schema. The first bar would thus be recognized by the reader as *part*(*pictorial_material*(), *bar*(1)). To the left of *bar*(*j) would be several attributes (*color, size, position,* etc.). The horizontal *position*() attribute would be linked through a *coord_sys*() rectangular coordinate system to a horizontal axis element *geometric_shape*(1) that is *part*() of *framework*(). This axis *geometric_shape*(1) is *associated*() with *text*() that *spells*() "New England" and is assigned to the first variable V_1. The *bar*(1) also has an *attribute*() of vertical *position*() which is linked through a *coord_sys*() to a vertical axis *geometric_shape*(2) that is *part*() of the same *framework*(). The location on the vertical axis line *geometric_shape*(2) that is indexed by the *position*() of the top of the *bar*() has *near*(*tick*(), *text*()) that *spells*() "70." We enumerate and assign a value of 70 to the second variable V_2. Finally, the variable names "Region of U.S." and "Average Temperature" would have been located through the *A*() function tied to the *part*() of the vertical and horizontal *geometric_shape*() axes that is *near*() the *text*() containing them.

To make my description more rigorous, I would have to collect all the predicate functions in a linked list. I chose a sentence format to make this complex sequence more readable. Nevertheless, we should be able to get an idea of how this system functions from my description. There are several critical aspects to note.

First, look-up and scale decoding is done for every object and part-object in the system. The reader must locate and examine text every time a direct evaluation on a categorical or continuous scale is required. This apparently inefficient process fits empirical data of Pinker (1990), Simken and Hastie (1987), and other researchers quite well. As we shall see, it is not a model we need for efficient decoding in an automated system. Once coordinates are known and scales calculated, every measurement of position is a simple affine transformation for a system that is capable of doing linear algebra in its head (obviously not human).

Second, the propositional system says nothing about the number of schemas required for its implementation. There are presumably bar graph schemas, line graph schemas, and so on. Each of these may be a close relative of another and all are presumably children of the general schema in Figure 14.2. This plethora of schemas probably fits the human data better than the system I will develop in the next section. As Pinker indicates, efficient decoding of graphics is a learned skill that improves with the acquisition of new schemas rather than the refinement of a single global algorithm.

Third, Pinker's coordinate system is driven by a computational vision model outlined in Marr and Nishihara (1978). This means that graphic evaluation is confined to rectangular and polar coordinates. Again, this may follow the human decoding model more closely. It may be next to impossible for a human to decode raw values in a graph represented by a projectively transformed logarithmic scale, for example. This is no more difficult for a machine than handling rectangular coordinates.

Fourth, Pinker's model has no provision for composing functions outside of the network. The bar dodging we see in Figure 14.1, for example, is a matter of *bar*(*position,dodge*()). This pattern is seen by humans in a variety of clustered bar charts, but inducing the rule for other graphs and coordinate systems is nontrivial. As Pinker (1997) discusses, people do not compose even simple functions in the way I am proposing.

None of these characteristics of Pinker's model makes it less rigorous or adequate for describing how we humans read graphics. Indeed, as I have said, it almost certainly fits experimental data better than the system I will propose in the next section. Nor does this imply that it would be futile to build a graphics reading system along the lines Pinker suggests. Pinker's model can be implemented in a closed system. One might learn a lot from unexpected results and from comparing machine to human data. This is a venerable tradition in cognitive psychology.

Two lessons, I believe, can be taken from examining this model, however. First, it is not always desirable to use the strategies people actually bring to well-defined problems as methods for solving these problems automatically. In engineering, we should use psychological research for guidance, but not as a template. Secondly, well-articulated psychological models based on empirical research give us a head start in defining the basic objects we need for an automated system. I am more impressed by the similarities of Pinker's model to the one I will propose than by the differences.

14.3 *A Graphics Grammar Reader Model*

Figure 14.3 presents my design of a graphics reader. The notation differs from Figure 14.2. I have adopted a subset of the Booch-Jacobson-Rumbaugh **Unified Modeling Language** (UML) notation (see Fowler and Scott, 1997). The triangular-shaped arrows represent "is a" relationships (inheritance). The diamond-shaped arrows represent "has a" relationships (aggregation). The hollow arrows represent interfaces. An interface is a specification for how a task is to be performed. This specification can be fulfilled by a variety of different implementations or devices. I use these interfaces to avoid making the objects they point to part of the system. Finally, italic type denotes abstract classes. These are classes that are containers for concrete classes. They specify how a class is to behave and what are its interfaces, but exist only as patterns for creating concrete classes. Using abstract classes helps to keep the design free of implementation details and provides an economical method for grouping classes that inherit from a common ancestor and whose differences in functionality are not substantively important.

The bold boxes for Image and Data show the input and output of the system. Image contains a bitmap or other representation of the graphic image. Data contains some representation of the table in Figure 14.1. The first thing we need is a Scanner. This object converts Image into an object discernible by the children of Reader. Since Reader has a Scanner, the converted graphic Image is now owned by the Reader.

Reader has three main components: an Identifier, a Measurer, and a Framer. The general strategy for converting geometric entities to numerical and textual tables is to measure extents or other aesthetic attributes and convert these to numbers or text. To do this, Measurer needs to have two packets of information. First Measurer must know how to identify an object in order to assemble a measuring strategy and methods. Second, Measurer must know about the coordinate system and frame that defines the dimensions on which graphs are measured. I will review these two in turn.

Identifier examines the shapes and attributes of objects and compares them to its list of known graphic elements. This is not a simple pattern matching or template procedure, however. Because Identifier knows about the coordinate system (through Reader), it is capable of knowing that a section of a divided bar in rectangular coordinates is the same object as a pie slice in polar coordinates. It uses an inverse polar-to-rectangular transformation to make this comparison. Identifier requires shape recognition methods for accomplishing its work, but because it has top-down information (like the rest of the system) about the array of shapes it is seeking, Identifier's methods can be customized for this purpose. Identifier supervises several children. AxisIdentifier, for example, looks for ordered text near rules and tick marks with an associated label. PointIdentifier looks for clouds of points inside a frame. It knows that a cloud may consist of points that do not look like geometric points, but it seeks to determine if they are a collection of similar atoms within a common pattern and grouped inside the frame. Finally, Identifier evaluates the votes of each of its children and picks the strongest vote. This follows the Pandemonium model described in Selfridge (1959) and later employed as a foundation for neural networks.

Framer is responsible for establishing the model underlying the graphic. It must associate variables with dimensions, set the coordinate system, and determine the scales on which dimensions are mapped. The first of these three tasks is accomplished by Modeler. Through Framer, Modeler can parse text and determine whether more than one variable name is associated with an axis or guide. Modeler, like the other agents in the system, knows where to look for an axis or guide because of the information provided by Identifier through Reader, the common parent. In addition to recognizing blends by parsing text, Modeler recognizes crossings by looking for perpendicular axes (after inverse transformation to rectangular coordinates). With legended variables, Modeler looks for all possible combinations of attributes to recognize a crossing. Modeler recognizes nestings by looking for subscales with different ranges on common variables. The CoordinateSetter depends on the presence of a Guide to determine coordinates. For example, a circular axis with appropriate ticks would signal CoordinateSetter that it is looking at polar coordinates. Additional methods for error checking (seeing that angles radiate from a central origin, for example) are available to CoordinateSetter to verify its hypothesis. Finally, Scaler computes scales by examining the spacing of tick marks on axes and their associated numerical labels. It inverse transforms the tick locations to see if the physical spacing of ticks in the transformed metric can be made proportional (after adjusting for arbitrary constant) to the numerical values at the ticks. Scaler, like Modeler, requires prior work by CoordinateSetter. Thus, Framer is usually given first priority by Reader and CoordinateSetter is given first priority by Framer.

The result of this process is that Measurer can do its work through a simple chain of coordinate and scale transformations without further reference to text or other cues in the scene. Measurer is an abstract class because it is a collection of different measuring objects that all return a common data structure. The actual measurements require location methods that are specific to the graphics being measured. For example, PointMeasurer requires a centroid computation to find the center of a *point* graphic. LinkMeasurer requires a skeletonizer to assure that the links are measured at their central mass (assuming they have thickness). ColorMeasurer requires a colorimeter. Once these readings are taken and collected, Measurer returns to Reader the information that Reader must pass to Data. This is the collection of numbers and text and field identifiers that is the dataset we seek.

How does this process work for the graphic in Figure 14.1? Let's consider AxisIdentifier first. This animal hunts around for an axis and barks when it finds one. The components it is looking for are a *rule*, *ticks*, tick *labels* (letters or numbers) and an axis *title* (*e.g.*, "Average Temperature"). The rule may be curved, so this little beast has to sniff along line segments that do not cross themselves and look for the associated elements attached to or near the line, much the way a contour-following algorithm works. When AxisIdentifier barks, it must then furnish to other clients the coordinates (in Image space) of the components of an axis. At this point, we are conversing in Image World coordinates, which I will call *w* coordinates.

How are these *w* coordinates and their object descriptors used by clients? Let's examine CoordinateSetter first. This calculating engine must examine one or more axis objects and try a number of inverse transformations of the plane that transform the axis rules to a set of orthogonal or parallel lines. In the case of Figure 14.1, an identity transformation yields the result immediately. At this point, we are conversing in rectangular coordinates, which I will call *r* coordinates.

AxisScaler examines the spacing of the tick marks on the plane in *r* coordinates and applies a set of inverse transformations (*log*(), *exp*(), etc.) to get them to be equally spaced. Then it uses TextConverter to convert the numerals near the ticks (located by AxisIdentifier) to numbers, assuming the scale is numerical. Through these operations, it can determine the scale transformation.

Again, for Figure 14.1 this would be an identity. At this point, we are conversing in scaled coordinates, which I will call s coordinates.

We still do not have data values, which I will call d coordinates. For this last step, which is an affine transformation, we need to bring in the scale values. A simple rescaling involves the transformation

$$d_i = s_i \left(\frac{d_{max} - d_{min}}{s_{max} - s_{min}} \right) + d_{min}$$

For the values on the horizontal axis, we need to remember that the character string labels correspond to the integers 1 through n. In the case of Figure 14.1, $n=8$, so $d_{min}=0$ and $d_{max}=9$.

The importance of inversion is nowhere more apparent than with coordinate systems. We *draw* the graphics in Chapter 10 through the composition chain $d \rightarrow s \rightarrow r \rightarrow w$. We *read* the graphics in Chapter 10 by inverting our transformations in the chain $w \rightarrow r \rightarrow s \rightarrow d$.

I will not discuss the remaining objects in Figure 14.3 with respect to the reading of the graphic in Figure 14.1. How does Reader recognize that the bars are dodging, and how does it link this information to the legend? Can Reader use the axis titles to infer whether blending is in the model? What text would it look for to identify this situation? Is AxisIdentifier fooled by the top and right axes or can it recognize that these are associated with the other two? How does color in the legend get linked to color in the bars? How are LegendIdentifier, ColorMeasurer, LegendScaler, and LegendModeler involved in this inference?

Additional questions are raised by scenarios involving other figures in this book. How does AxisIdentifier avoid thinking the *path* graphic in Figure 6.14 is an axis? Assume this path did not cross itself; could AxisIdentifier then recognize it as a graphic rather than a guide? What does Reader produce when there are no axes, such as in Figure 7.61? How does Reader approach facets, from simple Trellises to the complex polar graphic in Figure 11.16? Could Reader be modified to handle facets? If so, could Reader be modified to handle facet graphs, such as the tree in Figure 11.12? What problems are introduced by reading 3D graphics? Can this be done at all with the model I have developed? What does Reader do with Figure 15.1? Would it have to take a course with Ed Tufte or Bill Cleveland first?

Going through the scenarios necessary to understand parsing for these instances is the best set of exercises one can pursue in learning the aspects of the system in this book. The Reader is not only a useful application, it is also an exercise constructed to test the limits of a graphics grammar.

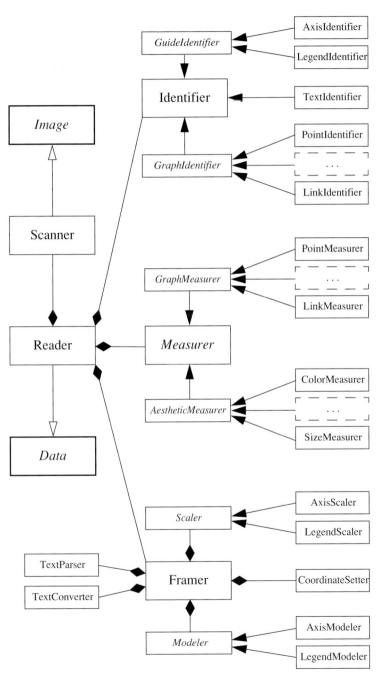

Figure 14.3 *A graphics grammar reader model*

14.4 Sequel

The next, final chapter will analyze two unusual graphics in detail in order to show how a specification and data contain the meaning of a graphic.

15

Semantics

Semantics is derived from the Greek $\sigma\eta\mu\alpha$, or sign. This same word underlies the title of Bertin's *Semiology of Graphics*. In linguistics, semantics involve questions of meaning. In this concluding chapter, I intend to show how the *grammar* of graphics can inform our understanding of the *meaning* of graphics. With Pinker (1990) and MacEachren (1995), I believe that understanding the meaning of a graphic is a lexical task. The syntactical information is expressed in its grammar and its semantic information is encapsulated in its associated data. We will examine this proposition through a detailed analysis of two statistical graphics.

15.1 Napoleon's March

Minard's "Figurative map of the successive losses of men in the French army during the Russian campaign, 1812-1813" is now one of the most famous statistical graphics, thanks to Tufte (1983). Tufte said of Minard's creation, "It may well be the best statistical graphic ever drawn." Tufte's devotion to this and other historical graphics is extraordinary; his books are worth owning for the quality of the reproductions alone. It would help during this discussion if you kept a copy of Tufte's book nearby. Also helpful is the fine analysis of this same graphic in Roth *et al.* (1997).

15.1.1 The Data

Table 15.1 shows the data behind Minard's graphic. I produced this table through a combination of digitizing the map itself, analyzing the annotations, and locating the geographic landmarks. Table 15.1 consists of three subtables – the city data, the temperature data, and the army data. I have omitted the data that define the rivers. There are other ways to organize these data, but I believe the structure of Table 15.1 is closest to the way Minard himself would have arranged the information. The data in Table 15.1 are designed to reproduce Minard's graphic, not to represent accurately the historical record.

Table 15.1 **Napoleon's March Data**

lonc	latc	city	lont	temp	date	lonp	latp	survivors	direction	group
24.0	55.0	Kowno	37.6	0	Oct 18	24.0	54.9	340000	A	I
25.3	54.7	Wilna	36.0	0	Oct 24	24.5	55.0	340000	A	I
26.4	54.4	Smorgoni	33.2	−9	Nov 9	25.5	54.5	340000	A	I
26.8	54.3	Molodexno	32.0	−21	Nov 14	26.0	54.7	320000	A	I
27.7	55.2	Gloubokoe	29.2	−11		27.0	54.8	300000	A	I
27.6	53.9	Minsk	28.5	−20	Nov 28	28.0	54.9	280000	A	I
28.5	54.3	Studienska	27.2	−24	Dec 1	28.5	55.0	240000	A	I
28.7	55.5	Polotzk	26.7	−30	Dec 6	29.0	55.1	210000	A	I
29.2	54.4	Bobr	25.3	−26	Dec 7	30.0	55.2	180000	A	I
30.2	55.3	Witebsk				30.3	55.3	175000	A	I
30.4	54.5	Orscha				32.0	54.8	145000	A	I
30.4	53.9	Mohilow				33.2	54.9	140000	A	I
32.0	54.8	Smolensk				34.4	55.5	127100	A	I
33.2	54.9	Dorogobouge				35.5	55.4	100000	A	I
34.3	55.2	Wixma				36.0	55.5	100000	A	I
34.4	55.5	Chjat				37.6	55.8	100000	A	I
36.0	55.5	Mojaisk				37.7	55.7	100000	R	I
37.6	55.8	Moscou				37.5	55.7	98000	R	I
36.6	55.3	Tarantino				37.0	55.0	97000	R	I
36.5	55.0	Malo-jarosewli				36.8	55.0	96000	R	I
						35.4	55.3	87000	R	I
						34.3	55.2	55000	R	I
						33.3	54.8	37000	R	I
						32.0	54.6	24000	R	I
						30.4	54.4	20000	R	I
						29.2	54.3	20000	R	I
						28.5	54.2	20000	R	I
						28.3	54.3	20000	R	I
						27.5	54.5	20000	R	I
						26.8	54.3	12000	R	I
						26.4	54.4	14000	R	I
						25.0	54.4	8000	R	I
						24.4	54.4	4000	R	I
						24.2	54.4	4000	R	I
						24.1	54.4	4000	R	I
						24.0	55.1	60000	A	II
						24.5	55.2	60000	A	II
						25.5	54.7	60000	A	II
						26.6	55.7	40000	A	II
						27.4	55.6	33000	A	II
						28.7	55.5	33000	A	II
						28.7	55.5	33000	R	II
						29.2	54.2	30000	R	II
						28.5	54.1	30000	R	II
						28.3	54.2	28000	R	II
						24.0	55.2	22000	A	III
						24.5	55.3	22000	A	III
						24.6	55.8	6000	A	III
						24.6	55.8	6000	R	III
						24.2	54.4	6000	R	III
						24.1	54.4	6000	R	III

Digitizing Minard's graphic revealed several anomalies. First, Minard gave no date for the –11 degree temperature measurement at Bobr (the dates are labeled on the temperature line at the bottom of the graphic). Second, Minard's temperature line indicates that the last retreating troops covered more than 50 miles in only one day (between Dec 6 and Dec 7). This is implausible. It also does not fit the contemporary descriptions of the events. One of Minard's sources (de Fezensac, 1849) wrote of those early December days,

> Imagine vast snow-covered plains stretching as far as the eye can see, deep pine forests, half-burned and deserted villages, and marching through this mournful countryside an immense column of miserable wretches, almost all without weapons, moving along rag-tag and bobtail, slipping on the ice at each step and falling down beside the carcasses of horses and the corpses of their comrades.

M. de Fezensac's detailed time line (with locations and events) does not match Minard's. It would appear Minard inconsistently amalgamated dates from the four sources he mentioned in his annotations to the graphic. Minard took other minor liberties with the numbers and the historical record. He combined some events in the campaign, as he says, "in order to make it easier to judge by eye the diminution of the army." For example, Minard drew one thin path for the final retreat west of Smorgoni and labeled it with numbers from 12,000 to 14,000 to 8,000 without changing its thickness.

Checking Minard's graphic against authoritative historical sources (*e.g.*, the statistical appendix in Chandler, 1966) makes several things clear. First, it must have taken him considerable effort to assemble these data from the published diaries, memoirs, and histories of the campaign that he cites in his comments. The authors of these works did not tabulate the troop losses consistently or in a readily usable form. Minard had to make quantitative inferences based on descriptions, estimates, and anecdotes. At best, the numbers printed alongside the paths in his map (especially the intermediate ones) are speculative. Second, he took liberties with the events in order to simplify his graphic. More happened in the campaign – routs, excursions, regroupings, bivouacs – than the graphic suggests. As Minard himself notes, he omitted major segments of the southern front. Altogether, his troop figures are about twenty percent short of the numbers reported in his sources.

One cannot argue that all these liberties are not significant. There are contemporary 19th century maps of the campaign that lack these imprecisions, including some in the works Minard cites in his annotations. Minard's graphic is even less accurate in its portrayal of the central army's movements. The army retraced its path during retreat in several places (*e.g.*, Mojaisk to Smolensk), but Minard kept the advance-retreat paths geographically separate. This was unnecessary because he used separate colors for advance and retreat and the paths would have superimposed nicely (as is shown, for example, in the revision of Roth *et al.*, 1997)

In short, Minard's graphic cannot be taken as an accurate geographic or statistical summary of the campaign. It is, as he says, a "figurative map," a popular chart (like ones in newspapers and magazines today) intended to make a political point. One that ignores details. These observations do not diminish the credit Minard deserves for a beautiful piece of work. Although he did not invent the idea of representing a variable by thickness of a path (Playfair, among others, had done that a century earlier), he used it to great effect. Minard was an engineer, not a statistician or cartographer. Despite the liberties he took, however, Minard's chart is not meaningless. It is well-formed and based on a clearly structured dataset. The test of this assertion is that a properly designed computer program can draw his graphic from the data and a properly structured specification. Now we will examine that specification.

15.1.2 The Graphic

Figure 15.1 shows the specification and a graphic that reproduces the deep structure and content of Minard's original. Tufte says, "*Six* variables are plotted: the size of the army, its location on a two-dimensional surface, direction of the army's movement, and temperature on various dates during the retreat from Moscow." Tufte's statement refers to variable sets or dimensions in the specification, because there is a blending. The six dimensions are: **survivors**, **longitude** (a blend of **lonp**, **lonc**, **lont**), **latitude** (a blend of **latp**, **latc**), **direction**, **temp**, and **date**.

In fact, there are *seven* dimensions in this plot. The seventh is **group**. This is not obvious from looking at the graphic. It only becomes apparent when we attempt to choose a graph for representing the troop movements from the data. In addition to *path*, possible candidates are *link* and *tile*. The last two are clearly inappropriate; they would require structures not easily computable from the original data and certainly not meaningful in terms of the variables. The *tile* graph would require polygon vertices describing the outline of the path. The *link.edge.tree* graph would require a scheme for producing the branching. Obviously, the physical movement of an army *is* a path. Our problem is that there is no single path that would describe the actual movements. It is clear that there are three paths required – each corresponding to collected divisions of the army (as Minard indicates in his annotations). These are: 1) the path of the central army group, 2) the path of the left flank taking the excursion northward between Kaunas and Vilnius, 3) another central army group consisting of the second and sixth corps that marched from Vilnius to Polotzk and rejoined the others at Bobr (I combined the remnant of this group with the central army's retreat west of the Berezina River because Minard provides only aggregate numbers after this point). It is likely that Minard chose not to assign a visible attribute to the **group** variable in order to keep the aesthetic simple and conserve color. His focus was on *overall* attrition. If we did not have to be explicit about specifying a graph correctly, we would have taken the structure of this part of the graphic for granted.

The frame specification for the upper graphic is based on the longitudes and latitudes of the cities (**lonc*latc**) through and around which the troops passed. The *position*() parameter for the *path* itself is based on the coordinates of the itinerary (**lonp*latp**). Each of the three *path* graphics is determined by setting *split*() to the value of **group**. Since **group** is categorical, this splits one *path* into three. Since Minard chose not to represent **group** through *size*, *shape*, *color*, *texture*, or any other aesthetic attribute, we must use the *split*() function explicitly to split the paths. Otherwise, the *path*() graphing function would display a jumble of paths.

The *size* of each segment of the *path* graphics is determined by **survivors**. And the *color* is determined by **direction** (advance or retreat). The advance is red and the retreat is black. Tufte's faithful reproduction shows the advance path in pale brown. The original was almost certainly bright red for two reasons. First, Minard said it was red in his annotations on the graphic. Second, red in a lithograph oxidizes and fades to brown in months under direct sunlight and in years under indirect light. Saturated reds fade faster than dull. Tufte's comment, "Minard's refined use of color contrasts with the brutal tones often seen in current-day graphics" is probably not historically correct. It is similar to the mistakes archaeologists once made in failing to notice that frescoes fade.

Unlike Minard's graphic, the two north-south black retreat paths are superimposed on the red advances in Figure 15.1. If Minard intended to show that these southerly retreats occurred earlier in time by putting them underneath the red paths, then this is puzzling. The black path from Polotsk to Bobr, for example, consisted primarily of the second corps under Marshal Oudinot. They rejoined the central army at the Berezina River near Bobr months after the central army had passed through the region on the way to Moscow. More likely, Minard did not want the black to cut the red path into sections because he wished to emphasize the drive toward Moscow in a single swath of red. We cannot do this without changing the definition of a path, however. A path wants to be drawn from beginning to end in sequence. In a statistical graphic, the choice of position cannot be made on the artistic merits. This is one of the few instances in the chart where Minard is graphically ungrammatical.

There remains the other major element in Minard's display: the temperature graphic below. This is defined by a second frame specification using **lonc*temp**. There are two coordinate transformations – one to resize the frame to be long and narrow (a *stretch* transformation) and one to position it below the upper frame (a *translate* transformation).

Ordinarily, we would use a *line* to represent temperature. I used a *path* instead because I wanted to modify each segment through another variable. As I discussed in Chapter 6, a *path* must be used in place of a *line* if we wish to modify the appearance of each separate segment. To do this, I added an eighth dimension to Minard's seven and realized it with *texture.granularity*(**days**). I did this because it is difficult to discern the pace of the armies' retreat from the **date** labels on the temperature graphic.

The **days** variable is created by differencing the lagged dates with themselves; the arithmetic is done by *diff*() after converting to numerical day-of-century values (numeric functions are overloaded to be able to handle string time variables). Notice that I had to fill in the missing value by linear interpolation using the *miss*() function before I could do this. Otherwise, the missing date between Nov 14 and Nov 28 would have caused missing values for **days** after using the *lag*() function. Once we have the **days** values, we use them to make each dash in the temperature line correspond to one day of marching. The implausible distance covered in the last day is immediately apparent.

The horizontal scale for the temperature graphic is linear in longitude and nonlinear in time – an ingenious linking of space and time on a single physical dimension. I have made this link more perceivable by supplementing the date annotations with the dash lengths. The two graphics (the march and the temperature) share a single horizontal dimension yet they vie for the vertical space in the display area. This is the same situation we encounter with bordered graphics, where we link on a common variable.

TRANS: **date** = *miss*(**date, lont,** "linear")
TRANS: **ldate** = *lag*(**date**, −1)
TRANS: **days** = *diff*(**date, ldate**)
FRAME: **lonc*latc**
GRAPH: *point*(*label*(**city**), *size*(0))
GRAPH: *path*(*position*(**lonp*latp**), *size*(**survivors**), *color*(**direction**),
            split(**group**))
GUIDE: *legend*(*color*(**direction**))
FRAME: **lonc*temp**
COORD: *stretch*(*dim1*,*dim2*,1.,.2)
COORD: *translate*(*dim1*, *dim2*, 0, -.5)
GRAPH: *path*(*position*(**lont*temp**), *label*(**date**), *texture.granularity*(**days**)
            color.brightness(.5))
GUIDE: *axis1*(*label*("Longitude"))
GUIDE: *axis2*(*label*("Temperature"))

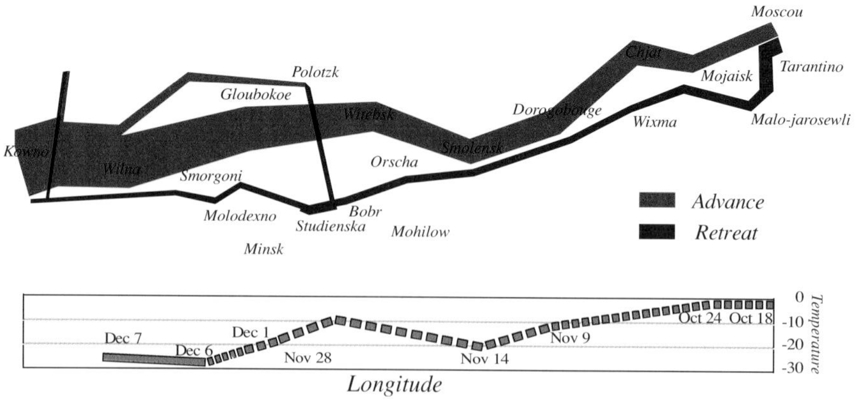

Figure 15.1 *Napoleon's Russian campaign (after Minard)*

15.1.3 The Meaning

Understanding the meaning of Minard's graphic is a matter of attending to the data and metadata underlying the graphic and then parsing the specification. There are other ways to specify this graph with a graphics algebra, but I have found none that is simpler and none that alters the substantive interpretation. The subtleties of this graphic (including Minard's errors and omissions) are revealed through a detailed analysis of the data in the light of the specification. Constructing a valid specification forces us to reconstruct the data properly.

Aside from the details that emerged from the process of producing Table 15.1, what is the main structure of the graph underlying this graphic? First of all, we know the data are geographic and temporal. We *could* hook up this specification to non-spatio/temporal data, but the *path* and *line* graphics would have a different meaning if this were the case. The *path* graphic is related to time only by indirection and only for half its extent (during retreat). The indirection is accomplished through the **date** variable.

Thus, Minard's graph is a *path* through geographical space linked to a meta-variable (temperature) through the time needed to cover the path. And his graphic is an aesthetically superb (better than mine) realization of that graph. What is unusual about the graphic is the positional sharing of the horizontal dimension (longitude) between the path frame and the temperature frame. A similar positional device is used to link panels of a SPLOM (see Figure 11.10), but Minard employs it in a geographic context.

What other data could we link to a geographical *path* specification? We could use this specification (as Minard did) to represent the campaigns of other armies. We could use it to represent trade routes in the Hellenistic era (Koester, 1982). We could use it to represent the resettling of refugees in Germany, Eastern Europe, and Russia after World War II (Barraclough, 1984). Or, we could use it to represent migrations, as in the following example. As I will show, however, migration data do not always allow us to use a *path*.

15.2 Monarch Butterfly Migration

In the early 1970's, Fred Urquhart and his associates at the University of Toronto began tagging Monarch butterflies (*Danaus plexippus*) in an effort to track their southward migratory movements in eastern North America. The tags returned to his laboratory pointed to a site somewhere in Mexico. This led Urquhart to advertise in Mexico for assistance in locating the site more precisely. Kenneth Brugger, a textile engineer working in Mexico, contacted Urquhart after seeing one of the advertisements in a Mexican newspaper. Brugger joined the team, and in January 1975 he and his wife found the site in the Sierra Madre mountains west of Mexico City. This spectacular discovery revealed trees veiled in orange by countless Monarchs waiting to return north in the spring.

Most newspapers, magazines, and Web sites covering this story have presented a graphic consisting of a tree whose root is anchored at the Mexican site and whose trunk splits just north of Mexico into four branches. This branching tree portrays the butterflies heading north and splitting into four major migratory routes. The data do not support such a graphic. With Minard's graphic, we might dispute the accuracy of his data but not his grammar. In this case, we may accept the data but we dispute the grammar. I will summarize the data and then present an alternative graphic based on grammatical rules.

15.2.1 The Data

The data underlying Figure 15.2 were collected in the first six months of 1997 by children, teachers, and other observers reporting to the Journey North Project under the auspices of the Annenberg/CPB Learner Online program (*www.learner.org*). Each data point is an observer's first sighting of an adult Monarch butterfly during the period of northward migration in 1977. The date of the sighting was coded in two-week intervals and the location of the sighting was given in latitude and longitude. I omitted a few observations from the West coast because these Monarch populations generally do not migrate to the same site in Mexico. Data and theory indicate that the butterflies are fenced in by the Rocky Mountains – both by climate and the lack of their critical nesting and food source, the milkweed.

There are other datasets on which we could build a migration graphic. Capture-recapture data arise when we capture a butterfly, tag it, release it, and capture it again. This allows us to infer survival, spatial distribution, and other aspects of a population distributed in space and time. It is particularly difficult with a fragile and dispersed migrating population such as Monarch butterflies, however. Further information on Monarch capture-recapture is available at *www.monarchwatch.org*, established by Orley R. Taylor at the University of Kansas Department of Entomology and co-sponsored by the University of Minnesota Department of Biology. Most recently, Wassenaar and Hobson (1998) have linked additional variables to Monarch data by analyzing chemical signatures in butterfly wings. This method has helped to identify the US origins of butterflies wintering in Mexico.

15.2.2 The Graphic

Figure 15.2 presents my alternative to the prevalent tree-form butterfly graphic. I will discuss this alternative first and then show why a *tree* graphic (or a *path*) is ungrammatical. The specification of Figure 15.2 is simpler than the one for Minard's. This graphic consists of a map of the continental U.S. overlaid with traces of the advancing front of Monarch northerly migration. The Journey North website has a map of the raw data plotted as colored points, one point for each sighting. Figure 15.2 shows more clearly the contours of the advance over time. These contours were computed by nonparametric smoothing.

Although I used the word contours to describe the butterflies' advance, the graphic I used in the specification is *line.smooth.quadratic.cauchy* instead of *contour*. This is because I chose to recognize the observations as containing random errors and thus ran the lines through the concentration of points at each different time interval rather than through their northernmost edges. Since the **date** scale is categorical, each smoother is computed separately on the subgroup of sightings occurring in each time interval.

Alternatively, I could have chosen *point*() to represent every separate sighting. This would have reproduced the original Journey North map. Or, I could have chosen *tile*() to aggregate the points into a regional representation of the concentration of sightings. Finally, I could have chosen *contour*(), as I mentioned earlier. As we shall see, however, there are other glyphs we cannot choose for these data, including the *path* graphic Minard used and the *tree* graphic used in the popular maps of the Monarch migration. The grammar of graphics prevents us from doing so.

FRAME: **lon*lat+lonp*latp**
GRAPH: *line.smooth.quadratic.cauchy*(*position*(**lonp*latp**), *color*(**date**))
GRAPH: *tile*(*shape.polygon*(**state**))

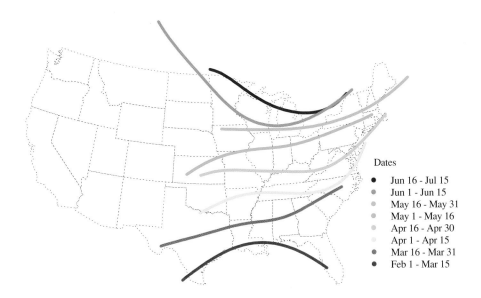

Figure 15.2 *Northerly migration of the Monarch butterfly*

15.2.3 The Meaning

The butterfly graphic shares substantial elements of meaning with Minard's. Both are migration graphics. There is an important difference, however. Minard used a *path* graphic to represent troop migration and I have used a *line* graphic to represent butterfly migration. In each case, the organization of the data constrains this usage.

I have already discussed why Minard's data require a set of *path* or *link.edge.tree* graphics based on a **group** variable. For the Monarch data, on the other hand, we cannot use a *path* or *link.edge.tree* graphic. The reason the Monarch data cannot support a *path* or *link* graphic is because there is no information to delineate the branching. To gather such information, we would have to tag butterflies and recapture them repeatedly along the northward migration route (not only at their final destination) to detect whether branching occurs. And if there were only four branches, we would expect to see large regions in central and northeastern U.S. devoid of Monarchs. The Journey North dataset suggests that the pattern is otherwise. The sightings are continuously distributed across the eastern U.S. in an advancing wave rather than in four widely separated branching migratory routes. Given the genesis of the data, we would have to call a tree representation not simply misleading, but meaningless.

15.3 Conclusion

Do we care whether we use a tree or contours to represent a migration? Don't both convey the same sense of movement in some direction? The answers to these questions depend on whether we intend to construct a graphic to represent *ideas* or to represent *variables*. Pictograms, ideograms, and thematic maps have their uses. Many abstract ideas are communicated especially well through figurative graphics (Herdeg, 1981; Lieberman, 1997). If we want to use graphics to represent magnitudes and relations among variables, however, we are not dealing with the grammar of ornament. We are dealing with the grammar of graphics.

Do we need a grammar of graphics for this task? Obviously, I think we do. Programs to draw graphics abound. They are built into spreadsheets, databases, and statistical packages. While many designers of these applications take pains to insure data integrity, fewer seem concerned about graphical mistakes, such as confusing pivoting with transposing. Graphical errors are subtle but serious, and remind one of Lincoln's saying that one can fool some of the people all of the time and all of the people some of the time. As with psychology, too many designers appear to consider themselves experts in graphics because they have good visual instincts. Just as psychological theory and experiments expose mistaken notions about graphical perception, however, the grammar of graphics exposes mistaken ideas about graphical structure.

15.3.1 *The Grammar of Graphics*

The grammar of graphics determines how algebra, geometry, aesthetics, statistics, scales, and coordinates interact. In the world of statistical graphics, we cannot confuse aesthetics with geometry by picking a tree graphic to represent a continuous flow of migrating insects across a geographic field simply because we like the impression it conveys. We can color a whole tree red to suit our design preferences, but we cannot use a tree in the first place unless we have the variables to generate one. By contrast, Minard took liberties with the data to influence the appearance of his graphic. His specification is tightly coupled to the data, however. We might disagree with his data manipulation, but we cannot call his graphic meaningless. For the Monarch data, on the other hand, the variables drive us toward a representation like that in Figure 15.2.

The rules I have been invoking to make these claims constitute what I call the grammar of graphics. It is important not to confuse this grammar with the particular language I have used to describe it. The grammar of graphics is not about whether *directedGraph()* is a better way to implement *link.edge.tree()*. It is not about whether *plot(smoother, method, data)* is preferable to *line.smooth.quadratic()*. It is not about whether a graphical system should use functions like *near()*, *enclose()*, or *intersect()* to definine geometric relations. It is not about Java. It is not even about whether a different syntactical system can produce many or all of the graphics shown in this book.

I can make these statements because I did not invent this grammar or even discover it by analyzing a collection of charts and deciding how they resemble each other. I began instead by constructing definitions of data, variables, and other primitives that underlie what we call statistical charts. These definitions are embedded in the mathematical history that determined the evolution of statistical charts and maps. One cannot separate that history from the functionality that we see in printed and computer charts today, as Collins (1993) and others have made clear.

Figure 2.1 summarizes the grammar of graphics. It tells us that we cannot make a graphic without defining and using the objects shown in that figure – in the implicational ordering denoted there. Its consequences are many. Figure 2.1 epitomizes not only the rules of graphics usage, but also the domain of statistical graphics. A graphic without a concept of a variable is not a statistical graphic. A graphic without an associated coordinate system is not a statistical graphic.

Everything after Figure 2.1 involves the details that follow from this general structure. These are most evident in the examples. We cannot flip a bar chart from vertical to horizontal without making assumptions about its domain and range. We cannot log the scale of a bar chart without re-aggregating the data. A *line* cannot be used to represent Minard's path. A *tree* cannot be used to represent the butterfly data. These assertions and others I have made in the previous chapters are grounded in the grammar of graphics that follows from Figure 2.1.

15.3.2 The Language of Graphics

We now have the outline for designing a language of graphics. A scatterplot is a point graphic embedded in a frame. A bar chart is an interval graphic bound to an aggregation function embedded in a frame. A pie chart is a polar, stacked, bar graphic mapped on proportions. A radar chart is a line graphic in polar parallel coordinates. A SPLOM is a crossing of nested scatterplots in rectangular coordinates. A trellis display is a graphic faceted on crossed categorical variables in a rectangular coordinate system.

If these descriptions make sense to you, then we have come a long way since Chapter 1. Deciding whether they are simpler than the ordinary language found in handbooks on statistical graphics is a matter of evaluating the parsimony and generality of the specifications at the head of the figures in this book. This effort should help us to see why statements like "a trellis employs small multiples" are too general to be useful and statements like "a pie slice is a wedge" are too particular.

Some of these specifications require study; they were not meant for light reading. Rather, they were designed to encapsulate the definitions and algorithms all of us use – consciously or unconsciously – when we create statistical graphics. The ultimate goal of this effort is to understand how graphics work by designing a system that can understand the content of graphics, commute effortlessly between the world of tabular data and the world of charts, and respond to creative and inquisitive users interacting through a graphical interface. By thinking about how to design such a system, we take steps toward understanding what graphics mean. And consequently, we may teach a computer to understand what they mean.

We return to the beginning. Grammar gives language rules. Graphics are generated by a language. The syntax of graphics lies in their specification. The semantics of graphics lies in their data.

15.4 Sequel

There is an important detail that does not appear in the Monarch specification. It is the connection between thousands of teachers and school children, outdoors in the spring searching for butterflies, and a Web site that provides them with the opportunity to share what they found. God is in the details.

References

Abelson, R.P. (1995). *Statistics as Principled Argument*. Hillsdale, NJ: Lawrence Erlbaum.

Allison, T. and Cicchetti, D. (1976). Sleep in mammals: Ecological and constitutional correlates. *Science, 194,* 732-734.

Alvey, N.G., Banfield, C.F., Baxter, R.I., Gower, J.C., Krzanowski, W.J., Lane, P.W., Leech, P.K., Nelder, J.A., Payne, R.W., Phelps, K.M., Rogers, C.E., Ross, G.J.S., Simpson, H.R., Todd, A.D., Wedderburn, R.W.M., and Wilkinson, G.N. (1977). *GENSTAT: A General Statistical Program*. The Statistics Department, Rothamsted Experimental Station. Harpenden, UK.

Anderson, E. (1935). The irises of the Gaspe Peninsula. *Bulletin of the American Iris Society, 59,* 2-5.

Anderson, J.R. (1983). *The Architecture of Cognition*. Cambridge: Harvard University Press.

Anderson, J.R. (1995). *Cognitive Psychology and its Implications* (4th ed.). New York: W.H. Freeman and Company.

Andrews, D.F. (1972). Plots of high dimensional data. *Biometrics, 28,* 125-136.

Andrews, D.F. and Herzberg, A.M. (1985). *Data: A Collection of Problems from Many Fields for the Student and Research Worker*. New York: Springer-Verlag.

Asimov, D. (1985). The grand tour: A tool for viewing multidimensional data. *SIAM Journal on Scientific and Statistical Computing, 6,* 128-143.

Baker, R.J., and Nelder, J.A. (1978). *GLIM*. Oxford, UK: Numerical Algorithms Group and Royal Statistical Society.

Bahrick, H.P., Bahrick, P.O., and Wittlinger, R.P. (1975). Fifty years of memory for names and faces: A cross-sectional approach. *Journal of Experimental Psychology: General, 104,* 54-75.

Banchoff, T.F. (1996). *Beyond the Third Dimension: Geometry, Computer Graphics, and Higher Dimensions*. New York: W.H. Freeman.

Barraclough, G., ed. (1984). *The Times Atlas of World History* (rev. ed.). London: Times Books Limited.

Becker, R.A. and Cleveland, W.S. (1987). Brushing scatterplots. *Technometrics, 29,* 127-142.

Becker, R.A. and Cleveland, W.S. (1991). Take a broader view of scientific visualization. *Pixel, 2,* 42-44.

Becker, R. A., Cleveland, W. S., and Shyu, M-J (1996). The design and control of Trellis display, *Journal of Computational and Statistical Graphics, 5*, 123-155.

Beniger, J.R., Robyn, D.L. (1978). Quantitative graphics in statistics: A brief history. *The American Statistician, 32*, 1-11.

Berlin, B., and Kay, P. (1969). *Basic Color Terms: Their Universality and Evolution.* Berkeley: University of California Press.

Bertin, J. (1967). *Sémiologie Graphique.* Paris: Editions Gauthier-Villars. English translation by W.J. Berg as *Semiology of Graphics*, Madison, WI: University of Wisconsin Press, 1983.

Bertin, J. (1977). *La Graphique et le Traitement Graphique de l'Information.* Paris: Flammarion. English translation by W.J. Berg and P. Scott as *Graphics and Graphic Information Processing*, Berlin: Walter de Gruyter & Co., 1981.

Besag, J. (1986). On the statistical analysis of dirty pictures. *Journal of the Royal Statistical Society, Series B, 3*, 259-302.

Beshers, C., and Feiner, S. (1993). AutoVisual: Rule-based design of interactive multivariate visualizations. *IEEE Computer Graphics and Applications, 13*, 41-49.

Biederman, I. (1972). Perceiving real-world scenes. *Science, 177*, 77-80.

Biederman, I. (1981). On the semantics of a glance at a scene. In M. Kubovy and J.R. Pomerantz (Eds.), *Perceptual Organization,* pp. 213-253. Hillsdale, NJ: Lawrence Erlbaum.

Bird, R., and De Moor, O. (1996). *Algebra of Programming.* Upper Saddle River, NJ: Prentice-Hall.

Blattner, M., Sumikawa, D. and Greenberg, R. (1989) Earcons and icons: Their structure and common design principles. *Human-Computer Interaction, 4*, 11-44.

Bly, S.A. (1983). Interactive tools for data exploration. *Computer Science and Statistics: Proceedings of the 15th Symposium on the Interface*, 255-259.

Bly, S.A., Frysinger, S.P., Lunney, D., Mansur, D.L., Mezrich, J.J., and Morrison, R.C. (1985). Communicating with sound. *Human Factors in Computing Systems: CHI 85 Conference Proceedings.* New York: ACM Press, 115-119.

Booch, G. (1994). *Object-oriented Analysis and Design* (2nd ed.). Redwood City, CA: Benjamin/Cummings Publishing.

Borg, I. and Groenen, P. (1997). *Modern Multidimensional Scaling: Theory and Applications.* New York: Springer-Verlag.

Borg, I. and Staufenbiel, T. (1992). The performance of snow flakes, suns, and factorial suns in the graphical representation of multivariate data. *Multivariate Behavioral Research, 27*, 43-55.

Boring, E.G. (1950). *A History of Experimental Psychology.* New York: Appleton-Century-Crofts.

Bornstein, M.H., Kessen, W., and Weiskopf, S. (1976). Color vision and hue categorization in young human infants. *Journal of Experimental Psychology: Human Perception and Performance, 2*, 115-129.

Bornstein, M.H. (1987). Perceptual categories in vision and audition. In S. Harnad (Ed.), *Categorical Perception: The Groundwork of Cognition.* Cambridge: Cambridge University Press, 287-300.

Boyer, R., and Savageau, D. (1996). *Places Rated Almanac.* Chicago, IL: Rand McNally.

Boynton, R.M. (1988). Color vision. *Annual Review of Psychology, 39,* 69-100.

Bregman, A. S. (1990). *Auditory Scene Analysis: The Perceptual Organization of Sound.* Cambridge, MA: MIT Press.

Breiman, L., Friedman, J.H., Olshen, R.A., and Stone, C.J. (1984). *Classification and Regression Trees.* Belmont, CA: Wadsworth.

Brewer, C.A. (1994). Color use guidelines for mapping and visualization. In A. M. MacEachren and D.R.F. Taylor (eds.), *Visualization in Modern Cartography,* pp. 123-147. Oxford: Pergamon Press.

Brewer, C.A. (1996). Guidelines for selecting colors for diverging schemes on maps. *The Cartographic Journal, 33,* 79-86.

Brewer, C.A., MacEachren, A.M., Pickle, L.W., and Herrmann, D. (1997). Mapping mortality: Evaluating color schemes for choropleth maps. *Annals of the Association of American Geographers, 87,* 411-438.

Brodlie, K.W. (Ed.) (1980). *Mathematical Methods in Computer Graphics and Design.* London: Academic Press.

Brodlie, K.W. (1993). A classification scheme for scientific visualization. In R.A. Earnshaw and D. Watson (Eds.), *Animation and Scientific Visualization: Tools and Applicaitons.* New York: Academic Press, 125-140.

Brooks, R. (1987). Planning is just a way of avoiding figuring out what to do next. Technical Report 303, MIT AI Labs.

Brown, G.W. (1986). Inverse regression. In S. Kotz and N.L. Johnson (Eds.), *Encyclopedia of Statistical Sciences, Vol 7.* New York: John Wiley & Sons, 694-696.

Bruckner, L.A. (1978). On Chernoff Faces. In P.C.C. Wang (Ed.), *Graphical Representation of Multivariate Data.* New York: Academic Press, pp. 93-121.

Buja, A., and Asimov, D. (1986). Grand tour methods: an outline. *Computer Science and Statistics: Proceedings of the 18th Symposium on the Interface,* 171-174.

Burns, E.M., and Ward, W.D. (1978). Categorical perception – phenomenon or epiphenomenon: Evidence from experiments in the perception of melodic musical intervals. *Journal of the Acoustical Society of America, 63,* 456-468.

Butler, D.M. and Pendley, M.H. (1989). A visualization model based on the mathematics of fibre bundles. *Computers in Physics, 3,* 45-51.

Carlis, J.V., and Konstan, J.A. (1998). Interactive visualization of serial periodic data. *Proceedings of the 11th Annual ACM Symposium on User Interface Software and Technology (UIST),* 29-38.

Carpendale, M.S.T., Cowperthwaite, D.J., and Fracchia, F.D. (1997). Extending distortion viewing from 2D to 3D. *IEEE Computer Graphics and Applications, 17,* 42-51.

Carr, D.B. (1994). Converting Tables to Plots. Technical Report No. 101, Center for Computational Statistics. Fairfax, VA: George Mason University.

Carr, D.B. and Nicholson, W.L. (1988). EXPLOR4: A program for exploring four-dimensional data using stereo-ray glyphs, dimensional constraints, rotation, and masking. In W.S. Cleveland and M.E. McGill, eds., *Dynamic Graphics for Statistics*. Belmont, CA: Wadsworth, pp. 309-329.

Carr, D.B., Littlefield, R.J., Nicholson, W.L., and Littlefield, J.S. (1987). Scatterplot matrix techniques for large N. *Journal of the American Statistical Association, 82*, 424-436.

Carr, D.B., Olsen, A.R., and White, D. (1992). Hexagon mosaic maps for display of univariate and bivariate geographical data. *Cartography and Geographic Information Systems, 19*, 228-236.

Carr, D.B., Olsen, A.R., Courbois, J-Y.P., Pierson, S.M., and Carr, D.A. (1998). Linked micromap plots: Named and described. *Statistical Computing & Statistical Graphics Newsletter, 9, 24-32*.

Carswell, C.M. (1992). Choosing specifiers: An evaluation of the basic tasks model of graphical perception. *Human Factors, 4*, 535-554.

Chambers, J.M. (1977). *Computational Methods for Data Analysis*. New York: John Wiley & Sons.

Chambers, J.M., Cleveland, W.S., Kleiner, B., and Tukey, P.A. (1983). *Graphical Methods for Data Analysis*. Monterey, CA: Wadsworth.

Chandler, D.G. (1966). *The Campaigns of Napoleon*. New York: The Macmillan Company.

Chelton, D.B., Mestas-Nunez, A.M., and Freilich, M.H. (1990). Global wind stress and Sverdrup circulation from the Seasat Scatterometer. *Journal of Physical Oceanography, 20*, 1175-1205.

Chernoff, H. (1973). The use of faces to represent points in k-dimensional space graphically. *Journal of the American Statistical Association, 68*, 361-368.

Chernoff, H. (1975). Effect on classification error of random permutations of features in representing multivariate data by faces. *Journal of the American Statistical Association, 70*, 548-554.

Chi, E.H., Konstan, J., Barry, P., and Riedl, J. (1997). A spreadsheet approach to information visualization. *Proceedings of the 10th Annual ACM Symposium on User Interface Software and Technology (UIST)*, 79-80.

Chomsky, N. (1956). Three models for the description of language. *IRE Transactions on Information Theory, 2*, 113-124.

Clarkson, D.B. and Jennrich, R.I. (1988). Quartic rotation criteria and algorithms. *Psychometrika, 53*, 251-259.

Cleveland, W.S. (1984). Graphs in scientific publications. *The American Statistician, 38*, 19-26.

Cleveland, W.S. (1985). *The Elements of Graphing Data*. Summit, NJ: Hobart Press.

Cleveland, W.S. (1993). A model for studying display methods of statistical graphics (with discussion). *Journal of Computational and Graphical Statistics, 2*, 323-343.

Cleveland, W.S. (1995). *Visualizing Data*. Summit, NJ: Hobart Press.

Cleveland, W.S., and Devlin, S. (1988). Locally weighted regression analysis by local fitting. *Journal of the American Statistical Association, 83*, 596-640.

Cleveland, W.S., Diaconis, P., and McGill, R. (1982). Variables on scatterplots look more highly correlated when the scales are increased. *Science, 216*, 1138-1141.

Cleveland, W.S., Harris, C.S., and McGill, R. (1981). Judgments of circle sizes on statistical maps. Unpublished paper. Murray Hill, NJ: Bell Laboratories.

Cleveland, W.S. and McGill, M.E. (1988). *Dynamic Graphics for Statistics.* Belmont, CA: Wadsworth.

Cleveland, W.S., McGill, M.E., and McGill, R. (1988). The shape parameter of a two-variable graph. *Journal of the American Statistical Association, 83*, 289-300.

Cleveland, W.S. and McGill, R. (1984a). Graphical perception: Theory, experimentation, and application to the development of graphical methods. *Journal of the American Statistical Association, 79*, 531-554.

Cleveland, W.S. and McGill, R. (1984b). The many faces of a scatterplot. *Journal of the American Statistical Association, 79*, 807-822.

Codd, E.G. (1970). A relational model of data for large shared data banks. *Communications of the ACM, 13*, 377-387.

Collins, B.M. (1993). Data visualization – has it all been seen before? In R.A. Earnshaw and D. Watson (Eds.), *Animation and Scientific Visualization: Tools and Applicaitons.* New York: Academic Press, 3-28.

Conway, J.H., and Guy, R.K. (1996). *The Book of Numbers.* New York: Springer-Verlag.

Cook, R.D. and Weisberg, S. (1994). *An Introduction to Regression Graphics.* New York: John Wiley & Sons.

Coombs, C.H. (1964). *A Theory of Data.* New York: John Wiley & Sons.

Copi, I.M. (1967). *Symbolic Logic* (3rd ed.). New York: Macmillan Co.

Coren, S., and Girgus, J.S. (1978). *Seeing is Deceiving: The Psychology of Visual Illusions.* Hillsdale, NJ: Lawrence Erlbaum.

Cornell, J.A. (1990). *Experiments with Mixtures: Designs, Models, and the Analysis of Mixture Data.* New York: John Wiley & Sons.

Cox, P.R. (1986). Population pyramid. In S. Kotz and N.L. Johnson (Eds.), *Encyclopedia of Statistical Sciences, Vol 7*. New York: John Wiley & Sons, 113-116.

Cressie, N.A.C. (1991). *Statistics for Spatial Data.* New York: John Wiley & Sons.

Cruz-Neira, C., Sandin, D.J., and DeFanti, T.A. (1993). Surround-Screen projection-based virtual reality: The design and implementation of the CAVE. *Siggraph '93 Conference Proceedings.* New York: ACM Press, 135-142.

Dallal, G., and Finseth, K. (1977). Double dual histograms. *The American Statistician, 31*, 39-41.

Date, C.J. (1995). *An Introduction to Database Systems* (6th ed.). Reading: MA: Addison-Wesley.

Dawson, R.J.M. (1995). The "unusual episode" data revisited. *Journal of Statistics Education, 3(3)*.

Dennis, J.E. Jr., and Schnabel, R.B. (1983). *Numerical Methods for Unconstrained Optimization and Nonlinear Equations.* Englewood Cliffs, NJ: Prentice-Hall.

Derrick, W.R. (1984). *Complex Analysis and Applications* (2nd ed.). Belmont, CA: Wadsworth.

Derthick, M., Kolojejchick, J., and Roth, S.F. (1997). An interactive visual query environment for exploring data. *Proceedings of the 10th Annual ACM Symposium on User Interface Software and Technology (UIST)*, 189-198.

De Soete, G. (1986). A perceptual study of the Flury-Riedwyl faces for graphically displaying multivariate data. *International Journal of Man-Machine Studies, 25*, 549-555.

deValois, R.L., and Jacobs, G.H. (1968). Primate color vision. *Science, 162*, 533-540.

Dierckx, P. (1993). *Curve and Surface Fitting with Splines*. Oxford: Clarendon Press.

Doane, D.P. (1976). Aesthetic frequency classifications. *The American Statistician, 30*, 181-183.

Doerr, A., and Levasseur, K. (1985). *Applied Discrete Structures for Computer Science*. Chicago: Science Research Associates.

Donoho, A.W., Donoho, D.L., and Gasko, M. (1988). MacSpin: Dynamic graphics on a desktop computer. In W.S. Cleveland and M.E. McGill, eds., *Dynamic Graphics for Statistics*. Belmont, CA: Wadsworth, pp. 331-351.

Draper, N.R., and Smith, H. (1981). *Applied Regression Analysis* (2nd ed.). New York: John Wiley & Sons.

Dunn, R. (1987). Variable-width framed rectangle charts for statistical mapping. *The American Statistician, 41*, 153-156.

Earnshaw, R.A., and Watson, D. (1993). *Animation and Scientific Visualization: Tools and Applications*. New York: Academic Press.

Edgar, G.A. (1990). *Measure, Topology, and Fractal Geometry*. New York: Springer Verlag.

Efron, B., and Tibshirani, R.J. (1993). *An Introduction to the Bootstrap*. New York: Chapman & Hall.

Egenhofer, M.J., Herring, J.R., Smith, T., and Park, K.K. (1991). A framework for the definition of topological relationships and an algebraic approach to spatial reasoning within this framework. *Technical Paper 91-7*, National Center for Geographic Information and Analysis/NCGIA.

Eimas, P. (1974). Auditory and phonetic coding of the cues for speech: Discrimination of the [r–l] distinction by young infants. *Perception and Psychophysics, 18*, 341-347.

Ekman, G. (1964). Is the power law a special case of Fechner's law? *Perceptual and Motor Skills, 19*, 730.

Ekman, P. (1984). Expression and the nature of emotion. In K. Scherer and P. Ekman (Eds.), *Approaches to Emotion* (pp.319-343). Hillsdale, N.J.: Lawrence Erlbaum.

Ekman, P., Friesen, W. V., & O'Sullivan, M. (1988). Smiles when lying. *Journal of Personality and Social Psychology, 54*, 414-420.

Emmer, M. (Ed.) (1995). *The Visual Mind: Art and Mathematics*. Cambridge, MA: MIT Press.

Epp, S.S. (1990). *Discrete Mathematics with Applications*. Belmont, CA: Wadsworth.

Estes, W.K. (1994). *Classification and Cognition.* Oxford: Oxford University Press.

Falmagne, J-C. (1985). *Elements of Psychophysical Theory.* Oxford: Oxford University Press.

Fan, J., and Gijbels, I. (1996). *Local Polynomial Modelling and Its Applications.* London: Chapman & Hall.

Fechner, G.T. (1860). *Elemente der Psychophysik.* Leipzig: Breitkopf & Härtel. English translation of Vol. 1 by H.E. Adler, New York: Holt, Rinehart and Winston.

Ferster, C.B., and Skinner, B.F. (1957). *Schedules of Reinforcement.* New York: Appleton-Century-Crofts.

de Fezensac, R.A.P.J. (1849). *Journal de la campagne de Russie en 1812.* Paris. English translation by L.B. Kennett as *The Russian Campaign, 1812*, Athens, GA: The University of Georgia Press.

Fienberg, S. (1979). Graphical methods in statistics. *The American Statistician, 33*, 165-178.

Fisher, P.F. (1994). Animation and sound for the visualization of uncertain spatial information. In H.H. Hearnshaw and D.J. Unwin (Eds.), *Visualization in geographical information systems.* New York: John Wiley & Sons, Inc., 181-185.

Fisher, R.A. (1915). Frequency distribution of the values of the correlation coefficient in samples from an indefinitely large population. *Biometrika, 10*, 507-521.

Fisher, R.A. (1925). *Statistical Methods for Research Workers.* London: Oliver and Boyd.

Fisher, R.A. (1935). *The Design of Experiments.* Edinburgh: Oliver and Boyd.

Flury, B., and Riedwyl, H. (1981). Graphical representation of multivariate data by means of asymmetrical faces. *Journal of the American Statistical Association, 76*, 757-765.

Foley, J.D., Van Dam, A., Feiner, S.K., and Hughes, J.F. (1993). *Introduction to Computer Graphics.* Reading, MA: Addison-Wesley.

Fortner, B. (1995). *The Data Handbook: A Guide to Understanding the Organization and Visualization of Technical Data* (2nd ed.). New York: Springer-Verlag.

Fowler, M., and Scott, K. (1997). *UML Distilled: Applying the Standard Object Modling Language.* Reading, MS: Addison-Wesley.

Freedman, D. and Diaconis, P. (1981). On the histogram as a density estimator: L_2 theory. *Zeitschrift für Wahrscheinlichkeitstheorie und verwandt Gebiete, 57*, 453-476.

Friedman, J., and Stuetzle, W. (1981). Projection pursuit regression. *Journal of the American Statistical Association, 76*, 817-823.

Friedman, J. (1987). Exploratory projection pursuit. *Journal of the American Statistical Association, 82*, 249-266.

Friedman, J. (1997). Data mining and statistics: What's the connection? *Computing Science and Statistics: Proceedings of the 29th Symposium on the Interface*, 3-9.

Friendly, M. (1994). Mosaic displays for n-way contingency tables. *Journal of the American Statistical Association, 89*, 190-200.

Funkhouser, H.G. (1937). Historical development of the graphical representation of statistical data. *Osiris, 3*, 269-404.

Furnas, G.W. (1986). Generalized fisheye views. *Human Factors in Computing Systems: CHI 86 Conference Proceedings*. New York: ACM Press, 16-23.

Gabriel, K.R. (1971). The biplot graphical display of matrices with application to principal component analysis. *Biometrika, 58*, 45-467.

Gabriel, K.R. (1995). Biplot display of multivariate categorical data, with comments on multiple correspondence analysis. In W.J. Krzanowski, Ed., *Recent Advances in Descriptive Multivariate Analysis*. Oxford: Clarendon Press, pp. 190-225.

Gamma, E., Helm, R., Johnson, R., Vlissides, J. (1995). *Design Patterns: Elements of Reusable Object-Oriented Software*. Reading, MA: Addison-Wesley.

Garner, W.R. (1970). The simulus in information processing. *American Psychologist, 25*, 350-358.

Garner, W.R. (1974). *The processing of Information and Structure*. Hillsdale, NJ: Lawrence Erlbaum.

Garner, W.R. (1981). The analysis of unanalyzed perceptions. In M. Kubovy and J.R. Pomerantz (Eds.), *Perceptual Organization*, pp. 119-139. Hillsdale, NJ: Lawrence Erlbaum.

Garner, W.R. and Felfoldy, G.L. (1970). Integrality of stimulus dimensions in various types of information processing. *Cognitive Psychology, 1*, 225-241.

Gibson, E.J. (1991). *An Odyssey in Learning and Perception*. Cambridge, MA: MIT Press.

Gibson, J.J. (1966). *The Senses Considered as Perceptual Systems*. Boston: Houghton Mifflin.

Gibson, J.J. (1979). *The Ecological Approach to Visual Perception*. Boston: Houghton Mifflin.

Glenberg, A.M. (1997). What memory is for. *Behavioral and Brain Sciences, 20*, 1-19.

Glymour, C., Madigan, D., Pregibon, D., and Smyth, P. (1996). Statistical inference and data mining. *Communications of the ACM, 39*, 35-41.

Goldstone, R. (1994). Influences of categorization on perceptual discrimination. *Journal of Experimental Psychology: General, 123*, 178-200.

Gomes, J., and Costa, B. (1998). *Warping and Morphing of Graphical Objects*. New York: Morgan Kaufmann.

Gonnelli, S., Cepollaro, C., Montagnani, A., Monaci, G., Campagna, M.S., Franci, M.B., and Gennari, C. (1996). Bone alkaline phosphatase measured with a new immunoradiometric assay in patients with metabolic bone diseases. *European Journal of Clinical Investigation, 26*, 391-396.

Gonzalez, R.C., and Wintz, P. (1977). *Digital Image Processing*. Reading, MA: Addison-Wesley.

Gould, S.J. (1996). *Full house: The spread of excellence from Plato to Darwin*. New York: Harmony Books.

Gower, J.C. (1995). A general theory of biplots. In W.J. Krzanowski, Ed., *Recent Advances in Descriptive Multivariate Analysis*. Oxford: Clarendon Press, pp. 283-303.

Green, P.J. and Silverman, B.W. (1994). *Nonparametric Rression and Generalized Linear Models: A Roughness Penalty Approach.* London: Chapman and Hall.

Gregory, R.L. (1978). *Eye and Brain* (3rd ed.). New York: McGraw Hill.

Gregson, R.A.M. (1988). *Nonlinear Psychophysical Dynamics.* Hillsdale, NJ: Lawrence Erlbaum.

Guttman, L. (1954). A new approach to factor analysis: The radex. In P.F. Lazarsfeld (Ed.), *Mathematical Thinking in the Social Sciences.* New York: Free Press.

Guttman, L. (1971). Measurement as structural theory. *Psychometrika, 36,* 329-347.

Guttman, L. (1977). What is not what in statistics. *The Statistician, 26,* 81-107.

Haber, R.B. and McNabb, D.A. (1990). Visualization idioms: A conceptual model for scientific visualization systems. In G.M. Nielson, B.D. Shriver, and L.J. Rosenblum, (Eds.), *Visualization in Scientific Computing,* pp. 74-93. Los Alamitos, CA: IEEE Computer Society Press.

Haber, R.N. and Wilkinson, L. (1982). Perceptual components of computer displays. *IEEE Computer Graphics and Applications, 2,* 23-35.

Haith, M.M. (1980). *Rules that Babies Look by: The Organization of Newborn Visual Activity.* Hillsdale, NJ: Lawrence Erlbaum.

Hand, D. (1996). Statistics and the Theory of Measurement. *Journal of the Royal Statistical Society, A, 159,* 486-487

Harary, F. (1969). *Graph Theory.* Reading, MA: Addison-Wesley.

Härdle, W. (1990). *Applied Nonparametric Regression.* Cambridge, UK: Cambridge University Press.

Harman, H.H. (1976). *Modern Factor Analysis,* (3rd Ed.). Chicago: University of Chicago Press.

Harnad, S. (1987). *Categorical Perception.* Cambridge, UK: Cambridge University Press.

Harris, J.E. (1987). Who should profit from cigarettes? *The New York Times.* Sunday, March 15, Section C, 3.

Hartigan, J.A. (1972). Direct clustering of a data matrix. *Journal of the American Statistical Association, 67,* 123-129.

Hartigan, J.A.(1975a). *Clustering Algorithms.* New York: John Wiley & Sons.

Hartigan, J.A. (1975b). Printer graphics for clustering. *Journal of Statistical Computation and Simulation, 4,* 187-213.

Hartigan, J.A. and Kleiner, B. (1981). Mosaics for contingency tables. In *Computer Science and Statistics: Proceedings of the 13th Symposium on the Interface,* 268-273.

Hartigan, J.A. and Kleiner, B. (1984). A mosaic of television ratings. *The American Statistician, 38,* 32-35.

Hastie, T. and Stuetzle, W. (1989). Principal curves. *Journal of the American Statistical Association, 84,* 502-516.

Hastie, T. and Tibshirani, R. (1990). *Generalized Additive Models*. London: Chapman and Hall.

Heckbert, P.S. (1990). Nice numbers for graph labels. In A.S. Glassner (Ed.), Graphics Gems. Boston: Academic Press, pp. 61-63.

Heckscher, W. (1958). *Rembrandt's Anatomy of Dr. Nicolaas Tulp*. New York: NYU Press.

Hedges, L.V. and Olkin, I. (1985). *Statistical Methods for Meta-Analysis*. Orlando, FL: Academic Press.

Heiberger, R.M. (1989). *Computation for the Analysis of Designed Experiments*. New York: John Wiley & Sons.

von Helmholtz, H. (1866). *Handbuch der Physiologischen Optik*. English translation by J. Southall as *Treatise on Physiological Optics, Vol III*, New York: Dover Books, 1962.

Herdeg, W. (Ed.) (1981). *Graphis Diagrams: The Graphic Visualization of Abstract Data*. Zürich, Switzerland: Graphis Press Corp.

Hill, M.A. and Wilkinson, L. (1990). Dissecting the Alaskan king crab with SYSTAT and SYGRAPH. *Proceedings of the Section on Statistical Graphics of the American Statistical Association*, 108-113.

Hollander, A.J. (1994). An exploration of virtual auditory shape perception. Unpublished Masters' thesis, Engineering, University of Washington.

Holmes, N. (1991). *Designer's Guide to Creating Charts and Diagrams*. New York: Watson-Guptill Publications.

Hopgood, F.R.A., Duce, D.A., Gallop, J.R., and Sutcliffe, D.C. (1983). *Introduction to the Graphical Kernel System (GKS)*. New York: Academic Press.

Hsu, J.C. (1996). *Multiple Comparisons: Theory and Methods*. New York: Chapman & Hall.

Hubel, D.H. and Wiesel, T.N. (1962). Receptive fields, binocular interaction, and functional architecture in the cat's visual cortex. *Journal of Physiology*, 166, 106-154.

Huber, P.J. (1972). Robust statistics: A review. *Annals of Mathematical Statistics*, 43, 1041-1067.

Huff, D. (1954). *How to Lie with Statistics*. New York: Penguin Books.

Hull, C.L. (1943). *Principles of Behavior*. D. Appleton-Century.

Hurley, C.B., and Oldford, R.W. (1991). A software model for statistical graphics. In A. Buja and P. Tukey (Eds.), *Computing and Graphics in Statistics*. New York: Springer Verlag.

Inselberg, A. (1984). The plane with parallel coordinates. *The Visual Computer*, 1, 69-91.

Jobson, J.D. (1992). *Applied Multivariate Data Analysis. Volume II: Categorical and Multivariate Methods*. New York: Springer Verlag.

Johnson, B.S. (1993). Treemaps: Visualizing Hierarchical and Categorical Data. Dissertation, The University of Maryland Department of Computer Science.

Johnson, M. H., and Morton, J. (1991). *Biology and Cognitive Development: The Case of Face Recognition*. Oxford, UK: Blackwell.

Jones, O. (1856). *The Grammar of Ornament*. Reprinted 1989, Dover Publications.

Jourdain, P.E.B. (1919). *The Nature of Mathematics.* London: T. Nelson. Reprinted in J.R. Newman, *The World of Mathematics.* New York: Simon and Schuster, 1956.

Judd, D.B. (1951). Basic correlates of the visual stimulus. In S.S. Stevens (Ed.), *Handbook of Experimental Psychology.* New York: John Wiley & Sons, 811-867.

Julesz, B. (1965). Texture and visual perception *Scientific American, 212,* 38-48.

Julesz, B. (1971). *Foundations of Cyclopean Perception.* Chicago: University of Chicago Press.

Julesz, B. (1975). Experiments in the visual perception of texture. *Scientific American, 232,* 34-43.

Julesz, B. (1981). Figure and ground perception in briefly presented isodipole textures. In M. Kubovy and J.R. Pomerantz (Eds.), *Perceptual Organization,* pp. 119-139. Hillsdale, NJ: Lawrence Erlbaum.

Julesz, B., and Levitt, H. (1966). Spatial chords. *Journal of the Acoustical Society of America, 40,* 1253.

Kahneman, D., and Tversky, A. (1979). Prospect theory: An analysis of decision under risk. *Econometrika, 47,* 263-291.

Kany, R. (1985). Lo sgardo filologico: Aby Warburg e i dettagli. *Annali della Scuola Normale Superiore di Pisa, 15,* 1265-83.

Kaufman, L. (1974). *Sight and Mind: An Introduction to Visual Perception.* New York: Oxford University Press.

Kennedy, W.J., and Gentle, J.E. (1980). *Statistical Computing.* New York: Marcel Dekker.

Knuth, D.E. (1969). *The Art of Computer Programming: Vol 1, Fundamental Algorithms.* Reading, MA: Addison-Wesley.

Koester, H. (1982). *Introduction to the New Testament (Vol. 1): History, Culture, and Religion of the Hellenistic Age.* Philadelphia: Fortress Press, and Berlin: Walter de Gruyter & Co.

Kosslyn, S.M. (1980). *Image and Mind.* Cambridge, MA: Harvard University Press.

Kosslyn, S.M. (1985). Graphics and human information processing: A review of five books. *Journal of the American Statistical Association, 80,* 499-512.

Kosslyn, S.M. (1989). Understanding charts and graphs. *Applied Cognitive Psychology, 3,* 185-225.

Kosslyn, S.M. (1994). *Elements of Graph Design.* New York: W.H. Freeman.

Kosslyn, S.M., Ball, T.M., and Reiser, B.J. (1978). Visual images preserve metric spatial information: Evidence from studies of image scanning. *Journal of Experimental Psychology: Human Perception and Performance, 4,* 47-60.

Kramer, G., (Ed.) (1994). *Auditory Display: Sonification, Audification and Auditory Interfaces.* Reading: MA: Addison-Wesley.

Krueger, L.E. (1982). Single judgments of numerosity. *Perception and Psychophysics, 31,* 175-182.

Krumhansl, C.L. (1979). The psychological representation of musical pitch in a tonal context. *Cognitive Psychology, 11,* 346-374.

Kruskal, J.B. (1964). Multidimensal scaling by optimizing goodness of fit to a nonmetric hypothesis. *Psychometrika, 29,* 1-27.

Krygier, J.B. (1994). Sound and Geographic Visualization. In Alan MacEachren and D.R.F. Taylor (Eds.), *Visualization in Modern Cartography*. New York: Pergamon Press, 149-166

Lancaster, P., and Salkauskas, K. (1986). *Curve and Surface Fitting: An Introduction*. London: Academic Press.

Lenstra, J.K. (1974). Clustering a data array and the traveling salesman problem. *Operations Research, 22*, 413-414.

Leung, Y.K., and Apperly, M.D. (1994). A review and taxonomy of distortion-oriented presentation techniques. *ACM Transactions on CHI, 1*, 126-160.

Levine, M.W., Frishman, L.J., and Enroth-Cugell, C. (1987). Interactions between the rod and the cone pathways in the cat retina. *Vision Research, 27*, 1093-1104.

Levine, M. W., and Shefner, J.M. (1991). *Fundamentals of Sensation and Perception* (2nd ed.). Belmont, CA: Brooks/Cole.

Lewandowsky, S., & Myers, W. E. (1993). Magnitude judgments in 3D bar charts. In R. Steyer, K. F. Wender, & K. F. Widaman (Eds.) *Psychometric methodology. Proceedings of the 7th European Meeting of the Psychometric Society in Trier* (pp. 266-271). Stuttgart: Gustav Fischer Verlag.

Lewandowsky, S., & Spence, I. (1989). Discriminating strata in scatterplots. *Journal of the American Statistical Association, 84*, 682-688.

Lewis, J.L., Askew, M.J., and Jaycox, D.P. (1982). A comparative evaluation of tibial component designs of total knee prostheses. *The Journal of Bone and Joint Surgery, 64-A*, 129-135.

Lieberman, H. (1997). Intelligent graphics. *Communications of the ACM, 39*, 38-48.

Ling, R.F. (1973). A computer generated aid for cluster analysis. *Communications of the ACM, 16*, 355-361.

Lisker, L., and Abramson, A. (1970). The voicing dimension: Some experiments in comparative phonetics. *Proceedings of Sixth International Congress of Phonetic Sciences*, Prague. Cited in J.R. Anderson (1995), *Cognitive Psychology and its Implications*. (p. 59). New York: W.H. Freeman.

Lockhead, G.R. (1992). Psychophysical scaling: Judgments of attributes or objects? *Behavioral and Brain Sciences, 15*, 543-601.

Lohse, G.L. (1993). A cognitive model for understanding graphical perception. *Human-Computer Interaction, 8*, 353-388.

Lohse, G.L., Biolsi, K., Walker, N, and Rueter, H.H. (1994). A classification of visual representations. *Communications of the ACM, 37*, 36-49.

Long, L.H. (Ed.) (1971). *The World Almanac*. New York: Doubleday.

Luce, R.D., and Tukey, J.W. (1964). Simultaneous conjoint measurement: A new type of fundamental measurement. *Journal of Mathematical Psychology, 1*, 1-27.

MacEachren, A.M. (1992). Visualizing uncertain information. *Cartographic Perspective, 13*, 10-19.

MacEachren, A.M. (1995). *How Maps Work*. New York: The Guilford Press.

Maindonald, J.H. (1984). *Statistical Computation*. New York: John Wiley & Sons.

Makridakis, S., and Wheelwright, S.C. (1989). *Forecasting Methods for Management* (5th ed.). New York: John Wiley & Sons.

Maling, D.H. (1992). *Coordinate Systems and Map Projections*. Oxford: Pergamon Press.

Marr, D. (1982). *Vision*. San Francisco: W.H. Freeman.

Marr, D., and Nishihara, H.K. (1978). Representation and recognition of the spatial organization of three dimensional shapes. *Proceedings of the Royal Society, 200*, 269-294.

Massaro, D.W. (1992). Broadening the domain of the fuzzy logical model of perception. In H.L. Pick, Jr., P. Van den Broek, and D.C. Knill (Eds.), *Cognition: Conceptual and Methodological Issues* (pp. 51-84). Washington, DC: American Psychological Association.

McLain, D.H. (1974). Drawing contours from arbitrary data points. *The Computer Journal, 17*, 318-324.

McNish, A.G. (1948). Terrestrial magnetism. *The Encyclopaedia Britannica, 21*, 959-970.

Meehl, P.E. (1950). Configural scoring. *Journal of Consulting Psychology, 14*, 165-171.

Meyer, B. (1988). *Object-Oriented Software Construction*. Englewood Cliffs, NJ: Prentice-Hall.

Mezrich, J.J., Frysinger, S., and Slivjanovski, R. (1984). Dynamic representation of multivariate time series data. *Journal of the American Statistical Association, 79*, 34-40.

Mihalas, D., and Binney, J. (1981). *Galactic Astronomy: Structure and Kinematics*. San Francisco: W.H. Freeman & Co.

Morton, H.C. and Price, A.J. (1989). *The ACLS Survey of Scholars: Final Report of Views on Publications, Computers, and Libraries*. Lanham, MD: University Press of America.

Munzner, T. (1997). Laying out large directed graphs in 3D hyperbolic space. *Proceedings of the 1997 IEEE Symposium on Information Visualization*. October 20-21, Phoenix, AZ.

Nadaraya, E.A. (1964). On estimating regression. *Theory of Probability and its Applications, 10*, 186-190.

Needham, T. (1997). *Visual Complex Analysis*. Oxford: Clarendon Press.

Nelder, J.A. (1965). The analysis of randomised experiments with orthogonal block structure (Parts I and II). *Proceedings of the Royal Society of London, Series A, 283*, 147-178.

Nelder, J.A. (1976). Scale selection and formatting. *Algorithm AS 96. Applied Statistics, 25*, 94-96.

Nelder, J.A., and Wedderburn, R.W.M. (1972). Generalised Linear Models. *Journal of the Royal Statistical Society, Series A, 135*, 370-384.

Neter, J, Wasserman, W., and Kutner, M.H. (1990). *Applied Linear Statistical Models* (3rd ed.). Homewood, IL: Richard D. Irwin.

Nielsen, D.R., Biggar, J.W., and Erh, K.T. (1973). Spatial variability of field-measured soil-water properties. *Hilgardia, 42*, 215-259.

Okabe, A., Boots, B., and Sugihara, K. (1992). *Spatial Tessellations: Concepts and Applications of Voronoi Diagrams*. New York: John Wiley & Sons.

Olson, J.M., and Brewer, C.A. (1997). An evaluation of color selections to accommodate map users with color-vision impairments. *Annals of the Association of American Geographers, 87*, 103-134.

O'Neill, R. (1971).Function minimization using a simplex procedure. *Algorithm AS 47. Applied Statistics, 20*, 338.

Papantonakis, A., and King, P.J.H. (1995). Syntax and semantics of GQL, a graphical query language. *Journal of Visual Languages and Computing, 6*, 3-25.

Papathomas, T.V. and Julesz, B. (1988). The application of depth separation to the display of large data sets. In W.S. Cleveland and M.E. McGill, eds., *Dynamic Graphics for Statistics*. Belmont, CA: Wadsworth, pp. 353-377.

Pinker, S. (1990). A theory of graph comprehension. In R. Freedle (Ed.), *Artificial Intelligence and the Future of Testing*. Hillsdale, NJ: Lawrence Erlbaum Associates, pp. 73-126.

Pinker, S. (1997). *How the Mind Works*. New York: W.W. Norton & Company.

Plateau, J. (1872). Sur la mesure des sensations physiques, et sur la loi qui lie l'intensité de ces sensations à l'intensité de la cause excitante. *Bulletins de l'Académie Royale de Belgique, 33*, 376-388.

Preparata, F.P., and Shamos, M.I. (1985). *Computational Geometry: An Introduction*. New York: Springer Verlag.

Press, W., Flannery, B., Teukolsky, S., and Vetterling, W. (1986). *Numerical Recipes: The Art of Scientific Computing*. New York: Cambridge University Press.

Rao, C.R. (1973). *Linear Statistical Inference and Its Applications* (2nd ed.). New York: John Wiley & Sons.

Reed, S.K. (1972). Pattern recognition and categorization. *Cognitive Psychology, 3*, 382-407.

Rips, L.J., and Collins, A. (1993). Categories and resemblance. *Journal of Experimental Psychology: General, 122*, 468-486.

Robinson, A.H. (1974). A new map projection: its development and characteristics. *International Yearbook of Cartography, 14*, 145-155.

Robinson, A.H. (1982). *Early Thematic Mapping in the History of Cartography*. Chicago: University of Chicago Press.

Robinson, A.H., Morrison, J.L., Muehrcke, P.C. (1995). *Elements of Cartography* (6th ed.). New York: John Wiley & Sons.

Rogers, D.F. and Adams, J.A. (1990). *Mathematical Elements for Computer Graphics* (2nd ed.). New York: McGraw-Hill.

Ronan, C.A. (1991). Measurement of time and types of calendars. In P.W. Goetz (Ed.), *Encyclopaedia Britannica, Vol. 15*. Chicago: Encyclopaedia Brittanica, Inc., pp. 432-435.

Rosch, E. (1975). Cognitive representations of semantic categories. *Journal of Experimental Psychology: General*, 104, 192-223.

Roth, M.A., Korth, H.F., and Silberschatz, A. (1988). Extended algebra and calculus for nested relational databases. *ACM Transactions on Database Systems, 13*, 389-417.

Roth, S.F., Kolojejchick, J., Mattis, J., and Chuah, M. (1995). SageTools: An intelligent environment for sketching, browsing, and customizing data graphics. *Conference on Human Factors in Computing Systems (SIGCHI '95).* Denver, CO, May 1995, 409-410.

Roth, S.F., Chuah, M.C., Kerpedjiev, S., Kolojejchick, J.A., and Lucas, P. (1997). Towards an information visualization workspace: Combining multiple means of expression. *Human-Computer Interaction Journal, 12,* 131-185.

Rothkopf, E.Z. (1957). A measure of stimulus similarity and errors in some paired associate learning tasks. *Journal of Experimental Psychology, 53,* 94-101.

Rubin, D.B. (1987). *Multiple Imputation for Nonresponse in Surveys.* New York: John Wiley & Sons.

Rugg, R.D., Egenhofer, M.J., and Kuhn, W. (1995). Formalizing behavior of geographic feature types. *Technical Report 95-7,* National Center for Geographic Information and Analysis/NCGIA.

Rumbaugh, J., Blaha, M., Premerlani, W., Eddy, F., and Lorensen, W. (1991). *Object-Oriented Modeling and Design.* Englewood Cliffs, NJ: Prentice-Hall.

Rumelhart, D.E. (1977). *An Introduction to Human Information Processing.* New York: John Wiley & Sons.

Russell, J.A., and Fernandez-Dols, J.-M. (Eds.) (1997). *The psychology of facial expression.* New York: Cambridge University Press.

Sacks, O. (1995). *An Anthropologist on Mars.* New York: Alfred A. Knopf.

Safire, W. (1997). *Watching My Language: Adventures in the Word Trade.* New York: Random House.

Sarawagi, S., Agrawal, R., and Megiddo, N. (1998). Discovery-driven exploration of OLAP data cubes. San Jose, CA: Almaden Research Center, IBM Research Division.

Sarkar, M., and Brown, M.H. (1994). Graphical fisheye views. *Communications of the ACM, 37,* 73-83.

SAS Institute Inc. (1976). *A User's Guide to SAS.* Raleigh, NC: Sparks Press.

Schmid, C.F., and Schmid, S.E. (1979). *Handbook of Graphic Presentation* (2nd ed.). New York: Ronald Press.

Schmid, C.F. (1983). *Statistical Graphics: Design Principles and Practices.* New York: John Wiley & Sons.

Schneider, B., Parker, S., Ostrosky, D., Stein, D., and Kanow, G. (1974). A scale for the psychological magnitude of number. *Perception & Psychophysics, 16,* 43-46.

Schneiderman, B. (1992). Tree visualization with tree-maps: A 2-d space-filling approach. *ACM Transactions on Graphics, 11,* 92-99.

Scott, D.W. (1979). On optimal and data-based histograms. *Biometrika, 66,* 605-610.

Scott, D.W. (1992). *Multivariate Density Estimation: Theory, Practice, and Visualization.* New York: John Wiley & Sons.

Selfridge, O.G. (1959). Pandemonium: A paradigm for learning. In D.V. Blake and A.M. Uttley (Eds.), *Symposium on the mechanization of thought processes* (pp. 511-529). London: H.M. Stationery Office.

Shepard, D. (1965). A two-dimensional interpolation function for irregularly spaced data. *Proceedings of the 23rd National Conference of the ACM,* 517.

Shepard, R.N. (1962). The analysis of proximities: Multidimensional scaling with an unknown distance function. I. *Psychometrika, 27*, 125-139.

Shepard, R.N. (1964). Circularity in judgments of relative pitch. *The Journal of the Acoustical Society of America, 36*, 2346-2353.

Shepard, R.N. and Carroll, J.D. (1966). Parametric representation of nonlinear data structures. In P.R. Krishnaiah (Ed.), *International Symposium on Multivariate Analysis*. New York: Academic Press.

Shepard, R.N. and Cooper, L.A. (1983). *Mental Images and their Transformations*. Cambridge, MA: MIT Press.

Shepard, R.N. and Metzler, J. (1971). Mental rotation of three-dimensional objects. *Science, 171*, 701-703.

Shiffman, H.R. (1990). *Sensation and Perception: An Integrated Approach*. New York: John Wiley & Sons.

Silverman, B.W. (1986). *Density Estimation for Statistics and Data Analysis*. New York: Chapman & Hall.

Simkin, D., and Hastie, R. (1987). An information processing analysis of graph perception. *Journal of the American Statistical Association, 82*, 454-465.

Simonoff, J.S. (1996). *Smoothing Methods in Statistics*. New York: Springer-Verlag.

Simonoff, J.S. (1997). The "unusual episode" and a second statistics course. *Journal of Statistics Education, 5(1)*.

Skinner, B.F. (1961). *Cumulative Record*. New York: Appleton-Century-Crofts.

Skinner, B.F. (1969). *Contingencies of Reinforcement: A Theoretical Analysis*. New York: Appleton-Century-Crofts.

Slagel, J.R., Chang, C.L., and Heller, S.R. (1975). A clustering and data reorganizing algorithm. *IEEE Transactions on Systems, Man, and Cybernetics, 5*, 125-128.

Smith, S., Bergeron, R., and Grinstein, G. (1990). Stereophonic and Surface Sound Generation for Exploratory Data Analysis. *Human Factors in Computing Systems: CHI 85 Conference Proceedings*. New York: ACM Press, 125-32.

Snyder, J.P. (1989). *An album of map projections*. US Geological Survey: Professional Paper 1453.

Spence, I. (1990). Visual psychophysics of simple graphical elements. *Journal of Experimenal Psychology: Human Perception and Performance, 16*, 683-692.

Spence, I., & Lewandowsky, S. (1991). Displaying proportions and percentages. *Applied Cognitive Psychology, 5*, 61-77

Spoehr, K.T. and Lehmkuhle, S.W. (1982). *Visual Information Processing*. San Francisco: W.H. Freeman and Company.

SPSS Inc. (1996). *SPSS Reference guide*. Upper Saddle River, NJ: Prentice-Hall.

Standing, L. (1973). Learning 10,000 pictures. *Quarterly Journal of Experimental Psychology, 25*, 207-222.

Stevens, A., and Coupe, P. (1978). Distortions in judged spatial relations. *Cognitive Psychology, 10*, 422-437.

Stevens, S.S. (1946). On the theory of scales of measurement. *Science, 103*, 677-680.

Stevens, S.S. (1961). To honor Fechner and repeal his law. *Science, 133*, 80-86.

Stevens, S.S. (1985). *Psychophysics: Introduction to its Perceptual, Neural, and Social Prospects.* New Brunswick, NJ: Transaction Books.

Stigler, S. (1983). *The History of Statistics.* Cambridge: Harvard University Press.

Stillwell, J. (1992). *Geometry of Surfaces.* New York: Springer-Verlag.

Stirling, W.D. (1981). Scale selection and formatting. *Algorithm AS 168. Applied Statistics, 30*, 339-344.

Stoyan, D., Kendall, W.S., and Mecke, J. (1987). *Stochastic Geometry and its Applications.* New York: John Wiley & Sons.

Stouffer, S.A., Guttman, L., Suchman, E.A., Lazarsfeld, P.F., Staf, S.A., and Clausen, J.A. (1950). *Measurement and Prediction.* Princeton, NJ: Princeton University Press.

Sturges, H.A. (1926). The choice of a class interval. *Journal of the American Statistical Association, 21*, 65-66.

Swayne, D.F., Cook, D., and Buja, A. (1998). XGobi: Interactive dynamic data visualization in the X Window system. *Journal of Computational and Graphical Statistics, 7*, 113-130.

Swets, J.A., Tanner Jr., W.P., and Birdsall, T.G. (1961). Decision processes in perception. *Psychological Review, 68*, 301-340.

Symanzik, J., Cook, D., Kohlmeyer, B. D., Lechner, U., Cruz-Neira, C. (1997). Dynamic Statistical Graphics in the C2 Virtual Environment. *Computing Science and Statistics, 29(2)*, 35-40.

Theus, M. (1998). MONDRIAN: Data visualization in Java. AT&T Conference on Statistical Science and the Internet, Madison, NJ, Drew University, July 12-14.

Thisted, R.A. (1988). *Elements of Statistical Computing: Numerical Computation.* New York and London: Chapman and Hall.

Tidmore, F.E. and Turner, D.W. (1977). Clustering with Chernoff-type faces. *Communications in Statistics - Theory and Methods, 12*, 397-408.

Tierney, L. (1991). *Lisp-Stat.* New York: John Wiley & Sons.

Tilling, L. (1975). Early experimental graphis. *The British Journal for the History of Science, 8*, 193-213.

Tobler, W. (1993). Speculations on the geometry of geography. In Technical Report 93-1, *Three Presentations on Geographical Analysis and Modeling.* National Center for Geographic Information and Analysis. Santa Barbara, CA.

Tobler, W. (1997). Visualizing the impact of transportation on spatial relations. Paper presented at the Western Regional Science Association meeting. Honolulu, Hawaii: February.

Travis, D. (1991). *Effective Color Displays: Theory and Practice.* New York: Academic Press.

Treinish, L.A. (1993). Unifying principles of data management for scientific visualization. In R.A. Earnshaw and D. Watson (Eds.), *Animation and Scientific Visualization: Tools and Applicaitons.* New York: Academic Press, 141-170.

Troje, N., and Bülthoff, H. (1996). How is bilateral symmetry of human faces used for recognition of novel views? Technical Report No. 38, Max-Planck-Institut für biologische Kybernetik.

Tufte, E.R. (1983). *The Visual Display of Quantitative Information.* Cheshire, CT: Graphics Press.

Tufte, E.R. (1990). *Envisioning Data.* Cheshire, CT: Graphics Press.

Tufte, E.R. (1997). *Visual Explanations.* Cheshire, CT: Graphics Press.

Tukey, J.W. (1958). Bias and confidence in not quite large samples. *Annals of Mathematical Statistics, 29,* 614.

Tukey, J.W. (1974). Mathematics and the picturing of data. *Proceedings of the International Congress of Mathematicians.* Vancouver: BC., pp. 523-531.

Tukey, J.W. (1977). *Exploratory Data Analysis.* Reading, MA: Addison-Wesley.

Turk, M., and Pentland, A., (1991) Eigenfaces for Recognition. *Journal of Cognitive Neuroscience, 3,* 71-86.

Tversky, A., and Kahneman, D. (1974). Judgments under uncertainty: Heuristics and biases. *Science, 185,* 1124-1131.

Tversky, B., and Schiano, D.J. (1989). Perceptual and cognitive factors in distortions in memory for graphs and maps. *Journal of Experimental Psychology: General, 118,* 387-398.

Upson, C., Faulhaber, T., Kamins, D., Schlege, D., Laidlaw, D., Vroom, J., Gurwitz, R., and vanDam, A. (1989). The application visualization system: A computational environment for scientific visualization. *IEEE Computer Graphics and Applications, 9,* 30-42.

Upton, G.J.G. and Fingleton, B. (1989). *Spatial Data Analysis by Example. Vol 2: Categorical and Directional Data.* New York: John Wiley & Sons.

US Department of Labor, Bureau of Labor Statistics, Office of Systems and Standards (1979). *Table Producing Language, Version 5: Language Guide and Print Control Language.* Washington, DC: Government Printing Office.

Velleman, P.F., and Hoaglin, D.C. (1981). *Applications, Basics, and Computing of Exploratory Data Analysis.* Belmont, CA: Duxbury Press.

Velleman, P.F., and Wilkinson, L. (1996). Nominal, ordinal, interval, and ratio typologies are misleading for classifying statistical methodology. *The American Statistician, 47.* 65-72.

Velleman, P.F. (1998). *Data Desk.* Ithaca, NY: Data Description Inc.

Wadsworth, H.M. Jr., Stephens, K.S., and Godfrey, A.B. (1986). *Modern Methods for Quality Control and Improvement.* New York: John Wiley & Sons.

Wahba, G. (1990). *Spline Models for Observational Data.* Philadelphia, PA: SIAM.

Wainer, H. (1995). A rose by another name. *Chance, 8,* 46-51.

Wainer, H. (1997). *Visual Revelations: Graphical Tales of Fate and Deception from Napoleon Bonaparte to Ross Perot.* New York: Springer-Verlag.

Wainer, H., and Francolini, C.M. (1980). An empirical inquiry concerning human understanding of two-variable color maps. *The American Statistician, 34,* 81-93.

Wallgren, A., Wallgren, B., Persson, R., Jorner, U., and Halland, J-A. (1996). *Graphing Statistics & Data.* Thousand Oaks, CA: Sage Publications.

Wassenaar, L.I., and Hobson, K.A. (1998). Natal origins of migratory monarch butterflies at wintering colonies in Mexico: New isotopic evidence. *Proceedings of the National Academy of Sciences 95(Dec. 22):15436.*

Watson, G.S. (1964). Smooth regression analysis. *Sankhya, Series A, 26,* 359-372.

Watson, J.B. (1924). *Behaviorism.* New York: W.W. Norton & Company.

Watt, R. (1991). *Understanding Vision.* London: Academic Press.

Webb, E.J., Campbell, D.T., Schwartz, R.D., Sechrest, L., and Grove, J.B. (1981). *Nonreactive Measures in the Social Sciences* (2nd ed.). Boston, MA: Houghton Mifflin.

Wegman, E.J. (1990). Hyperdimensional data analysis using parallel coordinates. *Journal of the American Statistical Association, 85,* 664-675.

Wertheimer, M. (1958). *Principles of Perceptual Organization.* In D.C. Beardslee and M. Wertheimer (Eds.), *Readings in Perception.* Princeton, NJ: Van Nostrand-Reinhold. (Originally published in German, 1923).

Whorf, B.L. (1941). Languages and logic. In J.B. Carroll (Ed.), *Language, Thought, and Reality: Selected Papers of Benjamin Lee Whorf* (233-245). Cambridge, MA: MIT Press.

Wilkinson, G.N., and Rogers, C.E. (1973). Symbolic description of factorial models for analysis of variance. *Journal of the Royal Statistical Society, Series C, 22,* 392-399.

Wilkinson, L. (1975). Similarity and Preference Structures. Unpublished dissertation, Yale University.

Wilkinson, L. (1979), Permuting a matrix to a simple pattern, *Proceedings of the Statistical Computing Section of the American Statistical Association,* 409-412.

Wilkinson, L. (1982). An experimental evaluation of multivariate graphical point representations. *Human Factors in Computer Systems: Proceedings.* Gaithersburg, MD, 202-209.

Wilkinson, L. (1983a). SYSTAT: System Statistics. *Proceedings of the Statistical Computing Section of the American Statistical Association,* 312-314.

Wilkinson, L. (1983b). Fuzzygrams. Paper presented at Harvard Computer Graphics Week. Cambridge, MA.

Wilkinson, L. (1988). Cognitive Science and Graphic Design. In *SYGRAPH: The System for Statistics.* Evanston, IL: SYSTAT Inc.

Wilkinson, L. (1992). Graphical displays. *Statistical Methods in Medical Research 1,* 3-25.

Wilkinson, L. (1993a). Algorithms for choosing the range and domain of plotted functions. In A. Buja and P. Tukey (Eds.), *Computing and Graphics in Statistics.* New York: Springer Verlag.

Wilkinson, L. (1993b). Comment on "A model for studying display methods of statistical graphics." *Journal of Computational and Graphical Statistics, 2,* 355-360.

Wilkinson, L. (1996). A graph algebra. *Computing Science and Statistics: Proceedings of the 28th Symposium on the Interface,* 341-351.

Wilkinson, L. (1997). *SYSTAT 7.* Chicago, IL: SPSS Inc.

Wilkinson, L. (1998). *SYSTAT 8.* Chicago, IL: SPSS Inc.

Wilkinson, L. (1999). Dot plots. *The American Statistician, 53.* In press.

Wilkinson, L., Blank, G., and Gruber, C. (1996). *Desktop Data Analysis with SYS-TAT*. Upper Saddle River, NJ: Prentice-Hall.

Wilkinson, L., Gimbel, B.R., and Koepke, D. (1982). Configural self-diagnosis. In N. Hirschberg and L.G. Humphreys (Eds.), *Multivariate Applications in the Social Sciences*. Hillsdale, NJ: Lawrence Erlbaum, 103-115.

Wilkinson, L., and McConathy, D. (1990). Memory for graphs. *Proceedings of the Section on Statistical Graphics of the American Statistical Association*, 25-32.

Winston, P.H. (1984). *Artificial Intelligence*. Reading, MA: Addison-Wesley.

Woodruff, A., Landay, J., and Stonebraker, M. (1998). Constant density visualizations of non-uniform distributions of data. *Proceedings of the 11th Annual ACM Symposium on User Interface Software and Technology (UIST)*, 19-28.

Young, T. (1802). The Bakerian lecture: On the theory of lights and colours. *Philosophical Transactions of the Royal Society, 92*, 12-48.

Young, M. P. & Yamane, S. (1992). Sparse population coding of faces in the inferotemporal cortex. *Science, 56*, 1327-1331.

Author Index

Subject Index

absolute scale 212
abstraction 4
Ada 4
address 57
aesthetic function 37
affine mapping 244
aggregation hierarchy 10
algebra 27, 65
algebraic form 66
Algol 4
annotation 341
APL 4
arcsine scale 226
area chart 87, 135, 265
aspect ratio 245
auto-correlogram 129
axis 35, 332
    limits 270
    scale break 333

bandwidth 170
bar chart 88, 123, 136, 137, 153, 183,
    261, 324
    clustered 136
    divided 137
    stacked 137
BASIC 4
binary operators 27
binary relation 24
binning, hexagon 190
biplot 148
blocking 279
bootstrapping 49
bounded regions 81
box plot 90
    bivariate 190

brush 7, 298
bubble plot 103, 141

C++ 4
cache, programming 201
call
    by name 30
    by value 30
cardinality 24
Cartesian product 24
case number 31
categorical scale 105, 215
categorical variable 30
chartjunk 114
charts 2
choropleth map 160
circumplex 151
clustered bar chart 136
co-domain of a function 25
coherence in 3D 281
color
    afterimages 127
    categorization 106
    choropleth maps 160
    legending blends 155
    naming 127
    shading 154
    splitting 154
command language 13
complex conjugate 267
components 55
composition of functions 26
conditional statistical estimation 172
confidence intervals
    mean 183